The Art of
Parallel Programming

The Art of
Parallel Programming

BRUCE P. LESTER

Maharishi International University
Fairfield, Iowa

PRENTICE HALL, Englewood Cliffs, New Jersey 07632

Library of Congress Cataloging-in-Publication Data

Lester, Bruce P.
    The art of parallel programming / Bruce P. Lester.
       p.   cm.
    Includes bibliographical references (p.   ) and index.
    ISBN 0-13-045923-2
    1. Parallel programming (Computer science)   I. Title.
  QA76.642.L47   1993
  005.1'1—dc20   92-38520
                                             CIP

Acquisitions editor: *William Zobrist*
Editorial/production supervision: *Raeia Maes*
Cover designer: *Bruce Kenselaar*
Cover credit: "Ambassador of Autumn" 1922
   by Paul Klee. Watercolor $10\frac{3}{8}$ x $13\frac{1}{8}$.
   Yale University Art Gallery/Gift
   of Collection Société Anonyme.
Prepress buyer: *Linda Behrens*
Manufacturing buyer: *Dave Dickey*

 Copyright © 1993 by Prentice-Hall, Inc.
A Simon & Schuster Company
Englewood Cliffs, New Jersey 07632

Printed in the United States of America

10 9 8 7 6 5 4 3 2

ISBN 0-13-045923-2

PRENTICE-HALL INTERNATIONAL (UK) LIMITED, *London*
PRENTICE-HALL OF AUSTRALIA PTY. LIMITED, *Sydney*
PRENTICE-HALL CANADA INC., *Toronto*
PRENTICE-HALL HISPANOAMERICANA, S.A., *Mexico*
PRENTICE-HALL OF INDIA PRIVATE LIMITED, *New Delhi*
PRENTICE-HALL OF JAPAN, INC., *Tokyo*
SIMON & SCHUSTER ASIA PTE. LTD., *Singapore*
EDITORA PRENTICE-HALL DO BRAZIL, LTDA., *Rio de Janeiro*

To My Father
Jay Lester

Contents

PREFACE *xv*

ABOUT THE AUTHOR *xxi*

1 WHY PARALLEL PROGRAMMING? 1

1.1   Sequential vs. Parallel   1

1.2   Parallel Computer Systems   2

1.3   Multiprocessor Architecture   3

1.4   Multicomputers   5

1.5   Parallel Programming   7

1.6   The Multi-Pascal Language   10

1.7   Parallel Algorithms   13

1.8   The Multi-Pascal Debugger and Performance
        Monitor   16

1.9   Parallelism in the Human Computer   17

        References   18

        Exercises   18

2 DATA PARALLELISM 19

2.1   FORALL Statements   20

    2.1.1   *Process Creation, 20*
    2.1.2   *Process Granularity, 22*
    2.1.3   *Optimal Group Size, 24*

2.2   Example: Parallel Sorting   26

2.3   Nested Loops   29

2.4   Example: Matrix Multiplication   31

2.5   Shared and Local Variables   34

    2.5.1   *Statement Blocks with Declarations, 35*
    2.5.2   *Scope of FORALL Indices, 39*

2.6   The FORK Operator   40

    2.6.1   *Process Termination, 41*
    2.6.2   *The JOIN Statement, 42*
    2.6.3   *Parallel List Processing, 43*

2.7   Amdahl's Law   44

    2.7.1   *Effects of Sequential Code on Speedup, 44*
    2.7.2   *Overcoming Initialization Overhead, 45*

2.8   Summary   47

    References   48

    Programming Projects   48

    1. Multiplying Polynomials, 49
    2. Merging Sorted Lists, 50

    Exercises, 50

3 MULTIPROCESSOR ARCHITECTURE 55

3.1   Bus-Oriented Systems   56

3.2   Cache Memory   57

    3.2.1   *Uniprocessor Caches, 57*
    3.2.2   *Multiprocessor Caches, 58*

3.3   Multiple Memory Modules   60

3.4   Processor–Memory Interconnection Networks   63

3.5   Influence of the Algorithm   65

    3.5.1   *Rank Sort, 66*
    3.5.2   *Matrix Multiplication, 67*

3.6   Memory Hot Spots 68

3.7   Summary 69

       References 70

       Exercises 70

4 PROCESS COMMUNICATION 73

4.1   Process Communication Channels 74

4.2   Channel Variables 75

       4.2.1 Reading and Writing Channels, 75
       4.2.2 Producer–Consumer Example, 77

4.3   Pipeline Parallelism 77

4.4   Solution to Linear Equations 80

       4.4.1 Back Substitution, 80
       4.4.2 Pipeline Algorithm for Back Substitution, 82

4.5   Channels and Structured Types 85

4.6   Bitonic Merge Sort 88

4.7   Summary 91

       References 91

       Programming Projects 92

       1. Prime Number Sieve, 92
       2. Bitonic Merge Sort, 93

       Exercises 94

5 DATA SHARING 97

5.1   Atomic Operations 98

5.2   Spinlocks 102

       5.2.1 Implementation of Spinlocks, 102
       5.2.2 Spinlocks and Structured Types, 103

5.3   Contention for Shared Data 104

       5.3.1 Histogram of a Visual Image, 105
       5.3.2 Effect of Contention on Performance, 107

5.4   Numerical Integration 108

5.5   Comparing Spinlocks and Channels 110

       5.5.1 Equivalent Power, 110

Contents

          5.5.2   *Busy-Waiting vs. Blocking, 113*
          5.5.3   *Semaphores, 113*

5.6   Summary   115

         References   116

         Programming Projects   116

          1. Saddle Point of a Matrix, 116
          2. Bucket Sort, 116

         Exercises   117

6 SYNCHRONOUS PARALLELISM 120

6.1   Solving a Differential Equation   121

6.2   Parallel Jacobi Relaxation   124

          6.2.1   *Synchronization by Process Termination, 124*
          6.2.2   *Barrier Synchronization, 126*

6.3   Linear Barrier Implementation   128

6.4   Binary Tree Implementation of Barriers   130

          6.4.1   *Tournament Technique, 131*
          6.4.2   *Tree Creation Algorithm, 132*
          6.4.3   *Performance, 134*

6.5   Local Synchronization   136

6.6   Broadcasting and Aggregation   140

          6.6.1   *Convergence Testing, 140*
          6.6.2   *Implementing Parallel Aggregation, 140*
          6.6.3   *Parallel Jacobi with Convergence, 142*
          6.6.4   *Improving the Performance, 145*

6.7   Summary   146

         References   147

         Programming Projects   148

          1. Red–Black Relaxation, 148
          2. Gaussian Elimination, 148

         Exercises   150

7 MULTICOMPUTER ARCHITECTURE 153

7.1   Processor Communications   154

          7.1.1   *Communication Link, 154*

   7.1.2 Routing and Congestion, 156
   7.1.3 Communication Delay, 159

 7.2 Multicomputer Topology 161

   7.2.1 Line and Ring Topology, 162
   7.2.2 Mesh Topology, 163
   7.2.3 Hypercube Topology, 165

 7.3 Broadcasting and Aggregation 168

 7.4 Hypercube Embeddings 174

 7.5 Summary 178

   References 179

   Exercises 179

8 *MESSAGE-PASSING PROGRAMS* *183*

 8.1 Communication Ports 184

   8.1.1 Communication Channels, 185
   8.1.2 Port Declarations, 187
   8.1.3 Comparison with Other Languages, 189

 8.2 Language Support for Message-Passing 190

   8.2.1 The PORT Declaration, 191
   8.2.2 Communication with the Main Program, 193
   8.2.3 The @ Primitive for Processor Allocation, 196

 8.3 Pipeline Programs on Multicomputers 197

 8.4 Communication Delay 199

   8.4.1 Basic Communication Model, 200
   8.4.2 Software Overhead, 202

 8.5 Multiple Port Communications 204

   8.5.1 Multiple Aggregation, 204
   8.5.2 Multiple Broadcast, 208

 8.6 Summary 212

   References 213

   Programming Projects 213

   1. Sorting on a Line Topology, 213
   2. Numerical Integration on a Mesh, 214
   3. Solving Linear Equations on a Hypercube, 214

   Exercises 215

9 DATA PARTITIONING 219

9.1   Communication Overhead 220

9.2   *N*-Body Problem in Astrophysics 222

     9.2.1   *Shared Memory Version, 223*
     9.2.2   *Partitioning the Data Array, 224*
     9.2.3   *N-Body Program on Ring Topology, 226*
     9.2.4   *Performance Analysis, 228*
     9.2.5   *Overlapping Communication with Computation, 231*
     9.2.6   *Virtual vs. Physical Topology, 231*

9.3   Matrix Multiplication 234

     9.3.1   *Partitioning the Matrices, 235*
     9.3.2   *The Algorithm, 236*
     9.3.3   *Simplified Version, 238*
     9.3.4   *Complete Program, 240*
     9.3.5   *Performance Analysis, 242*

9.4   Jacobi Relaxation 245

     9.4.1   *Multicomputer Algorithm, 245*
     9.4.2   *Performance Analysis, 250*
     9.4.3   *Alternate Partitioning Methods, 253*

9.5   Summary 254

     References 255

     Programming Projects 256

     1. Region Growing, 256
     2. Jacobi Relaxation on a Mesh, 258
     3. Gaussian Elimination, 258

     Exercises 259

10 REPLICATED WORKERS 261

10.1   Work Pools 262

10.2   Shortest Path Algorithm 264

     10.2.1   *Sequential Shortest Path Algorithm, 265*
     10.2.2   *Parallel Shortest Path Algorithm, 266*

10.3   Implementation of Work Pools 269

10.4   Eliminating Contention 270

     10.4.1   *Load Balancing, 272*
     10.4.2   *Termination Algorithm, 273*
     10.4.3   *Performance, 276*

10.5   *N*-Queens Problem 281

10.6   Summary   285

References   286

Programming Projects   287

1. Maze Search, 287
2. Traveling Salesman Problem, 288

Exercises   289

11   DISTRIBUTED TERMINATION DETECTION   292

11.1   Multicomputer Shortest Path Program   293

11.2   Work Pool Implementation   296

11.2.1   Message Acknowledgments, 296
11.2.2   Termination Detection Algorithm, 298

11.3   Getwork and Putwork   301

11.4   Performance Analysis   306

11.4.1   Factors Influencing Performance, 306
11.4.2   Communication Delay, 306
11.4.3   Load Balancing, 310

11.5   Work Compression   311

11.5.1   New Getwork Implementation, 311
11.5.2   Asynchronous Algorithms, 313

11.6   Summary   314

References   316

Programming Projects   316

1. Asynchronous Solution of Linear Equations, 316
2. Traveling Salesman Problem, 316

Exercises   317

**APPENDIX A: ADVANCED MULTI-PASCAL
FEATURES   320**

A.1   Environments   320

A.2   Channel Variables   325

A.2.1   Channel Variables in Expressions, 325
A.2.2   Channel Variables as Parameters, 326
*A.2.3   Combining Channels with Arrays, Records, and
Pointers, 327*

APPENDIX B: THE MULTI-PASCAL INTERPRETER AND DEBUGGING TOOL USER'S MANUAL   329

B.1   Getting Started   330

B.2   List and Input–Output Options   331

B.3   Overview of Interactive Commands   332

B.4   Setting Breakpoints   333

B.5   Processes and Processors   334

B.6   Stepping Through a Process   337

B.7   Writing and Tracing Variables   338

   B.7.1   *Writing Standard Variables, 339*
   B.7.2   *Writing Structured Variables, 340*
   B.7.3   *TRACE Command, 343*

B.8   Program Performance Statistics, 345

   B.8.1   *TIME Command, 346*
   B.8.2   *UTILIZATION Command, 349*
   B.8.3   *Sequential Execution Time, 349*
   B.8.4   *ALARM Command, 350*
   B.8.5   *VARIATION Command, 351*
   B.8.6   *DURATION Statement, 352*

B.9   Program Performance Profile   353

B.10   Simulation of Parallel Architectures   355

   B.10.1   *Specifying the Architecture, 355*
   B.10.2   *Communication Delays, 357*

B.11   Summary of Commands   359

   References   360

APPENDIX C: MULTI-PASCAL ERROR MESSAGES   361

   Features Not Supported   361

   Error Codes   361

   PC Version   364

   References   364

REFERENCES   365

INDEX   369

Preface

Parallel computing is playing an increasingly important role in computer science and offers great promise for future progress of computer technology. For this reason, most universities with extensive curricula in computer science are offering courses in this area. *The Art of Parallel Programming* is intended as a text for a first course in parallel computing taught at either the advanced undergraduate or beginning graduate level. The only prerequisites for the text are a knowledge of Pascal programming and data structures.

The author believes the best way to present a comprehensive overview of the entire field of parallel computing is through a study of parallel *programming*. Programming plays a central role in computing and brings together elements from many different areas, including algorithms, languages, and computer architecture. To write a parallel computer program, one must first formulate an efficient parallel algorithm. Then the algorithm must be expressed in a parallel programming language. To make the program perform well, the particular characteristics of the target parallel computer architecture must also be considered. Finally, one must have good techniques of debugging and performance evaluation to create a finished product.

Throughout the text there is a continual interplay among parallel algorithms, languages, architecture, and performance evaluation. This is in contrast to other textbooks in the field of parallel computing, which contain a more complete presentation of only one of these areas, such as parallel algorithms or parallel architectures. Another important difference between this text and other published texts in parallel computing is the level of the material. Most of the existing texts are more suited as reference manuals for researchers in the field or for intensive graduate courses. This text is suitable for a wider range of students as a general introduction and overview of parallel programming. Parallel computing is becoming widespread enough that it is important for this knowledge to be available in general courses for undergraduates as well as for graduate students.

This text is organized according to the major programming techniques for parallel programs, including both shared-memory and distributed-memory machines. As each new programming technique is introduced, the necessary parallel language support features are also introduced, and several parallel algorithms are used as examples to illustrate the technique. This text definitely uses a "hands-on" approach for the students. Every chapter has extensive programming projects in which the students write and debug their own parallel programs.

Software Accompanying the Text

All of the example parallel programs in the text use the parallel programming language "Multi-Pascal," which consists of a few of the standard parallel programming primitives added to the language Pascal. Accompanying the text is a software package that allows students to write their own Multi-Pascal programs and simulate the program performance on a wide variety of parallel architectures. This Multi-Pascal software package is itself written in standard Pascal and thus can run on any computer system, including PCs.

The availability of this software package is one of the things that makes this text unique as the basis for a course in parallel programming. The software is designed for student use and is interactive and user-friendly. The interactive system compiles Multi-Pascal programs and flags the syntax errors. The student can then specify some of the characteristics of the target parallel computer, including the total number of processors and whether it is a shared-memory multiprocessor or a distributed-memory multicomputer. For multicomputers, the overall topology can be chosen from among some of the common topologies such as mesh, hypercube, torus, and ring.

The Multi-Pascal software system will simulate the running of the student's program as it would behave on the chosen target architecture. The system has a powerful interactive debugger that allows students to set program breakpoints, step through the program, and display the values of program variables. The student can also monitor the program performance through processor utilization statistics and performance profiles. The simulation system charges overheads for process creation time, memory contention, and interprocessor communication delays. Comparison with performance of actual parallel computers has shown that the simulation system is quite realistic.

For purposes of a course in parallel programming, the use of this Multi-Pascal interactive system offers many advantages over the use of a real parallel computer. With a real parallel machine, the student is required to master a whole new and complex programming environment, which takes a considerable amount of time. Furthermore, a course that uses a real parallel machine will be forced to use a textbook that will almost certainly use a different programming language from the one used by the parallel machine. The students will then have the additional burden of translating between two different languages.

With the use of this text and the accompanying software package, the instructor is given a completely integrated and self-sufficient package for teaching a course in parallel programming. The text includes instruction in the Multi-Pascal language and the use of the interactive system to run Multi-Pascal programs. All of the sample algorithms in the text are written in Multi-Pascal, and the student exercises and programming projects can be done in Multi-Pascal and tested by using the interactive system.

The main philosophy behind this textbook is that to gain a real understanding of parallel programming, students must have the opportunity to write and test their own parallel programs. There are many important issues in parallel programming that do not even arise in sequential programming. Just reading about these issues and studying some abstract parallel algorithms in a book brings one level of understanding of these issues. However, when this reading is supplemented with the experience of writing parallel programs and seeing how they actually perform, a whole new level of understanding is achieved. In courses based on this text, it is anticipated that students will spend most of their time working on programming projects and exercises using the Multi-Pascal interactive system.

Organization of the Text

The text contains eleven chapters. It should be possible to cover the entire text in a one-semester course. The instructor also has the option of omitting some chapters and focusing more attention on the other chapters by assigning more of the exercises and programming projects. For courses in which the students have already had some previous exposure to parallel computer architecture or to concurrent programming, the instructor may choose to skip some of the material in the first half of the text and spend more time on the latter chapters that deal with the more sophisticated programming techniques.

The first half of the text (Chapters 1–6) is chiefly devoted to programming of shared-memory multiprocessors, while the second half (Chapters 7–11) focuses on distributed-memory multicomputers (with the exception of Chapter 10). Chapter 1 contains a brief introduction to the entire field of parallel computing, including a preview of the material covered in the text. Chapter 2 introduces the most important organizational technique for parallel programs—data parallelism. The chapter also contains coverage of two of the important sources of parallel program performance degradation: process creation overhead and sequential portions of code. Chapter 3 presents an overview of shared-memory multiprocessor architecture, with special emphasis on caching and memory system organization. The important performance issue of memory contention is introduced in this chapter.

Chapters 4 and 5 are concerned with the two major types of parallel process interaction: process communication (Chapter 4) and data sharing (Chapter 5), including the supporting parallel programming languages features. Chapter 4 discusses the syntax and semantics of process communication channels and their application in pipeline parallelism. Chapter 5 presents an explanation of the use of spinlocks and atomic operations for process data sharing. Special attention is given to the problem of contention for shared data and how to avoid performance problems through decentralization of the locked region. Chapter 6 covers the important organizational technique for parallel programs called *synchronous iteration*, which is the parallel form of iterative numerical programs. The chapter considers the implementation and efficiency of "barrier" synchronization and convergence testing, both of which play a major role in synchronous iteration.

Chapter 7 begins the second half of the text with an overview of distributed-memory parallel computers. The main topics covered in this chapter are multicomputer topology and communications. Chapter 8 then gives an overview of the message-passing programming style and its application for creating efficient programs for multicomputers. Also, this chapter introduces the language support features required for multicomputer programming. Chapter 9 focuses on how to achieve good performance in multicomputer programs. The technique of data partitioning is presented as the method for overcoming the potential performance degradation caused by communication delays. This chapter also contains extensive material on how to evaluate parallel program performance through a combination of complexity analysis and empirical testing.

Chapters 10 and 11 complete the text with a coverage of "replicated workers," a method for organizing parallel programs that produce computational tasks in a dynamic and unpredictable way. The two chapters mainly focus on the implementation of "work pools" that allow newly generated tasks to be collected and distributed to worker processes. The main issues that arise in this context are contention, load balancing, and termination detection. Chapter 10 deals with implementation of replicated workers on shared-memory machines, and Chapter 11 with distributed-memory machines. Appendix B contains a complete user manual for the Multi-Pascal software system.

All the chapters of the text are intended to be covered in sequence. However, there are two chapters that may be omitted without loss of continuity: Chapters 3 and 9. Also, the instructor has the option of covering Chapter 10 immediately after Chapter 6. If students have already had an advanced course in computer architecture covering aspects of parallel computer organization, then the instructor may choose to omit Chapter 3 and the first half of Chapter 7. Many operating system courses cover the topics of concurrent process communication and mutual exclusion. If students have had such a course, the instructor can move quickly through Chapter 2 and omit the first half of Chapter 5.

At the end of each chapter are exercises and programming projects for the students. Most of the exercises are rather straightforward—their purpose is to help the students review and integrate the material presented in the chapter. The programming projects require more creativity and more time to complete.

Ordering the Software Source Code

The software contained on the accompanying diskette is an executable version of the Multi-Pascal interactive system. This software should run on any IBM PC-compatible with the MS-DOS operating system. If the PC has an 8088 processor, then the program simulation may run slowly for large data sets, and therefore it will be necessary for students to use smaller data sets, especially during program development and debugging. For 286, 386, or 486 PCs, this should not be a problem. However, there are still some space limitations for program storage which may limit the size of data sets for some programs.

To overcome the space and time limitations of the PC version, the instructor may choose to order a copy of the source code of the Multi-Pascal system. Since this source code is written in standard Pascal, it will run on any computer. To order a copy of the source code, contact the author at the following address:

Dr. Bruce P. Lester
Computer Science Department
Maharishi International University
1000 N. 4th St., DB-1143
Fairfield, Iowa 52557

Acknowledgments

I wish to acknowledge the contribution of Dr. Gregory Guthrie to the design of the Multi-Pascal language and software package. He presented many helpful suggestions and ideas during the discussions we had about the language and software at MIU.

I also wish to thank the following individuals for their support and encouragement during the preparation of this text: Dr. Dwight Egbert, Robert Buck, Dr. Raman Mehra, Dr. K. C. Reddy, Francis Mosse, and Anne Bosold. Thanks are also due to Dr. Michael Weinless for sharing his computer equipment with me during preparation of the manuscript.

About the Author

Dr. Bruce Lester received his Ph.D. in Computer Science from M.I.T. in 1974, working in the research group of Professor Jack Dennis. Dr. Lester was a lecturer in the Department of Electrical Engineering and Computer Science at Princeton University for two years. He is an active researcher in the field of parallel computing and has published numerous research papers.

During 1979–1989, he was a faculty member at Maharishi International University (MIU), where he founded the Computer Science Department and became its chairman. The Computer Science Department offers both B.S. and M.S. degree programs. MIU is accredited to the Ph.D. level by the North Central Association of Schools and Colleges. The university is located on a 262-acre campus in Fairfield, Iowa, and has 800 students and 95 full-time faculty members.

Since 1989, Dr. Lester has been a visiting faculty member at MIU and a computer consultant.

1

Why Parallel Programming?

1.1 SEQUENTIAL VS. PARALLEL

Sequence is one of the most fundamental aspects of human activity and natural law. Each day, the darkness of the night is sequentially transformed into the brightness of the daytime, which then is sequentially transformed back into the darkness. Individual people each follow a daily routine of sequential steps of activity: getting up in the morning, having breakfast, going to work or school, having lunch, dinner, and so on. Human speech is sequential, and knowledge is expressed and communicated as a sequence of words, either spoken or written. The whole concept of time, which is so vital to the planning and execution of successful action, is based on the concept of sequence. Everywhere in nature and in human life, activity unfolds and expresses itself through the principle of sequence. Thus, it is natural that algorithms and computer programs were first formulated according to the concept of *sequence*. Even before the first electronic computers were built, the mathematical concept of an *algorithm* was defined as a finite *sequence* of operations.

However, as computer science has gradually matured, it has become increasingly clear, especially during the last ten years, that *sequential* is only part of the story. Human activity and natural law are not only sequential, but also highly *parallel:* action not only unfolds sequentially, but action occurs *simultaneously* everywhere at the same time. *Parallelism* is as important and fundamental as is sequentiality.

Individuals may speak and act sequentially, but individuals are part of organizations, which consist of many individuals all acting in parallel. Where would human life be today if it were not for the coordinated activity of many individuals working together all at the same time? The same principle holds for activity of nature: unfoldment of action and cycles in nature are certainly sequential, but nature functions everywhere at the same time with unbounded *parallelism*. Physical science now formulates the most fundamental laws of nature in terms of *fields:* force fields and matter fields. A *field* is an entity that functions everywhere at the same time with complete parallelism. Thus, a complete picture of human activity and the action of natural law in the universe strongly requires both concepts: sequential and parallel.

1.2 PARALLEL COMPUTER SYSTEMS

After 40 years of a complete focus on sequential programming, computer science has begun to recognize the importance of parallelism and parallel programming. Even though computer programs are sequential (a sequence of operations), tremendous increases in computing power have resulted by making that sequence faster and faster. The first electronic processor in the ENIAC computer in 1945 performed 1000 arithmetic operations per second. The latest RISC processors today can perform ten million arithmetic operations per second. These processors are still essentially sequential, but the sequence is now four orders of magnitude faster than it was 40 years ago. Through the increasing miniaturization of integrated circuit chips, this increasing sequential speed of processors is likely to continue, although perhaps not as rapidly as in the past.

Despite the growing computing power of VLSI processors, there is a wide range of important computational problems in science and engineering that require much greater computing speed. In some cases even several orders of magnitude more computing power is needed. Examples of such areas include aerodynamics, weather prediction, particle physics, signal processing used in geophysics, image processing in computer graphics, simulation of chemical reactions, and simulation of neural networks in biology. As one typical example, the solution of the Navier–Stokes equations used to aid in aircraft design is currently done on the largest available supercomputers, yet only an approximate solution can be computed. Computers with one or two orders of magnitude in increased computing power are needed immediately in this field.

In computer animation, the technique of *ray-tracing,* which produces the best-quality images, can usually not be used today because it is too computationally intensive for even the largest supercomputers. Another example of the need for greatly increased computing power is found in the field of particle physics. The current theories of subnuclear particles contain equations that predict the existence of a specific subnuclear particle called the "top quark." The solution to these equations requires so much computation that even the fastest supercomputer available today would require one full year of continuous computing.

One approach to producing this needed computing power is to custom design faster sequential processors by putting together large numbers of VLSI chips. However, the design and manufacture of these custom processors is extremely costly. About ten years ago, computer manufacturers began to discover that it was actually more economically attractive to put together many of the standard VLSI processors in one computer rather than custom designing an entirely new processor. If one needs 10 times more computing power, then use 10 processors. For 100 times more computing power, use 100 processors, and so on. This was the beginning of the widespread commercial introduction of *multiprocessor* computer systems.

As each new generation of faster VLSI sequential processors is developed, these standard processors can be combined in large numbers in multiprocessor computers to increase computing power to any desired level. Thus, parallel processing is not *opposed* to sequential processing; they work together in the same computer system. Progress in the design of faster VLSI processors will create the basic building blocks of faster and more powerful parallel processors. The companies that are now producing commercial multiprocessors, such as Intel, BBN, Sequent, Encore, Floating Point Systems, and Alliant, are continuing to incorporate the latest generation of powerful sequential processors into their multiprocessor computer systems. Even vector processing chip sets, which are in themselves highly parallel, are being combined in large numbers in multiprocessor computers. The progress in chip technology will continue to fuel progress in multiprocessor parallel computers.

1.3 MULTIPROCESSOR ARCHITECTURE

The basic concept behind the parallel computer is to simply have more than one processor in the same computer. Parallel computers may have as few as 10 processors or as many as 50,000. The key feature that makes it a "parallel" computer is that all the processors are capable of operating at the same time. If each processor can perform one million operations per second, then 10 processors can perform 10 million operations per second, 100 processors can perform 100 million operations per second, and so on.

The use of multiple parallel processors in the same computer system introduces some additional requirements on the architecture of the computer. For many processors to be able to work together on the same computational problem, they must be able to share data and communicate with each other. There are currently two major architectural approaches to fulfilling this requirement: shared memory and message passing. In shared-memory computers, usually called *multiprocessors*, all the individual processors have access to a common shared memory, allowing the shared use of various data values and data structures stored in the memory. In message-passing computer architectures, usually called *multicomputers*, each processor has its own local memory, and processors share data by passing messages to each other through some type of processor communication network. Each of these types of parallel computer architectures has certain advantages and disadvantages. We will consider the programming of both multiprocessors and multicomputers in this text.

Figure 1.1 shows a block diagram of the organization of a multiprocessor. All of the processors can compute in parallel, and each is able to access the central shared memory through a common bus structure. The common bus is responsible for arbitrating between simultaneous memory requests by several processors, and ensuring that all processors are served fairly with a minimum access delay. The activity of each processor is similar to the activity that is performed by the one processor in an ordinary sequential computer. Each processor continues to read data values from the shared memory, compute new values, and write them back to the shared memory. This computational activity is performed by all the processors in *parallel*. Thus, if there are n processors, then the computer system has a maximum computational capacity n times that of a single processor system.

The number of processors available in such systems today ranges up to a maximum of 50 to 100. One of the major difficulties with shared-memory multiprocessors is *memory contention* by the processors, which increases as more processors are added. When many

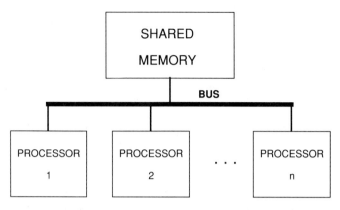

FIGURE 1.1   Multiprocessor computer organization with common bus.

of the processors try to access the shared memory within a very short time period, the memory will not be able to accommodate all the requests simultaneously, and some of the processors will have to wait while others are served. In the design of multiprocessors, much attention is given to reducing the possibility of memory contention.

A variety of techniques have evolved to help reduce the memory contention and make the system more efficient. One such technique is to allow each processor to have a local *cache memory*, which is used to hold copies of the most recently used memory values. Since each processor has its own local cache, these memory values can be accessed very rapidly with no possibility of contention. However, this introduces the *cache coherence problem*: there may be multiple copies of the same memory value in different caches, leading to the possibility of outdated values after an update. A variety of sophisticated cache coherence techniques have been developed on different systems to solve this problem. One such technique is for each processor to have a *snooping cache* that constantly monitors the common bus and immediately invalidates memory values that have been updated by other processors. The issue of multiprocessor cache memories is discussed in detail in Chapter 3.

Another technique for reducing memory contention in multiprocessors is to divide the shared memory into separate modules that can be accessed in parallel by different processors. The shared data is spread across many separate memory modules, thus reducing the probability of a simultaneous request to the same memory module by several processors. Figure 1.2 illustrates the general organization of a multiprocessor with multiple shared memory modules. Each of the n processors can access any of the m memory modules through a *processor–memory connection network*. This connection network is capable of a certain degree of internal parallelism, so that many processors may be accessing different memory modules simultaneously. The cost and performance of this type of multiprocessor depends on the internal design of the connection network. Some common designs such as butterfly, shuffle-exchange, crossbar, and omega networks are considered in detail in a later chapter.

The existence of multiple memory modules will improve the performance of a multiprocessor because many memory modules are capable of being accessed in parallel. This parallelism in memory access helps increase the parallelism in the activity of the processors: the chances of memory contention are greatly reduced. It is like going into a

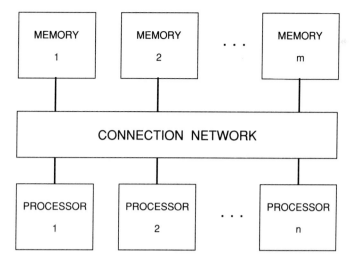

FIGURE 1.2   Shared memory with multiple modules.

bank where there are many tellers compared to a bank where there is only one teller. The increased number of tellers reduces the chance that you will have to wait to be served. In the same way, the increased number of memory modules reduces the chances that a processor will have to wait when it accesses the memory.

One important thing to remember about this type of multiprocessor is that the multiple memory modules together form a single shared memory, which is accessible to all the processors. The activity of the connection network is handled completely in the memory access hardware and is not visible to the programmer, who simply sees a contiguous central shared memory. Thus, the programming model is the same for Figures 1.1 and 1.2. There is one single memory address space seen identically by all the processors. These memory addresses are actually spread physically across the multiple memory modules, but this is hidden from the processors. When a processor reads or writes a specific memory address, the activity of the connection network and the selection of the proper memory module is handled automatically by the memory access hardware. Thus, when one is writing multiprocessor computer programs, the simple architectural model of Figure 1.1 is sufficient: just think of one simple shared memory directly accessible to all the processors.

1.4 MULTICOMPUTERS

Another approach to reducing memory contention in parallel processing computers is to eliminate the shared memory entirely, and provide a large local memory for each processor and a communication network for processor interaction via message-passing. This type of distributed-memory parallel computer is called a *multicomputer* and is illustrated in Figure 1.3. Each processor can compute in a self-sufficient manner, using the data stored in its own local memory module. Every processor can also send or receive data from any other processor, using the message-passing communication network.

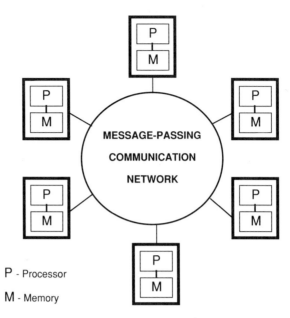

FIGURE 1.3 Multicomputer organization.

This basic multicomputer organization is fundamentally different from the multiprocessor organizations discussed earlier. A multicomputer behaves in a very different way from a multiprocessor, and requires a different conceptual programming model for software development. Now the processor knows the difference between local and remote memory modules. Each processor–memory pair behaves like a little self-sufficient uniprocessor computer. The processor can read and write data freely, using its own local memory. When processors want to exchange data, then this must be done through an explicit "message-passing" activity using the communication network. A processor has direct access only to its own local memory module, and not to the memory modules attached to other processors. However, any processor can read data values from its own local memory and send that data to any other processor. Therefore, the data can be freely shared and exchanged between the processors when desired.

There is a wide variety of different types of communication network topologies that have been developed for multicomputers. The goal of these topologies is to try to reduce the cost and complexity of the network, while rapid communication between processors is allowed. It is generally not possible in large multicomputers to provide a connection between every pair of processors, since this would require n^2 communication paths for n processors. To maintain a reasonable cost and allow the system to be easily scaled up to larger numbers of processors, the number of communication paths coming into each processor must be constant (independent of the total number of processors) or grow logarithmically with the total number of processors. The important multicomputer topologies are described in detail in Chapter 7, including hypercube, mesh, torus, and ring.

In this text, we make an important distinction between multiprocessors and multicomputers. The programming of these two major categories of parallel computers is quite different, and requires two different conceptual views of the underlying computer hardware. For programming multiprocessors, the conceptual view is that of Figure 1.1—many identical processors all accessing a single shared memory in parallel. For programming of multicomputers, the conceptual view is that of Figure 1.3—many parallel processors, each with its own private local memory, and a message-passing network to exchange data between processors. The programming of multiprocessors is actually much easier as a starting point because it more closely resembles the programming of uniprocessor systems, with which we are already familiar. Thus, the first half of this text focuses completely on multiprocessor programming. Multicomputer programming is more complex because the program must do explicit message-passing between the processors. This is further complicated by the fact that the processor interconnection topology must also be considered in planning of the program. A consideration of multicomputer programming begins in Chapter 8.

1.5 PARALLEL PROGRAMMING

This new type of computer architecture with large numbers of parallel processors places new requirements on the software. A computer program for an ordinary sequential computer has to provide a sequence of operations for the processor to follow. A computer program for a parallel computer must provide a sequence of operations for each processor to follow in parallel, including operations that coordinate and integrate the separate processors into one coherent computation. This necessity of creating and coordinating many parallel computing activities adds a new dimension to the process of computer programming. Algorithms for specific problems must be formulated in a way that produces many parallel streams of operations to be executed on different processors. Thus, although multiprocessor and multicomputer architectures have provided the potential for enormous increases in computing power at a reasonable cost, this potential can only be realized through a better understanding of parallel programming languages and parallel algorithm design.

To create programs for parallel computers, a useful conceptual tool is the notion of a *process*, which is essentially a sequence of operations that can be performed by a single processor. The *process* can be used as the basic building block of parallel programs: each processor executes a particular process at any given time. Informally, a *process* may be thought of as a subroutine or procedure that is executed by a specific physical processor. The availability of large numbers of physical processors means that large numbers of software processes may be executed by the computer hardware in parallel. Assuming that the activity of each process is contributing to the overall completion of a single computation, then the execution of that computation will be much faster than on a one-processor computer. For the *process concept* to be useful in creating programs for parallel computers, it must be added as an additional feature in parallel programming languages. Then the programmer can formulate and code parallel algorithms that are able to utilize the availability of many processors in a multiprocessor or multicomputer hardware.

To incorporate the process concept into a programming language, there must be some mechanism in the language for defining and creating new processes. There also should be some features in the language that allow sharing of data between parallel processes, so that the processes can interact with each other as they work toward computing some final overall result. Since the processes may execute at variable speeds on different physical processors, there must also be some language mechanism for synchronizing the processes. The concept of parallel processes and controlled process interaction actually originated in the late 1960s, when multiuser timeshared computer systems were first developed. Since multiple programs were active in a timeshared computer system at the same time, the concept of parallel processes was a useful organizational principle for designing operating systems for these computers, even though the hardware usually contained only one physical processor.

During the 1970s, a number of programming languages were developed that included features for creation and interaction of parallel processes, with application to the development of operating system software. These include Concurrent Pascal [Brinch Hansen, 1975], Modula [Wirth, 1977], Communicating Sequential Processes [Hoare, 1978], Distributed Processes [Brinch Hansen, 1978], and PLITS [Feldman, 1979]. The process concept was also found useful for real-time embedded systems and thus was included in the ADA language [U.S. Department of Defense, 1981]. The language Argus [Liskov and Scheifler, 1982] uses parallel processes for writing distributed database systems for computer networks.

As multiprocessors and multicomputers gained popularity during the 1980s, the process concept was added to a number of widely used application programming languages including Fortran, C, Pascal, and Lisp. For most commercially available parallel computers, this has been done by allowing special system calls in the language for creation, communication, and synchronization of processes. In the absence of standard parallel programming languages, each computer manufacturer created its own unique variation of such operating system calls. However, there have been a growing number of proposals for standard parallel programming languages. Two such languages that have been implemented on several commercial systems are Linda [Ahuja, Carriero, and Gelernter, 1986] and Multilisp [Halstead, 1985]. Although there is a wide variation in the exact syntax and semantics of parallel language features on current multiprocessors and multicomputers, they are all derived from a few simple conceptual ideas of which the process concept is the core.

To help gain a preliminary understanding of some of the principles of parallel programming, it will be useful to briefly consider a very simple example of a parallel program. Sorting is a computationally intensive activity, which is performed quite frequently on many computer systems. Since it is a familiar topic to most computer programmers, it is a good starting point for our discussion of parallel programming. Sorting on parallel computers has been studied quite thoroughly by researchers, and there is a wide range of parallel sorting algorithms that perform efficiently on various types of parallel computer architectures. A particularly simple one is based on a sequential sorting technique, which is itself actually not efficient at all: the Rank Sort.

Consider the problem of sorting a list of n numbers. In a Rank Sort program, the "rank" of each number in the list is defined as the total number of elements of the list that are less than that number. To compute the rank of some number x in the list, compare x to each element of the list, and keep a running total of the number of list elements that are less than x. In a fully sorted list, the "rank" of each element will just be its *actual* position in the list (if we assume that it is sorted in increasing numerical order). Therefore, it is obvious that in an unsorted list, the rank of each element is just its final position in the sorted version of that list. A Rank Sort computes the rank of each list element, and then uses this rank to place the elements in their proper sorted position.

To illustrate the Rank Sort, the following shows an unsorted list and the rank of each element of the list:

(Unsorted)

LIST	RANK
15	4
10	3
39	7
8	2
22	6
4	0
19	5
6	1

Notice that the RANK gives the exact ordering of the list elements. Once the *RANK* array is computed from the original unsorted list, the list elements are easily placed into their final sorted positions using $RANK[i]$ as an index for placing $LIST[i]$.

This Rank Sort algorithm is easily parellized because the rank of each list element can be computed independently by different processors. Processor 1 can compute $RANK[1]$ by taking $LIST[1]$ and comparing it with every other element in the list. While this computation is going on in Processor 1, Processor 2 can simultaneously be computing $RANK[2]$ by comparing $LIST[2]$ with every element in the list. If there are n elements in the *LIST* and n processors, then each Processor i can be assigned to compute $RANK[i]$ using element $LIST[i]$. This is illustrated in Figure 1.4 for a shared-memory multiprocessor.

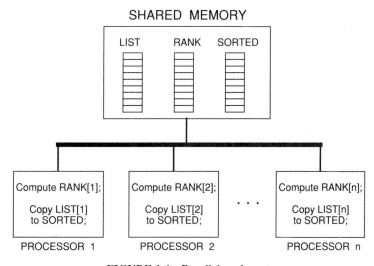

FIGURE 1.4   Parallel rank sort.

The three arrays *LIST, RANK,* and *SORTED* are placed in the shared memory, and are thus directly accessible to all the processors. Initially, the unsorted elements are located in array *LIST*. Processor 1 reads *LIST*[1] from the shared memory and then proceeds to compute *RANK*[1] by comparing *LIST*[1] with all other elements of the array *LIST*. After *RANK*[1] is computed, Processor 1 can write *LIST*[1] directly into its proper final sorted position in array *SORTED*. Since all the *n* processors compute in parallel, all of the *n* list elements will be placed into their final sorted position.

Many of the important properties of parallel programs are illustrated by this Rank Sort example as shown in Figure 1.4. The computational activity of each processor is called a *process*. Thus, a *process* is fundamentally different from a *processor*. A *processor* is a physical hardware device that has the capability of accessing the memory and computing new data values, whereas a *process* is much more abstract: a *process* is a computational *activity*. In order for a physical processor to do anything, it must have some *process* assigned to it—that is, the processor must have some computational activity to perform. In Figure 1.4, the "process" performed by Processor 1 is to "Compute *RANK*[1] and Copy *LIST*[1] to *SORTED*." The process for each processor to perform is defined by the program. Thus, "processor" is a hardware device, whereas "process" is a software concept. For now, a "process" can be informally defined as the *program code* run by a processor (although it will later become clear that this notion is not completely accurate).

The performance of parallel program is measured mainly by two important parameters: the Execution Time and the Speedup. The Execution Time, also called the "Parallel" Execution Time, is just the running time of the parallel program on the target parallel computer architecture. The "Sequential" Execution Time is defined as the running time of a sequential version of the same algorithm, executed with only one processor. The "Speedup" of the parallel program is the Sequential Execution Time divided by the Parallel Execution Time. Another important measure of program performance is the "Processor Utilization." For each processor, this is defined as the percentage of the time that the processor is actually running during program execution. With reference to the program as a whole, the Processor Utilization is defined as the average utilization over all the processors.

1.6 THE MULTI-PASCAL LANGUAGE

To teach the principles of parallel programming, this text uses a particular programming language called *Multi-Pascal*, developed by the author as part of a research project in the Department of Computer Science at Maharishi International University, Fairfield, Iowa. The design goal of Multi-Pascal was to create a language with a simple set of high-level parallel programming abstractions that have sufficient power to represent parallel algorithms for both multiprocessors and multicomputers. As the name implies, Multi-Pascal is an extension of the popular programming language Pascal, with the addition of features for creation and interaction of parallel processes. Multi-Pascal has many of the standard features for parallelism that are found in a variety of other parallel languages. Multi-Pascal also has a number of original and novel features designed to simplify the programming process by providing high-level parallel programming abstractions that help relieve the programmer from implementation details.

Programming languages have overall features that reflect characteristics of the underlying computer architecture. The two central hardware components of ordinary sequential computers are the memory and the processor. In ordinary programming languages like Pascal, C, or Fortran, there are two basic components of each program: the variables and the procedures. The *variables* contain the data values and are the software counterpart of the hardware memory. The *procedures* transform the data values, and are the software counterpart of the hardware processor. This correspondence between hardware structure and language features is to help the programmer produce efficient programs. To write efficient programs for parallel computers, it is also useful to have some overall aspects of parallel hardware architecture reflected in the parallel programming language.

Multi-Pascal is designed to be machine-independent and can run on a wide variety of parallel computers, including multiprocessors with shared memory and multicomputers based on message-passing between processors with local memory. Multi-Pascal has features that allow the dynamic creation of parallel processes to run on the physical processors. Recall from Figure 1.1 that multiprocessors have a shared memory that is accessible to all the processors. As a reflection of this hardware feature, Multi-Pascal allows data to be shared by parallel processes through the use of *shared variables*, which are a software abstraction of the shared memory found in multiprocessor computer hardware. In the Parallel Rank Sort program of Figure 1.4, the *shared variables* are the arrays *LIST, RANK*, and *SORTED*. These shared variables are stored in the shared memory. The following chart displays the correspondence between the major aspects of multiprocessors and the language Multi-Pascal:

Multiprocessor Hardware		**Multi-Pascal**
Processor	$\longrightarrow$	Process
Shared Memory	$\longrightarrow$	Shared Variables

In the case of multicomputers, each processor has a local memory, but there is no shared memory. As illustrated in Figure 1.3, the processors in a multicomputer use a network of communication channels to send messages to each other during computation. Intermediate data values produced during the course of a computation can be transmitted to other processors through these communication channels. As a software abstraction of these communication channels, Multi-Pascal has channel *variables*. A channel variable can be used to transmit data from one process to another. A process can write a data value into a channel variable, from which it can be read by another process running in parallel. Channel variables in Multi-Pascal are a conceptual software entity that allows communication between parallel processes via "messages" that are transmitted through the channels. The characteristics of channel variables are described in Chapter 4.

Because multicomputers have no shared memory, they require a different style of parallel programming. Instead of simply placing data values into the shared memory to be later retrieved by other processors, data values must be explicitly sent to other processors by using messages. This style of parallel programming is often called "message-passing" style. Since Multi-Pascal has channel variables as a built-in feature, the language can be used for writing message-passing style programs for multicomputers. Chapter 8 discusses this message-passing style in detail. The following chart shows the correspondence between the major aspects of multicomputer architecture and the features of Multi-Pascal:

Multicomputer Hardware		**Multi-Pascal**
Processor	$\longrightarrow$	Process
Local Memory	$\longrightarrow$	Local Variables
Communication Network	$\longrightarrow$	Channel Variables

Actually, channel variables can be also implemented on multiprocessors by using the shared memory. In these shared-memory multiprocessors, channel variables also serve an important function to help processes synchronize with each other and exchange data values. Simple shared variables alone, which can be freely read or written by parallel processes, are not sufficient for certain types of process interactions that are required in parallel programs on multiprocessors. To assist in process synchronization, Multi-Pascal also has the standard feature of *spinlocks*, which are especially useful in creating *atomic operations*. One of the most useful aspects of the Multi-Pascal language is that it is adaptable to both the *shared-memory* parallel programming paradigm and the *message-passing* parallel programming paradigm.

The current version of Multi-Pascal described in this text is not designed for single-instruction processor array architectures such as the Connection Machine [Hillis, 1986], in which each processor executes the same instruction simultaneously. Multi-Pascal also does not currently support vector processing, which is sometimes considered as an aspect of parallel processing.

This text describes the features and use of Multi-Pascal; it is accompanied by a software package that interprets and executes Multi-Pascal programs. This Multi-Pascal system includes an extensive interactive debugging tool and performance monitor. The system is capable of simulating the performance of Multi-Pascal programs on a wide variety of multiprocessor and multicomputer architectures, thus providing the programmer with direct experience of real parallel programming. This allows the student of parallel programming to gain experience with the interaction between algorithm and architecture, and become familiar with the opportunities and constraints imposed by various architectures.

Pascal has become the major language for education in computer programming, and is used in most universities for teaching students how to program. Likewise, the language Multi-Pascal is especially useful for education in parallel programming techniques. Multi-Pascal's set of commonly available parallel programming features is sufficient to enable students proficient in parallel programming in Multi-Pascal to easily adapt to other languages. Through a wide variety of programming exercises using the Multi-Pascal simulation system, students learn the important techniques and principles for organizing parallel programs for efficient execution on both multiprocessors and multicomputers. This knowledge can then be practically applied on specific parallel computers using other parallel programming languages that are supported on those machines.

1.7 PARALLEL ALGORITHMS

To utilize the enormous computing potential offered by the growth of parallel processing computer technology, it is necessary to devise parallel algorithms that can keep a large number of processors working in parallel toward the completion of one overall computation. In some cases, standard sequential algorithms are easily adapted to the parallel domain. In most cases, however, the computational problem must be reanalyzed at its basis, and entirely new parallel algorithms must be developed. During the last 15 years, there has been a considerable amount of research in the field of parallel algorithm design for a wide range of practical problems, including sorting, graph processing, solution of linear equations, solution of differential equations, and simulation. Some practical experience has been gained more recently with developing efficient parallel programs on multiprocessor and multicomputer hardware.

This text uses examples of parallel algorithms and programs chosen from a wide range of application areas, and designed to illustrate the major types of parallel programming techniques. When we look at the variety of parallel algorithms that have been developed so far, certain clear patterns begin to emerge, with a few simple organizational techniques recurring in different algorithms. One of the major goals of this text is to teach the student practical knowledge of applying these major organizational methodologies to writing parallel algorithms. The focus of the text is not on specific application areas, but more on general techniques that can be applied in a practical way in any application area. The following is a list of some categories of these techniques with a brief explanation of each:

1. Data Parallelism. A large number of different data items are subjected to identical or similar processing all in parallel. This type of parallelism is especially useful in numerical algorithms that deal with large arrays and vectors. The Parallel Rank Sort algorithm illustrated in Figure 1.4 uses data parallelism: each element of the unsorted list is processed in a similar way on a different processor. Rather than being just one single technique, data parallelism is really a large general class of techniques. Most parallel programs that achieve good performance use some form of data parallelism.

2. Data Partitioning. This is a special type of data parallelism in which the data space is naturally partitioned into adjacent regions, each of which is operated on in parallel by a different processor. There may be occasional exchange of data values across the region boundaries. This type of algorithm is especially suited to multicomputers because the computing activity of each processor is mainly concerned with its own local data region, and therefore the interprocessor communication is relatively infrequent.

For example, an iterative numerical algorithm using an 80 by 80 two-dimensional data array might be implemented on a multicomputer by partitioning the data array into 64 nonoverlapping regions, each consisting of a 10 by 10 array of numbers. On a multicomputer with 64 processors, each of the 64 regions can be stored in the local memory of one of the processors. The processors can then focus computation on their own local data region, while occasionally exchanging information with other processors through message-passing. The use of data partitioning in multicomputer programs is presented in Chapter 9.

3. Relaxed Algorithm. Each parallel process computes in a self-sufficient manner with no synchronization or communication between processes. Relaxed algorithms perform well on both multiprocessors and multicomputers, and can result in very large speedups. The Parallel Rank Sort of Figure 1.4 is an example of a *relaxed* algorithm. Notice that although the processors do access some common data, each processor can compute in a completely self-sufficient way without any reliance on intermediate data values produced by other processors. This complete self-sufficiency of each processor is one of the key features of *relaxed* algorithms that make them easy to program. Chapter 2 deals with the programming of relaxed parallel algorithms.

4. Synchronous Iteration. Each processor performs the same iterative computation on a different portion of data. However, the processors must be synchronized at the end of each iteration. This ensures that no processor is permitted to start the next iteration until all the other processors have finished the previous iteration. The synchronization of each iteration is necessary because data produced by a given processor during an iteration i is used by many other processors during iteration $i + 1$. Therefore, it is necessary that all processors complete iteration i before any of them can begin iteration $i + 1$.

When many of the standard numerical algorithms used in science and engineering are converted to parallel form, they result in *synchronous iteration*. This type of parallel program performs well on multiprocessors because the time required for synchronization of all the processors is relatively small. Thus, the *sychronization penalty* does not degrade the performance of the program very much. However, the synchronization penalty on a multicomputer is much higher due to the distributed nature of the processors. Therefore, synchronous iteration must be used with care on a multicomputer to create programs with good performance. The technique of synchronous iteration is described in detail in Chapter 6.

5. Replicated Workers. A central pool of similar computational tasks is maintained. There is a large number of worker processes that retrieve tasks from the pool, carry out the required computation, and possibly add new tasks to the pool. The overall computation terminates when the task pool is empty. This *replicated worker* technique is often useful for combinatorial problems, such as tree or graph searches. In such problems, large numbers of small computing tasks are generated dynamically as the overall computation progresses. Since it is not known in advance when or how many such tasks will be generated, it is convenient to organize the parallel program with a work pool. Whenever a new task is generated, it is simply added to the work pool, where it can later be picked up by any of the identical worker processes. This important parallel programming technique is discussed in Chapter 10 for multiprocessors and Chapter 11 for multicomputers.

6. Pipelined Computation. The processes are arranged in some regular structure such as a ring or two-dimensional mesh. The data then flows through the entire process structure, with each process performing a certain phase of the overall computation. These algorithms run well on multicomputers because of the orderly pattern of data flow and the lack of need for globally accessible shared data. Pipelined computation is presented in Chapter 4 for multiprocessors and Chapter 8 for multicomputers.

Through examples and programming exercises in this text, the student will gain a working knowledge of these and other important organization techniques for parallel algorithms. Then when approaching any type of parallel software development, the student will have a repertoire of useful methodologies for designing new algorithms that will run efficiently on parallel computers. The practical aspect of actually coding and debugging real parallel algorithms with the Multi-Pascal simulator is an essential part of any course that uses this text. It is only through the programming process that the various parallel programming techniques are really owned by the student in such a way that they can be applied in the future.

Another important aspect of running sample parallel programs using the Multi-Pascal simulation software is to gain experience with those things that can limit the amount of overall speedup achieved by a program. These efficiency issues certainly are of paramount importance in writing software for real parallel computers, but are often ignored in texts that deal with parallel algorithm design. Some parallel algorithms may appear to achieve a large theoretical speedup on paper, but when implemented on real systems result in a much smaller speedup, due to certain practical overheads such as memory contention and process creation time.

In this text, considerable attention is given to helping the student understand some of the major practical sources of degradation of parallel programs when run on real computers. The following is a list of some of the problems that may sometimes limit the performance of parallel programs:

1. Memory Contention. Processor execution is delayed while waiting to gain access to a memory cell currently being used by another processor. This problem may arise when global data values are shared by a large number of parallel processors. Memory contention is typically a problem only when there is shared memory, as in multiprocessors.

2. Excessive Sequential Code. In any parallel algorithm, there will always be portions of purely sequential code in which certain types of centralized operations are performed, such as initializations. In some algorithms, the sequential code may severely limit the maximum overall speedup that can be achieved.

3. Process Creation Time. In any real system, the creation of parallel processes requires a certain amount of execution time. If the created processes are relatively short in duration, the creation overhead may be greater than the time saved due to parallelism in some algorithms. This overhead is often completely ignored in texts and papers on parallel algorithms.

4. Communication Delay. This overhead occurs only in multicomputers because the processors interact with each other through message-passing communication. In some cases, the communication between two processors may involve forwarding by many intermediate processors in the communication network. The resultant communication delays may severely degrade the performance of some parallel algorithms.

5. Synchronization Delay. When parallel processes synchronize, it means that one process may be forced to wait for the other. In some parallel programs, the resultant delays may cause performance bottlenecks and a reduction in overall speedup.

6. Load Imbalance. In some parallel programs, computing tasks are generated dynamically in an unpredictable way and must be assigned to processors as they are generated. This results in the possibility that some processors may be idle while others have more computing tasks than they can handle. This type of load imbalance is especially common in Replicated Worker programs, which are discussed in Chapters 10 and 11.

1.8 THE MULTI-PASCAL DEBUGGER AND PERFORMANCE MONITOR

To write practical parallel programs that run efficiently and achieve a good speedup on parallel computers, it is necessary to have a thorough understanding of the major sources of performance degradation, of which a partial list is given in the previous section. This understanding will gradually develop through the wide range of programming exercises in this text that are designed to be run and tested using the Multi-Pascal simulation system. When one is writing a parallel program, it is often not possible to anticipate in advance where some performance bottleneck may appear in the program. When programmers become experienced with writing ordinary sequential programs, one important skill they have developed is the ability to isolate and remove bugs from their programs in a systematic way. Similarly, parallel programmers must develop a practical skill of isolating and removing performance bottlenecks that may severely limit the parallelism achieved by the program.

To help the student learn to eliminate performance bottlenecks, the Multi-Pascal simulation software has an interactive performance monitor that provides a range of tools for isolating portions of the program execution where bottlenecks exist. These tools are similar to the ones available on many real parallel computers. However, as an aid in learning, the use of these tools in the simulation system has been made very simple. One of the most useful performance features in the simulator is the ability to create a graph of processor utilization during any desired portion of the program execution and at any desired level of detail.

The Multi-Pascal simulation system also includes a variety of interactive debugging features that allow the execution of the parallel program to be carefully monitored to help isolate bugs. Again, these tools are similar to the ones that the programmer will find on parallel processing computers. Parallel programs can often be much more difficult to debug than sequential programs because of the difficulty of understanding the interaction of the many parallel streams of activity. Through repeated practice with the programming exercises in this text, the student will cultivate the ability to use interactive debugging tools to localize and remove bugs from parallel programs. This skill in debugging can be developed only through practice with coding and testing parallel programs. That is why the use of the simulation software with this text is a vital aspect of the learning process.

Another important aspect of learning practical parallel programming is to gain a familiarity with how various types of parallel algorithms will perform on different types of parallel architectures. A parallel algorithm that appears to achieve a high speedup on paper may perform very well on some architectures and poorly on others. Again the importance of practice and experience must be emphasized. The Multi-Pascal simulation system has features that allow the programmer to specify certain characteristics of the target multiprocessor or multicomputer architecture. In this way, the student will gain experience with the behavior of a wide range of parallel architectures with respect to specific classes of parallel algorithms. Through experience with optimizing the performance of various parallel algorithms for different target parallel architectures, the student will develop a practical understanding of how to write parallel software to run efficiently on different types of architectures.

1.9 PARALLELISM IN THE HUMAN COMPUTER

The advent of multiprocessor computer technology is just one more step of evolution of computer technology towards the perfected value of computing available in the human brain, which is the ultimate parallel computing hardware. The human brain has more than 100 billion neurons, all functioning together with massive parallelism. Even though the current style of computer architecture differs substantially from the computing architecture of the human brain, nevertheless computers may be understood as a limited reflection of the functioning of the human brain, which has unbounded computing potential. The human brain is really nature's own version of an enormously powerful parallel processing computer.

There is currently a large-scale research effort in the area of neural networks to try to understand and simulate some aspects of the computing processes that occur in the neurons of the brain. Although some of the results achieved so far are encouraging, it is becoming increasingly clear that the functioning of the human brain is much more complex and sophisticated than was once thought. The few basic things that are known about the chemical behavior of neuron firing are just beginning to scratch the surface of understanding the marvelous computing capabilities of the human brain. Although the activity of each individual nerve cell in the brain seems to occur much more slowly than the electronic gates that are the basic building blocks of electronic computers, the availability of massive parallelism in the brain creates its tremendous computing ability. Each of the 100 billion neurons in the brain may have synapse connections to as many as 1000 other neurons. It has been estimated that the human brain has an internal communication bandwidth of 10^{12}!

The study of the neurons in the brain and their interaction so far has failed to reveal the mechanisms of the powers of wholeness and wide comprehension of which the human brain is capable. The brain's abilities of complex pattern recognition, speech recognition, and natural language understanding make even the largest supercomputer available today seem like a child's toy by comparison. Furthermore, the brain's ability to do such things as complex logical deduction and creative planning seems to be far beyond anything that might even be imagined at this time for electronic computers.

It is becoming increasingly clear that a complete consideration of the computing capabilities of the human brain must also include the human mind and consciousness. In the field of artificial intelligence, which seeks to reproduce intelligent human activity in computers, the human mental thought process is often used as a model for creating computer programs. Even though a thought process must produce a corresponding pattern of activity in the neurons of the brain, it is often more instructive to consider the thought process directly. If the brain is considered as the "hardware" of the human computer, then perhaps the mind could be analogous to the "software," which ultimately guides the computing processes of the hardware.

In considering the computing capabilities of the human mind, one of its most striking characteristics is the ability to profoundly comprehend the subtle aspects of the functioning of natural law. The human mind has been capable of probing the properties of physical matter down to quantum mechanical level, where even the notion of *elementary particle* is replaced by quantum mechanical wave functions that are not completely localized in space and time. During the past ten years, quantum physics has finally begun to glimpse a completely *unified field* of natural law, whose excitations are the source of all the fundamental force fields and matter fields in the universe [Hagelin, 1987]. This unified field is described as a field of infinite energy that is always present everywhere in the universe, the ultimate source and governor of all activity. The unbounded parallelism of activity found in natural law, as discussed in the introduction to this chapter, has its basis in this unified field of natural law, which is itself a field of infinite parallelism.

Thus, the human mind and therefore also the human brain has the capability of comprehending the unbounded parallelism inherent in the functioning of natural law. Wallace [1986] states that the collective, massively parallel functioning of the neurons of the human brain is capable of producing a state of consciousness in the individual that can comprehend this most fundamental level of natural law. The human brain really is the ultimate parallel computer. It seems clear that the parallel architecture and computing ability of the human brain can be used as a reference point for creating a more comprehensive context for understanding the hardware and software of parallel computers in general. In this text which deals with the currently available technology of parallel computing, it is important to present this against a background of the most highly developed parallel computer in nature: the human brain computer.

REFERENCE NOTES

Hwang and Briggs [1984]* contains a comprehensive discussion of parallel computer architectures, including multiprocessors and multicomputers. Stone [1987] also has extensive material on parallel architectures, including memory system organization. Hockney and Jesshope [1988] discuss parallel architecture, languages, and algorithms.

Filman and Friedman [1984] has a survey of a variety of concurrent programming languages. Bertsekas and Tsitsiklis [1989] and Quinn [1987] contain material on many parallel algorithms for multiprocessors and multicomputers. The earliest publication of material on the Multi-Pascal language is found in Lester and Guthrie [1987].

A general introduction to the functioning of the brain is contained in Hubel [1984]. A discussion of the computing abilities of the human brain is contained in Lester [1987].

EXERCISES

1. Explain why progress in VLSI processor technology also produces progress in parallel computer technology.
2. Explain the difference between a multiprocessor and a multicomputer.
3. The performance of multiprocessors can be improved by splitting the shared memory into many memory modules. Explain how this performance improvement comes about.
4. Describe the difference between a *process* and a *processor*.
5. In the Parallel Rank Sort method illustrated in Figure 1.4, the number of processors must be the same as the number of elements in the list. Assume that the number of elements in the list is actually ten times larger than the number of processors in the computer. Describe a modification to handle this situation.

* Complete references are given in the list at the end of this text.

2

Data Parallelism

The most powerful and widespread technique for organizing parallel programs is *data parallelism*—generally defined as performing the same operation on every component of a data structure in parallel. The major application of parallel computing is to scientific and engineering problems, where large data structures are common, usually in the form of large multidimensional arrays of real numbers. The central core of most traditional sequential computer programs in these areas consists of a series of nested loops that perform complex manipulations of these large arrays to produce some numerical result. Today, most practical parallel application programs are created by reorganizing these sequential algorithms so that the nested loops can be parallelized. Usually this means that the parallelism in the program results from applying the same operation to different parts of the data array in parallel.

Data parallelism simply means that the structure of the parallelism corresponds to the structure of the data. In some cases, each individual item of data is processed in parallel. In other cases, the data structure is partitioned into groups of individual items, with each group being processed in parallel. Examples seen throughout this text will show that data parallelism is not only applicable to scientific "number crunching" algorithms, but also to many nonnumerical problems such as sorting, graph algorithms, and combinatorial search. All of these application areas have data structures consisting of large numbers of similar data items. In most cases these data items are stored in large arrays, but sometimes also in pointer structures such as linked lists.

Data parallel algorithms usually make heavy use of the *FORALL* statement, which is the parallel form of an iterative loop, where the iterations are all performed in parallel. It is natural that this type of parallelism has become predominant in the early stages of the growth of parallel processing. Programmers are already accustomed to using nested loop structures in their programs. It is a natural first step to think of parallelizing the loops for execution on a multiprocessor, with each processor performing a different loop iteration. However, as the examples in this text will make clear, iterative loops are not always amenable to immediate parallelization. Often some temporary values are accumulated and carried from one iteration to the next, so that the iterations must be done sequentially. In these cases, the sequential version of the algorithm must be substantially modified to create a parallel version, even often to the extent of actually creating a completely new algorithm.

Also, in parallelizing loops, certain complex performance issues arise, such as process creation overhead, memory contention, and synchronization delays. Through a series of simple examples, this chapter will begin to deal with some of these organizational issues for programs with data parallelism. For pedagogical reasons, the examples in this chapter will all be *relaxed* algorithms, defined as algorithms that require no synchronization between the parallel processes. The issue of process synchronization is discussed in Chapter 4.

This chapter serves as an introduction to the Multi-Pascal language and the process of parallel programming. It is interesting to see that even after presenting a few simple language constructs in Multi-Pascal, it is possible to create a wide range of parallel application algorithms from different areas. Once one becomes familiar with some of the important organizational techniques for parallel programs, the process of parallel programming can become as straightforward as ordinary sequential programming.

2.1 FORALL STATEMENTS

The most important building block of parallel programs is the *process*. Computational activity takes place when a process is assigned to a processor in the underlying parallel computer. Informally, a *process* may be viewed as a piece of "program code" assigned for execution on a given processor. Ordinary sequential computer programs can be understood as a special case of parallel programs, in which there is just one single process and one single processor. When such a sequential program starts to run on a computer, the processor starts to execute the body of the main program, starting from the first statement. Thus, this main program can be considered as the "process" being executed by the processor.

2.1.1 Process Creation

In Multi-Pascal programs, the program execution begins in exactly this same way: the main program becomes the first *process* and is assigned for execution to the first processor. The main program may contain any of the ordinary kind of statements that are found in sequential programs, such as assignments, loops, conditionals, and I/O statements. However, in Multi-Pascal there is also the possibility of a completely new kind of statement not found in sequential programs: a *process creation* statement. There are certain statements in Multi-Pascal whose execution will cause completely new processes to be created and assigned to other processors for execution. This is how parallel activity is initiated in the program: an existing process that is already running on a processor executes a "process creation" statement. The *created* process is sometimes called the "child" process, while the *creator* process is called the "parent" process.

The most powerful method of creating parallel processes in Multi-Pascal is the *FORALL* statement: a parallel form of a *FOR* loop in which all the loop iterations are executed in parallel rather than sequentially. Using *FORALL* statements, we can easily create hundreds of parallel processes, resulting in tremendous speedup in program execution. *FORALL* statements are especially useful when one is dealing with large arrays, which are very common in a wide variety of numerical computing methods used in science and engineering. For example, consider the following sequential program fragment that takes the square root of every element in an array:

```
PROGRAM Squareroot;
VAR  A:  ARRAY [1..100] OF REAL;
     i:  INTEGER;
BEGIN
 . . .

FOR  i := 1 TO 100 DO
   A[i] := SQRT( A[i] );
 . . .

END.
```

This program can be modified from this sequential form to a parallel form that operates on all the 100 array elements in parallel with 100 parallel processes:

```
PROGRAM ParallelSquareroot;
VAR  A:  ARRAY [1..100] OF REAL;
     i:  INTEGER;
BEGIN
 . . .

FORALL  i := 1 TO 100 DO
   A[i] := SQRT( A[i] );
 . . .

END.
```

The above *FORALL* statement creates 100 copies of the enclosed assignment statement and makes each one a separate parallel process with its own unique value of the index variable *i*. Each of these 100 processes may be executed on a different processor, all in parallel. This is illustrated in Figure 2.1. The main program running on Processor 0 is the "parent" process, and it creates 100 "child" processes for the 100 physical processors of the multiprocessor. The array *A* is stored in the shared memory, where it is easily accessible to all the physical processors. Each processor will work on a separate element of the array, all in parallel.

It will be useful to examine the role of the index variable *i* in more detail. In the case of the sequential *FOR* loop, the index *i* is a single INTEGER variable that takes on the value 1 during the first loop iteration, then value 2 during the second loop iteration, and so on. As each iteration of the loop begins, the index variable *i* is automatically incremented

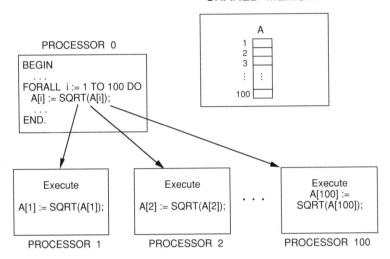

FIGURE 2.1 **Creating processes with FORALL.**

to the next value, and can be used inside the loop. This is part of the standard behavior of *FOR* loops in Pascal.

In the case of the *FORALL* statement, the index variable i is declared in the same way at the start of the program as an INTEGER variable. Therefore, variable i will be a single variable located in the shared memory. However, if the loop iterations are to be executed in parallel, then one single index variable i is not sufficient—all the values of i from 1 to 100 must be available simultaneously. This is automatically handled in the Multi-Pascal implementation by providing each processor with its own *local* copy of the index i. That is, Processor 1 has a local i with value 1, Processor 2 has a local i with value 2, and so on.

In the Parallel Square Root program above, the *FORALL* statement actually creates 100 child processes. The program code for each process is the same, just a copy of the body of the *FORALL*:

```
A[i] := SQRT( A[i] );
```

However, each child process is automatically given its own local copy of the variable i, and it is initialized to the proper value. Thus, although each processor will be executing the same code, the result will be different due to the differing values of the local index value i.

2.1.2 Process Granularity

An important issue that arises in the context of this example is the duration or execution time of each process, sometimes called the *granularity* of the process. In any computer system, there is always an overhead associated with creating a parallel process and dispatching it to a particular processor where it will be executed. For this overhead to be justified, the duration of the process must be much larger than the creation overhead. In the above Parallel Square Root example, the *FORALL* statement is implemented internally by increasing the index i from 1 to 100 and creating a process for each value of the index.

To create a new process, some computational activity is required, and therefore some computing time is consumed. The creation of a new process usually involves adding some new entries to the operating system tables, possibly changing some pointers, and the like. Typically, the activity of creating a process may require the execution of 30 to 50 machine-level instructions, or perhaps much more in some computer systems. When the *FORALL* statement in the above Parallel Square Root program is executed on Processor 0, the following computing activity will take place on Processor 0:

Create child process and give it to Processor 1;
Create child process and give it to Processor 2;
Create child process and give it to Processor 3;

.

.

.

Create child process and give it to Processor 100;

If the process creation time happens to be 10 time units in this system, then the *FORALL* statement requires $100 \cdot 10 = 1000$ time units on Processor 0 to create all of the processes. Suppose the assignment statement forming the body of each child process also requires 10 time units for execution. Since all of these child processes are executed in parallel on different physical processors, they require only an additional 10 units of overall time. However, the total elapsed time since the start of the *FORALL* statement is actually 1010. The parent process running on Processor 0 had to run for 1000 time units to create all the children, and then these children all ran in parallel in only 10 time units. Thus, the total time to execute the *FORALL* statement is 1010.

Now suppose the *FORALL* loop is replaced by a simple sequential *FOR* loop. Since it is sequential, the whole loop will simply be executed on Processor 0. Since the loop body requires only 10 time units, the whole *FOR* loop requires $100 \cdot 10 = 1000$ time units. Thus, with the *FORALL* statement above we have used 100 processors to do a task in 1010 time units, when we could have done it on one processor in 1000 time units! Not only have we failed to speed up the execution, but we have actually lengthened the execution time due to the process creation overhead.

Now suppose that instead of having such small granularity, the body of the *FORALL* statement has a large granularity of 10,000 time units. Since there are still 100 child processes created, the total process creation time on Processor 0 is the same as before: 1000 time units. However, each child process now runs much longer, so the second phase in which all the child processes run in parallel consumes 10,000 time units. Therefore, the total execution time for the *FORALL* is 11,000 time units. If this is changed to a sequential *FOR* loop, then each loop iteration requires 10,000 time units, resulting in a total execution time of $100 \cdot 10,000 = 1,000,000$ time units. Thus, the total speedup of the parallel *FORALL* statement over the sequential *FOR* loop is $1,000,000/11,000 = 91$. In this case with larger granularity processes, we have made good use of the 100 processors to speed up the program by a factor of 91.

To help overcome this granularity problem with *FORALL* statements, Multi-Pascal has a feature that allows several index values to be grouped together in the same process. For example, in the above Parallel Square Root, instead of creating 100 processes, it is possible to create 10 processes that each iterate through 10 values of the index variable *i*. In this way, there are 10 large-grain processes rather than 100 small-grain processes. In the *FORALL* statement, the keyword *GROUPING* may be used to group together a certain number of index values in each process as follows:

```
PROGRAM ParallelSquareroot;
VAR  A:  ARRAY [1..100] OF REAL;
     i:  INTEGER;
BEGIN
 ...

FORALL  i := 1 TO 100 GROUPING 10 DO
   A[i] := SQRT( A[i] );
 ...
```

The added notation *GROUPING* 10 causes the index values to be formed into groups of size 10 in each process. Thus, only 10 processes are created. The first process sequentially iterates through the index values 1 to 10, the second process iterates through 11 to 20, the third iterates through 21 to 30, and so on. In the previous version of Parallel Square Root, there were 100 processes that each ran for only a short time. Now in this new version, there are 10 processes that each run for a much longer time.

The general syntax of the *FORALL* statement is as follows:

```
FORALL <index-variable> := <initial> TO <final> {GROUPING <size>} DO
    <statement>;
```

where <initial>, <final>, and <size> may be any integer-valued expressions. The set braces "{ }" enclose optional entities. If *GROUPING* is omitted, then the default group size is 1. If <size> does not evenly divide the number of index values in the specified range, then the last child process will have less than <size> index values.

2.1.3 Optimal Group Size

The *FORALL* statement for the Square Roots was actually run on the Multi-Pascal interpreter and simulation system to see how long it takes for execution. The simulation system records the execution time of any Multi-Pascal program using simulated time units that correspond to 1 microsecond of execution time on a multiprocessor architecture with each processor having speed 1 MIP. The original version of this program with 100 processes requires 920 time units to execute. This is only slightly faster than the use of a sequential *FOR* loop, which requires 1011 time units. However, by using a *FORALL* with an index group size of 10 as shown in the new version above, the execution time is reduced to 200 time units.

Figure 2.2 shows a graph of the overall execution time of the following *FORALL* statement as the group size *G* is increased from 1 to 25:

```
FORALL i := 1 TO 100 GROUPING G DO
   A[i] := SQRT( A[i] );
```

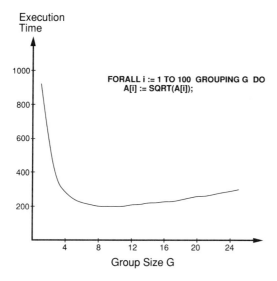

FIGURE 2.2   Effect of group size on FORALL execution time.

On the far left part of the graph, the small group size causes the sequential process creation in the parent to dominate the execution time. As the group size is increased from 1 to 5, this process creation time drops off sharply. However, as the group size is increased further, the execution time of the children starts to increase and will eventually dominate the execution time. For the group size 25 at the far right of the graph, there are only four child processes created. In this case, the process creation time by the parent is relatively short, but the children themselves must each handle 25 items. Notice in Figure 2.2 that the optimal group size seems to be approximately $G = 10$.

To derive a general algebraic expression for the optimal group size in an arbitrary *FORALL* statement, consider the following definitions:

n—Total number of index values in FORALL

G—Group size

c—Time to create each process

T—Execution time of the statement inside the FORALL

Using these parameters, we find that the total number of child processes created is n/G. The total time for creating all the processes is therefore cn/G. Each process does G executions of the statement inside the *FORALL*. Therefore, the execution time of each process is GT. Since all the processes are executed in parallel, the total execution time for the *FORALL* is as follows:

$$\frac{cn}{G} + GT$$

To minimize this execution time with respect to G, simply take the first derivative with respect to G and set it equal to 0. The result is as follows:

$$G = \sqrt{\frac{cn}{T}}$$

In the example of Figure 2.2, it turns out that c and T are approximately the same. Since $n = 100$, the above formula gives an optimal group size $G = 10$. Fortunately, the total execution time increases only very gradually as the value of G is varied around its optimal value. This is clearly illustrated in Figure 2.2. Therefore, it is not necessary to compute G exactly—an approximate guess will be sufficient for most programs. In *FORALL* statements with very short bodies, a good general rule of thumb is to simply use a group size equal to the square root of the total number of index values. For long bodies, the grouping may not be necessary at all.

Another circumstance for using the *GROUPING* is when the number of parallel processes greatly exceeds the total number of available physical processors on the target parallel computer. For example, consider the following *FORALL* statement:

```
FORALL i := 1 TO 100 DO
  Compute(i);
```

If we assume that the *Compute* procedure has a relatively large granularity, there appears to be no reason to use any index grouping in this statement. However, suppose the target multiprocessor has only 20 physical processors. One solution is to assign five processes to each physical processor. The system will consume extra time in creating all of those processes, and there will also be extra time taken to context switch the physical processor from one process to the next. If the programmer knows in advance that only 20 physical processors are available, these overheads can be significantly reduced by using the *GROUPING* feature as follows:

```
FORALL i := 1 TO 100 GROUPING 5 DO
  Compute(i);
```

This statement produces exactly 20 parallel processes, each with five index values. One process is automatically assigned to each of the 20 available physical processors. The total process creation time is reduced by a factor of five in this way, and the physical processors do not have to waste any time in switching between processes.

2.2 EXAMPLE: PARALLEL SORTING

To illustrate the use of *FORALL* statements in data parallelism, a simple parallel sorting algorithm will be used: the *Rank Sort*, which was briefly discussed in Chapter 1. In the Rank Sort, each element of a list is compared with every other element of the list to see which is larger. For an element e, the *rank(e)* is defined as the total number of elements less than e in size. It is obvious that the final position of element e in the fully sorted version of the list is just *rank(e)*. A Rank Sort can be done with two nested loops: the outer loop ranges over all the elements of the list to select the test element e, and the inner loop again ranges over all the elements in the list to compare them with e and keep a running total of the *rank* of e:

```
RANK SORT:
   For each element e in the list,
      Begin
        rank := 0;
        For each element t in the list,
           if e >= t then rank := rank + 1;
        Place e in position "rank" of final sorted list;
      End;
```

The outer loop in this sequential algorithm is easily parallelized by using a different processor for each element *e* in the list. If there are *n* elements in the original list called *values*, then this can be accomplished with the following *FORALL* statement:

```
FORALL i := 1 TO n DO
   Begin
     same as above, using e := values[i];
   End;
```

The inside part of this *FORALL* statement can be encapsulated into a Procedure called "PutinPlace." The resultant Multi-Pascal program for this Parallel Rank Sort is shown in Figure 2.3. The program begins in lines 18–19 by reading in the initial values to be sorted. Then the *FORALL* statement in line 20 creates one parallel process for each

---

```
1    PROGRAM RankSort;
2    CONST  n = 100;
3    VAR  values, final:  ARRAY [1..n] OF INTEGER;
4         i: INTEGER;

5    PROCEDURE PutinPlace( src: INTEGER);
6    VAR  testval, j, rank: INTEGER;
7    BEGIN
8      testval := values[src];
9      j := src;   (*j will move sequentially through the whole array*)
10     rank := 0;
11     REPEAT
12        j := j MOD n + 1;
13        IF testval >= values[j] THEN rank := rank + 1;
14     UNTIL j = src;
15     final[rank] := testval;  (*put value into its sorted position*)
16   END;

17   BEGIN
18   FOR  i := 1 TO n DO
19     Readln( values[i] );  (*initialize values to be sorted*)
20   FORALL  i := 1 TO n DO
21     PutinPlace(i);  (*find rank of values[i] and put in position*)
22   END.
```

FIGURE 2.3   Parallel Rank Sort.

element in the *values* array by calling Procedure PutinPlace. This is illustrated in Figure 2.4.

Since the arrays *values* and *final* are declared at the beginning of the main program, they are both accessible from within the Procedure PutinPlace, according to the usual Pascal scope rules. These arrays are stored in the shared memory, where they are accessible to all the processors. In Multi-Pascal, any variables declared at the beginning of the main program are *shared* variables, and can be directly referenced by any of the processes. The presence of process creation statements in Multi-Pascal does not change the scope rules for the interpretation of variable names that appear in the program.

Each of the 100 physical processors is assigned one of the index values from the *FORALL* loop, as shown in Figure 2.4. The result is a separate call to the Procedure PutinPlace by each processor. With reference to the code for Procedure PutinPlace in Figure 2.3, there are three local variables: *testval, j, rank*. In Pascal, each call to any procedure will create a new copy of all the local variables. The situation is the same in Multi-Pascal. As each processor calls Procedure PutinPlace, it gets its own copy of the local variables. Thus, the 100 parallel calls to Procedure PutinPlace will create 100 copies of the local procedure variables. This will allow all processors to execute in parallel without any interference. Later in this chapter, the issue of shared and local variables in Multi-Pascal is discussed more thoroughly.

The Procedure PutinPlace simply finds the rank of an element by scanning through the entire array *values*. After the rank is computed, the Procedure puts the element in its final sorted position in the array *final*. The PutinPlace procedure has a loop in lines 11–14 that moves an index *j* through the entire array and compares each element of the array with the *testval* to compute the rank. The value of *rank* is then used as an index in line 15 to put *testval* into its proper position in the sorted array *final*.

As the Rank Sort program is shown in Figure 2.3, it generates 100 processes that can all be executed in parallel on different processors, thereby producing a very large speedup.

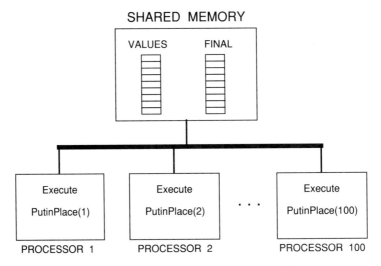

FIGURE 2.4   Execution of Parallel Rank Sort.

If there are less than 100 physical processors on the target multiprocessor architecture, the programmer may use a *GROUPING* option in the *FORALL* statement of line 20 to reduce the number of created processes to match the number of processors. For example, the following will create only 25 child processes:

```
FORALL i := 1 TO 100 GROUPING 4 DO
  PutinPlace(i);
```

Analysis of the sequential Rank Sort program shows that the execution time is $O(n^2)$ because it has two nested loops, each being executed n times. To characterize the general execution of programs, this text will sometimes use this standard *order* notation, as originally proposed by Knuth [1976]. For the reader unfamiliar with this notation, $O(n^2)$ simply means that the total execution time of the program is proportional to n^2, provided that n is sufficiently large. The formal definition is as follows:

> For any two functions f and g over the domain of natural numbers, the notation $O(f(n))$ denotes the set of all $g(n)$, such that there exist positive constants c and n_0 so that $|g(n)| < cf(n)$ for all $n > n_0$.

For example, $50n^3$ is $O(n^3)$ and $35n^2$ is $O(n^2)$. Also, $50n^3 + 60n^2$ is $O(n^3)$, and $30n^2 + 20n$ is $O(n^2)$.

Now consider the performance of the Parallel Rank Sort program. Using a multiprocessor with at least n processors as shown in Figure 2.4, all of the calls to Procedure PutinPlace will be executed in parallel on different processors. The heart of this Procedure PutinPlace is a single "repeat" loop that goes around for n repetitions. Therefore, the total execution time of each call to PutinPlace is $O(n)$. Since these calls are all executed in parallel, the total execution time of the whole parallel program is also $O(n)$. This is superior to the fastest known sequential sorting algorithms, which are all $O(n \log n)$. (*Note*: All logarithms in this text should be assumed to be base 2 unless otherwise noted.)

If the number of physical processors p is less than the number of array elements n, then the GROUPING option can be used to assign n/p elements to each processor. In this case, the total execution time is $O(n^2/p)$. If the number of available processors is $p = n$, then this expression reduces to the $O(n)$, which was calculated above. The problem of parallel sorting has been studied extensively during the past 10 years, and many useful algorithms have been developed that minimize the total amount of computation and offer good potential for large speedups. One example is the Bitonic Merge Sort, which has an execution time $O(\log^2 n)$. This is presented in Chapter 4 in the context of process communication techniques. The Rank Sort is chosen here as an example mainly because of its simplicity, not its efficiency.

2.3 NESTED LOOPS

FORALL statements may be nested to produce greater concurrency. For example, the following program fragment adds two multidimensional arrays:

```
PROGRAM SumArrays1;
VAR  i, j: integer;
     A, B, C:  ARRAY [1..20, 1..30] OF REAL;
BEGIN
 ...

FORALL  i := 1 TO 20 DO
   FORALL  j := 1 TO 30 DO
      C[i, j] := A[i, j] + B[i, j];
 ...

END.
```

In this example 600 processes are created: one for each element of the two-dimensional array. Each of the processes has its own appropriate values of both indices i and j. The outer *FORALL* causes the index i to range from 1 to 20, and the inner *FORALL* causes index j to range from 1 to 30. The nesting of these statements has the same overall effect as nesting of ordinary sequential *FOR* loops: all possible combinations of the two indices are generated. Since there are 20 different values of i and 30 different values of j, a total of $20 \cdot 30 = 600$ combinations are generated. Each combination will have its own unique child process that will be assigned to a physical processor for execution.

The dynamics of nested *FORALL* statements is such that it actually creates two generations of child processes. In the outer *FORALL*, the index i ranges from 1 to 20. This causes the creation of 20 child processes, one for each value of i. Each of these child processes will consist of an instance of the inner *FORALL* loop, with the appropriate value of i. When each member of this first generation of child processes is executed on its assigned physical processor, it will then create 30 more processes—one for each value of the index j. Thus, a total of 600 processes are created in the second generation. The parent process will then have 20 children and 600 grandchildren.

This multistage process creation greatly reduces the overall process creation time because the first generation of child processes are all executed in parallel on different physical processors. Instead of only one physical processor creating all the processes, there will be 20 physical processors all creating new child processes in parallel. Consider the general case of two nested *FORALL* loops, with the outer loop having n index values and the inner loop having m index values. If the time to create a single process is C, then the total time to create all the nm processes is $C(n + m)$. If they were all created by one parent process, then the total creation time would be Cnm, which is much larger.

In this example, the child processes have relatively short duration, since they each consist of only one assignment statement. Since there is a very large number of very short processes, this example suffers from the same granularity problem as the parallel Square Root example discussed previously. Therefore, the performance can be improved by grouping the values of j in the inner loop as follows:

```
PROGRAM SumArrays2;
VAR  i, j: integer;
     A, B, C:  ARRAY [1..20, 1..30] OF REAL;
BEGIN
 ...
```

```
FORALL  i := 1 TO 20 DO
   FORALL  j := 1 TO 30 GROUPING 6 DO
      C[i, j] := A[i, j] + B[i, j];
  ...

END.
```

In this new grouped version, the values of index *j* are put into groups of size 6. Thus, instead of 600 individual processes, there will be only 100 child processes generated. The granularity of each child process is six times larger than before, since each child must now iterate through six values of index *j*.

2.4 EXAMPLE: MATRIX MULTIPLICATION

Matrix multiplication is an important operation in linear algebra and is used frequently in many of the numerical techniques common in scientific and engineering computing. A *matrix* in this context is simply a two-dimensional array of real numbers. Multiplying two matrices involves a complex pattern of multiplying and adding numbers from the two matrices. This multiplication can best be understood by first considering the multiplication of two *vectors*. A *vector* is just a one-dimensional array of numbers.

To multiply two vectors, they must both have the same number of elements. The product of two vectors is computed by multiplying the corresponding elements in the two vectors and adding up all these results. Consider two vectors stored in arrays *X* and *Y*, each with *n* elements. The *vector product* is a single number defined as follows:

$$X[1] \cdot Y[1] + X[2] \cdot Y[2] + ... + X[n] \cdot Y[n]$$

This *vector product* can be computed by the following code:

```
sum := 0;
FOR k := 1 TO n DO
   sum := sum + X[k]*Y[k];
```

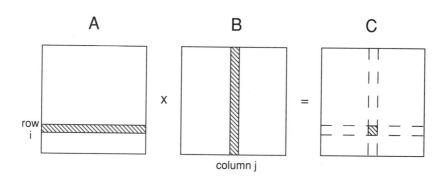

C[i, j] is computed as vector product of row i of A with column j of B.

FIGURE 2.5   Matrix multiplication.

Now consider the multiplication of two matrices A and B, each represented as an n by n array of real numbers. The product of A and B will be another n by n matrix C. Each element $C[i, j]$ in the matrix product is computed from the vector product of row i of A with column j of B. This is illustrated in Figure 2.5. Matrix A has n rows, each row being a vector with n elements. Matrix B has n columns, each column being a vector with n elements. The vector product of row 1 of A with column 1 of B gives element $C[1, 1]$ in the product matrix. The vector product of row 1 of A with column 2 of B gives $C[1, 2]$. The product of row 1 of A with column 3 of B gives $C[1, 3]$. Thus, the first row of A combined with all the columns of B gives the first row of C. Similarly, the second row of A multiplied times each of the columns of B will give the second row of C. This matrix multiplication operation is easily expressed as the following sequential computation:

Matrix Multiplication C = A * B:

```
FOR i := 1 TO n DO
  FOR j := 1 TO n DO
      compute C[i,j] as the vector product
         of row i of A with column j of B;
```

If there are enough processors available, then it should be possible to compute each of the above vector products on a different processor in parallel. Since there are n rows in A and n columns in B, there are n^2 vector products, whose results form the n^2 elements matrix C. If there are at least n^2 processors in the multiprocessor architecture, then the above sequential computation can be parallelized by changing the nested *FOR* loops to nested *FORALL* statements as follows:

Parallel Matrix Multiplication C = A * B:

```
FORALL i := 1 TO n DO
  FORALL j := 1 TO n DO
      compute C[i,j] as the vector product
         of row i of A with column j of B;
```

A complete program for the sequential matrix multiplication is as follows:

```
PROGRAM MatrixMultiply;
CONST  n = 10;
VAR  A, B, C:  ARRAY [1..n, 1..n] OF REAL;
     i, j, k: INTEGER;
     sum: REAL;
BEGIN
  ...

FOR  i := 1 TO n DO
  FOR  j := 1 TO n DO
    BEGIN
      sum := 0;
      FOR  k := 1 TO n DO
```

```
      sum := sum + A[i, k] * B[k, j];
    C[i,j] := sum;
  END;
 . . .


END.
```

In the above program, an inner *FOR* loop with index k is used to compute the vector product of row i of A with column j of B. The variable *sum* is used to accumulate the sum during the computation of this vector product. Since there are three nested loops, each with an index ranging from 1 to n, the total execution time of this matrix multiplication algorithm is $O(n^3)$.

Parallelism in this algorithm may be achieved by making the outer i loop a *FORALL*, thus creating a total of n parallel processes—one process for each value of i. If additional parallelism is desired, then the j loop may also be turned into a *FORALL*. For reasons that will be explained shortly, a slight modification is required in the parallel version: the inner *FOR* loop that computes the vector product is pulled up into a Procedure called "VectorProduct." The parallel matrix multiplication program is as follows:

```
PROGRAM ParallelMatrixMultiply;
CONST  n = 10;
VAR  A, B, C:  ARRAY [1..n, 1..n] OF REAL;
     i, j: integer;

PROCEDURE VectorProduct(i,j: INTEGER);
VAR sum: REAL;
     k: INTEGER;
BEGIN
  sum := 0;
  FOR  k := 1 TO n DO
    sum := sum + A[i, k] * B[k, j];
  C[i,j] := sum;
END;


BEGIN (*Body of Main program*)
 . . .

FORALL  i := 1 TO n DO
  FORALL  j := 1 TO n DO
    VectorProduct(i,j);  (*compute row i of A times column j of B*)


 . . .

END.
```

This program uses n^2 processors, thereby producing a high degree of concurrency and a large speedup over the sequential version of the program. The computational complexity of matrix multiplication is measured by the number of multiplications and additions, since they are the most time-consuming operations. To compute a single vector product requires n additions and n multiplications. The whole matrix multiplication algorithm computes n^2 such vector products. Therefore, the sequential MatrixMultiply program requires n^3 additions and n^3 multiplications. The total sequential execution time will thus be $O(n^3)$.

In the Parallel Matrix Multiply program shown above, all of the required n^2 vector products are computed in parallel by different physical processors. Therefore, the total program execution time is $O(n)$. If the multiprocessor has more than n^2 processors, then it is possible to speed up the matrix multiplication even more by applying several processors to each vector product. If there are n^3 processors available, then the parallel program execution time can be reduced to $O(\log n)$. In Chapter 6, a parallel method for computing the vector product is presented.

However, notice in the above parallel program that this parallel computation of the vector product cannot simply be achieved by changing the inner *FOR* loop (index k) to a *FORALL* statement. The iterations of this inner loop use the variable *sum* to accumulate the sum: *sum* is both read and written each time around the loop. Therefore, these sequential iterations cannot be just split among different processors to be performed in parallel. If this were done, the processors would all be trying to both read and modify the value of *sum*, thereby causing interference and generating an erroneous result. This important issue of conflicting references to shared variables by parallel processors is discussed in detail in Chapter 4.

2.5 SHARED AND LOCAL VARIABLES

Now it is important to understand why the vector product computation was pulled into a procedure in the above parallel matrix multiplication program. The reason has to do with the use of variables *sum* and k in the computation of the vector product. It is necessary for each parallel process to have its own local copy of these variables because they are used for temporary storage. The nested *FORALL* statements in the body of the main program create 100 parallel processes. Each process is assigned to compute the vector product of a specific row of A with a specific row of B. Each such parallel process uses variables *sum* and k during its computation. During the computation of the vector product, these variables are both read and modified during each loop iteration.

Consider the following erroneous parallel program, in which the vector product computation is not in a separate procedure:

```
PROGRAM ErroneousMatrixMultiply;
CONST  n = 10;
VAR  A, B, C:  ARRAY [1..n, 1..n] OF REAL;
     i, j, k: INTEGER;
     sum: REAL;

BEGIN
  ...

FORALL  i := 1 TO n DO
```

```
FORALL  j := 1 TO n DO
  BEGIN
    sum := 0;
    FOR  k := 1 TO n DO
      sum := sum + A[i, k] * B[k, j];
    C[i,j] := sum;
  END;
...

END.
```

In this erroneous program, there are 100 parallel processes created—one for each combination of the indices i, j. Since variable *sum* is declared at the start of the main program, it is a shared variable. There is only one copy of *sum*, and this copy is shared by all of the 100 processes. The code run by each physical processor involves the use of variable *sum* inside the *FOR* loop. Each time around the loop, a new value is written into *sum*, and then this value is read the next time around the loop. With all 100 processes trying to use the same memory cell *sum* in the shared memory, interference occurs. The value written by one process is quickly overwritten by other processes. Thus, none of the processes can compute a correct result.

For this parallel program to work correctly, each process must have its own unique local copy of variable *sum*. This situation is produced by using a Procedure VectorProduct, as shown previously. In the Procedure, the variable *sum* is declared at the start of the procedure. Therefore, each process will get its own local copy of *sum* when it calls the procedure. Instead of only one copy of variable *sum*, there are now 100 copies of *sum*. Thus, there is no interference in the vector product computation by each processor. The matrices A, B, and C are still globally shared by all the processors. There is no interference with respect to these matrices. Matrices A and B are only read by the processors and never written; therefore, no errors can occur (although some processors may experience an access delay). Matrix C is written by all the processors, but each processor writes to a different element of C; therefore, no errors can result with respect to C.

In any Multi-Pascal program, all the variables declared at the beginning of the main program are *shared variables*, directly accessible by all processes. If all the process creation statements are contained within the body of the main program, which is the case in all the example programs in this text, then there are no other shared variables. All variables declared locally within any procedure will be *local variables*, accessible only by the process that calls the procedure. However, Multi-Pascal does allow process creation statements to appear anywhere in the program, including inside the body of a procedure. In this case, it is possible for the locally declared variables of the procedure to become "shared" among a small group of processes. This aspect of the language is covered in Appendix A, which includes a discussion of some of the advanced features of Multi-Pascal.

2.5.1 Statement Blocks with Declarations

Since it is so important in parallel programs to be able to create local variables, Multi-Pascal has an additional feature to help in this regard: statement blocks with local declarations. This feature allows any group of statements in a Multi-Pascal program to be turned into a "block" with its own local variable declarations. A feature like this is available in many programming languages like C and Algol, but is not a standard feature of ordinary Pascal. In Multi-Pascal, creating a statement block with its own local declarations simply involves grouping the statements together within a *BEGIN-END* pair and preceding it with a standard *VAR* declaration section. The following program fragment illustrates the use of statement blocks:

```
PROGRAM Sample;
VAR A: ARRAY [1..10,1..10] OF REAL;
    x,p: REAL;
      ...

BEGIN (*Body of Main program*)
  ...

  x := A[i,4] * 3;
  p := Sqrt(x);

  VAR  x,y: INTEGER;  (*Start of statement block*)
       value: REAL;
  BEGIN
    value := 1;
    FOR x := 1 TO 10 DO
      FOR y := 1 TO 10 DO
        BEGIN
          A[x,y] := value;
          value := value * 2;
        END;
  END;                (*End of statement block*)

  Writeln(x);  (*Refers to "x" declared at start of main program*)
  Writeln(A[1,1]);
    ...

END.
```

In the above program fragment, the two initial assignments to variables *x* and *p* are executed first. These variables and the array *A* are defined in the main declaration section at the start of the program. The statement block inside the body of the main program is encountered after the two initial assignments to *x* and *p*. At this time, the *VAR* at the start of the statement block will cause a new local environment to be created containing the variables named in the declarations. Then the enclosed statements (inside the *BEGIN-END*) are executed using this new local environment. This *VAR* and *BEGIN-END* inside the main program is called a *statement block*.

A statement block behaves just as if a procedure call took place at that time. The local variables defined by the statement block behave just like local variables defined at the beginning of a procedure. Whenever a variable name is used in standard Pascal, there is a simple rule for determining the interpretation of that variable: first it is looked up in the local environment, and if it is not found, then the next outer level of enclosing variable definitions are checked, and so on. These same scope rules apply to variables in Multi-Pascal, with the addition of statement blocks having the ability to create a new local environment without making an explicit procedure call.

In this example, the variables *value* and *y* appear only within the local statement block. The variable declaration for *x* within the statement block supersedes the outer enclosing definition for variable *x*. Outside the statement block in the main program, any references to *x* will refer to the *REAL* variable declared at the start of the main program. However, reference to *x* inside the statement block will refer to the *INTEGER* variable declared at the start of the statement block. Thus after the statement block finishes, the *Writeln(x)* statement will write out the previous value of *x* as assigned before the statement block is executed.

When a statement block terminates, all local variables are destroyed as when a procedure body is terminated. Since the local variables *x, y, value* are all lost after the statement block is finished, the only effect of this block is to change the contents of the array *A*, which is declared at the start of the main program. The *Writeln(A[1, 1])* statement at the end will write out one of these new values assigned to the array. The general form of the statement block with local declarations is as follows:

```
VAR <declaration 1>;
    <declaration 2>;
        . . .
    <declaration m>;
BEGIN
  <statement 1>;
  <statement 2>;
      . . .
  <statement n>;
END;
```

A statement block is considered to be a single compound statement and may appear wherever an ordinary Multi-Pascal statement is allowed. Statement blocks may be nested and may appear within procedure or function bodies. However, procedures and functions may not be defined within a statement block—only variables may be defined. When a statement block is encountered during program execution, it behaves as if a procedure body were called at that point. The declarations create a local environment, which is destroyed after the enclosed statements are executed. The scope of the local declarations is only within the statement block itself. A procedure (or function) call within the statement block will take the execution temporarily into the procedure body, which is outside the scope of the local statement block declarations.

Recall from an earlier discussion that when a process executes a procedure call, the process gets its own unique copy of the local variables declared in that procedure. If many processes call the same procedure, they each get their own private copy of the local variables of that procedure. This is illustrated in the Rank Sort program of Figure 2.3: when the parallel processes call the procedure *PutinPlace*, they each get their own private copy of the variables *testval, j, rank*. There is a similar rule regarding execution of a statement block by multiple processes. Whenever any given process begins to execute a statement block with local declarations, a new private set of local variables is created for that process. Therefore, if parallel processes execute the same statement block, they each have their own set of variables that are declared local to that statement block.

The major application for statement blocks in Multi-Pascal is in the body of *FORALL* statements. Recall the Parallel Matrix Multiply program discussed in the previous section. In that program, a Procedure VectorProduct had to be used to create the necessary local variables *sum, k* used by each parallel process. Now this procedure can be replaced by the use of a statement block as follows:

```
1    PROGRAM ParallelMatrixMultiply_2;
2    CONST  n = 10;
3    VAR  A, B, C:  ARRAY [1..n, 1..n] OF REAL;
4         i, j: INTEGER;
5    BEGIN
     ...

6    FORALL  i := 1 TO n DO
7      FORALL  j := 1 TO n DO
8        VAR sum: REAL;
9             k: INTEGER;
10       BEGIN
11         sum := 0;
12         FOR  k := 1 TO n DO
13           sum := sum + A[i, k] * B[k, j];
14         C[i, j] := sum;
15       END;
     ...
```

In this new version, there are 100 parallel processes created by the nested *FORALL* statements. Each of these parallel processes begins its execution with line 8, the declaration part of the statement block. Each process as it begins will therefore create its own local copy of variables *sum* and *k* before executing lines 11–14. In this program, there is no interference between processes, and a correct result is produced. In this program, each process actually gets four local variables: *i, j, sum, k*. The nested *FORALL* statements automatically give each process a local copy of indices *i, j* with the proper initial value. The statement block declarations are responsible for giving each process a local copy of variables *sum, k*.

This statement block feature is often very useful in *FORALL* loops. Without statement blocks in *FORALL* loops, every variable that is modified in the loop must be an array reference using the loop variable as an index. An attempt to modify any scalar variable inside a *FORALL* will cause *all* the created processes to modify the same variable, thus causing interference as in the Matrix Multiply example described above. However, the use of a statement block with local declarations allows each *FORALL* process to have its own local copy of variables for modification.

This problem with *FORALL* statements may also be overcome by including a procedure call inside the *FORALL*, as was illustrated with the Parallel Matrix Multiply program. This technique is also used in the Rank Sort program shown in Figure 2.3. By calling the procedure *PutinPlace* in line 21, each process will then get its own unique copy of the local variables defined in that procedure. The use of statement blocks in *FORALL* statements saves the extra code required to define a whole separate procedure, and will be more convenient in some programs.

2.5.2 Scope of FORALL Indices

Recall that each process created by a *FORALL* statement gets its own unique local copy of the loop index variable. This loop index variable must be declared outside the *FORALL*, but it behaves as if it were defined locally within each process. In fact, the semantics of the behavior of a *FORALL* loop index is identical to what it would be if the index were actually defined in a local statement block within each process, except that the index is given a unique initial value in each process. For example, in the ParallelMatrixMultiply_2 program, the *FORALL* indices i, j must be declared globally in line 4 of the program. However, once inside the *FORALL* loops in lines 8–15, these indices behave as if they had been declared locally within the statement block along with the variables *sum, k*. This means that the scope of a local *FORALL* index is limited to the body of the *FORALL* statement.

Consider the following program fragment:

```
PROGRAM Sample;
VAR i: INTEGER;

  PROCEDURE Tree;
  BEGIN
    ...

  END;

BEGIN
  ...

  FORALL i := 1 TO 20 DO
    BEGIN
      ...

      Tree;
    END;
  ...

END.
```

The *FORALL* index i is defined globally at the start of the main program. Outside of the *FORALL* statement, the variable i behaves like any ordinary integer variable. However, within the *FORALL* body, the index i behaves as if it were defined as a local variable within the *FORALL*. Therefore, the scope of the local index i in each process does not include the Procedure Tree. When the Procedure Tree is called, the process will enter the body of the procedure, and temporarily lose access to its local *FORALL* index i. If it is necessary to use the local index within the Procedure, then it may be passed as a parameter to the Procedure.

Referring back to the Parallel Rank Sort program of Figure 2.3, we see that the procedure call in each process takes the form "PutinPlace(i)." The *FORALL* index *i* must be passed as an explicit parameter to the procedure because of the local scope rule. Similarly, in the original Parallel Matrix Multiply program of section 2.4, the procedure call has the form "VectorProduct(i,j)." Both *i* and *j* are *FORALL* indices, and therefore must be passed explicitly as parameters to the procedure.

FORALL indices have special properties and are treated in a special way in Multi-Pascal. Once a process is created and assigned its unique value of the *FORALL* index, this value cannot be changed within the process. Any attempt to change the value of this index in an assignment statement will result in a compiler error. Also, a *FORALL* index may not be used as the target of a *READ* statement, and may not be passed as a "Variable" parameter to procedures or functions. The *FORALL* indices may, however, be used in any context that does not change their value. For example, they may be used in any Multi-Pascal expression or to index an array. They may also be passed as a "Value" parameter to any procedure or function, as in the Parallel Rank Sort and Matrix Multiplication programs.

2.6 THE FORK OPERATOR

In most of the example programs in this text, the processes will be created using *FORALL* statements. However, there are some circumstances where it is useful to be able to turn an individual statement into a child process. This is done with another process creation primitive—the *FORK* operator. By preceding any statement with the *FORK* operator, it becomes a child process running in parallel with its parent. The general syntax of *FORK* is as follows:

```
FORK <statement>;
```

The <statement> can be any valid Multi-Pascal statement. This <statement> will become a child process that is executed on a different processor. The parent will continue execution immediately without waiting for the child in any way. Consider the following simple example:

```
   . . .

x := y * 3;
FORK  FOR i := 1 TO 10 DO  A[i] := i;
z := SQRT(x);
   . . .
```

After completing the execution of the assignment to variable *x*, the parent process will create a child process consisting of the *FOR* statement. While this child process is still running, the parent will execute the assignment to variable *z* and then continue to run in parallel with its child. The *FORK* operator may precede any statement in Multi-Pascal, causing that whole statement to be executed as a parallel process. For another example, *FORK* may be used in front of a procedure call as follows:

```
...

FORK   Normalize(A);
FORK   Normalize(B);
FORK   Normalize(C);
...
```

Three parallel processes are created in the above example, each consisting of a call to the procedure Normalize. While these calls to Normalize are executing, the parent process will continue to execute the remainder of its statements.

2.6.1 Process Termination

To understand the differences between *FORK* and *FORALL*, it is necessary to consider the issue of process termination more carefully. When does a process actually terminate? The answer is simple—a process terminates when it reaches the end of its code. With reference to the Rank Sort program of Figure 2.3, each process consists of a single statement, which is a call to Procedure PutinPlace. When this procedure call naturally reaches its end, then the corresponding process is automatically terminated. If the physical processors are identical, it would be expected that all the child processes will terminate at approximately the same time. However, slight variations in processor speeds, or other environmental influences may cause the termination times to be staggered somewhat. In any case, the parent process containing the *FORALL* will always wait for all the child processes to terminate. In Figure 2.3, this means that the execution of the main process will be suspended at line 21 until all the processes terminate. Then the main process will execute the "END" statement in line 22, and will itself terminate, thereby terminating the execution of the entire program.

Consider the general case of the following *FORALL* statement that creates *n* child processes:

```
FORALL i := 1 TO n DO
   <statement>;
```

The following sequence of actions results from this *FORALL:*

> Create the *n* child processes from <statement>
> Wait until all the *n* child processes have terminated
> Continue execution after the *FORALL*

The whole *FORALL* construct itself is just a single "statement" in the parent process. The execution of that *FORALL* statement begins by creating the child processes. Then the execution of that parent process is temporarily suspended while the children are running on their respective processors. When the children are all finished, then the execution of the parent process is resumed at the statement that follows the *FORALL*.

The situation is somewhat different for *FORK* statements. In this case there is only one child process created, and the parent continues execution immediately without waiting for the child to terminate. To understand more thoroughly the difference between *FORK* and *FORALL*, consider the following loop appearing in the main process:

```
FOR i := 1 TO n DO
   FORK <statement>;
```

Each iteration of the above loop will create a new child process from <statement>. As soon as each new child is created, the next loop iteration will proceed immediately. After all the *n* children are created, the *FOR* loop will end, and execution of main process will continue immediately at the statement following the *FOR* loop. Thus, the parent process will be executing in parallel with all of its *n* children. This situation is in contrast to a *FORALL* loop, which will cause the parent to wait until all the children terminate.

Although the parent process does continue with its execution while its *FORK*-children are still running, the parent is not permitted to terminate until all its children have terminated. If the parent reaches the end of its program code while one or more of its child processes is still running, the execution of the parent will be suspended until all the children terminate, and then the parent will also terminate. This behavior prevents a premature termination by the main program while some of its child processes are still computing.

2.6.2 The JOIN Statement

In some programs, it may be desirable for a parent to wait at some point for the termination of one or all of its *FORK* children. For this purpose, Multi-Pascal has the *JOIN* statement. If the parent has only one *FORK* child, then a *JOIN* executed by the parent will force it to wait for the child to terminate. If the child has already terminated, then the execution of *JOIN* will have no effect on the parent. One may think of the *JOIN* as the opposite of a *FORK*. *FORK* separates a child process from its parent, and *JOIN* brings the terminated child back together with its parent.

For example, consider the following portion of a parent process:

```
   . . .

FORK Normalize(A);
FOR i := 1 TO 10 DO
    B[i] := 0;
JOIN;
   . . .
```

The parent creates a *FORK* child consisting of a call to procedure Normalize. Then while the child is executing, the parent will execute the following *FOR* loop to initialize the array *B*. After this loop is finished, the parent executes the *JOIN* statement. If the *FORK* child has already terminated, the parent just continues execution after the *JOIN* immediately. However, if the child is still running, the parent will suspend execution at the *JOIN* until the child terminates, then continue following the *JOIN*.

If a parent has multiple *FORK* children, then the termination of any of these children will satisfy any *JOIN* in the parent. When executing a *JOIN*, the parent does not specify a particular child; any child will do. If the parent has multiple *FORK* children, it may execute multiple *JOIN* statements to wait for them all to terminate. The execution of each *JOIN* by the parent will match one single *FORK* child termination. If the parent mistakenly executes more *JOIN* statements than it has children, the parent will be suspended forever, resulting in an execution "deadlock" in the program.

Consider the following example of parent with multiple *FORK* children:

```
FOR i := 1 TO 10 DO
  FORK Compute( A[i] );
FOR i := 1 TO 10 DO
  JOIN;
```

The first *FOR* loop creates ten *FORK* child processes. Each child calls procedure Compute, using a different element of array *A* as a parameter. Then in the following *FOR* loop, the parent executes the *JOIN* statement 10 times, thus waiting for the termination of all 10 children. Without this second loop, the parent would just continue execution in parallel with all of its children. However, once the parent reached its end, it would not terminate until all children had terminated.

2.6.3 Parallel List Processing

The *FORK* operator is especially useful in implementing *functional parallelism*, in which many different computational activities are performed in parallel. This is in contrast to *data parallelism*, in which the same computation is applied in parallel to different data items. For example, four different procedures could all be executed in parallel as follows:

```
FORK ProcedureA;
FORK ProcedureB;
FORK ProcedureC;
FORK ProcedureD;
```

Another important use of the *FORK* operator is for parallel processing of data structures formed with pointers. For example, the following code applies a Procedure Compute to every element of a linked list in parallel:

```
PROGRAM ParallelListApply;
TYPE  pnttype = ^elementtype;
      elementtype = RECORD
                        data: REAL;
                        next: pnttype;
                    END;

VAR pnt, listhead: pnttype;

   PROCEDURE Compute(value: REAL);
     BEGIN
```

```
        . . .
      END;

BEGIN (*Main*)
  . . .

pnt := listhead;
WHILE pnt <> nil DO
   BEGIN
      FORK  Compute(pnt^.data);  (*Create child process*)
      pnt := pnt^.next;          (*Move to next list element*)
   END;
   . . .

END.
```

The use of the *FORK* operator preceding each call to procedure *Compute* causes the execution of that procedure to become a separate child process, which begins running immediately and allows the parent to continue executing the *WHILE* loop. Thus, the parent sequentially traverses the list structure by following pointers, and creates a child process for each data item in the list. If we assume that the execution time of the *Compute* procedure is large compared to the time to traverse the linked list, this program can result in a high degree of parallelism for a long list. Notice how simple it is to use the *FORK* operator in this program. The *WHILE* loop is allowed to continue at maximum speed, creating one child process on each iteration. Even though this is an example of data parallelism, trying to use a *FORALL* statement would be very cumbersome in this type of program.

2.7 AMDAHL'S LAW

2.7.1 Effects of Sequential Code on Speedup

One of the things that can severely limit the speedup achievable in parallel programs is sequential portions of the code, even if they are relatively short compared to the parallel portions. This fact is expressed in a well-known formula called *Amdahl's law*. Assume that a computation has a total of n operations, each requiring one time unit for execution. Assume further that a fraction f of the operations must be performed sequentially (where f is between 0 and 1). Therefore, fn operations must be done sequentially, and at most $(1-f)n$ operations may be parallelized. If this program is run on a parallel computer with p physical processors, then the minimum total execution time is clearly $fn + (1-f)n/p$. The total time to execute this program on a sequential computer is simply n. Dividing the sequential time by the minimum parallel time will give the maximum speedup achievable on any parallel computer with p processors, as follows:

$$\text{Maximum speedup} = \frac{1}{f + \dfrac{1-f}{p}}$$

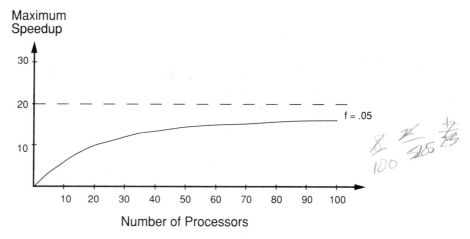

FIGURE 2.6   Effect of Amdahl's law.

This is Amdahl's law. As p approaches infinity, the value of this expression converges to $1/f$. This means that the proportion of sequential code in any parallel program can place severe limitations on the maximum achievable speedup. If, for example, a seemingly small fraction of the code must be executed sequentially, say 5 percent, then this will limit the maximum speedup to $1/0.05 = 20$, no matter how many processors are used. Figure 2.6 shows a graph of the maximum speedup as the number of processors grows from 1 to 100. The graph uses Amdahl's law; we assume that the fraction of sequential code is 5 percent.

Many parallel computers today contain 100 or more processors, and the next generation of parallel machines may contain 1000 or more processors. Amdahl's law tells us that to use these parallel machines effectively, the proportion of sequential code must be kept extremely small in a parallel program. For example, to achieve a speedup of 100, the sequential code must be less than 1 percent of the total.

Some people have used Amdahl's law as an argument against the feasibility of large-scale parallel processing. However, the examples of this chapter and future chapters show that there are some algorithms that involve almost no code that cannot be parallelized. Amdahl's law does warn us that there may be many types of programs that are not amenable to efficient execution on a parallel computer. Practical experience with real parallel computers during the past 10 years has shown that there are a large number of useful computational problems that can achieve good speedups of up to 100 or more. These results are encouraging for the future of parallel computing.

2.7.2 Overcoming Initialization Overhead

In the light of Amdahl's law, parallel programs must be very careful with initialization code. Any data-parallel program that deals with large data arrays must somehow initialize these arrays. The initialization is often difficult to parallelize because the program is dealing with external I/O devices and interfaces that are inherently sequential in behavior. Many commercial parallel computers, however, do have custom-designed disk interfaces with an extremely high bandwidth to help minimize the sequential initialization time.

One factor that helps greatly in overcoming the initialization problem is that programs executed on parallel computers are *computationally intensive*. This means that the amount of computation in the program is usually proportional to a power of the size of the data base—usually the square of the size of the data, but sometimes even higher powers. The Rank Sort program presented in this chapter has computation proportional to n^2. The Matrix Multiplication program is n^3. Since the initialization part of the program is always proportional to the size of the data (n), the fraction of the total computation needed for initialization will decrease dramatically as n increases. This means that Amdahl's law can be overcome by increasing the size of the data base.

Assume that the amount of computation required for initialization is cn, and the amount of computation in the body of the program is dn^2. Further, assume that the initialization code must be executed sequentially, but the remainder of the program can be highly parallelized. Then the fraction f of sequential code in Amdahl's law is as follows:

$$f = \frac{cn}{dn^2} = \frac{c}{dn}$$

As the size of the data base n grows larger, the fraction f gets smaller. Therefore, as n approaches infinity, the maximum speedup for a parallel computer with p processors, according to Amdahl's law, approaches p. Thus, the performance problems caused by initialization can be eliminated by using larger data bases. This is illustrated in the graph of Figure 2.7. For a multiprocessor with $p = 100$ physical processors, the graph shows the maximum speedup according to Amdahl's law as the size of the data base n grows. For data size $n < 200$, the sequential initialization does limit the maximum speedup, as seen in the figure. However, for data size $n > 500$, the loss due to initialization is less than 15 percent. Since the computer has only 100 physical processors, naturally the maximum speedup is limited to 100, no matter how large the data. (*Note*: The graph in Figure 2.7 assumes $c = d$; therefore $f = 1/n$.)

Experience with real parallel computers has shown that this technique of increasing the size of data has been utilized. The computationally intensive scientific and engineering problems solved on parallel computers are usually approximations to real physical sys-

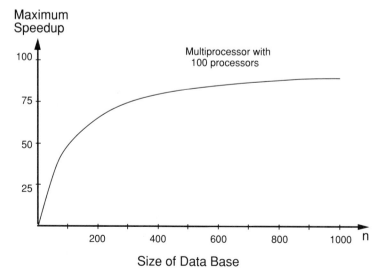

FIGURE 2.7   Growth of maximum speedup with size of data.

tems. In such programs, the programmer has a choice of the size of the data base, with larger data bases giving a more accurate approximation. For example, in simulation of particle systems, the number of particles is usually restricted by the processing power available in the computer. Real physical systems involve so many particles that no computer can ever consider all of them. Similarly, in solving the partial differential equations to compute the forces on an airplane wing, a grid of sample points is chosen for approximating the solution. If more processing power is available, then a more accurate solution can be obtained with a larger grid of data points.

As the number of processors on parallel computers grows, then larger data bases are used in the programs. As long as the computational part of the program can be highly parallelized, then the sequential initialization will not restrict the speedup. In our laboratory programming exercises in this text, however, the initialization may cause difficulties. Each programming exercise must begin with some sequential loops to initialize the data arrays, followed by a highly parallel computation on that data. The loss of speedup caused by the initialization can be minimized by increasing the size of the data base to the proportions that might be used on a real parallel computer. However, this will necessitate supplying the program with large amounts of input data, which is cumbersome in short programming exercises. Moreover, since the target parallel architecture is actually being simulated sequentially in the Multi-Pascal interactive software system, large data bases will cause the programming exercises to run for extremely long periods of time.

To overcome this initialization problem in the programming exercises, the best technique is to simply ignore the sequential initialization in computing the speedup, and focus attention on the computational part of the program. Techniques for doing this are included in Appendix B, which is a user's manual for the Multi-Pascal software package accompanying this text. This will allow small data bases to be used for testing purposes in the programming projects, and yet still achieve good speedups.

2.8 SUMMARY

The chapter has introduced one of the simplest organizational techniques for parallel programs: *relaxed data parallelism*. These programs usually contain a few nested *FORALL* statements that create large numbers of parallel processes to perform similar computations on each element in a large data base. Usually the data base consists of large multidimensional arrays of numbers. Sometimes the data base has a more complex structure, such as a tree or graph. The term *relaxed* means that the parallel processes can compute in a completely self-sufficient manner—they do not have to communicate or synchronize with each other. These relaxed data-parallel programs usually result in very large speedups, and are excellent candidates for execution on a wide range of parallel architectures.

One of the major purposes of this chapter has been to introduce the concept of parallel processes in Multi-Pascal, and explain the syntax and semantics of the process creation statements: *FORALL* and *FORK*. *FORALL* is a parallel form of a *FOR* loop, in which the loop iterations are executed in parallel rather than sequentially. The *FORK* operator can turn any statement into a detached parallel process that runs concurrently with its parent. Processes in Multi-Pascal can share data through the use of ordinary variable declarations that appear at the beginning of the program. These shared variables can be accessed by many processes in parallel. Processes may also gain their own private copies of variables by calling procedures or functions with local variable declarations. Statement blocks with local declarations may also be used for this purpose. Thus, parallel processes may have both shared data and local data.

Using these two important primitives for creating parallel processes in Multi-Pascal, a few simple parallel algorithms were presented, including Parallel Rank Sort and Parallel Matrix Multiplication, both of which achieve a high degree of parallelism and a large speedup over sequential algorithms. Both of these algorithms were easily derived from sequential algorithms by just parallelizing the iterative loops into *FORALL* statements. It was seen that this parallelization must be done carefully to avoid interference between the processes regarding the modification of shared variables. The use of procedure calls or statement blocks with local declarations was helpful in this regard to allow processes to have their own nonshared variables.

The important performance issue of *process creation overhead* was also discussed in this chapter and illustrated through several examples. The processes must have a large enough *granularity* to overcome the necessary overheads associated with process creation. One feature that is useful to help increase the process granularity in *FORALL* statements is the *GROUPING* primitive that combines several index values into the same process.

The performance limitations caused by sequential code are illustrated by Amdahl's law, which states that a fraction f of sequential code in a program will limit the speedup to $1/f$, no matter how many processors are used. This warns the programmer to be alert to keep sequential code to an absolute minimum. In this regard, sequential initialization of large data arrays can present a problem. However, in large parallel computers this can be overcome by using larger data bases, because the initialization time grows linearly with the data size, whereas the parallel portion of the program grows as a power of the data size. Other important performance degradation problems such as memory contention and communication delays will be discussed in future chapters.

REFERENCE NOTES

A comprehensive summary of parallel sorting algorithms is contained in Bitton, et al. [1984]. Quinn [1987] also has a good presentation of parallel sorting. The parallel Rank Sort technique can be found in Chandy and Misra [1988].

The use of local declarations to qualify individual statements in a Pascal-based parallel programming language is found in Sterling, Musciano, Chan, and Thomae [1987]. The *FORK–JOIN* primitives are widely used, such as in the UNIX operating system [Ritchie and Thompson, 1974].

The original presentation of Amdahl's law is in Amdahl [1967]. Further analysis and rebuttals of this law are found in Quinn [1987] and Fox, et al. [1988].

The parallel algorithm for merging sorted lists used in the programming project is found in Shiloach and Vishkin [1981] and Baase [1988].

PROGRAMMING PROJECTS

The programming projects in this text can be done by using the Multi-Pascal interactive software package that accompanies the text. The software includes features to help debug and monitor the performance characteristics of Multi-Pascal programs. A complete user's manual for the software package is found in Appendix B.

1. MULTIPLYING POLYNOMIALS

In this project, you will write and run a parallel program to compute the product of two polynomials. In addition, you will create a performance graph for the program showing the speedup as a function of the size of the polynomials.

The following is an example of a polynomial:

$$\text{Polynomial } A: \quad 6x^{10} + 4x^5 - 8x^2 + 2$$

In general a polynomial consists of a summation of *terms*. Each term consists of a *coefficient* and a *power* of x. When two polynomials A and B are multiplied together, each term in A must be multiplied by each term in B. When two terms are multiplied, the coefficients are multiplied and the powers are added. Consider the following example of multiplication of two terms:

$$6x^{10} \cdot 10x^8 = 60x^{18}$$

The following is an example of another polynomial:

$$\text{Polynomial } B: \quad 10x^8 + 3x^3$$

Multiplying this polynomial B by the previous polynomial A will result in a total of eight terms as follows:

$$60x^{18} + 18x^{13} + 40x^{13} + 12x^8 - 80x^{10} - 24x^5 + 20x^8 + 6x^3$$

To put this product polynomial in final form, the terms must be sorted in decreasing order of power, and terms with the same power must be combined by adding the coefficients. The following is the result:

$$60x^{18} + 58x^{13} - 80x^{10} + 32x^8 - 24x^5 + 6x^3$$

In a computer program, each polynomial may be represented in a simple data structure. Each term can be represented by a record with two components: coefficient and power. A polynomial can be stored in an array of such records. Your program will have the following four phases:

1. Initialize the two polynomials.
2. Take a cross-product of terms from the two polynomials to form a new polynomial, which will be stored in a new array.
3. Sort this new polynomial by power, using a Parallel Rank Sort.
4. Scan through the polynomial sequentially and combine terms with the same power.

The two middle phases of this program can be highly parallelized, and therefore should produce an excellent speedup for reasonably long polynomials. Your goal in this project is to minimize the total program execution time and produce the maximum speedup. Run and test the program, using the Multi-Pascal interactive system. Once the program is debugged, run it for a variety of polynomials of different lengths, and observe the increasing speedup for longer polynomials. Draw a graph of the speedup verses the polynomial length. Explain why the graph has this shape. (It will be helpful to ignore the initialization phase of the program in computing the speedup, by using the techniques described in Appendix B.)

2. MERGING SORTED LISTS

In this programming project you will write and run a parallel program to merge two sorted lists into a single sorted list. Your goal is to make the program as efficient as possible, to both minimize the parallel execution time and maximize the speedup.

At first consideration it may seem that merging sorted lists is an inherently sequential activity, with little opportunity for parallelism. However, there is a clever parallel technique that can produce a very large speedup for this problem. Assume that the two sorted lists are initially stored in arrays X and Y, and the final merged list is to be stored in array Z. The parallel algorithm is based on the following simple observation with respect to any data item $X[i]$ in the first sorted list:

> Consider merging $X[i]$ directly into its proper sorted position in the second list Y. Let $Y[j]$ be this proper position. Then the final position of $X[i]$ in the fully merged list must be $Z[i+j-1]$.

The above observation is easily justified. The first $i-1$ items in list X are all less than $X[i]$, and therefore must appear prior to $X[i]$ in the final sorted list Z. Also, the first $j-1$ items in list Y are all less than $X[i]$, and therefore must also appear prior to $X[i]$ in Z. Thus, there are exactly $i-1+j-1$ items that must appear prior to $X[i]$ in the final list Z. This gives the Rank of $X[i]$ as $i+j-1$. Therefore, $X[i]$ must be placed into position $Z[i+j-1]$. This simple observation leads to a highly parallel algorithm for merging the two sorted lists. For each item $X[i]$, scan list Y to locate its proper position j. This can be done most efficiently with a binary search of list Y. Then simply copy item $X[i]$ into position $Z[i+j-1]$. Naturally, the same thing can be done for each item $Y[k]$: perform a binary search on list X to find the proper position m, and then copy $Y[k]$ into position $Z[k+m-1]$.

The above discussion ignores the problem of duplicate items in the two lists. This can be easily solved by creating a slight asymmetry in the treatment of the two lists. When doing the binary search of list Y to find the location for $X[i]$, treat any items in Y that are equal to $X[i]$ as if they were greater than $X[i]$. However, when binary searching list X for $Y[k]$, treat equal items in list X as if they were less than $Y[k]$. This asymmetry will prevent equal items from the two lists from colliding on the same location in the merged list Z.

Based on the above discussion, your task in this project is to write a highly parallel program to merge any two sorted lists. Try to optimize the performance of the program to minimize the execution time and maximize the speedup. Observe how the speedup and processor utilization change as the list sizes are increased. In determining the speedup, ignore the sequential list initialization code by using the techniques described in Appendix B.

EXERCISES

1. Write a sequential FUNCTION that computes and returns the sum of the elements of a one-dimensional array. Write a main program that applies this function to each of four different

arrays, all in parallel. Be careful about conflicting use of global shared variables in your program.

2. To improve the visual quality of an image represented as a two-dimensional array of pixel values, a smoothing algorithm is sometimes applied. A simple smoothing algorithm is to replace the value of each pixel by the average of its immediate neighbors. Each pixel has eight immediate neighbors, including the diagonal neighbors. This algorithm replaces the value at each pixel by the average of nine pixels, consisting of itself and the eight neighbors.

In this exercise, you are to write and run a parallel program to apply this smoothing algorithm to an image. To simplify the programming, do not modify the pixels along the four outer boundaries of the image array.

3. Write a parallel program that searches a two-dimensional array for an occurrence of a given input number. Run the program using the Multi-Pascal interactive system. By varying the process granularity, try to minimize the total program execution time.

4. Consider the following portion of a program:

```
    . . .

FORK   x := x + 1;
FORK   y := 23 * z;
FORK   z := a[i] + a[j];
    . . .
```

Despite the parallelism in this statement, it is actually found that the total execution time can be reduced by removing the *FORK* operators, and thereby eliminating the parallelism. What is the explanation for this apparent contradiction?

5. The Parallel Rank Sort program given in Figure 2.3 creates n processes, one for each of the n elements of the array. Rewrite this program to run on a multiprocessor which has only $n/5$ physical processors.

6. A vector is represented by a one-dimensional array, and a matrix by a two-dimensional array. Recall that the product of two vectors A and B is a new vector C computed by multiplying the corresponding components of A and B, and then summing these products. The product of a matrix M with vector A is a new vector C, computed by multiplying A times each row of M. Each component of vector C is computed as follows:

$$C[i] = \text{vector product of } A \text{ with row } i \text{ of } M$$

Write a parallel program for computing the product of a 20 by 20 matrix with a vector having 20 elements.

7. Consider the following version of the Parallel Rank Sort in which the Procedure PutinPlace has been moved into the body of the main program as part of the *FORALL* loop:

```
PROGRAM NewRankSort;
CONST  n = 100;
VAR  values, final:  ARRAY [1..n] OF INTEGER;
     i: INTEGER;
     src, testval, j, rank: INTEGER;

BEGIN
FOR  i := 1 to n DO
  Readln( values[i] );  (*initialize values to be sorted*)
FORALL  src := 1 TO n DO
  BEGIN
    testval := values[src];
```

```
      j := src;    (*j will move sequentially through the whole array*)
      rank := 0;
      REPEAT
        j := j MOD n + 1;
        IF testval >= values[j] THEN rank := rank + 1;
      UNTIL j = src;
      final[rank] := testval;   (*put value into its final sorted position*)
    END;
  END.
```

    (a) This program has a serious problem and will not produce correct results. Explain the nature of this problem.

    (b) Indicate some slight modifications to this program that will correct the problem and allow the program to work correctly.

8. The Parallel Rank Sort program will actually not work correctly if the list of values to be sorted has any duplicates.

    (a) Explain the nature of the error which occurs for duplicates in the list.

    (b) Indicate a minor modification in the program that will correct this problem.

9. In the Parallel Matrix Multiplication program given in this chapter, there are n^2 processes created. Rewrite the program for a multiprocessor with only n physical processors. Be careful about the use of shared and local variables to make sure that there is no interference between the parallel processes.

10. Consider the following *FORALL* statement:

```
FORALL i := 1 TO 200 GROUPING size DO
        A[i] := 10*A[i];
```

Use the Multi-Pascal interactive system to compute the speedup achieved by this statement as the variable *size* is varied from 1 to 25. What is the optimal group size for maximizing the speedup? Explain the reasons for this general pattern of speedup variation. What is the reason for the increase at the beginning? What is the reason for the decrease at the end?

11. The *sequential execution time* of a *FORALL* statement is defined as the time to execute the same statement with the *FORALL* replaced by a *FOR*. The speedup of a *FORALL* statement is derived by dividing its execution time into the sequential execution time. Consider a *FORALL* statement that creates n parallel processes. The granularity of these processes is such that they each have an execution time that is 10 times as long as a single process creation time. Derive an algebraic expression in terms of n that gives the highest achievable speedup of this *FORALL* statement on a parallel computer with p processors. You should choose a *FORALL* group size that maximizes the speedup.

12. Consider the following program fragment:

```
PROGRAM Sample;
VAR  a,b: INTEGER;
BEGIN
  a := 4;
  b := 2;
  VAR t,a: INTEGER;
  BEGIN
    a := 7;
    t := 10;
    b := t + 5;
  END;
  Writeln(a,b);
END.
```

What will be the final values of variables (*a, b*) that are written out at the end? Explain the reasons for your answer.

13. Consider the following *FORALL* statement to produce a sum array *C* from arrays *A* and *B*:

```
FORALL i := 1 TO 50 DO
   C[i] := A[i] + B[i];
```

In an attempt to produce a similar statement using *FORK* to create the processes instead, the following *FOR* loop has been written:

```
FOR i := 1 TO 50 DO
  FORK  C[i] := A[i] + B[i];
```

When this statement is executed, however, it is found to produce an erroneous result for the sum array *C*. What is the reason for this error?

14. **(a)** In this problem you will write a parallel program to search a linked list for a given value. Each data item in the linked list is an array of *REAL* values. Your program should create a parallel process to search each array. The following type declarations and *Search* procedure should be used as the starting point for your program. Do not be concerned with initialization of the list.

```
PROGRAM SearchList;
TYPE   arraytype = ARRAY [1..100] OF REAL;
       pnttype = ^itemtype;
       itemtype = RECORD
                    data: arraytype;
                    next: pnttype;
                  END;

VAR  found: BOOLEAN;
     listhead: pnttype;


PROCEDURE Search(inarray: arraytype);
VAR i: INTEGER;
BEGIN
  FOR i := 1 TO 100 DO
    IF inarray[i] = value THEN found := TRUE;
END;
```

(b) Will this program achieve a reasonably good speedup for a list of length ten?

15. Consider the program in this chapter that uses the *FORK* operator to create parallel processes for applying a procedure to every element of a linked list. Rewrite this program to use a *FORALL* statement to create the processes instead of the *FORK* operator. This will require some slight reorganization of the program and the addition of a some new variables. Try to minimize the changes to the program.

16. This exercise provides practice with applying the scope rules for *FORALL* index variables (see section 2.5.2). Give the exact output of each of the following three programs:

```
PROGRAM Test1;
VAR i: integer;
BEGIN
  i := 25;
  FORALL i := 1 TO 10 DO
    Writeln(i);
```

```
    Writeln(i);
END.


PROGRAM Test2;
VAR i: INTEGER;

  PROCEDURE Print;
  BEGIN
    Writeln(i);
  END;

BEGIN
  i := 25;
  FORALL i := 1 TO 10 DO
    Print;
END.


PROGRAM Test3;
VAR i: INTEGER;

  PROCEDURE Print(val: integer);
  BEGIN
    Writeln(val);
  END;

BEGIN
  i := 25;
  FORALL i := 1 TO 10 DO
    Print(i);
END.
```

17. The following statement computes the sum of the elements in an array A:

```
FOR i := 1 TO n DO
  sum := sum + A[i];
```

In an attempt to compute this sum in parallel, the following statement is written:

```
FORALL i := 1 TO n DO
  sum := sum + A[i];
```

Explain why this *FORALL* statement produces an erroneous result for the sum.

18. For a particular algorithm, assume that 8 percent of the code is purely sequential and cannot be parallelized. Use Amdahl's law to draw a graph of the maximum speedup of this algorithm as the number of processors is varied from 1 to 30. On the same graph, also draw the maximum speedup curve for an algorithm with only 4 percent sequential code.

19. The graph of Figure 2.7 assumes that the multiprocessor has 100 processors. Recompute and redraw the graph, assuming that the multiprocessor has only 50 processors.

20. Consider a sequential program in which the total amount of computation is $O(n^3)$. Assume that in the parallel version of this program, the initialization must be sequential, and is therefore $O(n)$. However, the remainder of the program can be completely parallelized. Use Amdahl's law to derive a general algebraic expression for the maximum speedup of this program on a multiprocessor with p processors.

21. In light of Amdahl's law, explain why it is important for multiprocessor systems to have specially designed high-bandwidth disk I/O systems.

3

Multiprocessor Architecture

When a parallel program is executed on a particular multiprocessor, the overall machine architecture will have an important influence on the program performance. Certainly, the number and speed of the processors is of primary importance in determining the program performance. However, the processors must operate on data values stored in the memory, and the average speed of the processors will be reduced if they experience long delays in accessing these data values from memory. Therefore, the overall organization of the memory system is extremely important to program performance. This chapter surveys the major issues in multiprocessor architecture in relation to processor–memory interaction.

To write parallel programs that perform well on a chosen multiprocessor architecture, the programmer must be aware of the general design of the processor–memory interconnection system. In some machines, this may be a bus-oriented system, possibly with cache memories. In other multiprocessors, there are multiple memory modules connected to the processors with a switching network. In any multiprocessor architecture, there is always a possibility of memory contention problems, which may seriously degrade program performance. Sometimes the memory contention is inherent in the organization of the program itself, and will manifest in any target multiprocessor. In other parallel programs, memory contention may occur only with certain multiprocessor architectures.

This chapter surveys some of the important issues in multiprocessor architecture which affect memory contention. By gaining a general understanding of these issues, the programmer will then be equipped to evaluate specific target multiprocessors when the need arises. The major focus of the chapter is on the "programmer's view" of the processor–memory architecture. Those issues that affect program performance are considered, with special emphasis on the problem of memory contention. Only shared-memory multiprocessors are presented here. A detailed examination of multicomputers, the other major type of parallel computer architecture, is deferred to Chapter 7.

One major category of multiprocessor architecture is bus-oriented systems, in which a single shared-memory unit is connected to all the processors with a common bus. Because of the memory contention problem, bus-oriented systems can have only a limited number of processors. One hardware feature that greatly improves the performance of bus systems is cache memory, a small high-speed memory unit attached to each processor to hold recently used data values. The other major category of multiprocessors is those with multiple memory modules, connected to the processors with a switching network. Since the multiple modules may be accessed in parallel by different processors, the chances of memory contention are reduced.

3.1 BUS-ORIENTED SYSTEMS

In a uniprocessor computer system, it is important for the memory speed to be matched to the processor speed. A slow memory will cause the processor to spend much of its time waiting, thus reducing the performance of the computer. To improve average memory performance, various special mechanisms are used, such as cache memory and CPU registers, both of which take advantage of locality of memory access to decrease the average time to access data from the memory. Similarly, in parallel computers, the memory speed must be balanced with the processor speed to avoid undue memory access delays. In multiprocessor systems, this problem is especially acute, since all the processors are using the same globally shared memory. If many processors are accessing the shared memory simultaneously, then some processors may experience delays. When these delays become excessive, it is referred to as *memory contention*.

Memory contention is highly dependent on the specific memory architecture of the multiprocessor, and on the patterns of memory access by the program being executed. The same parallel program may have memory contention problems on some multiprocessors but not on others. However, there are some things in parallel programs that will cause memory contention on *any* multiprocessor. These things should of course be avoided. This chapter gives an overview of the general reasons for the occurrence of memory contention, and the various architectural features that influence memory contention. Then the influence of specific classes of parallel algorithms is discussed.

Recall from Chapter 1 that the basic architecture of a uniprocessor computer system consists of a processor (CPU) and memory with a *bus* connecting them. The bus is the pathway for the data to flow between the processor and memory. This bus architecture can be extended to handle multiple processors, as illustrated in Figure 1.1. The single common bus is shared by all the processors and used to access the single shared memory module. The bus and memory can service only one request at a time. To access any memory cell, a processor needs *exclusive* use of the bus for a short time period. Thus, the maximum bus speed or bus *bandwidth* will limit the number of processors that can effectively use the shared memory. For example, if the bus bandwidth is 50 MHz, and the average processor memory access rate is 5 MHz, then the bus will saturate at 10 processors. Even in a well-balanced system, in which the bus bandwidth exceeds the average processor memory access rate, there is still the possibility of memory contention during short bursts of highly memory intensive computation by many processors at the same time.

Buses operate electrically, and therefore high-speed buses require very rapid changes in voltages and currents. There are physical limitations to how quickly materials can change their voltages and currents. These limitations will place limits on the maximum bus speed. As more processors are addcd to the bus, then more electrical power is required, which also increases the switching time in the physical components. One technique that helps to increase the maximum speed is making the bus itself physically small, because voltages and currents can be changed more quickly over shorter distances. Current commercial bus-oriented multiprocessors are usually limited to 20–30 processors because of limitations in the bus speed. This may be increased in the future up to perhaps 50–100 processors, but is unlikely to increase beyond that unless some new breakthrough in bus technology occurs.

3.2 CACHE MEMORY

3.2.1 Uniprocessor Caches

In uniprocessor systems, one important technique for reducing the processor memory-access rate is the use of *cache memory*. A *cache memory* is a small high-speed memory connected directly to the processor. Frequently used data values are stored in the cache, where they can access much more quickly than data values stored in the larger but slower main memory. The size of the main memory in typical computer systems is measured in megabytes, whereas cache size is measured in kilobytes. Since the cache is much smaller, it can be built from much more costly but faster hardware technology than the main memory.

The basic principle behind cache memory in a uniprocessor system is illustrated in Figure 3.1. Each entry in the cache contains an address–data pair. The "address" corresponds to some real address in the main memory, and the "data" tells the contents of that main memory cell. For example, in Figure 3.1 the first cache entry says that memory address 1000 in the main memory contains data value 75. The second cache entry says that main memory address 3500 contains data value 2. These cache entries are copies of a few of the memory cells in the main memory. When the processor performs a memory access, it first checks the contents of the cache to see if the value is stored there. If so, the value is accessed at high speed from the cache, thus saving the need of a much slower access to the main memory itself. Since the cache is structured as an "associative" memory, all the cache entries can be searched in one operation at extremely high speed.

When a particular memory reference by a processor is found in the cache, this is called a cache "hit." If the memory reference is not in the cache, and therefore must go to the main memory, this is called a cache "miss." The cache memory has a limited size and cannot hold copies of all the main memory locations used by the program. Therefore, some cache misses are inevitable. However, studies show that computer programs exhibit a property called "locality" of memory access. This means that memory locations accessed in the immediate past are the ones most likely to be accessed in the immediate future.

Cache memory exploits this property of "locality" by storing all the most recently used memory values in the cache, because these are the ones most likely to be used in the immediate future. This greatly enhances the probability of a cache hit on each memory

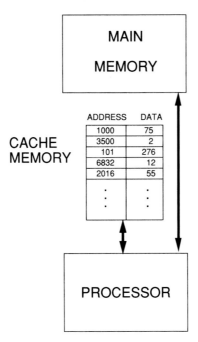

CACHE
MEMORY

ADDRESS	DATA
1000	75
3500	2
101	276
6832	12
2016	55

FIGURE 3.1 Cache memory in uniprocessor computer.

reference. Typical uniprocessor computer systems achieve a "hit" percentage of 90 percent for the cache. This means that only 10 percent of the processor memory references need go to the slower main memory. The average memory access time is thereby greatly reduced. When a cache miss occurs, and the main memory must be accessed, then that entry is copied into the cache, replacing a cache entry that has not been used recently.

The cache is much more useful for memory "read" operations than memory "write" operations. Each data item in the cache is a duplicate of one of the memory cells in the main memory. When a *write* operation takes place to an item in the cache, then the original copy in the main memory becomes outdated. There are two general approaches to dealing with this issue in the design of the cache. One approach is to immediately write the new value to the main memory at the same time it is written to the cache. This is called a *write-through* technique. The other major approach is to write the new value to the cache entry only, and allow the main memory location to become outdated temporarily. When the cache entry is finally replaced because it is not being used anymore, then the outdated copy in the main memory is updated. This is called a *write-back* approach. With either technique a time-consuming access to main memory is required. Fortunately, in typical computer programs only 20 percent of the total memory accesses are "write" operations, and 80 percent are "read" operations.

This simple conceptual view of the functioning of cache memory is sufficient for understanding its impact on program performance. Further discussion of the details of cache design are beyond the scope of this text. For an excellent introductory discussion of cache memory technology, the reader is referred to Stone [1987].

3.2.2 Multiprocessor Caches

The use of cache memory can be extended to multiprocessor systems, as illustrated in Figure 3.2. In this system, there is still one single shared memory with a common bus connecting it to each processor. However, now each processor also has its own private cache memory, which can store recently used values. Just as in the uniprocessor case, whenever a processor performs a memory access, it first checks its own local cache to see if the needed entry is there. Only if the entry is not found in the local cache does the processor attempt to access the main shared memory through the bus. These local caches greatly reduce the contention for the shared memory. If each processor has a hit percentage of 80 percent in its own local cache, then the average rate of access to the shared memory has been reduced by a factor of 5. This greatly reduces the chances of memory contention, and allows larger numbers of processors to be connected to the bus without overloading it.

The basic principle behind the use of cache memory in multiprocessors is the same as in uniprocessors. Each cache is a small high-speed memory containing "address–data" pairs as in Figure 3.1. For each memory reference by a processor, the local cache is first searched for the memory address. Only if the needed item is not found in the cache is it necessary to use the bus to access the shared memory. As this item is read from the shared memory, it is simultaneously copied into the local cache, so that it will be available there on subsequent accesses by the same processor.

One interesting issue in multiprocessor cache memory is that several copies of the same memory item may appear in different caches. For example, assume Processor 1 reads memory address 1000 from the shared memory. Then a copy is written into the local cache of Processor 1. If Processors 2 and 3 also read memory address 1000 from the shared memory, then their local caches will also have a copy. Thus, there are four different copies of the same shared memory cell 1000—one copy in the shared memory itself and three additional copies in the caches of Processors 1, 2, and 3. As long as all subsequent accesses to address 1000 are "read" operations only, then there is no problem with having multiple copies. Each processor can continue to perform read operations using its own copy in the local cache, without any need for accessing the shared memory.

However, if a processor performs a "write" operation to memory cell 1000, then a problem develops. All the copies must remain identical. It is not acceptable to change one copy while leaving other copies unchanged. Since they are multiple copies of the same

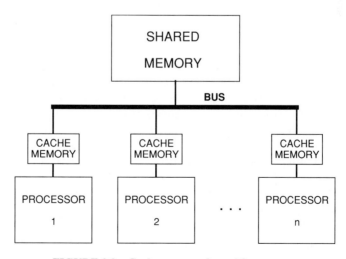

FIGURE 3.2   Cache memory in multiprocessor.

memory item, they must be kept consistent. This general problem of handling multiple copies of a memory item is called the *cache coherence* problem. There are many solutions to this problem which have been implemented in various commercial and experimental multiprocessor computers. All of the solutions, however, involve some additional overhead in the system and therefore degrade the performance somewhat.

In bus-oriented systems, one solution to the cache coherence problem is to require every "write" operation by any processor to be broadcast on the common bus. Each local cache will constantly monitor the common bus to see if any of its own memory entries has been written by another processor. Therefore, when a write operation is performed by any processor, all the cache memories will immediately find out, and update their own local copies of that memory item. Since all caches are directly connected to the common bus anyway, this broadcasting of "write" operations is very easy in a bus-oriented system. In fact, if the caches use a *write-through* policy, then every write operation will immediately go through the bus to the main memory. The other caches can easily monitor this bus traffic to see if any of their own entries have been updated by other processors.

3.3 MULTIPLE MEMORY MODULES

To further improve the performance of the multiprocessor memory systems, the shared memory can be divided into multiple modules, which can be accessed in parallel by different processors. Figure 1.2 shows a general structural model of such a multimodule memory access system in multiprocessor computers. The n physical processors all have access to a commmon shared-memory system. The memory consists of m individual memory modules. Some type of connection hardware will allow each processor to access any of the memory cells in any memory module. The memory system will still appear to the processors as one contiguous shared-memory space, accessed by the usual memory addressing mechanisms. Each memory reference by any processor is sent into the connection hardware, where it is automatically routed to the correct physical memory module. With this multimodule memory system, many memory requests can be handled simultaneously, thus reducing the chances of memory contention.

Memory contention can still arise in two ways in these systems. First, there may be some congestion in the connection hardware. This will vary considerably, depending on the technology used in the connection hardware. The second way in which memory contention can arise is when two or more processors are accessing the same memory module within a short time interval. Each memory module services memory requests sequentially, and has only one memory controller that services requests at a certain speed. Therefore, concurrent requests by different processors to the same memory module will cause delays.

It is often found that processors access consecutive memory addresses. This happens during access of large data arrays. The program is also stored in the memory, and it is usually accessed by each processor through consecutive memory addresses. To reduce memory contention in these situations, consecutive memory addresses are usually spread across different memory modules, as illustrated in Figure 3.3. In the figure, memory address 0 is found in memory module 0, memory address 1 is found in memory module 1, address 2 is in module 2, and address 3 is in module 3. Then address 4 wraps around and starts at module 0 again. In this way, the consecutive memory addresses are spread across the four memory modules. It is interesting to examine in detail how this spreading of memory addresses helps reduce memory contention during sequential access by each processor to consecutive memory addresses.

Module 0	Module 1	Module 2	Module 3
0	1	2	3
4	5	6	7
8	9	10	11
12	13	14	15
16	17	18	19
20	21	22	23
24	25	26	27
.	.	.	.
.	.	.	.
.	.	.	.

FIGURE 3.3   Spreading memory addresses across the modules.

Consider a parallel program that causes each of four physical processors to access consecutive memory addresses 0, 1, 2, 3, 4, ..., 100. This is illustrated in the timing diagram of Figure 3.4, which shows the memory address referenced by each processor during each time interval. Time flows from top to bottom in the figure.

From this memory reference diagram, it appears that a high degree of memory contention will result, because the processors are always referencing the same memory

Processor 1	Processor 2	Processor 3	Processor 4
0	0	0	0
1	1	1	1
2	2	2	2
3	3	3	3
4	4	4	4
5	5	5	5
6	6	6	6
7	7	7	7
8	8	8	8
.	.	.	.
.	.	.	.
.	.	.	.
100	100	100	100

FIGURE 3.4   Consecutive memory address pattern.

address. However, the spreading of the consecutive addresses in different modules, as shown in Figure 3.3, will eliminate the memory contention in this situation. When the four processors first start, there is some initial contention for memory address 0. Let us assume that Processor 1 is the first one to gain access to memory address 0, which is located in memory module 0. Processors 2–4 will have to wait for Processor 1 to finish. When Processor 1 goes on to its next memory address 1, then Processor 2 will be allowed access to memory address 0. Following Processor 2, then eventually Processor 3 and Processor 4 will gain access to memory address 0. This initial delay by each processor in accessing memory address 0 will shift the memory access pattern as shown in Figure 3.5.

Processor 1	Processor 2	Processor 3	Processor 4
0	*	*	*
1	0	*	*
2	1	0	*
3	2	1	0
4	3	2	1
5	4	3	2
6	5	4	3
7	6	5	4
8	7	6	5
9	8	7	6
10	9	8	7
11	10	9	8
.	.	.	.
.	.	.	.
.	.	.	.
100	99	98	97
	100	99	98
		100	99
			100

FIGURE 3.5   Skewing of memory access pattern to eliminate contention.

This initial shifting of the memory access pattern by each processor is enough to completely eliminate any remaining memory contention. In Figure 3.5, each horizontal line is one time interval in the program, with time flowing downwards. Notice in the figure that the processors no longer refer to the same memory address at the same time. In fact, a careful study of each time interval will show that no two processors ever refer to the same memory module during any single time interval.

There are several important factors that have contributed to this lack of memory contention in this example. First, consecutive physical memory addresses are distributed across the modules, as shown in Figure 3.3. Second, the processors are each referencing a sequence of consecutive memory addresses. Third, the processors are all performing their memory references at approximately the same rate. It turns out that these three conditions are satisfied in many parallel programs. It is quite common to have identical parallel processes all moving through shared data arrays sequentially, as is seen in many of the example programs in this text.

3.4 PROCESSOR–MEMORY INTERCONNECTION NETWORKS

The memory contention properties exhibited by multiprocessors also depend on the character of the processor–memory interconnection network. With reference to the general architectural diagram of Figure 1.2, the splitting of the shared memory into multiple modules greatly reduces the chances of memory contention. However, congestion may occur in the connection hardware even when processors are referring to different modules. There has been a great deal of theoretical and practical research in the design of processor–memory interconnection networks in multiprocessors [Siegel, 1984].

Figure 3.6 shows a *crossbar* network connecting eight processors to eight memory modules. Each memory module can service requests only one at a time. Therefore, simultaneous requests by many processors to the same memory module will result in contention. However, the crossbar network has the important property that contention never occurs in the interconnection network. The crossbar network can connect all of the processors simultaneously to different memories. The switches can be adjusted to allow

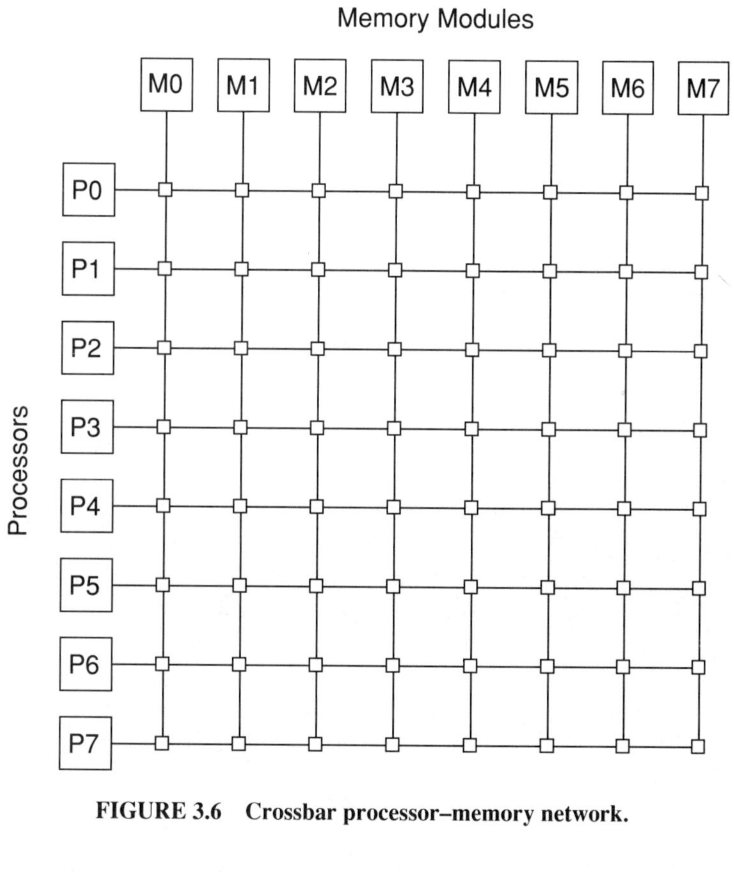

FIGURE 3.6   Crossbar processor–memory network.

any possible pattern of processor–memory connections to take place simultaneously, provided, of course, that the processors are not referencing the same module. This is because each processor–memory pair has its own switch in the crossbar. Thus, for n processors and n memory modules, the crossbar requires n^2 switches, and therefore has a cost $O(n^2)$.

For large numbers of processors, this $O(n^2)$ cost of the network may be prohibitively high. To reduce cost, many $O(n \log n)$ networks have been developed, such as the *butterfly* network illustrated in Figure 3.7. In this network, each processor has a path to every memory module. However, some paths conflict with each other, so that contention in the connection switch may occur even when the processors are referencing different memory modules. The butterfly network gets its name from the "butterfly" wings that appear in each stage of the network. At each successive stage of the network from left to right, the butterfly wings increase in size by a factor of two. In general, the number of stages required for n processors is $\log n$, with each stage having a total of $n/2$ switches. Therefore, the total number of switches required is $(n/2)\log n$. In Figure 3.7, 16 processors are connected to 16 memory modules using 32 switches. A crossbar network for this many processors and memories would require $16 \cdot 16 = 256$ switches.

Another switching network with cost $O(n \log n)$ is the *shuffle-exchange* network illustrated in Figure 3.8. This network gets its name because the connection pattern at each stage resembles a shuffle of a deck of cards. As with the butterfly network, the shuffle-exchange network has many paths between the processors and the memories, allowing many parallel memory accesses from the processors to be serviced simultaneously. Also as

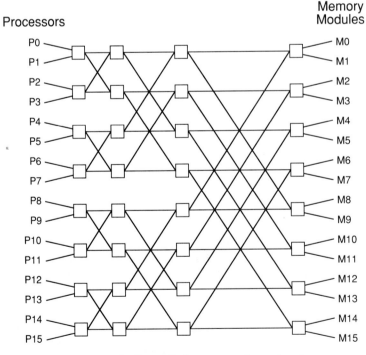

FIGURE 3.7   Butterfly interconnection network.

Processors

Memory
Modules

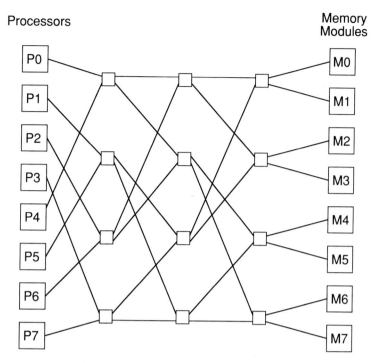

FIGURE 3.8   Shuffle-exchange network.

in the butterfly network, it is possible in the shuffle-exchange network for contention in the switch itself, even when processors are referencing different memory modules. This contention inside the switch cannot occur in the more costly crossbar network.

In both the shuffle-exchange and butterfly networks, each processor memory reference is sent directly into the interconnection network, where it is automatically routed by the switches to the proper memory module. When a processor sends a memory address into the switching network, the switches use the bits of the binary address to route the message along the proper path to the destination memory module. When the request reaches the memory module, the proper memory address is accessed. In the case of a "read" memory operation, the data value is then returned back through the switching network along the same path to the source processor.

3.5 INFLUENCE OF THE ALGORITHM

Now we consider the Parallel Rank Sort and Matrix Multiplication algorithms from Chapter 2 in the light of this discussion of multiprocessor architecture and memory contention. In both algorithms, there are some large shared data arrays that are read by all the parallel processes. Local caches should help reduce memory contention for the reading of the shared array. There is some writing to shared arrays in these algorithms, but the writing is relatively rare, and two different processes never write to the same location, thereby reducing the probability of write contention.

3.5.1 Rank Sort

Refer back to Figure 2.4 for the basic structure of the Parallel Rank Sort program. The two major data structures are the *values* array containing the original unsorted list, and the *final* array, where the sorted list will be created. Each processor takes one single list element from the *values* array and computes the rank by comparing it with all the other elements in *values*. Thus, each processor must scan through the entire *values* array, reading each element. The program is shown in Figure 2.3. The Procedure PutinPlace contains a "Repeat" loop with an index *j* that moves sequentially through the array *values*. This means that each processor is reading through all the elements of *values* in sequence. Ordinarily, a one-dimensional array like *values* will be stored in the physical memory in consecutive memory locations. Therefore, each processor will be reading sequentially through consecutive memory locations.

This is the same situation just discussed with respect to multiple memory modules. If the target multiprocessor architecture has multiple modules with address spreading as illustrated in Figure 3.3, then the reading of array *values* by all the processors will not cause memory contention. Since all the processors are executing the same Procedure "PutinPlace" (see Figure 2.4), it can be assumed that they will be moving sequentially through the array *values* at approximately the same rate. Therefore, all the conditions necessary for the contention-free reading of the array are satisfied, as discussed in section 3.3.

In addition to the *values* array, there is also another shared array, *final*. However, each process refers to this array only once at the very end of the Procedure PutinPlace, and each process refers to a different element of the array. Thus, no memory contention with respect to array *final* is to be expected. Besides the two shared arrays, each processor of course also has a few of its own private local variables; these are the local variables of the Procedure PutinPlace. Each processor will reference its local variables on every loop iteration. Since they are not shared by other processors, these local variables will end up in the cache memory of the processor using them. Therefore, no access to shared memory is required for reading these local variables, thus reducing the potential for contention. However, writing to the local variables in the cache is another matter. As discussed earlier, cache coherence requires some kind of "write-through" policy back to the shared memory.

With a multimodule memory system, the main factor in determining contention is whether large numbers of parallel memory requests go to the same memory module. This brief analysis of the Parallel Rank Sort program shows that this kind of behavior is not expected. However, for a bus-oriented system, a different kind of program analysis is required. In a bus-oriented system as shown in Figure 3.2, memory contention depends on the rate at which the processors refer to the shared memory, and whether the bus speed is sufficient to handle all the requests without delaying the processors. We can probably expect that the system is well designed, so that the bus has enough capacity to handle normal patterns of memory access by the processors.

One of the major issues in running a program on a bus system is the extent to which the cache memories will be effective in reducing the shared memory traffic to an acceptable level. Cache memory is especially effective if each processor continues to read from the same memory cells many times. After the first read, a copy is put in the local cache, where it can be accessed at high speed without burdening the shared memory. If a write operation is performed on a cache item, then an immediate write-through to shared memory using the bus is required.

With reference to the Rank Sort program in Figure 2.3, the main activity of each parallel process is to execute the "Repeat" loop in lines 11–14 as follows:

```
11    REPEAT
12      j := j MOD n + 1;
13      IF testval >= values[j] THEN rank := rank + 1;
14    UNTIL j = src;
```

Each time around this loop, there are nine references to program variables: four references to *j*, two references to *rank*, one to *testval*, one to *src*, and one to *values*. Seven of these nine references are "read" operations, and six of these seven reads are to variables that should already be stored in the cache. The read operation to the *value* array is the only one that needs to go through to the shared memory because it is always referring to an array element not previously referenced by this processor. The two "write" operations to local variables *j* and *rank* will cause a cache write-through back to the shared memory. Thus, of the nine memory references each time around the loop, six will be serviced from the cache. On the average, this means that one-third of the processor memory references will have to access the shared memory.

Whether this Rank Sort exhibits memory contention will simply depend on whether the bus bandwidth is sufficient to handle this traffic to the shared memory. This pattern of shared memory usage in the Rank Sort is not unusually high, and therefore it would be expected that a well balanced bus-oriented system could execute the program without significant degradation from memory contention.

3.5.2 Matrix Multiplication

Matrix multiplication is often used as one of the benchmarks programs for parallel computers. As can be seen in the parallel matrix multiplication program in Chapter 2, there is an opportunity for large numbers of parallel processes. For reference the basic structure of this program is repeated:

```
Parallel Matrix Multiplication  C = A * B:

    FORALL i := 1 TO n DO
      FORALL j := 1 TO n DO
        compute C[i,j] as the vector product
          of row i of A with column j of B;
```

The reading of the two matrices by the processes is reasonably distributed across the matrices. Each process reads one row of matrix *A* and one column of matrix *B*. When this program is applied to matrices with dimension $n \times n$, there will be n^2 parallel processes. Each row of *A* will be read by *n* processes, and each column of *B* will be read by *n* processes. This spreading of the reading across the matrices helps reduce the probability of memory contention. Generally, most parallel computers perform very well on the matrix multiplication program.

The reading of the matrices by each process also follows a "consecutive-sequential" pattern as seen in the Rank Sort, which is efficiently handled by multiprocessors with multiple memory modules. This means that a process may experience some initial delay when beginning to read its matrix entries, but after the first entry is read, the processes will have already established the "skewed" access pattern illustrated in Figure 3.5. Therefore, no additional contention should take place. Since there are n processes reading each row of A, a process may experience a delay *of* n memory accesses when reading the first element in its assigned row of A. However, no additional delays should be incurred for the remainder of the row. When the process reads its column of B, then another contention delay of n is also possible.

This initial contention delay was illustrated in Figure 3.5: since all four processors start with the same memory address 0, it requires four memory accesses before the "skewed" pattern is established. In general, with n processors, it requires n memory accesses to establish the skewed access pattern. Thus, the maximum memory contention delay will be n. In the Parallel Matrix Multiplication program, each process computes a complete vector product of a row of matrix A with a column of matrix B. This vector product requires n multiplications and n additions. A single addition or multiplication of real numbers generally requires at least ten times as much time as a single memory access. Therefore, a memory contention delay of n accesses is tolerable by the processes, without causing any significant performance degradation.

3.6 MEMORY HOT SPOTS

Both the Rank Sort and Matrix Multiplication programs are "relaxed" algorithms, which means that the parallel processes do not interact or communicate. As a general rule, relaxed parallel algorithms tend to minimize memory contention problems, especially in cases of data partitioning. In nonrelaxed algorithms, the processes interact with each other through shared communication or synchronization variables. This introduces the possibility of memory contention on these shared variables in some algorithms. Relaxed algorithms will serve as a test of whether the memory system of the target multiprocessor is balanced with the processor speed. Memory contention will usually arise only in relaxed algorithms if the data is not distributed properly across the memory modules, or if the memory access hardware has some bottlenecks.

Memory contention occurs when memory accesses from different processors fall within the same memory module during a short time interval. In locating potential sources of memory contention in a particular parallel algorithm, it may sometimes be difficult to determine whether certain memory accesses will fall in the same module. However, if the same program variable is accessed by many parallel processes, then certainly those accesses will fall in the same module! At first consideration, it may seem that this situation of parallel accesses to the same variable will be rare, especially parallel write accesses. However, there are actually certain types of variables in parallel programs that are written by large numbers of parallel processes. These are variables whose purpose is to help processes communicate and synchronize. These centralized communication and synchronization variables can sometimes be the source of severe memory contention, causing large performance degradation.

These variables that are accessed frequently by many processors are sometimes referred to as *memory hot spots*. Even in a well-designed memory system, memory hot spots will always cause contention. Also, this contention at the hot spot may cause a general congestion to develop in the whole processor–memory interconnection network. The congestion will then also slow down memory accesses to other modules, even those far away from the memory hot spot. This creation of memory hot spots through the use of communication and synchronization variables in parallel programs is a very important topic, and will be considered in detail in Chapter 5.

This type of memory contention involving communication and synchronization variables is not dependent on the particular memory architecture. It is a property of the parallel algorithm itself and will manifest itself on any parallel computer. For this reason, this type of memory contention is built into the Multi-Pascal interactive software system, so that programmers can learn to detect and avoid this performance bottleneck in their programs. In Chapter 5, several examples are given of programs that exhibit this type of memory contention, and systematic techniques are described to remove this contention.

3.7 SUMMARY

When writing parallel programs, it is important for the programmer to be aware of the general organization of the target multiprocessor architecture. The memory systems of multiprocessors do not always behave in an ideal manner, and sometimes exhibit memory contention that may degrade program performance. Computer manufacturers utilize a variety of hardware organization techniques to increase the capacity of the memory system and reduce chances of memory contention. However, by their very nature, multiprocessors will always have the potential for memory contention because the same centralized memory system is used in parallel by all the processors.

This chapter has discussed a variety of techniques that are used to improve the performance of multiprocessors, including high-speed buses, cache memory, multiple memory modules, and processor–memory interconnection networks. The use of these techniques in various multiprocessors will depend on the size and cost of the system and its intended application. Some computer manufacturers favor bus-oriented systems with smaller numbers of processors, and other manufacturers produce much larger systems with sophisticated processor–memory interconnection networks. The parallel programmer should be aware of the range of possibilities in multiprocessor architecture, and the general causes of memory contention in each of the major classes of architecture.

In bus-oriented systems, the processors are connected by a high-speed common bus to a single shared memory. Despite the high bandwidth of the bus, the processor memory requests can be handled only one at a time. Therefore, the number of processors that can be effectively connected to a particular bus is limited by its speed and the speed of the shared memory. Even in a well-balanced system in which the bus capacity exceeds the average processor memory access rate, memory contention may still occur during short bursts of memory-intensive activity by many processors in parallel.

One technology that helps reduce the rate of access to the shared memory is the use of high-speed cache memory. Each processor has its own private cache memory to store copies of recently used memory values. A large percentage of the processor memory requests can be serviced directly by its own local cache, thus eliminating the need to access the shared memory through the common bus. One problem that limits the cache efficiency is the need to maintain consistency of multiple copies of the same memory location in different caches. One technique to solve this cache coherence problem is to broadcast all write operations on the bus, so that they can be noted by all the caches. Cache memories are also important and useful in systems with processor–memory interconnection networks.

To improve the performance of the memory system, it can be split into multiple memory modules, all capable of operating in parallel. This allows many processors to access memory simultaneously, provided that they are referencing different memory modules. To help distribute the processor memory references more evenly among the modules, an address "spreading" technique is used to put consecutive memory addresses in different modules. This method is particularly useful in reducing contention during access to large data arrays and to program code stored in memory.

There is a wide variety of techniques for connecting the processors to the multiple memory modules, each with its own cost–performance characteristics. The best performance is achieved by the crossbar interconnection network. However, its $O(n^2)$ cost is usually prohibitive. There are many popular $O(n \log n)$ interconnection networks, including the butterfly and shuffle-exchange networks described in this chapter. These networks can support many parallel memory requests by different processors, provided that they go to different memory modules.

The chapter concludes with a short discussion of memory hot spots, arising from the use of communication and synchronization variables that must be accessed by many processors in parallel. These hot spots can cause severe congestion in the processor–memory network, and seriously degrade parallel program performance. This issue is very important to parallel program design and is discussed thoroughly in future chapters.

REFERENCES

For more detailed information on multiprocessor memory system organization see Hwang and Briggs [1984] and Stone [1987]. The discussion in this chapter of bus-oriented systems and the shuffle-exchange network is based on material in Stone [1987]. Desrochers [1987] also has an overview of parallel computer architecture.

EXERCISES

1. Describe a situation in ordinary life where delays result from contention for a shared resource. Explain how this contention is analogous to memory contention in multiprocessors. Describe a solution to the contention problem in ordinary life, and show how this kind of solution can also be applied to multiprocessors.

2. Consider two general techniques for connecting I/O devices to a bus-oriented multiprocessor:
   (a) The I/O devices are connected directly to the common bus and access the shared memory through the bus.
   (b) The I/O devices are connected to a separate I/O bus, which has direct access to memory locations in the shared memory.
      Either technique may produce additional memory contention and thereby degrade processor performance. Explain, for each technique, how it may increase contention. Which technique is expected to produce worse contention? Why?

3. In a uniprocessor system, cache memory is more useful with "read" memory operations than "write" memory operations. Explain the reason for this.

4. Under what circumstances will cache memory in a multiprocessor be most useful in reducing contention for the shared memory? Describe general charactertics of parallel programs which are most important with respect to improving performance through cache memory.

5. Give a detailed example of a situation where cache coherence becomes an issue. Show the contents of each cache and the memory references being performed by each processor as the cache coherence problem arises.

6. The solution described in this chapter for maintaining cache coherence is a write-through technique for each write operation to an item in the cache. To avoid the necessity of a write-through, some multiprocessors include a "tag" bit on each cache item, which will indicate whether additional caches also have a copy of the same item. A tag bit 1 indicates that there are no other copies, and a tag bit 0 indicates that there are additional copies.

During a write operation to any item in the cache, the tag bit is examined. If the tag is 0, then the usual write-through technique is used. However, if the tag is 1, then the write is performed locally in the cache only, without using the bus or shared memory. The shared memory will be updated later by using the standard cache write-back technique.

This technique does decrease the overhead associated with write operations. However, it necessitates an additional activity during read operations. If a cache miss occurs during a read operation by any processor, then the processor cannot simply go directly to the shared memory to read the required item. The processor must broadcast the read operation to all the other caches.

Describe in detail the reasons for this broadcast of the read operation. Give an example of a situation where this broadcast is necessary, and show what changes take place as a result of the broadcast.

7. In Figures 3.4 and 3.5, it is shown how consecutive memory addressing by several processors in parallel will result in no memory contention when multiple memory modules are used. There are several important conditions that must be satisfied for this contentionless access pattern to develop.

(a) Consecutive memory addresses are spread across the modules in sequence.
(b) Each processor is sequentially accessing consecutive memory addresses.
(c) The number of processors is less than or equal to the number of memory modules.
(d) The processors perform memory accesses at the same rate.

As long as these four conditions are met, the processors will quickly fall into a memory access pattern in which they move from one memory module to the next without any contention delays. No two processors will ever try to access the same module at the same time, except in the very beginning when a few contention delays may occur.

In the example of Figures 3.4 and 3.5, the processors all reference the same sequence of addresses and all begin executing at the same time. These two conditions are not actually necessary. As long as the four conditions listed above are met, the processors may start at any time, and may access any sequence of consecutive memory locations. When each processor first starts to access the memory, it may experience a few delays if it happens to start with a module currently being accessed by another processor. However, after a few such initial delays, the processor will quickly fall into step with the other processors and result in no additional contention.

Show in detail that the above claims are indeed true. Give a few detailed examples that illustrate how the contentionless pattern develops even in cases where processors begin at different times and on different memory addresses. Sketch out the steps of a simple proof (concise logical argument) that show conclusively that the above claims are true.

8. (a) Draw a butterfly interconnection network with eight processors and eight memory modules.
(b) Draw the last stage (rightmost stage) of a 32 by 32 butterfly network.

(c) In general, for n processors and n memories, how many stages are required in the butterfly network?

9. (a) In the butterfly network of Figure 3.7, give an example of two simultaneous processor–memory accesses by different processors to different memory modules, which result in contention and delays in the network.

(b) Repeat question (a) for three simultaneous accesses, which will all contend in the network. Repeat (a) for four simultaneous accesses.

10. Draw one stage of a shuffle-exchange network for connecting 16 processors to 16 memory modules.

11. In processor–memory interconnection networks, it is sometimes necessary for a particular processor to broadcast something to all the other processors. For the shuffle-exchange network of Figure 3.8, show how Processor P0 could utilize the network to broadcast an item to all the other processors. Which switches will be utilized, and how will the items move within the network? Try to minimize the amount of activity in the network to achieve the broadcast. (*Hint*: The broadcast can be done using only seven of the 12 switches.)

Assume that switches have the capability to duplicate items coming in from any of the four connections and send them out along any of the connections.

12. Some parallel computers have a hierarchical memory system. Processors are grouped in local clusters of 8–16 processors. Each local cluster has its own shared memory, accessible only to processors in that cluster. The clusters are all connected to a global shared memory that can be accessed by all processors. Access time to local cluster memory is faster than to the global shared memory.

An interesting performance anomaly sometimes results in such systems. Consider an application that uses relaxed data parallelism. The application is run on the computer, using one processor, then two processors, then three, and so on. As the number of physical processors used is increased, the execution time of the program naturally decreases. However, a point is reached when adding one more processor suddenly increases the overall program execution time dramatically. Adding still more processors after this increase will again begin to gradually decrease the execution time.

Explain a possible reason why this can occur in parallel computers with hierarchical memory systems.

13. Consider a relaxed parallel algorithm in which each process accesses some localized portion of the data base, with no overlap between processes. Therefore, each data item is accessed by at most one process during program execution. Such an algorithm appears to have no possibility of memory contention, since there can never be multiple processes accessing the same data item. However, in some parallel computers such an algorithm may result in memory contention. Explain the reason for this. Can this memory contention occur in bus-oriented systems? Can it occur in multiprocessors with multiple memory modules?

4

Process Communication

The parallel algorithms presented so far in this text have all been *relaxed*: each parallel process operates independently without interacting with other processes. In some cases the processes do share parts of a central data base, but the data is read and not written. In a relaxed parallel algorithm, no process ever writes a value that is intended for use by another parallel process. These types of algorithms were considered first because they are simplest and yet produce very good speedups on a wide range of parallel architectures.

In this chapter we begin to consider the issue of process communication and interaction. We describe a special feature of the Multi-Pascal programming language called the *channel variable*, which is used for process communication and synchronization. A channel variable, as its name implies, collects data values from writer processes and "channels" them into reader processes. Channel variables allow parallel processes to exchange and share data values in a controlled way that prevents the possibility of timing-dependent errors. This chapter describes the complete syntax and semantics of channel variables in Multi-Pascal.

The availability of channels for process interaction will open up several new important classes of parallel algorithms in this chapter and the following ones. This chapter introduces the concept of pipelined algorithms, in which a series of parallel processes connected by channels form a long "pipeline" for data to flow and be transformed. Each process represents one stage of processing of the data. Initial data values flow in one end of the pipeline, and the final computed results flow out the other end. If the pipeline is full of data, then each process can continue to operate in parallel, receiving new data values from one neighboring process and sending data values to its other neighbor.

An important example of a pipeline algorithm is presented: a practical method for solving a triangular system of linear equations through *back substitution*. In this algorithm, each equation is assigned to one process in the pipeline, and computed values of the unknowns flow down the pipeline from one process to the next. This pipeline method achieves an $O(n)$ speedup over the sequential form of back substitution. To illustrate a more complex communication pattern among processes, the Bitonic Merge Sort algorithm is briefly described. This efficient parallel sorting algorithm has an $O(\log^2 n)$ execution time, and forms the basis for many sorting algorithm for parallel computers.

4.1 PROCESS COMMUNICATION CHANNELS

In ordinary sequential programs, once the input data is specified, the instructions of the program are executed one at a time in a specific sequence. For the same input data, the sequence of instruction execution is always the same. However, execution of parallel programs involves many parallel processes all being executed at the same time. The sequence of instruction execution in each process is well defined, but the relation between execution of instructions in different processes is not known. For example, consider the following example with two parallel processes:

```
FORK FOR i := 1 TO 20 DO sum1 := sum1 + a[i];
FORK FOR j := 1 TO 20 DO sum2 := sum2 + b[j];
JOIN; JOIN;
```

The first process adds the first 20 elements of array a, and the second process adds array b. Each process has a specific sequence of instruction execution, but the relation between the two processes is unknown. Since the processes are executed on different physical processors, their relative speeds cannot be guaranteed to be identical. Thus, the first process may proceed much faster and reach element 15 of the array, while the second process is still on element 8 of its array. Or the situation may be reversed, with the second process executing faster. Because of unpredictable delays and environmental influences that affect real processors in any multiprocessor computer system, one can never be sure how fast parallel processes will execute in comparison to one another.

In the above example, since the two processes are independent, the relative timing of their execution is not important. The parent process will wait for both child processes to terminate before continuing. Thus, if one is faster than the other, the overall correctness of the program is not affected. However, when parallel processes use common shared variables, the situation becomes more complex. In the examples of parallel programs given in previous chapters, the parallel processes were always relatively independent with little interaction between the processes. In this chapter, our consideration is extended to programs where parallel processes interact during their execution through shared variables. For this purpose a new type of variable is introduced called a *CHANNEL* variable, specifically designed to help coordinate process interaction and communication.

Consider the case of two parallel processes $P1$ and $P2$. During its execution, $P1$ computes a value and writes it into variable C, where it is read by $P2$ and used for further computation. This is illustrated in Figure 4.1. Since $P1$ and $P2$ are parallel processes, the relative order of their internal execution is not known in advance. Thus, there is no way to be certain that $P1$ will write the value into C before $P2$ reads it, except by letting $P1$ run to completion and then executing $P2$. However, this eliminates the parallelism.

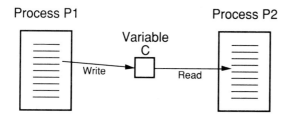

FIGURE 4.1   Communication between parallel processes.

This type of process communication occurs in many parallel programs: one process is computing some values that are to be used by other parallel processes. To handle this situation, a *CHANNEL* variable has the property that it can be "empty." When any process attempts to read an empty channel, the process execution is automatically suspended until some other process writes a value into the channel. By making shared variable *C* a *CHANNEL* variable that is initially empty, process *P*2 will be required to wait if it attempts to read variable *C* before process *P*1 has written the value into *C*. Thus, the process communication is guaranteed to be correct.

4.2 CHANNEL VARIABLES

In some cases when processes are communicating, a process will be sending not just a single value to another process but a whole sequence of values. This type of interaction is sometimes called *producer–consumer*, where the *producer* process is computing data values and sending them to a *consumer* process for further computation. To facilitate this general type of parallel programming technique, Multi-Pascal has *CHANNEL* variables. Conceptually, a channel acts like a first-in-first-out queue of values. As values are written to the channel, they are saved in a queue until they are read by some other process. In Figure 4.2, the channel *C* is drawn as a long "pipe" to illustrate this property. As values are written by Process *P*1, they enter the pipe on the left and travel toward the right, where they can be read by Process *P*2. If several values are written by Process *P*1, they are all saved inside the pipe, and can be read by Process *P*2 at any time.

4.2.1 Reading and Writing Channels

A value may be written into a channel variable in the same way a value is written into any variable—the name of the channel variable is simply used on the left side of an assignment statement, as in the following example for channel *C*:

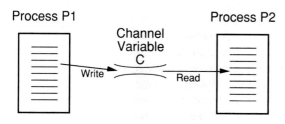

If P2 arrives at *Read* first, it will wait until P1 executes *Write*.

FIGURE 4.2   Communication using channel variable.

```
C := 10;
```

The above statement will write the value 10 at the end of the internal queue of channel C. Of course, the right side of the assignment may contain any valid Pascal expression as in the following:

```
C := x + i * 2;   (* x and i are scalar variables *)
```

The above statement computes two times i, adds x, and writes the resultant value into channel C. Channel variables have a component type that determines what type of value they can hold. In the assignment statement, the value computed by the expression on the right must match the type of the channel according to the same rules as ordinary Pascal variable types. The component type of a channel variable is declared in the declaration section of the program along with the other variable declarations. The general syntax of a channel declaration is as follows:

```
<channel-name>:   CHANNEL OF <component-type>;
```

The component-type may be any ordinary Pascal type such as *INTEGER, REAL, CHAR,* or *BOOLEAN.* Thus, a channel variable may be *CHANNEL OF INTEGER, CHANNEL OF REAL, CHANNEL OF CHAR,* or *CHANNEL OF BOOLEAN.* To read a value from a channel variable, simply use the channel name on the right side of an assignment statement as in the following example:

```
x := C;
```

The above assignment statement reads a value from the front of the queue of values stored in channel C and writes this value into variable x. The type of variable x must match the component-type of channel C. For example, if C is *CHANNEL OF REAL,* then x must be of type *REAL.* Each write to a channel will add a new value to the internal queue, and each read of the channel will completely remove a single value from this internal queue.

When a process executes a read operation to a channel that is currently empty, then the execution of that process is automatically delayed until a value is written into the channel by another process. For example, if a Reader Process executes the assignment "$x := C$" while the channel C is empty, the execution of that process will be automatically suspended. Later when some other process finally writes a value into channel C, then the execution of the Reader Process will be automatically resumed at this same assignment statement "$x := C$". Since there is now a value in channel C, the assignment will execute successfully, and the Reader Process will continue to the next statement. This is one of the main values of a channel: it has the ability to delay a Reader Process until the necessary values are supplied by a Writer Process. Each channel has unlimited capacity for storing any number of values. Therefore, writer processes are never delayed.

To determine if a given channel currently contains any values, a boolean-valued expression may be created by using the name of the channel followed by a question mark, as in the following example for channel C:

```
IF C?
  THEN x := C   (*Read the channel*)
  ELSE x := 0;  (*Do not read the channel*)
```

The expression "C?" will evaluate to TRUE if the channel C currently contains any values and FALSE if the channel is empty. Any process may evaluate this boolean expression "C?" without fear of being delayed. The process executing the "C?" operation will not be suspended if the channel is empty. One of the important uses of this empty channel test is to allow a reader process to determine if there is anything in a channel before committing itself to a read operation. In the above example, the process first checks the channel C and attempts to read the channel only if it actually contains a value.

4.2.2 Producer–Consumer Example

Channels are especially useful for the Producer–Consumer parallel programming paradigm, which is often used for systems programming. This is illustrated in Figure 4.3, which shows a program segment that uses a channel for communication of values between a Producer process and a Consumer process. The procedure *Producer* will produce an integer value through some unspecified internal computation, then write this value into the channel *commchan*. Similarly, the procedure *Consumer* will read a value from channel *commchan*, and then use it in some unspecified internal computation.

The producer process continues until some special *endmarker* value is produced (in this case −1). The consumer process also continues to loop and read values from the channel until the *endmarker* value is detected. Figure 4.4 illustrates the general behavior of this Producer–Consumer program. The channel variable *commchan* is used to buffer values being sent from the Producer process to the Consumer process. If the Producer is faster, then the channel will store the extra values until the Consumer eventually catches up. If the Consumer is faster, then it may find sometimes that the channel is empty. Each time this happens, the channel will automatically force the Consumer to wait until something is written into the channel by the Producer.

Examples later in the chapter illustrate how this producer–consumer style of parallel programming can be useful for some types of applications.

4.3 PIPELINE PARALLELISM

A special case of the producer–consumer paradigm is *pipelining,* in which a series of processes form a linear "pipeline," with each process consuming from its left neighbor and producing for its right neighbor. Generally in pipeline-style parallel algorithms, a sequence of data values flows through the pipeline and is transformed by the processes at each stage of the pipeline. Each process receives a series of data values from its left neighbor, transforms them, and sends the resultant values to its right neighbor. Each initial data value entering the pipeline thereby undergoes a series of successive transformations until it finally emerges as an output value at the end of the pipeline. The parallelism arises from the fact that each process in the pipeline is performing transformations at the same time, but on different data values.

```
PROGRAM Producer-Consumer;
CONST endmarker = -1;
VAR commchan: CHANNEL OF INTEGER;

    PROCEDURE Producer;
    VAR inval: INTEGER;
    BEGIN
      REPEAT
          ... (*Compute new item "inval" for the channel*)

        commchan := inval; (*Write into channel*)

      UNTIL inval = endmarker;
    END;


    PROCEDURE Consumer;
    VAR outval: INTEGER;
    BEGIN
      outval := commchan; (*Read from channel*)
      WHILE outval <> endmarker DO
        BEGIN
          ... (*Utilize "outval" in some computation*)

          outval := commchan; (*Read next value from channel*)

        END;


BEGIN (*Main*)

  FORK Producer;  (*Producer Process*)

  FORK Consumer;  (*Consumer Process*)

END.
```

FIGURE 4.3   Producer–consumer communication with channel.

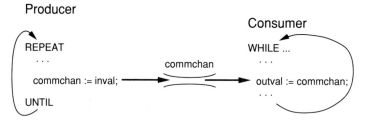

FIGURE 4.4   Producer–consumer interaction.

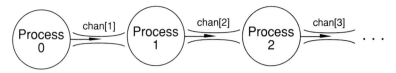

FIGURE 4.5 Process pipeline.

Figure 4.5 illustrates the general structure of a process pipeline. Each process acts as both a producer and a consumer. The process consumes from the channel on its left, and produces into the channel on its right. To facilitate the programming of pipeline algorithms, an array of channels can be used. Multi-Pascal allows several channels to be grouped together in arrays, in the same way that ordinary variables can be grouped together in arrays. For example, several *CHANNEL OF INTEGER* can be grouped into an array as follows:

```
VAR chan:  ARRAY [1..20] OF CHANNEL OF INTEGER;
```

To reference elements in this array of channels, the usual subscripting is used, just like subscripting of any ordinary array. "chan[1]" is the first channel of the array; "chan[2]" is the second channel of the array, and so on. For example, the following statement will write the value 10 into channel "chan[1]":

```
chan[1] := 10;  (*Write into "chan[1]"*)
```

Similarly, the following will read a value from "chan[1]" into the *INTEGER* variable x:

```
x := chan[1];
```

Arbitrary expressions may also be used in the array subscripts, as with ordinary arrays. For example, the following will read a value from *chan*[5] into x:

```
i := 5;
x := chan[i];  (*Read from "chan[i]"*)
```

This array of channels can conveniently be used to facilitate programming of a process pipeline, as illustrated in Figure 4.5. The processes are numbered sequentially from left to right in the pipeline. Process 1 reads from *chan*[1] on its left and writes to *chan*[2] on its right. Similarly, Process 2 reads from *chan*[2] and writes to *chan*[3]. In general, each Process k in the pipeline will read from *chan*[k] and write to *chan*[k + 1]. The following Procedure can be used as the basis for each process in the pipeline. The process will read m values from its left channel and write m values to its right channel:

```
PROCEDURE PipeProcess(mynumber: INTEGER);
VAR inval,outval,i: INTEGER;
BEGIN
  FOR i := 1 TO m DO
    BEGIN
       inval := chan[mynumber]; (*Read from left channel*)

       ... (*Use "inval" to compute "outval"*)
```

```
      chan[mynumber+1] := outval; (*Write to right channel*)
    END;
  END;
```

When the above procedure is called to create each process in the pipeline, it will be given the process number "mynumber" as a parameter. This "mynumber" will tell the process which channels to use for input and output in the pipeline. Input comes from *chan*[*mynumber*], and output goes to *chan*[*mynumber* + 1].

In general, the *relaxed* parallelism studied in previous chapters leads to a much greater speedup than the *pipeline* style. In *relaxed* parallelism, there are very large numbers of parallel processes created—the only limitation is the size of the data base and the number of available physical processors. With pipelines, the number of parallel processes is limited by the number of successive transformations performed on the data. Even increasing the number of input data items or increasing the number of physical processors will not increase the potential speedup of a pipeline style algorithm. Nevertheless, there are some algorithms that are very naturally expressed in a pipeline style, and do produce some good speedups. Pipelining is one of the major classes of parallel program organization, and should be thoroughly understood by the parallel programmer.

4.4 SOLUTION TO LINEAR EQUATIONS

The parallel pipeline programming technique can be adapted to solving a system of linear equations using an important numerical method called *back substitution*. Linear systems of equations are extremely important in many areas of scientific and engineering computing. The mathematical formulas used in these areas often result in a system of linear equations that must be solved numerically. Often systems of nonlinear equations must also be solved in various areas of scientific and engineering computing. However, the solution technique for these nonlinear equations usually involves the repeated solution of a system of linear equations, which is derived from the nonlinear equations. Chapter 6 illustrates one such important numerical computing technique for solving a common differential equation.

4.4.1 Back Substitution

A system of linear equations specifies a relationship among a group of *unknowns,* usually denoted $x_1, x_2, ..., x_n$. The general form of the system of equations is as follows:

$$a_{11}x_1 + a_{12}x_2 + a_{13}x_3 + \cdots + a_{1n}x_n = b_1$$

$$a_{21}x_1 + a_{22}x_2 + a_{23}x_3 + \cdots + a_{2n}x_n = b_2$$

$$a_{31}x_1 + a_{32}x_2 + a_{33}x_3 + \cdots + a_{3n}x_n = b_3$$

$$\cdot \qquad \cdot \qquad \cdot \qquad \quad \cdot \qquad \cdot$$

$$\cdot \qquad \cdot \qquad \cdot \qquad \quad \cdot \qquad \cdot$$

$$\cdot \qquad \cdot \qquad \cdot \qquad \quad \cdot \qquad \cdot$$

$$a_{n1}x_1 + a_{n2}x_2 + a_{n3}x_3 + \cdots + a_{nn}x_n = b_n$$

The values of the a and b terms are already known, and the computer is asked to determine the numerical value of the unknowns $(x_1, x_2, \ldots, x_n)$, which will make all the equations true simultaneously. A special form of this system of equations that is especially easy to solve is called *lower triangular* form. A lower triangular system has all the a values equal to zero in the upper right part of the equations. Specifically, $a_{ij} = 0$ if $j > i$. The following is the general structure of a lower triangular system with all the zero terms eliminated:

$$a_{11}x_1 \qquad\qquad\qquad\qquad\qquad = b_1$$

$$a_{21}x_1 + a_{22}x_2 \qquad\qquad\qquad\qquad = b_2$$

$$a_{31}x_1 + a_{32}x_2 + a_{33}x_3 \qquad\qquad\quad = b_3$$

$$a_{41}x_1 + a_{42}x_2 + a_{43}x_3 + a_{44}x_4 \qquad = b_4$$

$$\cdot \qquad \cdot \qquad \cdot \qquad \cdot \qquad\qquad \cdot$$

$$\cdot \qquad \cdot \qquad \cdot \qquad \cdot \qquad\qquad \cdot$$

$$\cdot \qquad \cdot \qquad \cdot \qquad \cdot \qquad\qquad \cdot$$

$$a_{n1}x_1 + a_{n2}x_2 + a_{n3}x_3 + a_{n4}x_4 + \cdots + a_{nn}x_n = b_n$$

In the original system, the equations have a "rectangular" shape. With all the upper right terms eliminated, the system now has a "triangular" shape, hence the name *lower triangular* system of equations. Notice that in equation i, the only terms present are those involving unknowns $x_1, x_2, \ldots, x_i$. Each successive equation adds one more unknown, until the last equation involves all the n unknowns. When a system has this lower triangular form it is easily solved by considering the equations one at a time starting from the top. Equation 1 is easily solved to determine the numerical value of unknown x_1:

$$x_1 = \frac{b_1}{a_{11}}$$

The second equation can be solved for unknown x_2 as follows:

$$x_2 = \frac{(b_2 - a_{21}x_1)}{a_{22}}$$

Since all of the values on the right side are already known, this equation gives the required numerical value for unknown x_2. Since the values of x_1 and x_2 are now known, the third equation can be solved to determine the numerical value of x_3:

$$x_3 = \frac{(b_3 - a_{31}x_1 - a_{32}x_2)}{a_{33}}$$

Clearly, this method can be continued through each equation to successively compute the value of each of the n unknowns. In general, by the time equation i is reached, the values of the unknowns $x_1, x_2, \ldots, x_{i-1}$ are already known. Then equation i can be used to compute the value of x_i. The general form of equation i is as follows:

$$a_{i1}x_1 + a_{i2}x_2 + \cdots + a_{ii}x_i = b_i$$

Therefore, the value of x_i can be determined as follows:

$$x_i = \frac{(b_i - a_{i1}x_1 - a_{i2}x_2 - \cdots - a_{i,i-1}x_{i-1})}{a_{ii}}$$

The method just described for solving a lower triangular system is called *back substitution*. It is easily encoded into a sequential computer program. The a_{ij} terms can be stored in a two-dimensional array A, the b terms in a one-dimensional array B, and the unknowns in a one-dimensional array x. The sequential algorithm is as follows:

```
Sequential Back Substitution:

  FOR i := 1 TO n DO
    BEGIN (*Solve equation i for value of x_i *)
      sum := 0;
      FOR j := 1 TO i-1 DO
        sum := sum + A[i,j]*x[j];
      x[i] := (B[i] - sum) / A[i,i];
    END;
```

The above sequential algorithm can be parallelized, but it must be done carefully. The outer *FOR* loop cannot simply be changed to *FORALL*. The inner loop computes the value of $x[i]$ using the previously computed values of $x[1]$, $x[2]$, ..., $x[i-1]$. Therefore, all values of i cannot be considered in parallel. Clearly, the equations must be considered sequentially, and cannot all be solved in parallel. However, there still is a good opportunity for parallelism in this back substitution method.

4.4.2 Pipeline Algorithm for Back Substitution

To begin to structure a parallel algorithm, first assign each equation to a different process. Process i is assigned equation i and will therefore compute the value of $x[i]$. Thus, Process i requires the values $x[1]$, $x[2]$, ..., $x[i-1]$. These values are computed by Processes 1, 2, ..., $i-1$. If the processes are all arranged in a pipeline numbered from left to right, then Process i in the pipeline will need all the values computed by processes to its left in the pipeline. This is illustrated in Figure 4.6. After Process 1 at the far left computes $x[1]$, it knows that all other processes to its right will need that value. So it can just send $x[1]$ down the pipeline to the right, where it will eventually reach all the other processes. Similarly, after Process 2 finishes the computation of $x[2]$, it knows that all the processes to its right will need this value. Therefore, Process 2 can send it down the pipeline to the right.

Assume now that each Process i in the pipeline will send its computed value $x[i]$ to the right down the pipeline. Each process in the pipeline can now expect to receive all its needed values coming down from the left. With reference to Figure 4.6, it is seen that a

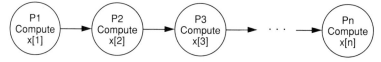

FIGURE 4.6 Process pipeline for back substitution.

Process i anywhere in the pipeline will receive the values $x[1], x[2], ..., x[i-1]$ from the processes on its left. To make the algorithm work correctly, however, it is necessary to ensure that the values come down the pipeline in the proper sequence. This is done by having each process send through all previous values, and then add its own value to the end. As Process i receives its needed values $x[1], x[2], ..., x[i-1]$ from the left, it will send these through to the right down the pipe, followed by its own computed value $x[i]$ at the very end. Thus, each successive process in the pipeline will add one new value to the flow of x's down the pipeline.

The following is a description of the computing activity performed by each process in the pipeline:

```
Pipeline Process i:

   sum := 0;
   FOR j := 1 TO i-1 DO
     BEGIN
        Read value of x[j] from left;
        Send value of x[j] to the right;
        sum := sum + A[i,j]*x[j];
     END;
   x[i] := (B[i] - sum) / A[i,i]; (*Compute x[i]*)
   Send x[i] to the right;
```

Notice that this code for Process i is almost the same as the inner *FOR* loop in the original program for sequential back substitution given above. The only change is the use of the pipeline to read the values of $x[1], x[2], ..., x[i-1]$. Notice also that the process uses each of these values immediately as it comes in from the left. As soon as some $x[j]$ is received, it is immediately multiplied by $A[i,j]$ and added into the partial sum. Then at the end, this partial sum is used to compute the final value of $x[i]$, which is then sent down the pipeline to the other processes.

The complete Multi-Pascal program is shown in Figure 4.7. The array of channels called "pipechan" is used to form the pipeline. The processes are created from the Procedure "PipeProcess". Each process is passed its index number i as a parameter, and computes one unknown $x[i]$ using equation i from the original system of linear equations. The program uses n physical processors to solve a system of n equations. The overall execution time is $O(n)$. The sequential program has execution time $O(n^2)$. The speedup achieved by the parallel program is thus $O(n)$. This Pipeline Back Substitution algorithm is a useful practical method for solving lower triangular systems of linear equations. It is used commonly in practice on a wide range of multiprocessors and multicomputers.

Some insights into the dynamics of this program can be gained through the performance profile of Figure 4.8, created by using the "profile" command in the Multi-Pascal interactive system (see Appendix B). To allow the profile to fit within the width of the page, a system of 30 linear equations was used, requiring 31 physical processors. Each horizontal line in the profile represents 60 time units. The blank area in the upper right of the profile results from the process creation time. Before a physical processor is assigned its process, the profile shows blank space for that processor. Notice that even after each process is created, it still has to wait some time before it gets into full operation. This is

```
PROGRAM BackSubstitution;
CONST n = 50;
VAR  A: ARRAY [1..n,1..n] OF REAL;
     B,x: ARRAY [1..n] OF REAL;
     pipechan: ARRAY [1..n+1] OF CHANNEL OF REAL;
     i: INTEGER;

PROCEDURE PipeProcess(i: INTEGER);
(*Solves Equation i to compute x[i]*)
VAR j: INTEGER; sum,xvalue: REAL;
BEGIN
  sum := 0;
  FOR j := 1 TO i-1 DO
    BEGIN
      xvalue := pipechan[i];   (*Read x[j] from the left*)
      pipechan[i+1] := xvalue; (*Send x[j] to the right*)
      sum := sum + A[i,j]*xvalue;
    END;
  x[i] := (B[i] - sum) / A[i,i]; (*Compute value of x[i]*)
  pipechan[i+1] := x[i];         (*Send x[i] to the right*)
END;

BEGIN

  ...  (*Initialize arrays A and B*)

FORALL i := 1 TO n DO  (*Create the pipeline processes*)
  PipeProcess(i);

END.
```

FIGURE 4.7 Parallel back substitution.

because each process (except Process 1) must wait for the value of $x[1]$ to be received from its left neighbor before beginning computation. Since the value of $x[1]$ originates in Process 1 and then gradually moves to the right down the pipeline, each successive process in the pipeline has to wait for a little extra time before beginning.

Notice also in the profile that higher-numbered processes do more computation. This results from the "triangular" shape of the system of equations, with higher-numbered equations involving more terms. The triangular shape of the equations is reflected in the triangular shape of the computational region in the right portion of the profile. The large area of dots in the lower left represents idle time for the processors. The average processor utilization is 37 percent. However, the program does achieve a reasonable overall speedup of 11.

The $O(n)$ execution time also becomes clear from the profile. The execution time is dominated by the highest-numbered processor n, which has to compute the value of $x[n]$ using $x[1]$, $x[2]$, ..., $x[n-1]$. This requires n additions and n multiplications, and is therefore $O(n)$. The time for the first value $x[1]$ to reach processor n is also $O(n)$—thus the overall program execution time is $O(n)$. This analysis is confirmed by the performance

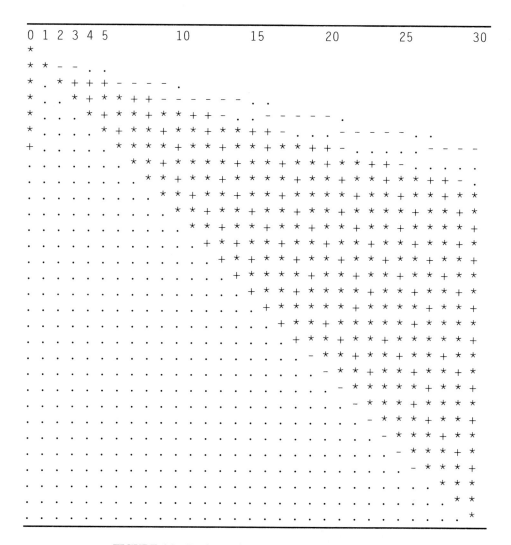

FIGURE 4.8   Performance profile for back substitution.

graph of Figure 4.9, which shows the program speedup for increasing values of n, determined by running the program with the Multi-Pascal interactive software. The graph indicates that the actual program speedup is approximately $.37n$.

4.5 CHANNELS AND STRUCTURED TYPES

In this section, some of the more sophisticated aspects of channel usage in Multi-Pascal are discussed. The discussion so far has focused on channel variables whose component type is one of the four simple Pascal data types: *INTEGER, REAL, CHAR, BOOLEAN*. Multi-Pascal allows the component type of a channel to be any valid type in standard Pascal, including arrays, records, or pointers. The following are examples of channel declarations with component types *ARRAY* and *RECORD*:

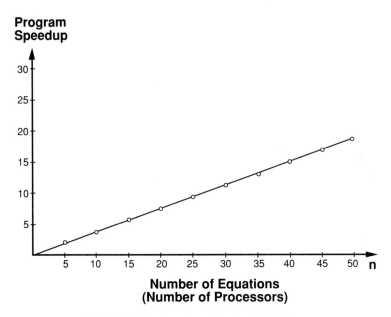

**Program
Speedup**

**Number of Equations
(Number of Processors)**

FIGURE 4.9   Speedup of back substitution.

```
C:   CHANNEL OF ARRAY [1..10] OF REAL;
D:   CHANNEL OF RECORD
                left, right:  INTEGER;
                center: REAL;
            END;
```

It is also permitted in Multi-Pascal to have a channel whose component type is a pointer, as in the following example:

```
TYPE
   item:  RECORD
                x, y: INTEGER;
            END;
VAR
   E:  CHANNEL OF ^item;
```

All of the same rules for channel usage discussed so far also apply to channels of array, record, or pointer. To write a new value into a channel, use the name on the left side of an assignment, with an expression on the right side whose type is identical to the component type of the channel. For example, the following writes a new value into a *CHANNEL OF ARRAY*:

```
TYPE  artyp = ARRAY [1..10] OF REAL;
VAR
   C: CHANNEL OF artyp;
   a: artyp;
   ...
```

```
BEGIN
  ...

  C := a;
```

In the above assignment, the current contents of array *a* are written into the end of channel *C*. Each item in channel *C* will be a whole array with 10 real values. Notice that the type of variable *a* matches the component type of channel variable *C*. Similarly, the channel can be read with the following statement:

```
a := C;
```

It is not permitted to use a subscript with a *CHANNEL OF ARRAY*: the expression *C*[3] is not valid Multi-Pascal syntax. To get at the third element in the array, one must first read the whole array from the front of channel *C* into an ordinary array variable such as *a*, and then use the expression *a*[3]. The only operations that can be performed with a *CHANNEL OF ARRAY* is reading or writing a whole array from the channel. It is not permitted to read or write one element in the array. The rules are similar for records, as shown in the following example:

```
TYPE  rectyp = RECORD
                 left, right:  INTEGER;
                 center: REAL;
               END;
VAR  D: CHANNEL OF rectyp;
     e: rectyp;
  ...

BEGIN
  ...

  D := e;
```

A whole record may be read or written from a *CHANNEL OF RECORD* by using the channel variable name in an assignment with an ordinary variable having the same record type. As with arrays, it is not permitted to qualify a *CHANNEL OF RECORD*; the expression *D.left* is a syntax error. A whole record must be read or written to the channel as a single operation. The general rule for channel variables is as follows:

The component type of a channel may be any valid type in standard Pascal.

As seen in the pipeline examples of this chapter, Multi-Pascal also allows an array of channels. The pipeline programs all use a one-dimensional array of channels, but multidimensional arrays are also permitted, as in the following sample declaration:

```
A: ARRAY [1..10, 1..20] OF
   CHANNEL OF REAL;
```

The above variable *A* is a two-dimensional array of channels: each element in the array is a separate channel of real numbers. The array *A* contains 200 individual channels that can be selected by using subscripts. Reading and writing from each channel is done as usual, using the channel on the left or right side of an assignment. The following assignment statements will read a value from channel *A*[3, 2] and write the value into channel *A*[4, 3] (variable *p* is an ordinary *REAL* variable):

```
p := A[3,2];   (*read channel*)
A[4,3] := p;   (*write channel*)
```

Additional examples of combining channel variables with other Pascal data types are given in Appendix A, including records with channel components, and pointers to channel types. Appendix A also discusses passing channels as procedure parameters, and the use of channels in expressions.

4.6 BITONIC MERGE SORT

As an example of the application of multidimensional arrays of channels, this section considers the Bitonic Merge Sort, which is an efficient parallel sorting algorithm with execution time $O(\log^2 n)$. This algorithm requires a programming technique called *phased-array* communications, in which each process goes through a series of computational phases, using a different channel for communication during each phase. In the pipeline programs described earlier in the chapter, each process had two fixed communication partners, always receiving data from its left neighbor and sending data to its right neighbor. In the Bitonic Merge Sort, each process will have a series of different communication partners, with the precise sequence of partners being critical to the correctness of the program. To maintain the proper sequence, each process needs its own array of channels, one for each communication partner.

The Bitonic Merge Sort is based on an organizational principle that is similar to the classic Merge Sort, with which the reader may be familiar. During each step of a Merge Sort, small sorted sublists are "merged" in pairs to form half as many sorted sublists of twice the length. For a list of length *n*, repeating this merge step log *n* times results in a fully sorted list. The Bitonic Merge Sort is very similar, except instead of using fully sorted sublists, it uses partially sorted sublists called "bitonic" lists. A list that is not sorted will have a number of local maxima or minima. A *local maximum* is defined as a list item both of whose immediate neighbors are lower in value. Similarly, a *local minimum* has neighbors with higher value. The endpoints of the list are not considered as local maxima or minima since they have only one neighbor. A *bitonic list* is defined as a list with no more than one local maximum and no more than one local minimum.

One important type of bitonic list has the first half sorted in ascending order and the second half in descending order. This type of list has one local maximum in the center of the list and no local minimum. The heart of the Bitonic Merge Sort is an operation on a bitonic list called a *binary-split*. By assigning one process to each item in the list, this binary-split can be done in parallel with just a few computational steps by each process, independent of the size of the list. To simplify the remainder of this discussion, let us assume that the length of the list *n* is an exact power of two. The list items and their corresponding processes are numbered $0 \ldots n - 1$. The binary-split operation is defined as follows:

1. Each process in the first half of the list is assigned a "partner," which is the process in the same relative position from the second half of the list. This means that each Process i in the first half is assigned to Process $i + n/2$ in the second half.
2. Each pair of partner processes compare their assigned list items. If the process from the first half of the list has a larger item, then the processes exchange items; otherwise nothing is done.

It is clear that this binary-split tends to reorder the list items, such that smaller items move more toward the beginning, and larger items toward the end. When applied to a bitonic list, the binary-split results in a new list with the following remarkable properties, which we will just state and not prove:

1. Each item in the first half of the list is less than every item in the second half.
2. The first half and the second half of the list are each a bitonic list of length $n/2$.

As an example, consider the following bitonic list with one local maximum in the center:

10 20 30 40 50 60 70 80 75 65 55 45 35 25 15 5

Applying the binary-split to this list results in the following list:

10 20 30 40 35 25 15 5   75 65 55 45 50 60 70 80

Notice that this list satisfies property 2 above, since the first half of the list is now a bitonic list with one local maximum (40), and the second half is a bitonic list with one local minimum (45). Property 1 above is also satisfied by this new list.

Now what happens if the binary-split is now recursively applied to the two halves of the list? The answer is that after $\log n$ levels of recursion, the list will be fully sorted. This leads to the possibility of a parallel algorithm to sort any bitonic list through repeated application of the binary-split to smaller and smaller sublists. All that is needed to formulate the algorithm is a method for each process to choose its partner process at each stage. This can be done by considering the binary form of the identification number of each process, and examining the bits from left to right. The partner is determined by simply reversing the bit. Since there are n processes, each process has $d = \log n$ bits in its identification number. Assume that the bit positions are numbered from right to left: $0, 1, \ldots, d - 1$. The following procedure is followed by each process:

```
(Ascending) Sort of Bitonic List:

   (* Process idenfication number is "myid" *)
   For j := d-1 Downto 0 Do (* Use bit j of myid *)
     Begin (* Binary-Split *)
       Determine Partner process by reversing bit j of myid;
       Send copy of my list item to Partner;
```

```
    Receive Partner's copy;
    If bit j of myid is 0 Then
        Retain smaller of the two items
      Else Retain larger of the two items;
End;
```

This parallel algorithm will sort any bitonic list into ascending order. Through a minor modification of changing the 0 to a 1 in the "If" statement, it is transformed into a descending sort. This algorithm can be used to merge any pair of bitonic lists into a single bitonic list by applying an ascending Sort to the first list and a descending Sort to the second list. This parallel Merge algorithm requires one process for each item in the two lists, and has execution time $O(\log n)$. This Merge algorithm is the heart of the Bitonic Merge Sort. By applying it to adjacent pairs of bitonic sublists, the result is half as many bitonic sublists of twice the length.

Now consider starting with an unsorted list with n items, and assign one process to each item. Any list with only two items is always a bitonic list. Therefore, this unsorted list consists of $n/2$ bitonic lists of length 2. By applying the parallel Merge to pairs of adjacent lists, the result is $n/4$ bitonic lists of length 4. After $\log n$ repetitions of the parallel Merge, the list is completely sorted. It is interesting that there is a very simple method of formulating this sorting algorithm based on examining and comparing the $d = \log n$ bits of the process identification numbers. To complete this Bitonic Merge Sort, the above sorting algorithm for bitonic lists is enclosed in an outer loop that scans through the bits of the process identification number from right to left:

```
Bitonic Merge Sort:

  (* Each process "myid" runs this code *)

  For i := 1 To d Do (* Use bit i of myid *)
    (*Perform parallel Merge of adjacent bitonic sublists*)
    For j := i-1 Downto 0 Do
      Begin (* Binary-Split *)
        Determine Partner process by reversing bit j of myid;
        Send copy of my list item to Partner;
        Receive Partner's copy;
        If (bit j of myid = bit i of myid) Then
            Retain smaller of the two items
          Else Retain larger of the two items;
      End;
```

This algorithm performs $d(d + 1)/2$ repetitions of the Binary-Split, which has a constant execution time. Therefore, the total execution time of this parallel Bitonic Merge Sort is $O(\log^2 n)$, which is superior to the $O(n)$ time achieved by the Rank Sort presented in Chapter 2. The coding of this Bitonic Merge Sort is interesting in Multi-Pascal because it requires each process to have its own private array of channels for communicating with its many potential partners. This issue is considered in Programming Project 2.

4.7 SUMMARY

This chapter is our first exposure to nonrelaxed algorithms, defined as algorithms that require process interaction. In relaxed algorithms, the parallel processes may access shared data, but it is generally only read-type access. When processes begin to modify shared data that is intended for use by other parallel processes, then special language mechanisms are required to ensure that the data is fully modified before it is read by the target process. Since parallel processes may run at varying speeds on different processors, there is no way to guarantee such a requirement without some additional language mechanism. This new mechanism introduced in this chapter is the *channel variable*. Channel variables can store a sequence of values to allow a writer process to proceed ahead of a reader process. The values will then later be fed to the reader process one at a time as needed. If the reader is faster and tries to read an empty channel, it will be suspended until some other process writes into the channel.

Channel variables are ideal for the classic producer–consumer parallel programming paradigm. The properties of the channel variable guarantee correct communication between the producer and consumer. By connecting producers and consumers in a linear chain using channels, a *pipeline* is created with a good potential for parallel processing. In pipeline algorithms, a stream of data values passes through the pipe from one end to the other, with each process performing some specific transformation on the data. An automobile assembly line is an example of the pipeline principle, where the partially assembled autos are analogous to the data values, and the workers are analogous to the parallel processes.

A well-known pipeline algorithm was given for solving a triangular system of linear equations, based on the standard sequential *back substitution* technique. In this pipeline method, each process computes the value of one of the unknowns, and then sends it down the pipeline for the rest of the processes to read. As each process receives unknown values on the left, it both passes them on to the right and incorporates them into its internal computation. As time progresses, more and more of the processes become active. The speedup of the parallel algorithm over the sequential back substitution method is $O(n)$. This parallel pipeline method for linear equations is used frequently in practice.

The complete syntax and semantics of channel variables are described in this chapter. Channels can be composed with other Pascal data types, including structured types. An array of channels is allowed, and also a channel whose component type is an array. Similarly, channels can be composed with record types. The Bitonic Merge Sort algorithm was presented to illustrate the use of a two-dimensional array of channels for process communication. Channel variables are used extensively in the example programs in all the following chapters of this text.

REFERENCE NOTES

The concept of having named communication channels for sending information between processes is quite common in parallel programming languages. The UNIX programming environment [Ritchie and Thompson, 1974] has "pipes" for sending data between processes. The language Occam [Inmos, 1985] has channel variables for passing data from a sending to a receiving process. These Occam channels have capacity for only one message and will block the writer process when the channel is full. The language Poker allows each process to have named "ports" that behave like Multi-Pascal channels, except that only one writer and one reader process are allowed for each port [Snyder and Socha, 1986].

The Producer-Consumer parallel programming paradigm appears in Dijkstra [1968a]. The use of channels in Multi-Pascal for writing pipeline algorithms originally appeared in Lester and Guthrie [1988]. The pipeline back substitution algorithm is described in Bertsekas and Tsitsiklis [1989]. The sequential Bitonic Merge Sort was originally developed by Batcher [1968]. The parallel version given in this chapter is similar to the one that appears in Fox, et al. [1988]. See Bitton, et al. [1984] for a comprehensive summary of parallel sorting algorithms.

The prime number sieve algorithm described in programming project 1 is a variation of the one found in Bokhari [1987].

PROGRAMMING PROJECTS

1. PRIME NUMBER SIEVE

In this project you will write a parallel version of the classic Sieve of Eratosthenes for computing prime numbers. The program is highly efficient and can achieve very large speedups.

The first step is to consider a sequential program for the Sieve of Eratosthenes. To compute the prime numbers from 1 to n, the basic data structure is a simple boolean array called *Prime* with n elements. The program initializes all the array elements to the value TRUE. The remainder of the program will gradually change array elements from TRUE to FALSE. At the end, all remaining array elements that are still TRUE will indicate prime numbers. The program is shown below:

```
PROGRAM Sieve;
CONST n = 100;
VAR Prime: ARRAY [1..n] OF BOOLEAN;
    i,num,loc: INTEGER;

BEGIN
FOR i := 1 TO n DO
  Prime[i] := TRUE;
FOR num := 2 TO Trunc(Sqrt(n)) DO
  IF Prime[num] THEN
    BEGIN
      loc := num + num;
      WHILE loc <= n DO
        BEGIN
          Prime[loc] := False;
          loc := loc + num;
        END;
    END;
END.
```

The program has a FOR loop that scans the array fr[...]
Each element that still has value TRUE when the scan reac[...]
such prime identified is the number 2. For each such prin[...]
program), an inner *WHILE* loop will change all multiples [...]
the array. The variable *loc* is used to step through the array[...]
process will eliminate all nonprime numbers in the array[...]
with value TRUE at the end of the program are prime nu[...]

Your job is to write a parallel version of this Siev[...]
program is parallelized by partitioning the array *Prin*[...]
creating one parallel process to work on each portion. M[...]
that all the elements up to the square root of *n* are contain[...]
assigned to the first portion is almost identical to the sequential program. [...]
main difference is that the *WHILE* loop stops when it reaches the end of the first portion of
the array. The other portions will be handled by their own processes.

All processes begin by initializing their own portion to TRUE. This can all be done in
parallel. Then the first process begins to search for the first TRUE value, which of course is
2. This number 2 is then broadcast to all the other processes. As each process receives this
number, it begins to step through its own portion in jumps of size 2, thereby changing all
the even numbers to FALSE. Then the first process loops around again to search for the
next TRUE value, and again broadcasts this to the other processes, where it is used to step
and change TRUE to FALSE. In this parallel version, there is a separate process to step
through each portion of the array in parallel.

Broadcasting each "step" number to all the processes can be made more efficient by
having the first process send it to the second process only. The second process sends it to
the third, and the third to the fourth, and so on. By passing the "step" number through a
process pipeline in this way, the overall execution time is reduced.

Another important issue is how each process determines the starting point for
stepping after it receives a given "step" number *num*. It will take steps of size *num*, but
where should it start? The answer is at the first number in its portion of the array that is
evenly divisible by *num*. Assuming that the first element of the array in this portion is
Prime[*first*], then the following technique will locate the starting point:

```
remainder := first MOD num;
if remainder = 0 then starting point is "first"
  else starting point is (first DIV num + 1) * num
```

Write this parallel version of the Sieve program and run it, using the Multi-Pascal
system. Test the program for correctness, and then experiment with different size arrays to
see how much speedup can be achieved. You should see that very large speedups can be
achieved for big arrays.

2. BITONIC MERGE SORT

In this project you will write a program for the Bitonic Merge Sort, as described in
this chapter. The main issue will be how to implement the comparing and possible
exchange of values of partner processes. If there are *n* processes, then each process

on number has $d = \log n$ bits. Therefore, each process has exactly d potential
, and needs its own array of d channels, one for each partner. To compare values
given partner, the process sends a copy of its value to the partner and receives a copy
the partner's value. Then the process can easily compare the values and retain the
maller or larger of the two values, as needed. To ensure the correct sequence of partners,
the array of channels is necessary.

Run and test the program, using the Multi-Pascal interactive system. Compare the
performance to the Rank Sort for a range of values of n.

EXERCISES

1. In the Producer–Consumer example of Figure 4.3, the end of the communication is indicated by
   a special *endmarker* value in the channel. An alternate method of controlling the communication
   is to let the first value sent through the channel be a count of the total number of subsequent
   values that will be sent through the channel. Rewrite the Producer–Consumer example, using
   this new technique.

2. Write a program containing two processes—a Reader process and a Writer process. The Reader
   process reads a sequence of values from the user and sends them to the Writer process through a
   channel. The Writer process reads the values from the channel and writes them out to the
   terminal screen. The end of the sequence of values is denoted by a special end-of-stream value.

3. Consider changing the Producer–Consumer communication of Figure 4.3 to eliminate the
   necessity for the *endmarker* value by having the Consumer check for an empty channel as
   follows:

```
BEGIN (*Consumer Process*)
  WHILE commchan? DO
    BEGIN
      outval := commchan;
      ... (*Utilize "outval" in some computation*)

    END;
```

   Explain why this modification may work correctly for some Producer and Consumer procedures
   but not for others. Describe a possible communication scenario that causes an error in the
   program.

4. Write a program to read 10 values from a channel and write them in the same sequence into a
   different channel. This can be done with a single loop.

5. Write a program to count the number of items in a channel, such that the channel is returned to its
   original state after counting. This can be done by first writing a special "endmarker" symbol into
   the channel, and then reading the values sequentially from the channel until the endmarker is
   encountered. As each value is read, it is also written into the channel. This guarantees that after
   the endmarker is removed, the channel will be returned to its original state.

6. Consider a general form of a pipeline program, in which a long sequence of data values continues
   to flow through the pipeline from beginning to end. In this general pipeline, different types of
   operations may be performed by different processes. Assume that the specific operation performed by each Process i requires T_i time units. Let Process k be the one with the largest such
   time. Explain why the time T_k limits the performance of the pipeline, even if all the other T_i are
   much less than T_k.

7. In this chapter, the following Sequential Back Substitution program is given:

```
FOR i := 1 TO n DO
  BEGIN (*Solve equation i for value of xi *)
    sum := 0;
    FOR j := 1 TO i-1 DO
      sum := sum + A[i,j]*x[j];
    x[i] := (B[i] - sum) / A[i,i];
  END;
```

In attempting to parallelize this program, suppose that the outer *FOR* loop is changed to *FORALL*.

(a) Explain why this does not produce a correct parallel program. Show in detail how an erroneous computation might occur in this case.

(b) Consider a target multiprocessor having the property that the process creation time is much greater than the execution time for each iteration of the inner *FOR* loop. For these special circumstances, the parallel program will actually produce the correct answer. Explain in detail the reasons for this.

8. It is stated in the chapter that the Parallel Back Substitution program has an execution time $O(n)$. Provide a detailed explanation and justification for this statement, based on the structure of the program code.

9. An execution profile for the Back Substitution program is shown in Figure 4.8. From the characteristics of this profile, it is possible to conclude that the process creation overhead actually did not influence the execution time of the program.

(a) Explain in detail the justification for this statement about the process creation overhead.

(b) If the process creation overhead were much larger, then it would begin to influence the program execution time. Approximately how large must the creation overhead be for this to happen?

10. In a pipeline program with p processes, a sequence of n data values flows through the pipeline from beginning to end. Each process in the pipeline performs a transformation on each data value that requires T time units, and then sends it to the next process. The communication time between processes is C time units. The program ends when all the n data values have passed all the way through the pipeline. Assuming a negligible process creation overhead, derive an algebraic expression for the program execution time, speedup, and average processor utilization.

11. Consider the following declarations:

```
TYPE  artyp = ARRAY [1..20] OF INTEGER;
      rectyp = RECORD
                    a, b: INTEGER;
                    c: REAL;
               END;
VAR  achan:  CHANNEL OF artyp;
     rchan:  CHANNEL OF rectyp;
```

For each of the following tasks, write a series of statements to accomplish that task. Include declarations for all variables used:

(a) Remove all the items currently in channel *achan*.

(b) Write out the value of components *a* and *b* of the first item in channel *rchan*.

(c) Create an array containing the numbers 101 to 120 and write this array into channel *achan*.

(d) Create a record of *rectyp* by reading in three values; then write this record into channel *rchan*.

(e) Write out the fifth and tenth elements in the array at the front of channel *achan*.

12. Consider the following declaration:

```
VAR  a: ARRAY [1..10, 1..20] OF CHANNEL OF CHAR;
```

For each of the following tasks, write a series of statements to accomplish that task. Include declarations of all variables used.

(a) Write the letters "A" and "B" into each of the channels in array a.

(b) Clear out the contents of all the channels in array a.

13. (a) Give an example of a bitonic list with 16 elements.

(b) Apply the Binary-Split operation to the list of part (a), and show the resultant list. Then continue to apply the Binary-Split recursively to the two halves of the list, showing the list after each level of recursion.

(c) Apply the algorithm given in section 4.6 for sorting a bitonic list to a list with 16 elements. Create a table that shows, for each of the 16 processes, the sequence of binary identification numbers of its partners in the algorithm.

(d) Explain in detail the logic behind the use of individual bits in the algorithm for sorting a bitonic list. Why is bit j reversed to get the Partner? Why is the value of bit j used to determine which item to retain?

14. One of the most interesting aspects of the Bitonic Merge Sort algorithm is the comparison of bit i with bit j of the process identification number, to determine whether to retain the smaller or larger of the two items. Explain in detail the reasons for this, and the mechanics of how it operates during the execution of the algorithm.

5

Data Sharing

When parallel processes access shared data, it is important that the operations performed on this data do not conflict with each other as a result of the parallelism; each operation performed by a process must maintain its own integrity despite the operations being performed by other processes. This chapter describes an important Multi-Pascal feature called *spinlocks*, which are useful to help coordinate the sharing of data values and data structures by parallel processes. Spinlocks can be used to guarantee exclusive access to shared data, and ensure the integrity of parallel operations. This chapter describes techniques for using spinlocks to solve this classic "mutual exclusion" problem for parallel access to shared data.

The important concept of "atomic operations" is introduced in this chapter. An atomic operation performed by a process is defined as an operation that cannot be interrupted by other processes. A single atomic operation on shared data will usually involve a series of incremental changes to the data. If other processes are allowed to read or write the shared data before the whole series of changes is complete, then an error may result. For example, adding a new element to a linked list involves reading and modifying several pointers. If one process is adding an element to the list, and another process is allowed to read the pointers in an intermediate state, then an error may result. The purpose of atomic operations is to prevent this kind of interference between parallel processes. The "atomic" nature of the operation will guarantee that no other process can access the relevant shared data values until the whole operation is complete.

To create an atomic operation, the basic requirement in the programming language is some mechanism to make processes wait. In Multi-Pascal this can be accomplished with a *spinlock*, which creates a "locked gate" through which processes can pass only one at a time. When a process passes through the "gate," it is automatically locked to prevent other processes from entering. After the process finishes its atomic operation, the gate is unlocked again to allow another process to enter. Spinlocks are a very common feature in other parallel programming languages.

One performance issue that inevitably arises in this context is contention. By their very nature, atomic operations require some degree of exclusive access to shared data elements. Therefore, a single process performing such an operation may cause a large number of other processes to wait. There is a possibility that the contention for the exclusive use of the shared data may result in a performance bottleneck. This issue is discussed thoroughly in this chapter, and a general technique is described for minimizing the performance degradation resulting from atomic operations: "decentralization" of the access mechanism to the shared data. This allows multiple parallel processes to access different parts of the shared data, and thus reduces the process waiting time.

5.1 ATOMIC OPERATIONS

To understand the motivation for mutual exclusion and atomic operations, let us first consider the simple operation of reading and writing of an individual shared variable by parallel processes. For simple nonstructured variables, this problem is solved by the memory access controller at the hardware level in the computer. Even if many parallel processes attempt to read or write a single memory cell at the same time, the memory controller will arbitrate the parallel requests and cause other processes to wait while each process is allowed to access the memory cell one at time.

For example, assume that a variable X contains the value 20 and two processes try to access the variable in parallel: process A is reading the value from X, and process B is writing a new value of 30 into X. The memory controller will guarantee that the read and write operations will each maintain their own integrity; either the read will occur first and then the write, or the write and then the read. Thus, the final value of variable X will always be 30, and process A will read either 20 or 30. It would certainly be erroneous if the read and write collided in such a way that process A read some number halfway between 20 and 30, like 25.

The memory controller in the hardware will thus guarantee the integrity of individual read and write operations performed by parallel processes on shared variables. However, it is often the case that a process will perform a more complex high-level operation on shared data involving several memory accesses. For example, consider the following Multi-Pascal statement for incrementing a shared variable n:

```
n := n + 1;
```

This statement first causes a read of variable n to get the old value, followed by a write to n of the new value. The read and write are logically part of the same operation, but it is possible that some other parallel process can access variable n between the read and write. For example, consider two processes A and B, each trying to increment n using a statement like the above. If the initial value of n is 20, the correct final result should be 22. However, consider a possible scenario in which process A reads the value of 20 from n, and then process B reads the same value 20 before A gets a chance to write the new value back. Then process A adds 1 to its value of 20 and writes back 21 into n. Similarly, process B

adds 1 to its value of 20 and writes back 21 into *n*. Thus, the final value of *n* is an erroneous 21 instead of the correct 22. This scenario is illustrated in Figure 5.1.

This potential program error is an example of what is generally called a *timing-dependent error*—the actual occurrence of the potential error during a particular execution of the program depends on the relative timing of the processes involved. Only under certain relative timing relationships will the error be detected through a test run of the program. Such timing-dependent bugs in parallel programs are often very difficult to detect, and are best located through analysis of the program structure rather than running the program with test cases. However, to help the programmer locate timing-dependent errors, the Multi-Pascal interactive software has a special "Variation" feature that will create randomly selected variations in processor speed. Details are given in Appendix B.

As an example of how this type of error could actually arise in a real program, consider the following program segment to search an array for a given value and record the total number of occurrences of that value in the array:

```
PROGRAM Search;
VAR  A: ARRAY [1..200] OF INTEGER;
     i, val, n: INTEGER;

 BEGIN
  ...

n := 0;
Readln(val);
FORALL i := 1 TO 200 GROUPING 10 DO
  IF A[i] = val THEN n := n + 1;
Writeln('Total occurrences: ', n);
  ...
```

Each parallel process created by the *FORALL* statement will search a different part of the array for the value in variable *val*. Each time this value is found, the variable *n* will be incremented with the intention that *n* will accumulate a count of the total number of occurrences. However, actually running this program will result in an error when the number of occurrences of *val* is large enough to cause two processes to attempt to increment *n* at the same time.

The problem in the above Parallel Search can be eliminated by using a *spinlock*. At any given time during program execution, the spinlock itself will have a state, which is

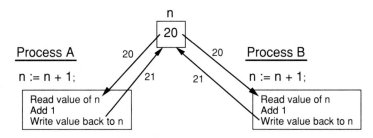

FIGURE 5.1   Error with shared data.

either "locked" or "unlocked." To modify the state of a spinlock, there are two simple operations—*Lock* or *Unlock*. The *Lock* operation changes the spinlock into the "locked" state, and the *Unlock* operation changes it to the "unlocked" state. The *Lock* operation has one more very important property: if the spinlock is already "locked," then the process will automatically wait until it is unlocked by another process. Therefore, spinlocks provide a mechanism for one process to make other processes wait. This can be used to create a new Parallel Search program that works correctly:

```
PROGRAM Search;
VAR  A: ARRAY [1..200] OF INTEGER;
     i, val, n: INTEGER;
     L: SPINLOCK;

BEGIN
  ...

n := 0;
Readln(val);
FORALL i := 1 TO 200 GROUPING 10 DO
  IF A[i] = val THEN
    BEGIN
      Lock(L);   (*Enter and lock the spinlock*)
      n := n + 1;
      Unlock(L); (*Unlock the spinlock to allow another to enter*)
    END;
Writeln('Total occurrences: ', n);
  ...
```

In the above program, each process must execute "Lock(L)" before performing the update of variable *n*. After any process executes this "Lock(L)" operation, then all other processes will find that *L* is now in the "locked" state. If any of them try to perform their own "Lock(L)" operation, they will automatically be forced to wait. Eventually, the first process will finish the "n := n + 1" instruction and will execute the "Unlock(L)" instruction. This will again place the spinlock *L* into the "unlocked" state. If there are any processes waiting at the "Lock(L)" instruction, one of them will be allowed to pass by, causing the spinlock *L* to again go into the "locked" state. In this way, the spinlock guarantees that only one process at a time can update variable *n*, thus ensuring the correct operation of the program.

The operation of the spinlock in this program is illustrated in Figure 5.2. The "Lock(L)" and "Unlock(L)" operations create a kind of "fence" around the instruction "n := n + 1," such that only one process at a time may be inside the fence to modify *n*. Time flows from top to bottom in the figure, showing the successive stages of activity. At the top of Figure 5.2, Process *P5* is the first to arrive, and finds the spinlock *L* in the "unlocked" state. When Process *P5* executes the "Lock(L)" operation, this has two effects: Process *P5* is allowed to pass by, and the spinlock *L* is changed to the "locked" state. In the next stage shown in Figure 5.2, Process *P5* is now executing the "n := n + 1" instruction. While this is happening, three more processes *P1*, *P2*, and *P7* execute "Lock(L)" in an attempt to pass through. Since the spinlock *L* is now in the "locked" state,

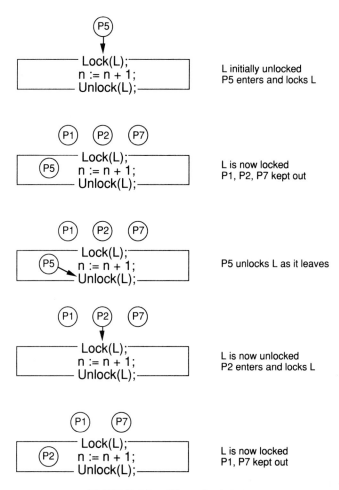

FIGURE 5.2   Effect of spinlocks.

all three of these processes will automatically have their execution suspended. Finally, Process *P5* leaves the enclosed region by executing the "Unlock(L)" operation. This returns the spinlock *L* to the "unlocked" state. One of the three waiting processes will now be allowed to enter the enclosed region. In this way, the processes will be allowed to modify the variable *n* only one at a time.

The increment operation in the Parallel Search program is a specific example of an important concept in the field of parallel programming: the *atomic* operation. An *atomic* operation is performed by a single parallel process and cannot be interrupted by any other process. Incrementing the value of *n* in the Parallel Search is one example of an operation that must be atomic for the program to work correctly. Other parallel programs may have more complex atomic operations involving reading and writing of many different variables.

Every parallel programming language has special features designed to help create atomic operations. Examples of such features are semphores [Dijkstra, 1968a, 1968b], locks [Shaw, 1984], critical regions [Brinch Hansen, 1983], and monitors [Hoare, 1974].

In every case, the goal of these features is to allow one process to access and modify some shared data, while at the same time preventing other processes from reading or writing this data until the modification is finished. This requirement is sometimes called the classic *mutual exclusion* problem of parallel programming: the use of shared data by one process must "exclude" all other processes. This "exclusion" property guarantees that the operation performed is atomic.

5.2 SPINLOCKS

5.2.1 Implementation of Spinlocks

To understand the effect of spinlocks on the performance of parallel programs, it is necessary to know something about how they are implemented in a multiprocessor. The most important implementation issue is how the processes are suspended when attempting a "Lock" operation on a spinlock that is already in the "locked" state. In most multiprocessor systems, this is done with a form of process suspension called *busy waiting*: the process keeps computing, but is stuck inside a small loop that keeps on examining the state of the spinlock. As long as the spinlock remains in the "locked" state, the process continues in the loop. This is the source of the name *spin*lock. Processes are forced to "spin" while waiting for the lock to open.

The spinlock itself is easily implemented as a program variable associated with an ordinary memory cell. Memory value 0 represents the "unlocked" state, and memory value 1 represents the "locked" state. The *Unlock(L)* operation is easily performed by writing a 0 into the memory cell as follows:

```
Unlock(L):   Write 0 into L;
```

The *Lock(L)* operation is slightly more complex because the spinlock must both be examined and modified. The operation is often performed with the help of a special machine instruction called "TestandSet." This instruction will return the current value of a memory cell and also set the memory cell to 1. These two phases of the TestandSet instruction are executed by the multiprocessor hardware in an uninterruptable manner. When any processor executes this instruction, both the "test" and "set" phases are performed together by the hardware, without any possibility of intervention by other processors. This *atomic* nature of the TestandSet instruction is crucial to its usefulness in implementing spinlocks. The *Lock(L)* operation is implemented as follows:

```
Lock(L):

  Repeat
    X := TestandSet(L);  (*Read old state and set to "locked"*)
  Until X = 0;      (* Terminate loop if L was "unlocked" *)
```

The above *TestandSet* instruction will read the current state of the spinlock *L* and store this in variable *X*. As the current value of *L* is read, it is also immediately set to the value 1, which represents the "locked" state. Thus, X remembers the old state of the spinlock. There are two important cases to consider in this implementation. First, assume that the spinlock is initially in the "unlocked" state. Then the TestandSet instruction will read a 0 into X, and also set the spinlock to the "locked" state. This allows the loop to end immediately. However, other processes will now find the spinlock in the "locked" state. When any other process executes this "Lock(L)" operation, it will also perform *TestandSet(L)*. This causes variables X to receive the value 1, which is the current value of the spinlock L. Thus, all subsequent processes entering a "Lock(L)" operation will continue to *busy-wait* inside the loop.

Eventually, the first process that already passed through its "Lock(L)" operation will execute an "Unlock(L)" operation. This will change the value of spinlock L to 0. If there are several processes busy-waiting inside the "Lock(L)" operation, the first one to execute its "TestandSet(L)" instruction will read a 0, but immediately set L back to 1 again. This process will now escape from its loop. However, all the other processes will now find that L is locked again, and will continue inside their loops. In this way, many processes will be suspended inside the "Lock(L)" operation, and released one at a time by each "Unlock(L)" operation.

5.2.2 Spinlocks and Structured Types

In Multi-Pascal, "SPINLOCK" is a built-in data type. In the declaration section of the main program or any procedure, any variable name may be declared as having type "SPINLOCK." Once a variable is declared in this way, it can be used in *LOCK* or *UNLOCK* operations in the program. Multi-Pascal restricts the use of *LOCK* and *UNLOCK* to spinlock variables. Attempting to apply these operations to variables of other types will result in a compiler error. In the ordinary usage of *LOCK* and *UNLOCK* for creating atomic operations, they are always used as a pair, surrounding a few statements of the program. However, the Multi-Pascal language does not require that they be used in this restricted pattern. The compiler will allow either of these two operations to appear anywhere in the program, provided that they are applied to valid spinlock variables.

The SPINLOCK data type may be combined with the structured types—arrays and records. Just as one can have an "Array of Integer" or "Array of Boolean," it is also possible to have an "Array of Spinlock." The indexing of such an array follows the same standard Pascal rules as the indexing of any array. For example, consider the following declarations:

```
VAR  G:  ARRAY [1..10] OF SPINLOCK;
     H:  ARRAY [1..10,1..10] OF SPINLOCK;
```

The following are all valid operations for these arrays:

```
Lock(G[3]);
Unlock(H[1,5]);

i := 2;
Lock(G[i]);
Unlock(G[i+5]);
```

Similarly, the SPINLOCK data type may also be used as a component of a Record type, as in the following declaration:

```
VAR  item:   RECORD
                data: INTEGER;
                L: SPINLOCK;
             END;
```

For this record declaration, the following are valid operations:

```
Lock(item.L);
Unlock(item.L);
```

Pointers can also be combined with spinlocks. In Pascal, a pointer can be defined to point to any of the other data types. This same rule applies in Multi-Pascal. It is possible to have a pointer to a spinlock type. The following is a valid Multi-Pascal declaration:

```
TYPE itempnt = ^itemtype;
     itemtype = RECORD
                   data: INTEGER;
                   L: SPINLOCK;
                   next: itempnt;
                END;
VAR head: itempnt;
```

By using the above declarations, it is possible to create a linked list, in which each list item has its own private spinlock. This issue is explored further in some of the exercises at the end of this chapter. Spinlocks may also be used as procedure or function parameters, and behave in the same way as other Pascal parameters. Using a spinlock as a *VAR* parameter will cause the parameter name to become an alias for the spinlock that is passed as an argument in the procedure call. Using a spinlock as a value parameter will cause it to get a copy of the state of the spinlock argument in the procedure call.

5.3 CONTENTION FOR SHARED DATA

To prevent parallel processes from interfering with each other during access to shared data, it is necessary to create atomic operations by using spinlocks. However, in some programs these atomic operations can increase the overall program execution time by forcing processes to wait for access to shared data. During an atomic operation by a given process *A*, all other processes are prevented from accessing that shared data. This may severely reduce the parallel activity in the program and thereby reduce the overall speedup of the program. Even a relatively short atomic operation can cause a program performance bottleneck, if that operation is performed very often by a large number of parallel processes. For example, consider an atomic operation that requires 10 times units. If there are 50 parallel processes each performing this atomic operation, then a total of 500 time units is required.

5.3.1 Histogram of a Visual Image

This situation of parallel processes slowing each other down when accessing shared data is sometimes called *contention*. To illustrate programming techniques for data sharing and how contention can arise, we consider the computation of a histogram of pixel intensity for a two-dimensional image. Computing the histogram is a very common technique used in image processing as a part of some larger overall process, such as identifying objects in the image. Image processing algorithms usually offer a great potential for parallel processing, since different parts of the image can be processed in parallel. Image processing is one of the major application areas for parallel computers.

For simplicity, the image will be represented as a two-dimensional array of integral intensity values, whose range is from 0 up to some known maximum intensity. Figure 5.3 shows a sequential program for computing the histogram of an array *image*. The histogram is built up in an array *hist*. The program begins by reading in the two-dimensional array of pixel intensities that range from 0 up to *max*. The histogram is created by using two nested loops that scan through the image. For each pixel, the intensity is used to increment the appropriate element of the histogram.

This histogram program can be parallelized by changing the outer sequential *FOR* loop into a *FORALL* statement. This will create one parallel process for each row of the image. This Parallel Histogram program is shown in Figure 5.4. Notice also that the variables *j* and *intensity* have been pulled into each process as a local variable declaration. This is necessary because all of the processes refer to these variables.

```
PROGRAM Histogram;
CONST n = 20;   (*dimension of the image*)
      max = 10; (*maximum pixel intensity*)
VAR image:  ARRAY [1..n, 1..n] OF INTEGER;
    hist:  ARRAY [0..max] OF INTEGER;
    i,j,intensity: INTEGER;
BEGIN
FOR i := 1 TO n DO   (*Input the image array*)
  BEGIN
    FOR j := 1 TO n DO
      Read(Image[i,j]);
    Readln;
  END;
FOR i := 0 TO max DO   (*Initialize histogram*)
   hist[i] := 0;
FOR i := 1 TO n DO
  FOR j := 1 TO n DO
    BEGIN
      intensity := image[i,j];
      hist[intensity] := hist[intensity] + 1;
    END;
END.
```

FIGURE 5.3   Sequential program for histogram.

```
PROGRAM ParallelHistogram;
CONST n = 20;    (*dimension of the image*)
      max = 10; (*maximum pixel intensity*)
VAR image:  ARRAY [1..n, 1..n] OF INTEGER;
    hist:   ARRAY [0..max] OF INTEGER;
    L:   ARRAY [0..max] OF SPINLOCK;
    i:  INTEGER;
BEGIN
  ...  (*Initialize the image array*)

FOR i := 0 TO max DO
   hist[i] := 0;
FORALL i := 1 TO n DO
   VAR j,intensity: INTEGER;
   BEGIN
     FOR j := 1 TO n DO
       BEGIN
         intensity := image[i,j];
         Lock(L[intensity]);
           hist[intensity] := hist[intensity] + 1;
         Unlock(L[intensity]);
       END;
   END;
END.
```

FIGURE 5.4 Parallel program for histogram.

Another problem is also created by parallelizing the program. Now the histogram array is being accessed and updated by all the processes in parallel. Recall from an earlier section that when two parallel processes both try to increment the value of a variable, an error can sometimes be produced. This problem is solved by making each update an *atomic* operation. One technique is to use a single spinlock *L* as follows:

```
BEGIN
  intensity := image[i,j];
  Lock(L);
    hist[intensity] := hist[intensity] + 1;
  Unlock(L);
END;
```

This method does make the update of *hist* an atomic operation and ensures correctness of the program. However, each process performs these updates quite frequently, resulting in a contention problem. To reduce the contention, an array of spinlocks can be used. Each element of the *hist* array will have its own spinlock. This allows each element of the *hist* array to be locked individually, instead of locking the entire array. Thus, as long as processes are updating different elements of the *hist* array, they can still continue to execute in parallel. Only when two processes happen to collide on the same array element will some contention result.

5.3.2 Effect of Contention on Performance

In Figure 5.4, *L* is declared as an array of spinlocks with the same dimension as the *hist* array. After each process examines a pixel, it will use the "intensity" to select the proper element of *hist* to update. Before performing the update, it will first lock this element with the instruction "Lock(L[intensity])." Two processes may find the same pixel intensity in different parts of the image, and then try to update the same histogram element in parallel, thus causing contention and forcing one process to wait for the other. In this program there are *n* parallel processes created, and there are *max* separate elements in the histogram array. The likelihood of contention arising in this program depends on the ratio *n/max*.

Each process consists of a *FOR* loop that accesses one element of the histogram array during each loop traversal. An important parameter that influences the contention is the fraction of time *f* during each loop iteration that a process spends inside the atomic operation. The *load factor*, defined as *fn/max*, gives the ratio of the demand for atomic operations to the available supply. As the load factor grows, the contention problem becomes worse. Using the Multi-Pascal system, the Histogram program was executed with 60 processes working on a 60 by 60 image array created with a random number generator. The load factor was varied by changing the value of *max*. The result is shown in Figure 5.5. The vertical axis is the execution time of the parallel portion of the program, ignoring the initialization and process creation time. The horizontal axis is the load factor. The number of processors and the size of the image array are held constant throughout the graph. Therefore, the increase in execution time is completely a result of contention for access to the *hist* array.

At load factor 1, the total demand for access to the histogram array by the 60 processes exactly equals the ability for that demand to be satisfied through the atomic operations. However, due to the random nature of processor access to the histogram array, it is likely that some contention will occur. In Figure 5.5, it is seen that contention at load factor 1 has increased the execution time by about 28 percent. At load factor 2, the demand

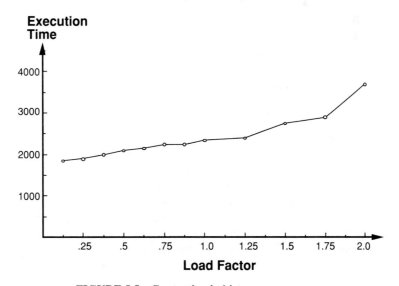

FIGURE 5.5   Contention in histogram program.

is twice as much as the supply; therefore, contention is expected to become a major problem. In the figure, it is seen that the execution time has basically doubled by the time load factor 2 is reached.

5.4 NUMERICAL INTEGRATION

To further illustrate the techniques for creating atomic operations with minimal contention, this section describes a parallel program for *numerical integration*. Numerical integration is a common operation performed in scientific and engineering computing. Many of the mathematical formulas used in this type of computing are in the form of differential equations or integral equations. Solving these equations sometimes requires the computation of a numerical integration.

An application of numerical integration is illustrated in Figure 5.6. The curved line shows the velocity of a vehicle as a function of time. To determine the total distance traveled by the vehicle from time a to b, the total area under the curve must be computed, as indicated in the figure. The computation of this area can be done with a numerical integration. For any function $f(t)$, a definite integral from a to b is represented with the following notation:

$$\int_a^b f(t)\, dt$$

If $f(t)$ is the velocity of a vehicle, then this definite integral gives the total distance traveled by the vehicle from time a to b. In another area of application, the function $f(t)$ might represent the current into a capacitor in an electronic circuit. In this case, the above integral will give the total change in voltage across the capacitor during the time interval from a to b.

This definite integral can be approximated numerically by sampling the function f at the two endpoints a and b, and n internal points, spaced w units apart. Using the standard trapezoid rule, the following formula results for the integral:

$$w[f(a)/2 + f(a + w) + f(a + 2w) + \cdots + f(a + nw) + f(b)/2]$$

Velocity

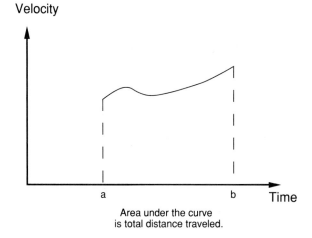

Area under the curve
is total distance traveled.

FIGURE 5.6 Application of numerical integration.

The above formula provides a general computational technique for approximating the area under any curve $f(t)$, and thus can be used as the basis of a computer program for numerical integration. With this computational method, the function f to be integrated is sampled at a series of points, and the values of the samples are added. The general structure of the sequential program is as follows:

Sequential Numerical Integration:

```
    sum := 0;
    t := a;
    FOR i := 1 TO n DO
      BEGIN
        t := t + w;              (*Move to next point*)
        sum := sum + f(t);    (*Add sample point to sum*)
      END;
    sum := sum + (f(a) + f(b)) / 2;
    answer := w * sum;
```

To create a Parallel Numerical Integration program, a portion of the curve to be integrated is assigned to each process. Our first impulse might be to have all the processes add their sample points into a single shared *sum* variable, using a spinlock to ensure the integrity of the addition operation. However, this centralization of the sum leads to a contention problem that may degrade performance. A better solution is to *decentralize* the sum into a number of local sum variables, which are then added into a global sum at the end. While running in parallel, the processes will compute and sum the sample points in their own portion, using a "localsum" variable. Then the local sums are added into a "globalsum" with an atomic operation. This technique is illustrated in Figure 5.7.

The complete program is shown in Figure 5.8. The central component of the program is the Procedure Integrate that forms the body of each process. After computing its own starting position along the curve, the procedure has a *FOR* loop to sum the sample points of the function using a "localsum" variable. The constant *numpoints* tells the number of sample points in the region assigned to each process. Since there are *numproc* processes, the total number of sample points is *numproc*numpoints*. At the end of Procedure Integrate, the *localsum* is added to the *globalsum* by using an atomic operation. As this program appears in the figure, a total of 40 physical processors are required. Running the program with the Multi-Pascal interactive system results in an overall speedup of 25. The potential for contention has been minimized in this program by using the "localsum" variable for each process. Thus, the program achieves good performance.

This Parallel Numerical Integration program helps to illustrate the general techniques described in this chapter for creating atomic operations, while at the same time avoiding any performance degradation from contention. Since the processes in this program do use an atomic operation to update the global sum, there is some possibility for contention. However, since each process performs only one such update, there is no serious performance degradation. The basic principle used here and in the Histogram program presented earlier is to *decentralize* the atomic operation to reduce contention problems. In the case of the Histogram, the decentralization is achieved by using separate lock for each element of the histogram array. In the Numerical Integration, the shared sum variable is decentralized into a number of local sums.

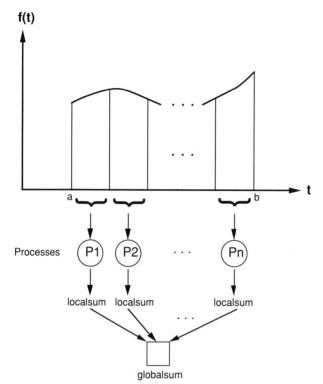

FIGURE 5.7 Parallel form of numerical integration.

5.5 COMPARING SPINLOCKS AND CHANNELS

The last two chapters have introduced two important mechanisms for coordinating the orderly interaction of parallel processes. Channels allow producer processes to communicate a series of data items to consumer processes. Spinlocks allow the creation of atomic operations, so that processes do not interfere when accessing shared data items. Both channels and spinlocks have their own area of applicability, and both are useful in writing parallel programs. However, a closer analysis of their behavior shows that actually they are not both completely necessary—either one can be used to simulate the other. This section explores the similarity and differences between channels and spinlocks, and presents general criteria for determining when to use each.

5.5.1 Equivalent Power

A spinlock has the ability to create atomic operations because it can force any process to wait by being in the "locked" state. This is the key feature in implementing atomic operations: forcing many processes to wait at the "Lock" operation, and then allowing exactly one of them to proceed after an "Unlock" operation is performed. Channels also have this ability to make a process wait: when a channel is empty, the Reader process will be forced to wait until something is written into the channel. This mechanism can be used to create atomic operations.

```
PROGRAM NumericalIntegration;
CONST numproc = 40;  (*number of processes*)
     numpoints = 30; (*number of points per process*)
VAR a,b,w,globalsum,answer: REAL;
    i: INTEGER;
    L: spinlock;


FUNCTION f(t: REAL): REAL; (*Function to be integrated*)
BEGIN
   ...  (*Compute value of f(t)*)

END;


PROCEDURE Integrate(myindex: INTEGER);
VAR localsum,t: REAL; j: INTEGER;
BEGIN
  t := a + myindex * (b - a)/numproc; (*My starting position*)
  FOR j := 1 TO numpoints DO
    BEGIN
      localsum := localsum + f(t); (*Add next sample point*)
      t := t + w;
    END;
  localsum := w * localsum;
  Lock(L);
    globalsum := globalsum + localsum; (*atomic update*)
  Unlock(L);
END;


BEGIN
   ... (*Initialize values of end points "a" and "b"*)

w := (b - a) / (numproc * numpoints); (*Distance between points*)

FORALL i := 0 TO numproc-1 DO  (*Create processes*)
    Integrate(i);

answer := globalsum + w/2 * (f(b) - f(a)); (*Add end points*)
END.
```

FIGURE 5.8   Parallel numerical integration.

In all the channel examples of the previous chapter, there was always one Reader process and one Writer process for a given channel. However, Multi-Pascal does not restrict the usage of channels in this way. Many different processes may write to the same channel, and many processes may read from the channel. Also, any process may be both a writer and reader of the same channel. The Lock and Unlock operations on spinlocks can be simulated with a channel by initializing the channel with one single data item. To "Lock" the channel, a process simply reads that data item out of the channel. This means that any other processes attempting to "Lock" by also reading the channel will find that the channel is empty and be forced to wait. When the first process finishes its atomic operation, it performs an "Unlock" by writing the data item back into the channel. This allows exactly one of the waiting processes to read the data item and continue into the atomic operation. In this way, the processes can be forced to execute the atomic operation one at a time. Further details of this implementation are considered in the exercises at the end of this chapter.

In the same way that channels can be used to simulate spinlocks, the reverse is also true. Spinlocks can be used to create process communication queues that behave like channels. A channel is simply a parallel-access FIFO queue: writing to the channel adds an item to the tail of the queue, and reading the channel removes an item from the head of the queue. By using spinlocks to ensure that modifications are atomic, it is possible to implement a parallel-access queue that behaves like a channel. Further details of the implementation will be considered in the exercises at the end of this chapter.

Even though it is possible to simulate channels in this way, it is of course much easier to just use channels directly when they are needed in the program. The simulation is much more cumbersome to use from a programming point of view, and is also not as efficient as the internal implementation of channels in the language. Channel variables are included in the Multi-Pascal language for a reason: process communication is quite a common activity in parallel programs. Whenever processes need to send and receive data items from each other, channel variables are the best language feature to implement this communication. The programming of such communication is made much simpler by the availability of channel variables as a built-in feature of Multi-Pascal.

On the other hand, spinlocks also have their place in particular contexts. The advantage of spinlocks is that their internal implementation is simpler and less time-consuming than channels. The reason is that channels perform a much more complex function, and therefore require many more operations in their internal language implementation. Earlier in this chapter, it was shown that spinlocks can easily be implemented with one memory cell and a "TestandSet" machine language instruction. The "Lock" operation is implemented with a simple loop containing two instructions, and the "Unlock" operation is one instruction. In the case of implementing channels, an internal queue of data values must be maintained and modified. This requires many more instructions. Reading or writing of a channel will require a much longer time than executing a "Lock" or "Unlock" operation.

In the Multi-Pascal interactive system that accompanies this text, a Lock or Unlock operation consumes two time units, and a channel read or write operation consumes five time units. Of these five time units, a process is given *exclusive* access to the channel for three of the time units. Any internal channel implementation must maintain a queue of data values. Modification of this queue must be an atomic operation. Therefore, each reader or writer process must be given a short time period, during which it has exclusive access to a channel. Actually, through a more sophisticated implementation, it is possible to allow a read and a write operation to occur simultaneously. This is because these operations modify two different ends of the internal queue. For this reason, the Multi-Pascal interactive system does allow a read and a write to occur in parallel to the same channel. However, a read operation will exclude other readers, and a write operation will exclude other writers. This "exclusion" feature has been put into the Multi-Pascal interactive system to make it behave in a more realistic manner, more like an implementation on a real multiprocessor.

5.5.2 Busy-Waiting vs. Blocking

One more important difference between channels and spinlocks is the method used to make processes wait. They both have the ability to suspend process execution. When a process executes a Lock operation on a spinlock that is already in the "locked" state, then the process is forced to wait through a technique called *busy-waiting*. The internal implementation of the "Lock" operation will keep the process spinning in a tight loop, continually examining the spinlock, until it is unlocked by another process. This busy-waiting can be implemented easily on multiprocessors, and is the usual technique used in spinlocks.

Channels also will make a process wait when it attempts to read an empty channel. When any process executes a read operation to an empty channel, the process execution is suspended until some other process writes an item into the channel. In the internal implementation of channels, this is done by putting the Reader process into the *BLOCKED* state, so that it is no longer executed by the physical processor. The execution of that process by the physical processor completely ceases, leaving the processor free to do something else, such as perhaps executing a different process for some time. When a Writer process finally puts an item in the channel, this will cause the "Blocked" Reader process to go into the *READY* state. This change of state of the Reader process is a signal to the physical processor that it can now begin to execute it again.

This mechanism of process-blocking has both advantages and disadvantages compared to busy-waiting. The advantage of busy-waiting is simplicity of implementation, which results in less execution overhead. The disadvantage of busy-waiting is that it ties up the physical processor in doing useless work, just continuing to spin in a tight loop for possibly long periods of time. The advantage of process-blocking is that it releases the physical processor to do something else. However, this is at the cost of a more complex implementation that creates additional overhead for the program. Changing the state of a process to *BLOCKED* and then to *READY*, and switching the physical processor require some extra execution time in the implementation.

To clearly differentiate between busy-waiting and process-blocking in the Multi-Pascal interactive system, the state of each process is indicated as one of the following: RUNNING, SPINNING, BLOCKED, READY. *RUNNING* means that the process is currently being executed by its physical processor. *SPINNING* indicates that the process is suspended inside a "Lock" operation. *BLOCKED* indicates that the process is waiting on an empty channel, or in the case of a parent process, waiting for its children to terminate. *READY* indicates that the process is fully prepared to be executed, but is currently not being executed by its physical processor.

5.5.3 Semaphores

Research on parallel programming over the past two decades has discovered a number of useful primitives for coordinating the activity of parallel processes and guaranteeing atomic access to shared data structures. One of the oldest and most well-known such primitive is the *semaphore*, originally proposed by Dijkstra [1968a]. A *semaphore* is an integer-valued variable that is restricted to nonnegative integers. There are two valid operations on a semaphore, called *signal* and *wait*, defined as follows:

```
For a semaphore S,

Wait(S):   If S > 0 then S := S - 1
           else suspend execution and wait for Signal operation on S.

Signal(S): If a process is waiting on S, then release the process
           else S := S + 1;
```

Both the *Wait* and *Signal* operations themselves are guaranteed to be atomic by the underlying language implementation. A semaphore can be used to guarantee atomic access to a shared data structure by preceding access to the shared data with a *Wait*(S) operation, and then performing a *Signal*(S) operation after the access is finished. Initializing the value of S to one guarantees that only one process at a time gains access to the shared data. The use of semaphores has become especially popular in the field of operating system design.

Semaphores can easily be simulated by Multi-Pascal channel variables. Simply replace the semaphore by a channel, use a write-channel operation for *Signal*, and use a read-channel operation for *Wait*:

```
TYPE Semaphore = CHANNEL OF INTEGER;
VAR  S: Semaphore;

  ...

  PROCEDURE Wait(VAR S: Semaphore);
  VAR dummy: INTEGER;
  BEGIN
    dummy := S;  (*Read from the channel*)
  END;

  PROCEDURE Signal(VAR S: Semaphore);
  BEGIN
    S := 1;  (*Write to the channel*)
  END;
```

In the channel simulation of the semaphore, the *value* of the semaphore is simply represented by the number of items currently stored in the channel. Each *Wait* operation removes an item from the channel, thus reducing the semaphore value. Each *Signal* operation adds a new item to the channel, thus increasing the semaphore value. If a *Wait* operation is performed on an empty channel (semaphore value 0), then the process execution is suspended at the statement *dummy* := S until some other process executes a *Signal* and puts an item into the channel.

5.6 SUMMARY

This chapter deals with mechanisms for data sharing using spinlocks. The main requirement for modifying shared data is to make sure that the modification is completed before any other process can interfere. The required *exclusion* of other processes is accomplished by locking a spinlock, thus forcing other processes to wait when attempting to lock the same spinlock. In this context, an *atomic operation* is defined as a tranformation of data that cannot be interrupted by other parallel processes; the transformation appears like an "atom," that is, unbreakable. Several examples are given of the application of atomic operations, including incrementing a shared counter and updating a global sum.

The mutual exclusion of parallel processes resulting from atomic operations creates a sequential bottleneck in the program execution. In some programs with heavy usage of shared data objects, this may lead to contention problems and resultant degraded performance. The contention problem is not just a property of spinlocks; it will result with any language primitive designed to guarantee atomic operations. There are many specific types of solutions to the contention problem that are applicable in different programs. However, the one general rule is to *decentralize* the data and its access control mechanism. This decentralization allows multiple parallel processes to access different parts of the shared data in parallel, thus reducing contention. One example is dividing a shared counter variable into many separate counters that are combined later. Another example is reducing the granularity of the mutual exclusion region in a shared linked list: exclusion is performed separately on each list element rather than on the list as a whole.

To further illustrate atomic operations and contention, a Parallel Histogram program is presented. In this program, parallel processes examine different portions of a visual image, while updating a shared histogram array. Each array element is protected with its own spinlock, selected from an array of spinlocks. If the number of processes grows too large in comparison to the number of spinlocks, then contention will result. A general technique is presented in this context for analyzing programs for potential contention problems. The most important parameter in this analysis is the proportion of its time that each process spends inside an atomic operation. If the total access requirements of all parallel processes begin to approach the throughput capacity of the atomic operation, then contention must be the result.

The final example of the chapter is Numerical Integration—computing the area under a curve between two boundary points. This numerical computing technique requires that the value of the function be sampled at regular intervals, and the sample values be added together. In the parallel program, each process is assigned a portion of the curve for sampling and adding. At the very end, each process updates a global sum variable to compute the final answer. By allowing each process to first compute its own local sum, the potential for contention is eliminated from this program.

Chapters 4 and 5 together have presented a complete discussion of the two important features of Multi-Pascal for coordinating process interaction: channels and spinlocks. Channels are used for process communication, and spinlocks for atomic operations on shared data. Subsequent chapters give further examples of the use of these language features. For reasons that will be discussed later, spinlocks are allowed only in multi-processors. When Multi-Pascal is implemented on a multicomputer, only channels are allowed, not spinlocks.

REFERENCES

The important parallel programming issue of mutual exclusion and its solution using semaphores was formally introduced by Dijkstra [1968a, 1968b]. The term "atomic operation" is popular in the literature on concurrency in data base systems [Liskov and Scheifler, 1982].

A discussion of computing the histogram of a visual image is found in Ballard and Brown [1987]. A numerical integration program for the Encore multiprocessor is found in Brawer [1989]. Bitton, et al. [1984] contains a discussion of parallel bucket sorting.

PROGRAMMING PROJECTS

1. SADDLE POINT OF A MATRIX

A *saddle point* of a two-dimensional array is defined as an element that is the smallest in its column and the largest in its row. In this project you will write a program to input a two-dimensional array, find the saddle point, and write out its location in the array. If the array has no saddle point, then this message should be written by the program.

For large arrays, there is clearly a good potential for parallelism in this program. For a given array size, try to maximize the speedup in your program. Run and test the program, using the Multi-Pascal interactive system.

2. BUCKET SORT

The principle behind a Bucket Sort is best illustrated by an example. Suppose a list of names is to be sorted. One bucket is set up for each letter of the alphabet. The first letter of each name in the list is then used to distribute all the names into the buckets. The "A" bucket contains all the names that begin with "A." The "B" bucket contains all the names that begin with "B," and so on, up to the "Z" bucket. After the distribution step, then each bucket is internally sorted. In the final step, the names from the buckets are appended together to form the sorted list. The "A" bucket comes first, followed by the "B" bucket, then the "C" bucket, and so on.

There is clearly a good opportunity for parallelism in the Bucket Sort. The distribution step can be parallelized by assigning processes to different portions of the original list. After the distribution step, the sorting of the individual buckets can be done in parallel. Parallelism can also be applied to the final appending phase by having a different process copy each bucket into the final sorted list.

The performance of both the sequential and parallel versions of the Bucket Sort will depend on the evenness of the distribution phase. If there are a large number of buckets and each bucket gets approximately an equal number of items, then a large speedup can be achieved. However, if most of the items go into a few of the buckets, then the sorting phase will have a highly imbalanced processor load, thereby limiting the speedup.

Your job is to write and test a Multi-Pascal program to perform a Parallel Bucket Sort. For simplicity, use an array of integer values for sorting. Assume that your program knows in advance the range of numerical values in the array. This total range is just divided by the number of buckets to get the size of the range for each bucket. Then the proper bucket for each value can be determined by a simple division operation.

One important issue in your program is the use of each bucket by many processes in parallel during the distribution phase. You will have to deal with the exclusion problem and the contention problem. The other interesting issue is the technique for achieving parallelism during the final appending phase of the algorithm. The parallelism requires that each process know in advance where to put its values into the final sorted array. To achieve this knowledge in each process, the processes must perform a brief communication step prior to the append phase. During this step, each process receives the information it needs from the other processes to determine where to write its values into the final array. The starting point in the final array for each process is simply the sum of the bucket sizes of all its predecessor processes.

EXERCISES

1. Consider the following program, which attempts to use a parallel technique for computing a power of two:

```
PROGRAM Power2;
VAR value, power: INTEGER;

BEGIN
  Write('Power of Two: ');  (*Assume power is greater than 0*)
  Readln(power);
  value := 1;
  FORALL i := 1 TO power DO
    value := 2 * value;
  Writeln('Answer is ',value);
END.
```

Enter and run this program on the Multi-Pascal simulator. (For this exercise, the only concern is correctness of the answers. The issue of speedup is considered in another exercise.)
   (a) Why are the answers produced by the program incorrect?
   (b) Use the "Variation" option in the Multi-Pascal system to vary the processor speed. Why does this variation change the answer produced by this program?
   (c) Add "Lock" and "Unlock" operations to make the program run correctly. Test your modification, using the Multi-Pascal simulator.

2. Before doing this exercise, first do exercise 1(c).
   (a) Explain why the actual speedup of this program is so low even though there are a large number of parallel processes created.
   (b) In an attempt to increase the speedup, use the *GROUPING* option in the *FORALL* statement and run the program on the Multi-Pascal simulator. Explain why the speedup is still very low.

3. In this chapter, the following implementation method for the "Lock" operation is given:

```
Lock(L):

  Repeat
    X := TestandSet(L);  (*Read old state and set to "locked"*)
  Until X = 0;     (* Terminate loop if L was "unlocked" *)
```

For this implementation to work correctly, the "TestandSet" must be a single machine language instruction that is indivisible—when executed by any physical processor, it cannot be interrupted in the middle by another processor.

Describe in detail how an error may result if "TestandSet" is not indivisible. Describe a specific scenario of how an error may result in this case.

4. In the *Lock*(*L*) implementation in Section 5.2.1, a busy-waiting technique is used to repeatedly examine the contents of a memory cell. When there are many processes busy-waiting in this way on the same spinlock, a memory contention problem may result in the multiprocessor memory access hardware, according to the principles described in Chapter 3. However, if the multiprocessor system has a cache memory for each processor, then this memory contention can be alleviated by adding the following instruction inside the repeat loop of *Lock*(*L*): WHILE L <> 0 DO;

Explain how this modification to *Lock*(*L*) alleviates the contention.

5. In some programs, a process may require access to several locked data objects at the same time. The process may be performing an update that involves several data objects, which each have their own spinlock for protection. In this case, the process must perform a "Lock" operation on each one, perform the modification, and then "Unlock" each spinlock. If several processes are performing multiple "Lock" operations in this way, an interesting problem may occur in the program called *deadlock*. To illustrate this problem, consider the following scenario with two processes and two spinlocks:

```
     Process 1                Process 2

        . . .                    . . .

     Lock(A);                 Lock(B);
     Lock(B);                 Lock(A);
        . . .                    . . .

     Unlock(B);               Unlock(A);
     Unlock(A);               Unlock(B);
```

(a) Describe an execution scenario for the above processes which results in a *deadlock*—a situation in which both processes are suspended forever.

(b) Indicate a minor modification to the two processes that will still allow them to "Lock" both spinlocks and perform their atomic operation, but will never result in a deadlock.

(c) This same problem may result with many processes and many spinlocks. It can be completely eliminated through a simple technique of having the programmer give some arbitrary numbering scheme to all the spinlocks. Then each process must be coded to correspond to the following rule: whenever multiple spinlocks are to be locked at the same time, the "Lock" operations must be performed on the spinlocks in increasing numerical order. Show that this technique solves this deadlock problem.

6. Write a Multi-Pascal procedure that inserts a new item into an ordered, linked list. Assume that this procedure may be called by many processes in parallel to modify a single shared list. To reduce the possibility of contention, use a separate spinlock for each list item, rather than a single spinlock for the whole list.

7. Write a Multi-Pascal program to find the minimum element in an array of integers. Assume that the array is large enough to efficiently employ parallel processes in the program. Write the parallel program to minimize the total parallel execution time. Be sure to carefully consider the two important performance issues—process granularity and contention for shared data. Run and test your program, using the Multi-Pascal interactive system.

8. A stack is created from the following three procedures:

Push(stack,x)   puts item x on top of stack
Pop(stack,y)   removes top item from stack and returns it in y
Clear(stack)   initializes stack to empty

Write the above three procedures in Multi-Pascal. Assume that many parallel processes may be using a given stack at the same time. Test your procedures, using the Multi-Pascal interactive system. Use test cases with large numbers of parallel processes accessing the stack.

9. Another method for performing numerical integration is *Simpson's Rule*. To integrate a function f between two points a and b, sample the function at n internal points, spaced at distance w. The formula for the numerical integral is as follows:

$$(w/3)[\,f(a) + 2f(a + w) + 4f(a + 2w) + 2f(a + 3w) + 4f(a + 4w)$$
$$+ \cdots + 2f(a + (n - 1)w) + 4f(a + nw) + f(b)]$$

In this formula, the n must be odd. Modify the Numerical Integration program of Figure 5.8 to use Simpson's Rule.

10. In the Numerical Integration program of Figure 5.8, it appears that there should be some contention when the processes all update the "globalsum" variable. However, when this program is run on the Multi-Pascal interactive system, there is actually no contention at all during the updating.

   The reason for this is the method used by the Multi-Pascal system to create the processes. The processes are created one at a time by the parent process. There is a certain "creation time" consumed by the parent as it creates each process. Explain how this method of creating the processes results in lack of contention during the updating of the "globalsum" variable.

11. At the beginning of this chapter, a program is given for searching an array, based on the use of a spinlock. Rewrite the program without any spinlock, instead using a channel as the mechanism for creating the atomic operation.

12. Write two procedures *Readchan* and *Writechan* that simulate a Multi-Pascal *CHANNEL OF INTEGER* by using a linked list with Head and Tail pointers. A spinlock should be used to provide mutual exclusion where necessary.

6

Synchronous Parallelism

The main practical application of parallel computing is for large-scale numerical problems arising in science and engineering. These problems typically involve large multidimensional arrays, which present a good opportunity for data parallelism because different elements of the arrays can be processed in parallel. Numerical computing techniques on these arrays are usually iterative, with each iteration leading to another step of progress toward the final solution. This is especially true of numerical solution of large systems of equations. Generally, each iteration uses the data produced from the previous iteration, and the program gradually converges to a solution with the desired accuracy.

In such iterative numerical algorithms, there is an opportunity for parallelism within each iteration. Many parallel processes can be created to work on different parts of the array. However, after each iteration, the processes must be synchronized because the values produced by one process are used by other processes on the next iteration. This style of parallel programming is called *synchronous parallelism*.

In synchronous parallelism, the overall structure of the program often consists of a *FORALL* loop that creates a large number of parallel processes to operate on different portions of the data array. The processes are iterative and synchronize with each other at the end of each iteration. The purpose of this synchronization is to ensure that all processes finish the current iteration before any process can begin the next iteration. Thus, all the new data values produced during each iteration are available to all processes during the next iteration. This chapter presents a variety of different process synchronization techniques that can be used in such programs.

Process synchronization may introduce a performance bottleneck into the program. By its very nature, synchronization is opposed to parallelism because the processes must be brought together under some kind of centralized control that makes sure they are all there. This introduces the possibility of contention and delays in process execution. As the various synchronization techniques are presented in this chapter, their performance will be analyzed and compared. Several of the techniques introduce a linear delay proportional to the number of processes. A binary tree technique produces a delay that is proportional to the logarithm of the number of processes. For some types of algorithms, it is also possible to use a local synchronization technique, in which each process synchronizes with only a few of its immediate neighbors. This technique requires a constant time that does not grow with the number of processes.

This chapter also describes an important subclass of synchronously parallel algorithms: *Compute, Aggregate,* and *Broadcast* (CAB). In CAB programs, the process synchronization is also used to aggregate local data values from the processes into global data that is broadcast back to all the processes. The ordinary synchronization techniques are easily adapted to perform this aggregation and broadcasting. The CAB technique is especially useful for iterative numerical algorithms that must continue until some global convergence criterion is met. The aggregation phase is used to collect information from all the processes to determine if the global criterion has been met. Then the broadcast phase will send information back to each process, telling it whether to terminate or perform additional iterations.

An important numerical application program will be used to illustrate these techniques for synchronous parallelism: a parallel version of a standard numerical algorithm called *Jacobi Relaxation* for solving a differential equation. The performance of the various synchronization techniques will be compared by using this application.

6.1 SOLVING A DIFFERENTIAL EQUATION

Many of the most widely used numerical computing techniques use large multidimensional arrays as the primary data structure. By operating on many elements of these arrays in parallel, it is usually possible to create highly parallel versions of these popular numerical algorithms. One such numerical computing algorithm is the Jacobi Relaxation algorithm for solving an important type of differential equation called Laplace's equation. As an example of the application of this algorithm, consider a two-dimensional conducting metal sheet with a voltage applied at the four boundaries. The voltage differs along the boundary, but is held constant at each particular position on the boundary. To determine the resultant pattern of voltages at all the internal points of the sheet, one must solve Laplace's equation for all the internal points.

Let $v(x, y)$ represent the desired function that tells the voltage at each point (x, y) on the metal sheet. Then Laplace's equation has the following form:

$$\frac{\partial^2 v}{\partial x^2} + \frac{\partial^2 v}{\partial y^2} = 0$$

Laplace's equation is a *linear partial differential equation*, an important class of equations that arise quite frequently. This equation can be solved numerically by considering a two-dimensional grid of points on the surface of the metal sheet. This is illustrated in Figure 6.1. To get a more accurate solution to the equation, the number of points in the grid can be increased, but this also increases the amount of computation required. By applying Laplace's equation to this grid of points, the equation is converted from a differential

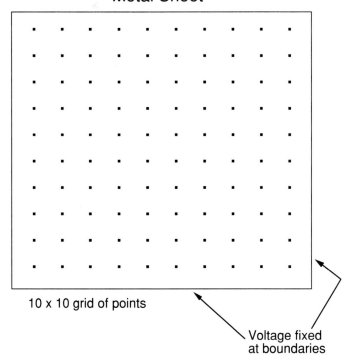

FIGURE 6.1 **Grid of points for Laplace's equation.**

equation to a *difference equation*, which can be solved numerically on a computer. Let the voltage at a particular grid point (i, j) be denoted $V(i, j)$. Applying Laplace's equation to this grid results in the following *difference equation*, which relates the voltage at neighboring points in the grid:

$$V(i, j) = \frac{V(i - 1, j) + V(i + 1, j) + V(i, j - 1) + V(i, j + 1)}{4}$$

This difference equation provides a very simple relationship between the voltages at neighboring points: the voltage at each point is simply the average of the voltage at its four neighboring points. This relationship is illustrated in Figure 6.2. The difference equation provides a simple computational technique for solving the equation. The first step is to select some initial values for the voltage at each point on the grid. Since the voltage at all the boundary points is held constant, then these voltages are already known. The initial value for all the internal points can be arbitrarily set to zero initially. Then the following iteration is repeated many times on these values: recompute the value at each point in the grid from the average of its four neighboring points. This computational method is called *Jacobi Relaxation*. Figure 6.2 illustrates the general idea behind this method.

It seems clear enough intuitively that if we want all the values at the grid points to equal the average of their neighbors, then iteratively replacing each value by the average of

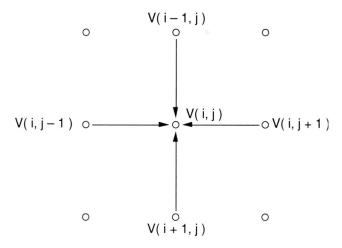

V(i – 1, j)

V(i, j – 1)   V(i, j)   V(i, j + 1)

V(i + 1, j)

FIGURE 6.2   Computing voltage at each point.

its neighbors will eventually achieve this goal. Since the boundary points are all held at their proper fixed value, they will act as a fixed reference to help determine the values of all the internal points, which will change on each iteration. This iterative technique has been analyzed mathematically and found to gradually converge to a more and more accurate solution with each successive iteration. For further details on this and other iterative methods for solving differential equations, the reader is referred to Bertsekas and Tsitsiklis [1989] and Hageman and Young [1981].

The Jacobi Relaxation algorithm for solving Laplace's equation begins with a two-dimensional array of real numbers representing the voltage at the grid points on the metal sheet. To get a more accurate solution, the number of points in the array is increased, which also increases the amount of computation required. After initializing this two-dimensional array, the Jacobi technique is extremely simple: recompute the value at each point in the array, using the average of the four immediate neighboring points. This recomputation is repeated for many iterations until the solution converges to some desired accuracy.

It is obvious that this algorithm is highly amenable to parallelism because the recomputation at each point is completely independent and can be performed in parallel with all other points. The only difficulty is that each iteration depends on the values computed by the previous iteration, so the iterations cannot be performed in parallel. A sequential Jacobi Relaxation algorithm is given in Figure 6.3. The program is quite straightforward. The array *A* holds the initial values for all points. The main iterative loop performs *numiter* iterations. During each iteration, a new value is computed for each point as the average of four immediate neighbors—above, below, left, and right. As each new value is computed, it is stored in temporary array *B* to avoid interfering with the rest of the calculations. After all new values have been computed, the temporary array *B* is written back to *A* before the next iteration. It is an important property of Jacobi Relaxation that during each iteration, all the new values are computed by using current values. New values replace old values only after all new values are computed.

```
PROGRAM Jacobi;
CONST n = 32;           (*Size of the array*)
      numiter = ... ; (*Number of iterations*)
VAR A,B: ARRAY [0..n+1,0..n+1] OF REAL;
    i,j,k: INTEGER;

BEGIN
FOR i := 0 TO n+1 DO   (*Initialize array values*)
  BEGIN
    FOR j := 0 TO n+1 DO
      Read(A[i,j]);
    Readln;
  END;
B := A;
FOR k := 1 TO numiter DO
  BEGIN
    FOR i := 1 TO n DO
      FOR j := 1 TO n DO (*Compute average of four neighbors*)
        B[i,j] := (A[i-1,j] + A[i+1,j] + A[i,j-1] + A[i,j+1]) / 4;
    A := B;
  END;
END.
```

FIGURE 6.3   Sequential Jacobi Relaxation program.

One interesting aspect of this program is the technique used to hold the boundary points constant. The array A has index values ranging from 0 to $n + 1$, but the program iterates only over values 1 to n. This leaves all four boundaries of the array unchanged. Since the temporary array B is copied back to array A after each iteration, the boundary values must be initialized in array B. This is done by copying the whole array A into array B during program initialization.

6.2 PARALLEL JACOBI RELAXATION

The most obvious technique for parallelizing the Jacobi Relaxation is to change the inner *FOR* loops to *FORALL* loops. This will create parallelism during each iteration. The outer *FOR* loop cannot be changed into *FORALL* because the iterations must be sequential. A second technique for parallelizing this program is to pull the outer iterative loop inside the parallel processes. Each process will continue to iterate internally, but will synchronize with all other processes at the end of each iteration. These two techniques will now be described in detail.

6.2.1 Synchronization by Process Termination

The basic requirement for a parallel version of the Jacobi Relaxation is that each iteration be completed before the next one begins. This property is part of the definition of this algorithm, and must be preserved for the algorithm to work correctly and converge to a proper solution. Despite this restriction, there is still a good opportunity for parallelism within each iteration. The new value at each point is computed from the values of the four neighbors. This computation for each point can be performed in parallel with all other points. By changing the two inner *FOR* loops to *FORALL*, this parallelization within each iteration is accomplished. All of the parallel processes will terminate after computing the new value for their assigned point. Then at the beginning of the next iteration, a new set of processes will be created.

The computing activity of each process in this case is illustrated in Figure 6.2; each process just computes a single average. The processes will all be relatively short in duration, thus possibly producing a granularity problem. To avoid this and simplify the parallel program, we will create a process to handle each row of points. This is done by parallelizing the *i* loop only. The parallel program is shown in Figure 6.4. The inner index *j* must be changed into a local variable within each process. Notice also that the copy operation of moving the newly computed values from *B* back to *A* has also been parallelized. Although this is done with one single assignment statement in the sequential version, the underlying implementation of this array copy operation requires many sequential steps.

```
PROGRAM ParallelJacobi;
CONST n = 32;
      numiter = ...;
VAR A,B: ARRAY [0..n+1,0..n+1] OF REAL;
    i,j,k: INTEGER;

BEGIN
  ... (*Read in initial values for array A*)

B := A;
FOR k := 1 TO numiter DO
  BEGIN

    (*Phase I - Compute new values*)
    FORALL i := 1 TO n DO (*Create process for each row*)
      VAR j: INTEGER;
      BEGIN
        FOR j := 1 TO n DO
          B[i,j] := (A[i-1,j] + A[i+1,j] + A[i,j-1] + A[i,j+1]) / 4;
      END;

    (*Phase II - Copy new values back to A*)
    FORALL i := 1 TO n DO (*Copy new values from B back to A*)
      A[i] := B[i];

  END;
END.
```

FIGURE 6.4   Parallel Jacobi Relaxation.

The original sequential program of Figure 6.3 has an execution time of 45202 time units for each iteration. The parallel version requires 2100 time units per iteration: a speedup of 21.5 over the sequential version. Although the parallel version creates 32 processes to operate on the 32 rows, the speedup is only about 21 because of the process creation overhead. During each iteration, all of the 32 processes must be created in the first *FORALL*, then terminated, and recreated again in the second *FORALL*. The program incurs a large process creation overhead every time around the outer iterative loop. This accounts for the 33 percent loss in program speedup.

This Parallel Jacobi Relaxation program achieves process synchronization by allowing the processes to terminate and then recreating them again. There are actually two such synchronizations during each iteration: one after Phase I and another after Phase II. During Phase I, the first set of 32 processes is created by the first *FORALL* to operate on the 32 rows of the array *A*. The *FORALL* statement terminates only after all 32 processes terminate. Therefore, the structure of the *FORALL* statement itself is used to synchronize the processes. This synchronization is necessary before Phase II can begin, in which the newly computed values in array *B* are written back into array *A*. It is important that all the new values be computed before any copying takes place. This property is ensured by separating the two phases in two different *FORALL* statements.

Similarly, it is necessary for all the copying of *B* back to *A* to be completed before the array *A* is used again on the next iteration. The 32 processes doing the copying in Phase II are synchronized at the end of the second *FORALL* statement. Thus, within each iteration, there are two synchronization operations, produced through the technique of *process termination* and recreation. The execution time overhead of this technique is the product of the process creation time with the number of processes. For a program with n processes, this synchronization method has execution time $O(n)$.

6.2.2 Barrier Synchronization

The Multi-Pascal system uses a relatively small process creation overhead of 10 time units. However, most real parallel computers have an overhead that is considerable larger. For this reason, the approach of terminating and then recreating processes is unacceptable in many systems. To provide cheaper synchronization of processes, some systems include a *Barrier* operation in the parallel programming language. A *Barrier* is a point in the program where parallel processes wait for each other. The first processes to execute the *Barrier* statement will simply wait until all the other processes have arrived. After all the processes have reached the *Barrier* statement, then they are all released to continue parallel execution. The effect of a *Barrier* is illustrated in Figure 6.5. Time flows from top to bottom in the figure, with asterisks indicating time periods during which the process is executing.

This Barrier synchronization technique can be applied to the Parallel Jacobi Relaxation program. Instead of terminating and recreating the processes, only one set of processes is created initially. Recall from the previous version that the processes must be synchronized twice during each iteration: after the new values are computed from the old values, and again after the new values are written back over the old values. This can be accomplished by using two *Barrier* operations inside each process. The program is shown in Figure 6.6.

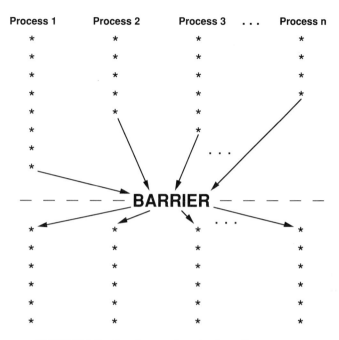

FIGURE 6.5 **Barrier synchronization of processes.**

The most notable feature of this new program is the fact that the *FORALL* statement is now on the outside. The 32 processes are created only once, with one assigned to each row. Then the iterations from 1 to *numiter* are done with a *FOR* loop inside each process. In this program the process creation overhead is only incurred once. The processes must still synchronize twice during each iteration, but now this is done with a *Barrier* instead of through process termination and recreation.

After each process computes the new values for its assigned row, then the *Barrier* is executed. This causes all the processes to wait for each other and synchronize before any is allowed to continue. After this synchronization, then all the new values have been computed. The next step is to copy the new values from array *B* back to array *A*. This is done with a single assignment in each process that copies a whole row. After the copying operation, the processes must again synchronize with a *Barrier* before beginning the next iteration, which uses array *A*.

The performance of this program will be highly dependent on the time required to execute the *Barrier* operation. By using the *Barrier* synchronization, the process creation time has been eliminated, but a new overhead has been introduced: executing the *Barrier* operation. In the subsequent sections, we examine two implementation techniques for Barriers, and analyze their efficiency. A linear time technique is described, whose execution time is proportional to the number of processes. Then a logarithmic time method is presented.

```
PROGRAM Jacobi_Barrier;
CONST n = 32;
      numiter = ... ;
VAR a,b: ARRAY [0..n+1,0..n+1] OF REAL;
    i,j: INTEGER;

BEGIN
  ...  (*Read in initial values for array A*)

B := A;
FORALL i := 1 TO n DO (*create one process for each row*)
  VAR j,k: INTEGER;
  BEGIN
    FOR k := 1 TO numiter DO
        BEGIN
          FOR j := 1 TO n DO (*Compute average of four neighbors*)
            B[i,j] := (A[i-1,j] + A[i+1,j] + A[i,j-1] + A[i,j+1]) / 4;
          Barrier;
          A[i] := B[i];
          Barrier;
        END;
  END;
END.
```

FIGURE 6.6   Jacobi Relaxation with Barrier synchronization.

6.3 LINEAR BARRIER IMPLEMENTATION

The Multi-Pascal programming language does not have an explicit Barrier statement. However, barriers are easily implemented by using spinlocks or channels. One implementation using spinlocks and one implementation using channels are described in the next several sections. The purpose of this discussion is to gain an understanding of the overall methodologies used to implement barriers and their complexity. The techniques described are quite general and could be implemented with any of the standard synchronization primitives available in other parallel languages, such as semaphores or monitors. Some of the exercises in this chapter will ask the student to express these Barrier implementations using semaphores, instead of spinlocks and channels.

All of the Barrier implementations will be expressed as Multi-Pascal procedures. In the Parallel Jacobi Relaxation program of Figure 6.6, the "Barrier" operation can simply be interpreted as a call to a procedure called "Barrier," which implements the operation by using standard Multi-Pascal features. One of the simplest implementation techniques is to use a *counting variable* to record the total number of processes that have arrived at the Barrier so far. When the count reaches the required number, then all the processes are released, and the count is reset to 0. As each arriving process executes the Barrier procedure, it tests and increments a global counting variable. If the count has not yet reached n, then the process goes into a suspended state within the Barrier procedure. As processes gradually arrive at the Barrier, they each become suspended and the count grows. Finally, the last process to arrive finds that the count has reached *n*, and then releases all of the suspended processes.

The Barrier procedure will have two distinct phases. During the *Arrival Phase*, processes are counted as they arrive at the Barrier. After all the processes have arrived, the Arrival Phase is terminated, and the *Departure Phase* begins. During the Departure Phase, the processes are released from the Barrier one at a time. Counting also occurs during the Departure Phase, so it will be known when all the processes have been released. To separate the activity of the phases, two different spinlocks are used: *Arrival* and *Departure*. Each spinlock is used to make the counting an atomic operation during their corresponding phases. The Multi-Pascal procedure for the Barrier is shown in Figure 6.7.

```
PROGRAM Jacobi_Barrier;
CONST n = 32;

VAR ...

    count: INTEGER;
    Arrival, Departure: SPINLOCK;

PROCEDURE Barrier;
BEGIN

  (*Arrival Phase - Count the processes as they arrive*)
  Lock(Arrival);
    count := count + 1;
  IF count < n
      THEN Unlock(Arrival)    (*continue Arrival Phase*)
      ELSE Unlock(Departure); (*terminate Arrival Phase*)

  (*Departure Phase - Count the processes as they leave*)
  Lock(Departure);
    count := count - 1;
  IF count > 0
      THEN Unlock(Departure) (*continue Departure Phase*)
      ELSE Unlock(Arrival); (*terminate Departure Phase*)

END;

BEGIN (*Main Program*)

count := 0; (*Initialize "count" and spinlocks*)
Unlock(Arrival);
Lock(Departure);
  ...

END.
```

FIGURE 6.7   Barrier implemented with spinlocks.

The most interesting feature of this Barrier procedure is the unusual use of "Unlock" at the end of each atomic operation. Notice in Figure 6.7 that both the Arrival and Departure phases begin with a "Lock" operation on their corresponding spinlock. During the Arrival Phase, the *count* variable in incremented as the processes arrive. During the Departure Phase, the *count* variable is decremented as the processes leave the Barrier. However, there must be some mechanism to ensure that the Arrival Phase is completed before the Departure Phase begins. This is accomplished by keeping the spinlock *Departure* in the "locked" state during the Arrival Phase. Any processes that reach the start of the Departure Phase will thereby get stuck at the *Lock(Departure)* statement, which begins the Departure Phase. When the last process finally exits the Arrival Phase, it executes *Unlock(Departure)*. This opens up the spinlock *Departure*, and allows the execution of the Departure Phase to begin.

For this double-locking mechanism to work correctly, spinlock *Arrival* must be initially "unlocked" and *Departure* must be initially "locked." At the end of the Barrier procedure, the last process to leave the Departure Phase must make sure that the spinlocks are reset properly for the next Barrier. That is why the last process to exit the Departure Phase, which identifies itself through a *count* value 0, will execute *Unlock(Arrival)*. The reader can verify from the code in Figure 6.7 that at the start of the Arrival Phase, *Arrival* = unlocked and *Departure* = locked, whereas at the start of the Departure Phase, *Arrival* = locked and *Departure* = unlocked. This double-locking is absolutely necessary in this procedure to separate the two Phases and ensure correct behavior. The exercises for this chapter explore this issue more thoroughly.

The performance of this Barrier implementation is limited by the contention for the *count* variable during the atomic increment and atomic decrement operations. Using the Multi-Pascal interactive system, it is determined that each atomic operation requires about 10 time units. Thus, the total time for all n processes to increment the *count* during the Arrival Phase is $10n$. Similarly, the total time for the Departure Phase is also $10n$. Therefore, the overall time for the Barrier synchronization of the n processes is $20n$. The multiplier may vary on different parallel computers, but this *counting variable* method always has execution time $O(n)$.

6.4 BINARY TREE IMPLEMENTATION OF BARRIERS

There have been two synchronization techniques presented so far, both with linear time complexity: the process termination method and the barrier implementation based on a counter variable. In both methods, the linear behavior results from the fact that a single centralized entity is used to coordinate the synchronization. This centralized entity must handle each of the n incoming processes individually, even if only for a brief time period. Thus, the total time required for synchronization is always $O(n)$.

The performance bottleneck caused by the centralized entity is just another example of the general problem of contention for shared resources in a parallel system. In the past, we have seen that contention can be reduced through *decentralization*. In the case of synchronization, decentralization can be achieved by allowing the arriving processes to synchronize among themselves in small groups, and then have the groups come together in a centralized fashion. When such a decentralization technique is applied in a multilevel fashion, the result is a tree structure. A tree is both centralized and decentralized at the same time: it is decentralized at the leaves and centralized at the root. Therefore, the tree structure provides the ability to perform a centralized activity in a decentralized fashion.

6.4.1 Tournament Technique

By creating a binary synchronization tree for the arriving processes at a Barrier, the execution time can be reduced to $O(\log n)$—proportional to the logarithm of the number of processes. The technique used is sometimes called a *tournament* technique. In a tournament, all the players come together in the first round and match up in pairs. The winner of each pair then goes on to the next round, where all the winners again match up in pairs. After each round, the total number of players is reduced by a factor of two, until eventually only one winning player remains. The tournament technique creates a binary tree structure with all the initial players at the leaves, and the final winning player at the root.

The tournament technique can be adapted to creating a synchronization Barrier for a group of n processes. Each process has its own private channel for receiving messages from other processes. At each stage of the tournament, the processes "play" and select a winner from each pair by sending messages. To gain an intuitive understanding of this method, first imagine that all the n processes have reached the Barrier. They are numbered 0 to $n - 1$. The pairing of processes and selection of winners are done by using the binary form of the process numbers. During the first round, each process determines its partner by reversing the rightmost bit in its own process number. Therefore, process 000 is paired with 001, process 010 is paired with 011, process 100 is paired with 101, and so on. The winner from each pair is simply the process with a 0 in the rightmost bit position. Therefore, the winners are 000, 010, 100, and so on. To indicate its defeat, each losing process will send a message to its winning partner.

All the $n/2$ winning processes now go on to the next round of play. Since they were winners in the previous round, all these processes have a 0 in the rightmost bit position. On this second round, the pairing and selection of winners is done by using the next bit in the process number: the second bit from the right. Again, the processes determine their partners by reversing their own second bit, and the winner is the one with bit 0. The losing processes again indicate defeat by sending a message to their winning partner. Now all the $n/4$ winners from this second round go on to the third round. For the third round, the next bit in the process number is used. Clearly, after $\log n$ rounds, one overall winning process will remain, and that will be process number 0.

Figure 6.8 shows a diagram of the tournament for eight processes, numbers 0 to 7. The wiggly diagonal lines represent the sending of a message by the losing process, and the upward solid line represents the receipt of the message by the winning process. The binary tree structure is clearly seen in this figure. For n processes, the number of levels in the tree is $\log n$. An important property of this tree is that every process contributes at least one message to the completion of the tree structure. Thus, process 0 can reach the root of the

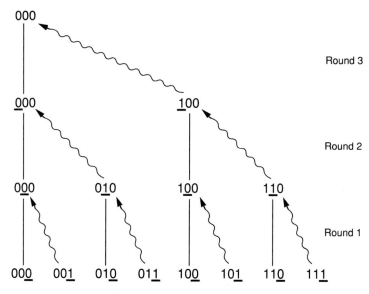

FIGURE 6.8 Binary tree synchronization.

tree only after *all* the processes have arrived at the Barrier. If some of the processes arrive at the Barrier late, then the tree will be held up at some level waiting for a message from that late process.

6.4.2 Tree Creation Algorithm

The binary numbering scheme suggests a very simple algorithm for generating this tree. Each process examines its bits from right to left. For each bit, if it is a 1 then reverse it to get the partner's number, and send him a message. However, if the bit is a 0, then wait for a message from your partner. After receiving the message, then move on the next round by considering the next bit to the left. To formulate the algorithm, two special functions will be needed to operate on the binary bit positions:

> Bit(i, p)—extracts the value of the pth bit position in the number i. (Bit positions are numbered from right to left in increasing multiples of 2.)
>
> ClearBit(i, p)—returns the number obtained by changing the pth bit position in number i from 1 to 0.

From right to left, the bit positions p are numbered 1, 2, 4, 8, 16, and so on. The function $Bit(i, p)$ is used to examine the bits of each process number during the successive rounds. By imbedding this function in a loop that doubles p, the attention can be moved from one bit to the next. The function $ClearBit(i, p)$ is used by the losing processes to determine the process number of their winning partner. By having each process execute the following simple algorithm using its own process number *mynumber*, the binary synchronization tree is generated:

```
position := 1;
WHILE (Bit(mynumber,position) = 0) AND (position < n) DO
  BEGIN
    Receive message from losing partner;
    position := position * 2;
  END;
IF mynumber <> 0 THEN
  BEGIN
    WinningPartner := ClearBit(mynumber,position);
    Send message to WinningPartner;
    Wait for reply message;
  END;
```

This simple algorithm creates the binary synchronization tree and brings all the processes together into the final root of the tree formed by process 0. Process 0 is unique in that it is the only process that is always a winner, and therefore gets some special treatment in the above algorithm. In any Barrier implementation, it is necessary to have all the processes wait inside the Barrier until all other processes have arrived. To meet this requirement in the binary tree, each process will go into a wait state after it loses. Thus, as the tree builds up toward the root, all losing processes get stuck waiting in lower levels of the tree. Eventually, every process will lose (except process 0). Therefore, when process 0 finally receives all its required messages from its losing partners, every other process will be stuck in a wait state at some lower level of the tree.

To release all the waiting processes, the tree creation will just be reversed from the root down. On the way down, the winner processes will move back down the tree, sending messages to their losing partners, who are waiting at each level of the tree. This is illustrated in Figure 6.9. As each loser receives a message and wakes up, then it also

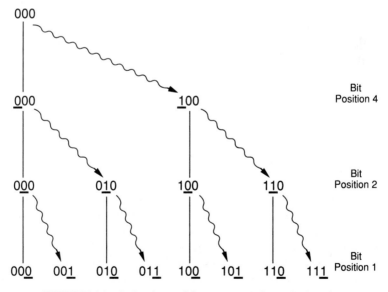

FIGURE 6.9 Releasing waiting processes from the barrier.

assumes the role of a winner and moves down to the next level to release its losing partners. For example, process 100 lost to process 000 in creating the tree, and therefore is released by a message from process 000. Then process 100 moves down to the next level and sends a message to release process 110, who was its losing partner at that level.

The algorithm for creating this downward binary tree is very similar to the upward one. To make the tree move downward, the bit positions are considered from left to right. Thus, the variable *position* starts at a high value and is divided by 2 each time around the loop. The other important change is that the Winning process must compute the number of its losing partner at each level and send it a message. A new function is needed for this purpose:

> SetBit(i, p)—returns the number obtained by changing the *p*th bit position in number *i* from 0 to 1.

The following is the algorithm for creating the downward tree and releasing all the waiting processes from the Barrier:

```
(*position is already set at a high value by the creation algorithm*)
WHILE position > 1 DO
  BEGIN
    position := position DIV 2;
    LosingPartner := SetBit(mynumber,position);
    Send message to LosingPartner;
  END;
```

6.4.3 Performance

The two algorithms for creating the two phases of the binary synchronization tree can now be combined into a Multi-Pascal procedure to implement the Barrier operation. The three special functions *Bit, ClearBit, SetBit* are implemented in Multi-Pascal as follows:

```
Bit(i,p):        i DIV p MOD 2
ClearBit(i,p):   i - p
SetBit(i,p):     i + p
```

The complete Barrier procedure is shown in Figure 6.10 in the context of the Jacobi Relaxation program. An array of channels *synchan* is used to give each process its own channel for receiving incoming messages. When the processes call the Barrier procedure, they pass their *FORALL* index value as a parameter. Inside the Barrier procedure, this establishes a unique number *me* and a unique channel *synchan*[*me*] for each process. The concept of the binary sychronization tree is quite simple, and this tree creation algorithm has only a few instructions. However, the dynamical behavior of the algorithm is quite intricate and may require some study by the reader. Several of the exercises in this chapter deal with this algorithm, and should help clarify its behavior.

The execution time for this binary tree implementation of Barriers is $O(\log n)$, compared to the previous method, which was $O(n)$. Using the timing of the Multi-Pascal interactive system, the exact execution time for the tree Barrier is $80 \log n$. Because of this large constant multiplier, there must be more than 16 processes for this technique to perform better than the linear method. One reason for the large multiplier is the difficulty of performing bit operations in Pascal. Some languages such as C have explicit bit manipulation operations, which are much more efficient and would result in a much lower multiplier. Also, if the Barrier routine can be written in assembly language using the machine instructions for bit manipulation, then the multiplier of 80 could be reduced considerably.

```
PROGRAM Jacobi_Barrier;
CONST n = 32;

VAR ...

    synchan: ARRAY [0..n-1] OF CHANNEL OF INTEGER;

PROCEDURE Barrier(me: INTEGER);
VAR position,dummy:INTEGER;
BEGIN
position := 1;
WHILE (me DIV position MOD 2 = 0) AND (position < n) DO
  BEGIN
    dummy := synchan[me];  (*Receive message from losing partner*)
    position := position * 2;
  END;
IF me <> 0 THEN
  BEGIN
    synchan[me-position] := 1; (*Send message to winning partner*)
    dummy := synchan[me];      (*Wait for reply*)
  END;
WHILE position > 1 DO
  BEGIN
    position := position DIV 2;
    synchan[me+position] := 1; (*Send message to previous loser*)
  END;
END;


BEGIN (*Main Program*)

  ...

FORALL i := 1 TO n DO (*create one process for each row*)
  ...

  Barrier(i-1);
  ...

  Barrier(i-1);
  ...

END.
```

FIGURE 6.10   Barrier implemented with binary tree.

One important feature of the Barrier procedure shown in Figure 6.10 is that it works only if n is an exact power of two. A few minor modifications to the algorithm can generalize it to work for any value of n. This issue is considered in the exercises for this chapter.

This dynamic tree creation algorithm is an important one in the field of parallel programming. It has several other applications besides Barrier synchronization. As we see later in this chapter, it can also be used for broadcasting data to a group of processes, or aggregating data from processes. The reader may recall that a similar bit-reversal technique was used in the Bitonic Merge Sort to pair up processors for comparison and exchange of values. This dynamic tree creation technique also bears some similarity to the principles underlying one of the important processor–memory interconnection networks, the *butterfly* network, presented in Chapter 3.

6.5 LOCAL SYNCHRONIZATION

As discussed at the beginning of this chapter, the need for process synchronization arises in some iterative algorithms because data produced during one iteration by a given process is used by other processes during the next iteration. If all the processes are synchronized after each iteration, then they all must finish the iteration before any can begin the next iteration. This ensures the correctness of the parallel form of the iterative algorithm. In the first half of this chapter, we have discussed a number of methods for achieving this global synchronization of all processes, including both linear and logarithmic time performance.

Some iterative algorithms have a useful property that allows the synchronization time to be reduced to a small constant that is independent of the number of processes. This is achieved by local synchronization of processes with only a few neighboring processes, thus avoiding the time-consuming global synchronization of all processes. In many algorithms, the data produced by a given process during a particular iteration is used by only a few neighboring processes on the next iteration. Therefore, the processes need be synchronized in only this local neighborhood to ensure correctness of the algorithm. The local synchronization can be done in a short time that is dependent only on the size of the local neighborhood.

The Jacobi Relaxation algorithm has this useful local behavior. Recall that the value computed for each point during a given iteration is just the average of the four surrounding points from the previous iteration. Thus, this algorithm exhibits locality. This locality property was illustrated in Figure 6.2. When a process changes the value of any point during a given iteration, this change affects only a few nearby points on the next iteration. Recall from the overall structure of the Parallel Jacobi program presented in Figure 6.6 that each process is assigned to a single row of the array. When computing the new values for all the points in this row, the process must also use the values from the immediately adjacent rows above and below. The following is the main computational loop used by each process:

```
FOR j := 1 TO n DO (*Compute average of four neighbors*)
  B[i,j] := (A[i-1,j] + A[i+1,j] + A[i,j-1] + A[i,j+1]) / 4;
```

Recall that the variable i is the *FORALL* index, and is used by each process as its row index in the array. The above loop computes the new values for row i by letting the loop index j range from left to right along the row. Notice that the only row indices that appear in this loop are i, $i - 1$, and $i + 1$. Thus, on each iteration, process i uses values from its own row and the immediately neighboring rows above and below. As long as processes $i - 1$ and $i + 1$ have finished the previous iteration, then process i can proceed with its computation for row i. Therefore, in the Parallel Jacobi Relaxation program, the global Barrier synchronization can be replaced by a *local synchronization*, in which each process synchronizes only with its two adjacent neighbors.

Any two processes A and B can sychronize with each other by simply exchanging messages: process A sends a message to process B, and process B sends a message to process A. To facilitate this message exchange in the Jacobi program, each process will be assigned two channels, called *higher* and *lower*. Channel *higher* will receive messages from the neighboring process whose number is higher, and channel *lower* will receive from the lower-numbered neighbor. These channels will be structured in two arrays, with *higher*[i] and *lower*[i] assigned to process i. To synchronize with its lower and higher neighbor, each process i first sends messages to both neighbors, then reads its return messages as follows:

```
higher[i-1] := 1;   (* send message to process i-1 *)
lower[i+1] := 1;    (* send message to process i+1 *)
dummy := lower[i];  (* receive message from process i-1 *)
dummy := higher[i]; (* receive message from process i+1 *)
```

Since each process receives the message from the higher-numbered neighbor in channel *higher*, process i must write into *higher*[$i - 1$] when sending a message to process $i - 1$. Similarly, process i must write to channel *lower*[$i + 1$] when sending a message to process $i + 1$. The names *higher* and *lower* identify the *source* of the messages. It is important for the processes to *send* messages first before receiving. Since all processes execute the same code, attempting to receive first will lead to a deadlock. It is also important to send to *both* neighbors before receiving from either. Exchanging with one neighbor and the exchanging with the other can actually lead to a global sequencing of all local synchronization. This subtle issue is dealt with in one of the exercises for this chapter.

A few additions to the message exchange are necessary to account for boundary conditions. The processes assigned to rows 1 and n will have only one neighbor. The complete local synchronization technique is shown in the procedure LocalBarrier in Figure 6.11. Each process first checks to see if the particular neighbor exists before attempting to exchange messages with it. Figure 6.11 gives the complete Parallel Jacobi Relaxation program. Each process performs its local synchronization by calling procedure LocalBarrier. This is done in the same two positions of the process as in the global Barrier synchronization. In this new version, the execution time for the LocalBarrier procedure is a small constant that is not dependent on the total number of processes.

It is important to remember that this local synchronization can be used only if the algorithm exhibits a locality property on each iteration. If each process uses data produced by only a few immediate neighbors, then it need synchronize only with those neighbors

```
PROGRAM Jacobi_Barrier;
CONST n = 32;
     numiter = ... ;
VAR a,b: ARRAY [0..n+1,0..n+1] OF REAL;
    i,j: INTEGER;
    higher, lower:  ARRAY [1..n] OF CHANNEL OF INTEGER;

PROCEDURE LocalBarrier(i: INTEGER);
VAR dummy: INTEGER;
BEGIN
  IF i > 1 THEN higher[i-1] := 1;  (*send to Process i-1*)
  IF i < n THEN
    BEGIN
      lower[i+1] := 1;             (*send to Process i+1*)
      dummy := higher[i];          (*receive from Process i-1*)
    END;
  IF i > 1 THEN dummy := lower[i]; (*receive from Process i+1*)
END;

BEGIN
 ...  (*Read in initial values for array A*)

B := A;
FORALL i := 1 TO n DO (*create one process for each row*)
  VAR j,k: INTEGER;
  BEGIN
    FOR k := 1 TO numiter DO
        BEGIN
          FOR j := 1 TO n DO (*Compute average of four neighbors*)
            B[i,j] := (A[i-1,j] + A[i+1,j] + A[i,j-1] + A[i,j+1]) / 4;
          LocalBarrier(i);
          A[i] := B[i];
          LocalBarrier(i);
        END;
  END;
END.
```

FIGURE 6.11   Jacobi Relaxation with local synchronization.

after each iteration. However, in algorithms with more global data flow, then a global Barrier must be used. Notice in the Jacobi algorithm that there is a global data flow after a series of iterations. A change made by one process in its row will propagate changes to the adjacent rows above and below on the next iteration. On the following iteration, these changes will then propagate one step further to adjacent rows of these neighbors. After each iteration, the changes will propagate one row further until the entire array is affected. Thus, the Jacobi Relaxation does have global flow of data between processes. However, during each *iteration*, the flow is only local, thereby requiring only local synchronization after each iteration.

Using the timings of the Multi-Pascal interactive system, the LocalBarrier procedure requires a constant 60 time units to perform the local synchronization. For a large number of processes, this can result in a significant time saving over the global Barrier methods, which are either $O(n)$ or $O(\log n)$. This Parallel Jacobi program of Figure 6.11 with its 32 processes requires 1579 time units for each iteration, compared to 2191 for the best global Barrier method. This local synchronization therefore has reduced the overall program execution time by 27 percent. For larger numbers of processes, the time savings will be even greater.

To summarize the relative performance of the three Barrier implementations presented in this chapter, Figure 6.12 shows the speedup achieved by each method for a range of values of n. The speedup was computed by first running the sequential Jacobi program of Figure 6.3 for each value of n to determine the average execution time per iteration. Then the execution time per iteration for each of the three Barrier methods was divided into the sequential time to determine the speedup. As expected, the local synchronization method is superior for all values of n. Comparing the two global Barrier methods, we find that the Counting Variable method performs better for $n < 20$, and the Binary Tree method performs better for $n > 20$. This crossover point for these two global methods will vary in different multiprocessor computers, depending on the relative execution times of the instructions used in the implementations.

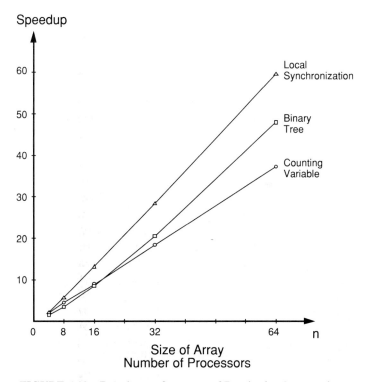

FIGURE 6.12   Relative performance of Barrier implementations.

6.6 BROADCASTING AND AGGREGATION

The methods for implementing Barriers can also be adapted to a new type of activity that is important in some parallel algorithms: aggregating data from processes and broadcasting the results back to the processes. This activity of aggregation and broadcasting of intermediate results forms the basis for a new class of parallel algorithms called *Compute, Aggregate,* and *Broadcast* (CAB). CAB algorithms are usually iterative. Each process goes through a *Compute* phase. Then each process will contribute some data into an aggregation phase that creates some global data values. This global data is then sent back to each process in the *Broadcast* phase. These Compute, Aggregate, and Broadcast phases are repeated in each iteration.

To illustrate this CAB organizational method, a new version of the Jacobi Relaxation algorithm will be developed by introducing a convergence test after each iteration.

6.6.1 Convergence Testing

In all the various versions of Jacobi Relaxation programs given so far in this chapter, a fixed and predetermined number of iterations is used, as specified in a constant at the beginning of the program. For the Jacobi algorithm and also for a wide variety of other iterative numerical algorithms, it is often difficult in advance to know how many iterations will be necessary. When solving such application problems with a computer, usually the user will have in mind a certain desired accuracy in the numerical solution. The program will then continue to iterate until the desired accuracy is achieved. In such programs, the number of iterations is not predetermined, but depends on the convergence rate of the particular data set being used on each run.

In the case of the Jacobi Relaxation algorithm, the accuracy of the computed solution is usually determined by how much change takes place in the array values after each iteration. Intuitively, one can see that initially during the first few iterations, large changes will be taking place in the values at various points. As the computing continues, gradually the changes will become less as the array values converge towards a solution. The usual method of measuring the accuracy after each iteration is to use the maximum change that has taken place among all the array points during that iteration. The iterations will continue until this maximum change goes below a certain critical tolerance that is specified by the user. For a sequential Jacobi Relaxation, this technique is shown in Figure 6.13.

The main outer loop in the program is now a *REPEAT* loop rather than a *FOR* loop. During each iteration, a new value is computed for each point and written into $B[i, j]$. The change is then computed by subtracting the old value $A[i, j]$ from this new value. As the rows and columns of the array are covered by the inner nested *FOR* loops, the maximum change is recorded in the variable *maxchange*. Then at the end of the iteration, this *maxchange* is compared with the desired tolerance to see if another iteration is necessary.

6.6.2 Implementing Parallel Aggregation

This convergence testing technique can also be applied in the parallel version of the Jacobi algorithm. In the basic parallel version of Figure 6.6, each process has its own *FOR* loop to

```
PROGRAM Jacobi;
CONST n = 32;
      tolerance = .01;
VAR A,B: ARRAY [0..n+1,0..n+1] OF REAL;
    i,j: INTEGER;
    change,maxchange: REAL;

BEGIN
    ...    (*Read in initial values for array A*)

B := A;
REPEAT (*compute new values until desired tolerance is reached*)
   BEGIN
     maxchange := 0;
     FOR i := 1 TO n DO
       FOR j := 1 TO n DO
         BEGIN (*compute new value and its change over old value*)
           B[i,j] := (A[i-1,j] + A[i+1,j] + A[i,j-1] + A[i,j+1]) / 4;
           change := ABS( B[i,j] - A[i,j] );
           IF change > maxchange THEN maxchange := change;
         END;
     A := B;
   END;
UNTIL maxchange < tolerance;
END.
```

FIGURE 6.13   Sequential Jacobi Relaxation with convergence test.

count the fixed number of iterations. To add a convergence test, this *FOR* loop must be replaced by a *REPEAT* loop in each process that continues until the desired tolerance is reached in the solution. Recall that each process is assigned to a single row of the array, and therefore can determine the changes that take place in this row after each iteration. However, the convergence test must be a *global* one: the changes in all rows must be considered to determine termination of the algorithm. Therefore, the changes from each row must be collected globally after each iteration to see if the desired tolerance is reached. Even one point in the whole array that has a large change on a given iteration will cause the whole program to continue running for more iterations.

This global aggregation of changes computed in the various processes is easily accomplished by using the Barrier, which is already in the program for synchronization purposes. To synchronize the processes after each iteration, the Barrier implementations collect and then release all the processes. During the collection phase, information from the processes can be aggregated, and then returned or "broadcasted" back to the processes during the release phase.

Figure 6.13 shows that the criterion for termination is whether the change in all of the array points is less than the given *tolerance*. In the parallel version, each process can test whether the changes in its assigned row are all less than the tolerance. This information can then be passed to the Barrier in the form of a Boolean variable *mydone*, which is true if all the changes in that row are less than the tolerance. If all processes have a *true* value for their *mydone* variable, then all changes in the array are less than the desired tolerance, and the program should terminate. To allow these individual values of *mydone* to be aggregated from all the processes, each process will pass the Boolean value to the Barrier. As the Barrier is performing the synchronization, it will also collect all these Boolean values. If all the collected values are *true*, then the Barrier will return a *true* value to each process to tell it to terminate.

To perform this aggregation and broadcasting, the Barrier procedure will be replaced by a function *Aggregate(mydone)*, where *mydone* is the Boolean described above. The function will perform the barrier synchronization in the same way as before, except that in addition it will also aggregate all the Boolean values and broadcast the result back to each process. Since *Aggregate* is a function, it can return a Boolean back to each process which tells whether or not to continue for another iteration.

Either of the Barrier techniques presented in this chapter can be adapted to this purpose. Consider the Counting Variable method originally shown in Figure 6.7. As each process enters the Barrier it goes through an Arrival Phase, during which it increments the global *count* variable. After all the processes have passed through this Arrival Phase, the Departure Phase begins. As processes pass through the Departure Phase, they decrement the *count* and exit the Barrier. This method is easily modified to aggregate a Boolean value *mydone* from each process. A new Boolean variable is introduced, *globaldone*. As each process passes through the Arrival Phase, it merges its own *mydone* value into the *globaldone* value. During the Departure Phase, this *globaldone* value is then passed back to each process as it departs.

Figure 6.14 shows an *Aggregate* function based on the Counting Variable method. The function performs a Barrier synchronization for all the *n* processes that call it. In addition, the function computes the logical *AND* of all the Boolean parameters *mydone* from each process. Only a few simple additions have been made to the original Barrier procedure. These additions are shown in boldface in Figure 6.14. The additional statements are just involved with the use of the *globaldone* variable.

6.6.3 Parallel Jacobi with Convergence

The Aggregation Barrier technique can be used as the basis for a parallel Jacobi Relaxation with convergence testing as shown in Figure 6.15. Each process has a *REPEAT* loop that continues to perform iterations until the variable *done* is set to *TRUE*. The value of *done* is computed by the *Aggregate* function at the end of each iteration. Each process passes one parameter to *Aggregate*: its own contribution to the convergence test. As each process computes the new values of the points in its own row, the variable *maxchange* is used to accumulate the maximum change in any point of that row. This *maxchange* is then compared with the specified *tolerance*, and the resultant Boolean value is passed to *Aggregate* as a parameter.

As described in the previous section, the *Aggregate* function collects all the Booleans from all processes, computes the logical *AND*, and returns the resultant Boolean as the value of the function. Thus, the local variable *done* in each process will be set to the global result of the termination test. If any process contributes a *FALSE* to the aggregation, then all processes will receive a *FALSE*, and will continue for another iteration. Only after all

```
PROGRAM Jacobi_Conv;
VAR   ...

   count: INTEGER;
   Arrival, Departure: SPINLOCK;
   globaldone: BOOLEAN;


FUNCTION Aggregate(mydone: BOOLEAN): BOOLEAN;
BEGIN

  (*Arrival Phase - Count the processes as they arrive*)
  Lock(Arrival);
    count := count + 1;
    globaldone := globaldone AND mydone; (*aggregation step*)
  IF count < n
      THEN Unlock(Arrival)    (*continue Arrival Phase*)
      ELSE Unlock(Departure); (*terminate Arrival Phase*)

  (*Departure Phase - Count the processes as they leave*)
  Lock(Departure);
    count := count - 1;
    Aggregate := globaldone;  (*return "done" flag to process*)
  IF count > 0
      THEN Unlock(Departure) (*continue Departure Phase*)
      ELSE BEGIN
        globaldone := TRUE;  (*reset for next Aggregation*)
        Unlock(Arrival);     (*terminate Departure Phase*)
      END;

END;


BEGIN (*Main Program*)

count := 0; (*Initialize "count" and spinlocks*)
Unlock(Arrival);
Lock(Departure);
globaldone := TRUE;  (*Initialize global flag*)
  ...
```

FIGURE 6.14   Aggregation and broadcasting barrier.

processes pass the termination test individually will the global termination test succeed. Notice in Figure 6.15 that the first call to the Barrier procedure still remains. However, the second Barrier has been replaced by the Aggregate function, which performs both synchronization and global termination testing.

```
PROGRAM Jacobi_Conv;
CONST n = 32;
      tolerance = .01;
VAR A,B: ARRAY [0..n+1,0..n+1] OF REAL;
    i,j: INTEGER;

PROCEDURE Barrier(me: INTEGER);
  ... (*same as before*)


FUNCTION Aggregate(mydone: BOOLEAN): BOOLEAN;
  ... (*see Figure 6.14*)


BEGIN
  ... (*Read in initial values for array A*)

B := A;
FORALL i := 1 TO n DO (*Create the processes*)
  VAR j: INTEGER;
      change,maxchange: REAL;
      done: BOOLEAN;
  BEGIN
    REPEAT
      maxchange := 0;
      FOR j := 1 TO n DO (*Compute new value for each point in my row*)
        BEGIN
          B[i,j] := (A[i-1,j] + A[i+1,j] + A[i,j-1] + A[i,j+1]) / 4;
          change := ABS( B[i,j] - A[i,j] );
          IF change > maxchange THEN maxchange := change;
        END;
      Barrier;
      A[i] := B[i];
      done := Aggregate(maxchange<tolerance);
    UNTIL done; (*Iterate until global termination is indicated*)
  END;
END.
```

**FIGURE 6.15   Parallel Jacobi Relaxation with convergence
test.**

The sequential version of Figure 6.13 and this new parallel version of Figure 6.15
were both run on the Multi-Pascal interactive system. For each iteration, the sequential
version requires about 68000 time units. The parallel version requires 3200 time units per
iteration—a speedup of about 21, using 32 processors. The loss of processor efficiency is
due to the performance bottleneck created by the Barrier and Aggregation. As we have
seen in earlier sections of this chapter, this bottleneck may be minimized by using more

efficient Barrier methods. Each global Barrier method will have a corresponding Aggregate method. For more than 20 processes, both the Barrier procedure and Aggregate function should use the *binary tree* method, which requires time proportional to the logarithm of the number of processes. The exercises at the end of this chapter will deal with this issue of converting the binary tree Barrier method to the corresponding Aggregate method.

However, the Local Barrier method has no corresponding Aggregate method. Aggregation definitely requires that *all* processes come together. In the Local Barrier method as applied to the Jacobi algorithm, processes synchronize only with their immediate neighbors after each iteration. This type of local synchronization is not sufficient to globally aggregate values from all the processes. Therefore, the Aggregate function must use one of the global Barrier methods. It is possible to minimize the overall performance reduction caused by the global aggregation, as is discussed in the next section.

6.6.4 Improving the Performance

Earlier in this chapter it was shown that the synchronization overhead in the Jacobi Relaxation can be reduced by using a local barrier for each process. In the Jacobi algorithm, each process uses values produced by its immediate neighbors on the previous iteration. Therefore, it is sufficient for each process to synchronize locally with the two processes assigned to the rows above and below. This local barrier technique reduces the synchronization time to a small constant that is independent of the number of processes.

Trying to use local barriers in a Jacobi Relaxation with convergence testing becomes somewhat more complex. The convergence testing requires a global aggregation function, which is essentially equivalent to a global Barrier. If this global aggregation is done after each iteration, then the global synchronization cost is paid on each iteration. However, the impact of the aggregation can be reduced by performing the convergence test only after several iterations. A whole series of m iterations can be performed by using the highly efficient local barrier method for process synchronization. Then the global aggregation can be performed at the end of the m iterations to see if the desired tolerance has been reached in the solution. In this way, the overhead required for the global aggregation is averaged over the m iterations. If the desired tolerance has not been reached, then another m iterations are performed, followed by another global aggregation. The general structure of each process i is as follows:

```
REPEAT
  FOR k := 1 TO m DO
    BEGIN
      Compute new values for row i;
      Record "maxchange" in values;
      LOCAL_BARRIER;
      Copy new values over old values;
      LOCAL_BARRIER;
    END;
  Compute "done" from global Aggregation;
UNTIL done;
```

For large numbers of processes, this technique of combining local barriers with global convergence testing results in a considerable performance improvement. Recall that the best global barrier techniques require time $20n$ or $80 \log n$. Therefore, the global aggregation requires aproximately the same time. By using $m = 10$, this aggregation is performed only once every ten iterations, thereby reducing the average overhead per iteration to $2n$ or $8 \log n$. The Jacobi program with global aggregation after every iteration (Figure 6.15) requires 3200 time units per iteration. This new version with local barriers achieves an average of 2000 time units per iteration, which is a 37 percent improvement. One hidden overhead in this new version results from the extra iterations that may be performed even after the desired tolerance is reached in the solution. Because the program tests convergence only every m iterations, some unnecessary iterations may be performed during the last set of m iterations. Thus the value of m—the number of iterations per set—should not be increased too far in an effort to further reduce the average aggregation cost.

Both versions of the Jacobi with convergence testing illustrate the Compute, Aggregate, and Broadcast type of parallel algorithm. During the "Compute" phase, each process computes the new array values from the old. The "Aggregate" phase collects the local tolerance test from each of the processes. The "Broadcast" phase returns the global termination condition back to all the processes. Aggregation and Broadcasting are time-consuming operations that require time at least $O(\log n)$. Therefore, the frequency of these operations relative to the duration of the Compute phase should be minimized. In this Jacobi example, we have seen how the performance can be greatly improved by increasing the duration of the Compute phase to include many iterations.

6.7 SUMMARY

This chapter presents an important major class of parallel algorithms: iterative synchronous algorithms. Most sequential numerical algorithms and a wide variety of other algorithms, consist of a series of iterations on large data arrays. Parallelism can be achieved by assigning processes to different portions of the data array. In some cases, the processes can continue to operate independently, leading to a *relaxed* algorithm that achieves a very large speedup. However, many algorithms require that the data produced by a given process during one iteration be used by other processes during the next iteration. In such algorithms, the processes must perform some type of synchronization after each iteration. The purpose of this chapter has been to describe a variety of methods for achieving this process synchronization with a minimum of computational overhead.

The first method for synchronization is just to let the processes terminate after each iteration and then to be recreated at the start of the next iteration. This method is useful for systems with a low process creation overhead. However, in systems with a large process creation overhead, this process termination method is unacceptable. For these systems, a synchronization "barrier" can be used to synchronize the processes after each iteration. An $O(n)$ Barrier technique using spinlocks is described, based on a counting variable. In the *counting variable* method, processes are counted as they pass through the Arrival Phase of the Barrier. The last process to pass through the Arrival Phase will open up the Departure Phase to release all the processes.

To achieve an $O(\log n)$ Barrier, a binary tree technique is used. As they enter the Barrier, the processes pair up and select a winner. The winners then pair up in the next round. This "tournament" style reduces the number of processes by a factor of two after each round. The eventual overall winning process sits at the root of the tournament tree. Then the winner starts back down the tree, releasing its previously losing partners from the blocked state. Eventually, all processes are released and return to computation. This dynamic tree technique eliminates the performance bottleneck that arises in the $O(n)$ methods due to centralization. The decentralization in the tree method increases parallelism and reduces the contention for shared channels. This binary tree technique is useful if the number of processes is very large.

The Jacobi Relaxation algorithm is used in this chapter to illustrate the application of all these synchronization techniques. This algorithm is used to solve an important differential equation called Laplace's equation. The Jacobi algorithm actually has the useful property that each process uses data from only neighboring processes. Therefore, after a given iteration, each process need synchronize only with its two immediate neighbors. This leads to a highly efficient LocalBarrier synchronization method, which requires only a small constant time, independent of the number of processes.

All the global Barrier synchronization methods are easily adapted to perform another important function: global aggregation and broadcasting. This is the basis of a major class of parallel algorithms called Compute, Aggregate, and Broadcast. When a global convergence test is added to the Jacobi Relaxation program, the result is a CAB algorithm. The convergence test is applied locally by each process, and then the local results are aggregated globally and the result is broadcast back to each process. For algorithms that exhibit a locality property like the Jacobi algorithm, it is possible to combine LocalBarriers with global aggregation and broadcasting. The result is a highly efficient parallel program that achieves an excellent speedup.

REFERENCES

A thorough discussion of the sequential Jacobi Relaxation algorithm is found in Jennings [1977]. Stone [1987] describes performance issues in the parallel implementation of this algorithm, with special emphasis on Barriers and the synchronization of the processes. Parallel Jacobi Relaxation is also discussed in Quinn [1987] and Hockney and Jesshope [1988].

Brawer [1989] presents material on the application of Barriers in parallel programs and their implementation using locks and semaphores. Baase [1988] gives a parallel tournament algorithm for finding the largest element in an array. Stone [1987] uses a parallel tournament technique for solving a variety of recurrence relations.

Fox, et al. [1988] has a comprehensive discussion of solving Laplace's equation on a multicomputer, including the important concept of "local synchronization." The *Compute, Aggregate,* and *Broadcast* parallel programming technique is described in Nelson and Snyder [1987]. The Red–Black Relaxation algorithm described in the programming projects can be found in Ortega [1985]. Parallel methods for Gaussian Elimination in a system of linear equations are presented in many references [see Heller, 1978].

PROGRAMMING PROJECTS

1. RED–BLACK RELAXATION

In the Jacobi Relaxation algorithm for solving Laplace's equation, each iteration computes new values for all array points using the old values from the previous iteration. There are other types of relaxation algorithms for solving Laplace's equation that use new values more quickly as they are created. This allows changes taking place in one part of the array to propagate more quickly to other parts of the array, thereby achieving a faster convergence.

One such technique is called *Red–Black Relaxation*. The two-dimensional data array is considered as a checkerboard, with alternating "red" and "black" squares. Each data point is one "square" of the checkerboard. Any relaxation algorithm always computes a new value for each point from the four immediate neighboring points—above, below, left, and right. In a checkerboard, each red point has only black neighbors, and each black point has only red neighbors. In Red–Black Relaxation, the computation of new values is alternated for the red and black points. First, new values are computed for all the red points, using the current values of the neighboring black points. Then new values are computed for all the black points, using the newly computed values of the red points. Then the red points are again recomputed, using the new values of the black points.

In Red–Black Relaxation, each iteration has two phases: the red phase and the black phase. During the red phase, new values are computed for all red points, and similarly for the black phase. It is required that the red phase be complete before the next black phase begins. Similarly, the black phase must be complete before the next red phase begins on the following iteration. Therefore, in any parallel form of this algorithm, it is necessary to synchronize processes after the red phase and again after the black phase.

Your job is to write a Multi-Pascal program that performs Red–Black Relaxation on a two-dimensional data array of real numbers, like that used in the Jacobi Relaxation programs of this chapter. Create one process for each row of the array, as is done in the sample Jacobi programs of this chapter.

You are to write three versions of the Red–Black Relaxation and compare their execution times. Versions 1 and 2 carry out a fixed number of iterations that is determined by a constant in the program. Version 1 uses a global barrier technique for process synchronization. Version 2 uses a local barrier technique. Version 3 carries out a variable number of iterations that is determined by a convergence test. Version 3 uses a local barrier for synchronization, combined with a global aggregation function to perform the convergence test.

During program debugging, use a very small data array to reduce program execution time. When testing the program performance, set a breakpoint that interrupts the program after each iteration. When comparing the execution times of the three versions, compare the time for a single iteration. By focusing on a single iteration, there is no need to let the programs run to completion, which is very time consuming for a large data array.

2. GAUSSIAN ELIMINATION

In a wide range of scientific and engineering applications of computers, it is necessary to be able to solve a system of linear equations. One of the popular techniques is called

Gaussian Elimination. For simplicity, assume that there are *n* equations and *n* unknowns. Then the coefficients of each equation will form an *n* by *n* array of real numbers. The most computationally intensive step in Gaussian Elimination is to convert this array into *upper triangular* form, which means that all positions to the left of the main diagonal are 0. For example, the following array is in upper triangular form:

$$
\begin{array}{ccccc}
3 & 5 & 2 & 30 & 21 \\
\\
0 & 1 & 17 & -3 & -49 \\
\\
0 & 0 & 33 & -6 & 2 \\
\\
0 & 0 & 0 & 9 & 12 \\
\\
0 & 0 & 0 & 0 & 13
\end{array}
$$

Once the array is in this upper triangular form, then it can be solved with the Back Substitution method described in Chapter 4. The first step in converting an array *A* to upper triangular form is to scan down all the numbers in column 1 and find the maximum. Assuming that this maximum occurs in row *i*, the next step in the algorithm is to exchange the whole of row *i* and row 1 in the array *A*. The element $A[1, 1]$ now in the upper left corner of the array is called the *pivot* element. Next the following two steps are carried out for each row *i* in the array (except row 1):

(1) Compute a multiplier by dividing the negative of the pivot element by the value in position 1 of row *i* as follows: $-A[1, 1]/A[1, i]$.

(2) For each element in any column *j* of this row, multiply it by the multiplier for this row and add the corresponding element in column *j* of row 1.

After repeating the above steps for each row in the array (except row 1), the array now has all zeroes in the first column, except possibly in the upper left corner. Now column 1 and row 1 of the array are in proper form and can be completely ignored and left unchanged in the subsequent transformations. The next step in the algorithm is just to focus attention on the subarray formed by rows 2 to *n* and columns 2 to *n*. Using this square subarray, the exact same process as described above is repeated, except the focus is on column 2 and row 2. This will place row 2 and column 2 in proper final form. Then the algorithm focuses on the square subarray with upper left corner in position (3, 3). This process is repeated until the entire array is in upper triangular form.

Write a parallel program in Multi-Pascal to transform an array of real numbers to upper triangular form. Try to minimize the execution time and maximize the speedup of the program by limiting the sequential aspects of the program and locating all the potential parallelism. It is suggested that your program use the process termination technique of synchronization: use an outer iterative loop with a series of *FORALL* statements inside to create groups of parallel processes for each phase of the computation.

Test the program on the Multi-Pascal system for correctness by first using a small array of perhaps 3 by 3. Then determine the speedup achieved by your program for the following array sizes: 20 by 20, 30 by 30, and 40 by 40. For an *n* by *n* array, an efficient version of this algorithm should achieve a speedup of $(.3n)$. Initialize the values in the array by using the following:

```
FOR i := 1 TO n DO
  FOR j := 1 TO n DO
    A[i,j] := i+j;
```

EXERCISES

1. Semaphores are a popular synchronization primitive in parallel programming languages. Chapter 5 has a complete definition of semaphores and their associated operations—*wait* and *signal*. Assume that instead of channel variables, Multi-Pascal has semaphore variables. Rewrite the Barrier procedure for the Counting Variable Method to use semaphores instead of spinlocks.

2. Chapter 5 defines the popular synchronization primitive called *semaphores* with their associated operations—*wait* and *signal*. Using an array of semaphores instead of an array of channels, rewrite the Barrier procedure that uses the dynamic binary tree method.

3. In the "Counting Variable" barrier method, two spinlocks are used to control the two phases of the barrier. For the method to function correctly, the initial state of the spinlocks must be as follows:

> Arrival—unlocked
>
> Departure—locked

Assume that both spinlocks are initially in the unlocked state. Describe a detailed scenario that results in a malfunction of the Barrier.

4. Consider the following attempt to create a simple Barrier procedure using a single spinlock:

```
(*global shared variables*)
VAR count: INTEGER;
    L: SPINLOCK;

PROCEDURE Barrier;
BEGIN
  Lock(L);
    count := count + 1;
  Unlock(L);
  While count < n DO; (*Busy-wait until all processes arrive*)
END;
```

Although this method may appear to work, it actually has a serious error. Describe the nature of this error. Give a detailed scenario which results in erroneous behavior of this Barrier procedure.

5. In this chapter it was shown how the "Counting Variable" Barrier procedure could be modified to perform aggregation and broadcasting of Boolean values. Each process passes a Boolean parameter to an Aggregate function, which *AND*s them all together and returns the resultant Boolean as the value of the function. Another technique is to create a special "Aggregate"

process having a channel to which all the processes write their Boolean. The Aggregate process computes the AND of all the Booleans and then sends a copy of the result back to each process, using an array of channels, with one element of the array assigned to each process. Write and test this Aggregation process, using the Multi-Pascal interactive system.

6. Convert the binary tree Barrier procedure into an Aggregate function that also achieves the same $O(\log n)$ performance. Test the function, using the Multi-Pascal interactive system.

7. Figure 6.13 shows a sequential Jacobi Relaxation with convergence test. Convert this to parallel form, using the process termination method of synchronization. Turn the variable *maxchange* into an array, and have each process write its maximum change into the corresponding element of the array. After the processes terminate, the array can then be aggregated to determine global convergence. Run and test the program, using the Multi-Pascal interactive system. To save execution time, use a smaller value of *n* during testing.

8. The binary tree Barrier procedure of Figure 6.10 works only if *n* is an exact power of 2. Indicate some simple modifications to this procedure so that it will work correctly for any value of *n*. If *n* is not a power of 2, then in some of the rounds, some winning processes may find that they have no losing partners in the tournament. In this case they just declare themselves to be the winner and go on to the next round. Some relatively minor modifications to the procedure can accomplish this. Test the new procedure, using the Multi-Pascal interactive system. Use a *FORALL* that generates a few processes to call the Barrier procedure.

9. In the tournament technique for creating a Barrier, it is interesting that the number of rounds that each process wins is exactly equal to the number of "trailing" zeroes in its binary process number. "Trailing" zeroes are defined as all those encountered when moving from the right until the first bit 1 is reached.

   (a) Explain the reason behind this trailing zero property.

   (b) Write a function *FindTrail(i)* that computes and returns the number of trailing zeroes in the binary form of *i*.

   This trailing zero property can be utilized to make the tree creation procedure more efficient. The procedure uses a new integer array *trailzero* that contains the number of trailing zeroes for each process. That is, *process i* finds out how many trailing zeroes it has by looking in *trailzero[i]*. In the Barrier procedure, this allows the *WHILE* loops to be changed to *FOR* loops.

   (c) Write a new Barrier procedure that makes use of the array *trailzero*.

   (d) Use the Multi-Pascal interactive system to run and test the function from part (b) and the procedure from part (a). Use a *FORALL* to create a few processes for testing purposes. Each process must first call the function *FindTrail* to initialize the array. Then it can call the Barrier procedure. In a real parallel program, the processes would have to call *FindTrail* only once, but the Barrier would be called many times.

10. The Jacobi Relaxation program of Figure 6.11 uses a Local Barrier technique for synchronization. Consider the following modified form of the LocalBarrier procedure:

```
PROCEDURE LocalBarrier(i: INTEGER);
VAR dummy: INTEGER;
BEGIN
  IF i > 1 THEN dummy := lower[i];
  IF i < n THEN
    BEGIN
      dummy := higher[i];
      lower[i+1] := 1;
    END;
  IF i > 1 THEN higher[i-1] := 1;
END;
```

Show that this new procedure will result in a program deadlock.

11. The Jacobi Relaxation program of Figure 6.11 uses a LocalBarrier technique for synchronization. Consider the following modified form of the LocalBarrier procedure:

```
PROCEDURE LocalBarrier(i: INTEGER);
VAR dummy: INTEGER;
BEGIN
  IF i > 1 THEN
    BEGIN
      higher[i-1] := 1;
      dummy := lower[i];
    END;
  IF i < n THEN
    BEGIN
      lower[i+1] := 1;
      dummy := higher[i];
    END;
END;
```

This new procedure appears more simple than the other form, and it does achieve the desired local synchronization. However, it has the extremely undesirable property that it forces all the local barriers to execute sequentially, one at a time. This defeats the purpose of having a local barrier.

Explain in detail why this procedure causes the local barriers to occur in sequence, and therefore has execution time $O(n)$ for the synchronization of all n processes.

7

Multicomputer Architecture

Parallel processing computer architecture is often divided into two major categories: *multiprocessors* and *multicomputers*. A *multiprocessor* is characterized by a shared memory—a single shared memory address space used by all the processors. In a *multicomputer*, each processor has its own local memory, and interaction between processors is through message passing. In a multiprocessor all the data used by the program is stored in the shared memory and is accessible to all the processors there. However, in a multicomputer the data must be distributed among the local memories of the processors. A processor cannot directly access the local memory of other processors, but may send or receive blocks of data from other processors through the processor interconnection network. Since access to a processor's own local memory may be several orders of magnitude faster than the network delay time, the performance of a program is critically dependent on the placement of data in the various local memories.

To effectively program a multicomputer, it is necessary to have some overall knowledge of the hardware architecture. Simply taking an efficient multiprocessor program and running it on a multicomputer will usually result in poor performance. The basic language features and programming techniques used on multiprocessors can be adapted to multicomputer programming. However, this requires an understanding of the general organization of multicomputer hardware, and how it differs from a multiprocessor. The focus of this chapter is on those aspects of multicomputer architecture that will affect program performance, and therefore should be known by the programmer. On the basis of this knowledge, the following chapter then begins to discuss multicomputer programming techniques.

In a multicomputer, each processor has its own private physical memory module for storing and retrieving data during computation. In addition, each processor has one or more direct connections to other processors, through which data may be transmitted. If a processor does not have a direct connection to another processor, they may still communicate by having the intermediate processors forward the data. Data transmission between processors requires a significant amount of time, and forwarding data between distant processors requires even more time. Thus, if there is frequent communication between processors during the execution of a program, the resultant communication delays may significantly increase the program execution time.

The overall pattern of the direct processor connections is usually called the multicomputer *topology*. For a particular algorithm, the execution delays resulting from communication will depend on the specific *topology*. This chapter considers several of the most important multicomputer topologies, including line, ring, mesh, torus, and hypercube. The relationships among the various topologies is described, and their relative suitability for different classes of algorithms. Two important parameters that characterize each topology are the *connectivity*, which is the number of direct connections per processor, and the *diameter*, which is the maximum number of intermediate connections required for distant processors to communicate. The connectivity is important because it influences the cost of the hardware. The diameter is important because it influences the program performance.

The chapter is divided into three major sections. The first section discusses processor-to-processor communication, and the various sources of communication delay. The next section describes the properties of the various multicomputer topologies. The final section considers the relationship between the multicomputer topology and the communication patterns used in different types of algorithms.

7.1 PROCESSOR COMMUNICATIONS

In a multicomputer, each processor has a separate local memory module for storing its data and program code. The processor together with its memory form a kind of self-sufficient little computer. The heart of every ordinary sequential computer is just the processor and the memory. The activity of each processor–memory pair in a multicomputer is very much like an ordinary sequential computer. The processor executes a series of instructions as determined by the program code stored in the memory. Each instruction may involve reading or writing of data values from the memory. This resemblance of each processor–memory pair to a complete computer is the origin of the name "multi"computer.

7.1.1 Communication Link

In order for all the processor–memory pairs to work together on a single computational problem, they must be able to communicate and exchange data during computation. This is accomplished with a hardware communication network that connects the processors together, and allows data to be transmitted from any processor to any other processor. The basic building block of this communication network is a direct processor-to-processor communication link, as illustrated in Figure 7.1. Each processor–memory pair is connected to its own *communication interface*, which is a piece of hardware capable of transmitting and receiving data through a *communication link*.

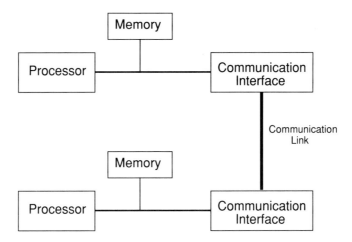

FIGURE 7.1 Processor communication link.

The function of a communication interface with respect to the processor is similar to an input–output (I/O) interface in an ordinary computer. The I/O interface receives input or output commands from the processor, and then interfaces with a specific device, such as a printer or disk drive, to carry out the commands and send or receive data. The I/O interface frees the processor from having to deal with the low-level details of hardware control of the input–output device, thereby leaving the processor to continue computation while input or output is being performed. Often the I/O interface has Direct Memory Access (DMA), which allows it to read or write data directly from the memory without any attention from the processor. The function of a communication interface in a multicomputer is similar—it is just a new type of input–output interface. The only difference is that the data is being sent through a communication link, rather than to an I/O device.

With reference to Figure 7.1, the communication link is *bidirectional*, which means that data can flow in either direction. Each communication interface is capable of both transmitting or receiving data. The communication link is simply an electrical connection capable of carrying a sequence of bits from one communication interface to the other. One may think of this link as a "pipe"—bits that are pushed one at a time into one end of the pipe flow through the pipe, and eventually arrive at the other end. At any given time, one of the communication interfaces will be the *receiver* and the other the *sender*. The basic unit of communication is a *packet* or *message*, which consists of many bits of data. The sender transmits the bits of the message one at a time through the communication link, until they are all properly received at the other end.

It is obvious that there is some time consumed by each message transmission. The communication link has a certain maximum bandwidth, which is usually measured in bits per second. Typical bandwidth for such a communication link might be 10 megabits/second. If a message packet contains 50 bytes, then it will require 40 microseconds for transmission. This time is significant when compared to the processor speed, which may require 1–10 microseconds to execute an instruction.

In addition to the actual physical transmission of the data bits, the communication interfaces must also perform other functions to ensure that the data is sent and received correctly. The raw data bits of the message are packaged together in a packet with a header at the beginning for identification information, and a checksum at the end for error detection. Therefore, some time is consumed in the two communication interfaces to create and decode this header and checksum. If there is an occasional transmission error resulting from noise in the electronic media of the communication link, then a retransmission of the message will be requested by the receiver. This error detection and correction may also add some time to the average communication delay.

7.1.2 Routing and Congestion

Each communication interface may have several links connecting it to several different processors, as illustrated in Figure 7.2. The processor in the center of the figure has four direct communication links to other processors. These other processors in turn have direct links to additional processors. These nine processor–memory pairs together with all the indicated communication links form a *communication network*. Each processor may communicate directly with its immediate neighbors by using the direct communication links. Processors without direct connections may also communicate by having the messages forwarded by intermediate communication interfaces. For example, Processor 0 may

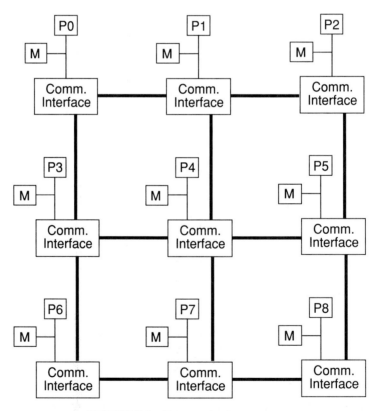

FIGURE 7.2   Communication network.

transmit a message to Processor 2 by sending it directly to the communication interface of Processor 1, which will forward it to the communication interface of Processor 2. Therefore, if the time to transmit through a single communication link is T time units, then the total time for Processor 0 to send a message to Processor 2 is $2T$ time units.

For some processor pairs, there may be alternative paths in the network. P0 can send a message to P5 via any of the following paths: P0–P1–P2–P5, P0–P1–P4–P5, P0–P3–P4–P5. All of these possible paths require the message to travel through three communication links. Therefore, the total communication delay from P0 to P5 is $3T$. To allow each message to be routed properly to its destination, each message packet will contain the destination processor number as part of the "header." The general format of a message packet is shown in Figure 7.3.

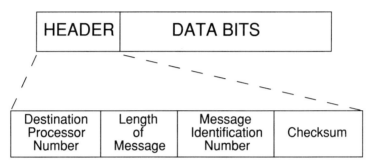

FIGURE 7.3   Format of message packet.

As each interface receives a message, it examines the destination processor number. Every interface knows its own processor number and also its relative position in the whole network with respect to the other processor numbers. If the received message is destined for its own processor, the communication interface will store the message in the memory and send a special "message received" signal to the processor. If the message is destined for some other processor, the interface will choose one of its connecting links to send the message to one of its neighboring communication interfaces. Knowing its own position in the network and the destination processor number, the interface will select a direction for forwarding the message which will move it towards its destination.

There is a wide variety of routing algorithms that may be used by the interfaces to choose a path for forwarding messages between distant processors. The two general categories are *static routing* and *dynamic routing*. In static routing, each message between a particular pair of processors will always follow the same route. All the routes may be computed initially and stored in fixed *routing tables* in each communication interface. Whenever a message arrives at an interface, it simply examines the "destination processor number" in the message header, and performs a table lookup to choose a communication link for forwarding the message. With static routing, the tables never change. However, with dynamic routing, the routing tables may be adjusted periodically to improve performance based on information about current network traffic and congestion. One disadvantage of dynamic routing is that messages sent from a given source to the same destination may arrive in different order than they were sent. This can be corrected at the receiving node, but does require additional time and message buffering space.

The main goal of any routing method is to minimize the total communication delay between sender and receiver. If the message traffic in the network as a whole is relatively low, then minimal delay results from choosing a path with a minimum number of connecting links. If there are several such paths, as was illustrated in the network of Figure 7.2, then one may be chosen randomly. This "randomization" technique will help to evenly distribute the message traffic through alternate paths in the network. If the random path selection is done once at the beginning and stored in fixed routing tables, then the result is static routing. If new random choices are made as time progresses, then the result is a dynamic routing algorithm. Dynamic routing has the advantage that it can respond to changes in the network traffic patterns to help avoid congestion, and the resultant additional delays.

If there are several messages moving through the network at one time, there is a possibility of some additional delays if two messages converge on the same interface within a short time interval. Each interface has a limit to the rate at which it can handle messages. If the message arrival rate exceeds this limit, then some delays will result. For example, in Figure 7.2, consider the situation where processor P1 is sending a series of messages to processor P7 at the opposite side of the network. The most direct path for this communication is P1–P4–P7. However, suppose at the same time processor P3 is sending a series of messages to processor P5. The most direct path for this communication is P3–P4–P5. Thus, both communication paths pass through processor P4. This communication scenario is illustrated more clearly in Figure 7.4.

If both of the source communication interfaces 1 and 3 are sending messages at their maximum communication rate, then interface 4 will not be able to handle all the traffic. If each interface can handle r messages per second, then messages will be converging on interface 4 at a rate of $2r$ per second. Thus, the two interfaces 1 and 3 will find that interface 4 is busy half the time. The result is that the messages will have to be queued at the source

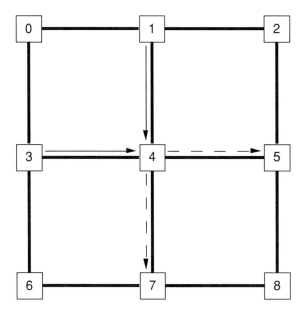

FIGURE 7.4   Congestion in communication network.

interfaces 1 and 3 while waiting for an opportunity for transmission to interface 4. Therefore, each interface must have some buffer space for queuing messages that are in transit. Such situations where messages build up and are delayed is sometimes called *congestion*.

Congestion at one interface in a communication network can quickly spread to neighboring interfaces. The situation is much like the flow of automobile traffic in a network of roads in a city. Each intersection is analogous to a communication interface, and each road that connects intersections is analogous to a commmunication link. Each intersection has a maximum capacity for handling traffic flow. If the flow of autos from its connecting roads exceeds that capacity, then the result is congestion: the traffic will back up along the roads. Eventually, the traffic may back up so far that neighboring intersections are also affected, causing further congestion. One solution to this problem is for the police, who may know about the congested intersections, to begin to reroute traffic around the congested area. This solution can also be adopted in a multicomputer communication network. The routing algorithm used by each communication interface can take congestion into account. Detailed consideration of such routing algorithms is beyond the scope of this text. For further discussion of this issue see Tanenbaum [1989].

Whether or not congestion occurs depends both on the structure of the communication network and the behavior of the particular parallel algorithm being executed at the time. Some algorithms have relatively infrequent communication, and thus will not cause any congestion. Other algorithms may have some periods during which large numbers of messages are generated by different processors, thus temporarily causing some congestion in parts of the network. Because of the time delays required for communication, algorithms are always designed with the goal of minimizing the amount of communication. One way to reduce the execution time overhead associated with communication is to improve the characteristics of the communication network, by adding more direct connecting links and increasing their bandwidth, and also increasing the speed of the communication interfaces. The other complimentary technique is to design the algorithm to suit the topology of the particular network on which it is running, with the goal of minimizing the frequency of communication and the distance traveled by each message.

7.1.3 Communication Delay

The communication time for a message to travel through the network has three major components: transmission time, processing time, and waiting time. The *waiting time* results from delays due to congestion in the communication network, as has already been discussed. The *transmission time* is the time required for the physical transmission of the bits of the message through the communication links. If the message plus the header contains a total of L bits, and each communication link has bandwidth B, then the transmission time per link is L/B. The *processing time* component of the communication delay results from the necessity to perform some computation within each interface for every message. This computation includes error detection using the checksum, and routing decisions based on the source and destination processor numbers. Let us use P to denote the average processing time required per message at each interface. If a message has to traverse m links from source to destination, then the sum of the transmission time and processing time components is $m(L/B + P)$.

In most multicomputer systems, communication is done with a fixed packet size. Messages that exceed this fixed size are broken into several packets, which are transmitted in sequence. This fixed packet size allows fixed-size buffers to be used in the communication interfaces, and generally tends to simplify the internal processing of the communication interface. It also has the advantage of reducing the transmission time for long messages. To understand this phenomenon, assume for now that the processing time is negligible compared to the transmission time, which is therefore the dominant term in the communication delay. If a message containing L bits is segmented into k packets, then each packet contains L/k bits. The time to transmit a single packet through a communication link with bandwidth B is $L/(kB)$. To transmit the entire message through a single communication link requires that all k packets be transmitted, and therefore requires a total time L/B, which is exactly the same as the time to transmit the same message in unsegmented form.

However, when the message has to traverse a path with multiple links, then the segmentation may considerably reduce the total communication time. As soon as each packet is completely received by a communication interface, the packet is immediately transmitted to its next destination on the path. This immediate forwarding of each packet results in a *pipelining* effect, in which the successive packets follow each other along the communication path like a long "worm" moving through the ground. The decreased transmission time results from the parallelism of having many communication links all operating at the same time, using different packets of the message. If the message has k packets, then k links may be functioning in parallel, resulting in an expected transmission speedup factor k. The actual speedup is slightly less than this because of the time required to "fill the pipeline" when the message transmission first begins.

Let T denote the time $L/(kB)$ for each packet to traverse a single communication link. Then the total time required to get all the k packets started along the path is $(k-1)T$. Once this "worm" is fully created, the tail packet will still have to traverse all of the m links between the source and destination processors. The total time for this traversal is mT. Since the tail is the last packet to arrive at the destination, the total communication time is just the sum of the "worm" creation time and the tail traversal time: $(k-1)T + mT = (m+k-1)T$. The time to communicate the unsegmented message was already computed as $mL/B = mkT$. Therefore, the speedup factor resulting from the segmentation is $mk/(m+k-1)$. For example, if the path length m is 12 and the number of packets k is 5, then a communication speedup factor of 3.75 is achieved by using segmentation.

Using this formula for the speedup, one might conclude that continuing to increase k will continue to increase the speedup. The ultimate in this direction will be a packet size of 1 bit, which according to the calculation made above will minimize the communication delay. This has been proposed as a viable communication method and is called *cut-through* routing. In this method, each bit of the message is passed on by the communication interface as soon as it is received. Athas and Seitz [1988] have developed an alternative called *worm-hole* routing, which uses a very small packet size.

The major factor in most multicomputer systems, which prevents this segmentation technique from being taken to its ultimate in this way, is the processing time required at each communication interface. There is generally a large fraction of the processing time that is independent of the packet size. This introduces a component of the communication delay for a message that grows in proportion to the total number of packets. As the packet size is reduced, the transmission time is reduced as described above. However, the processing time is increased. If the packet size is reduced too much, then the increase in processing time will outweigh the corresponding decrease in transmission time. The designers of each multicomputer system will try to balance these two factors to select an optimal packet size for that system. Another factor that tends to limit the minimum packet size is the requirement for adding a small header to each packet. The packet must have a certain minimum size in order to justify the overhead of transmitting the header.

Thus the relationship between the transmission time and processing time components of the communication delay are important parameters in understanding the performance characteristics of any multicomputer. One factor that influences the processing time is how much is done in hardware and how much in software. To reduce the hardware cost, some systems will use a simpler communication interface and involve the processor in some of the higher-level communication functions, such as error detection and routing. This is accomplished by having the communication interface send an interrupt to the processor after each packet has been physically received from the communication link. This interrupt will cause the processor to temporarily suspend execution of the program, and spend a brief time performing some computation to check for errors and make a routing decision. After this brief interruption, the processor will issue the necessary command to the communication interface and then return to executing the program. In such multicomputer systems, the *processing time* component of the communication delay will be one or two orders of magnitude higher than if the processing is done completely in the interface hardware. Also, this requirement to interrupt the processor for each message may significantly slow down the processor and degrade program performance if there is frequent communication.

7.2 MULTICOMPUTER TOPOLOGY

As with all computer architecture, there is a cost–performance tradeoff in the design of the processor communication network in a multicomputer. The delay encountered by a message in traveling between processors will depend on the average communication delay required for transmission along each communication link, and also on the total number of links traversed between the source and destination processors. The number of links traversed will depend to a great extent on the overall structure of the communication network, sometimes called the *topology* of the multicomputer. One important parameter of a multicomputer topology is the number of incident links on each interface, called the *connectivity* of the topology. This is an important factor in determining the cost of the network. Another important parameter is the *diameter* of the topology, defined as the maximum number of links required to transmit a message between the most distant processors. The diameter will be an important factor in the performance of the network.

This section describes a variety of multicomputer topologies with increasing degrees of sophistication. The simpler topologies have lower connectivity and therefore a higher diameter. The more complex topologies have higher connectivity and therefore a lower diameter. These topologies will present a hierarchy of increasing cost and improving performance. It is very important for the parallel programmer to be familiar with the qualities and behavior of various multicomputer topologies. Each topology has its own performance characteristics, and the parallel algorithm must be tailored to suit the particular topology in order to achieve maximum performance. All of the multicomputer topologies described in this section are available in the Multi-Pascal interactive software system that accompanies this text.

7.2.1 Line and Ring Topology

In a *Line* multicomputer topology, the communication interfaces are connected in a straight line, as illustrated in Figure 7.5. It is assumed in the figure that each numbered circle contains a processor, memory, and communication interface. Each line between a pair of circles represents a direct communication link in the network. The detailed internal structure of each component of the network is omitted from this and all future diagrams in this chapter. Only numbered circles with connecting lines are shown in the diagrams. Since it is the processors that are actually the real source and destination of each message, we will refer to "communication" between the processors and "connections" between the processors. When these terms are used, it is assumed that in reality it is the communication interfaces that are physically connected and physically communicating.

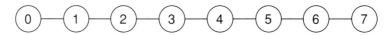

FIGURE 7.5   Line topology.

When two processors are directly connected in a given topology, they are said to be *adjacent* processors. To compare the relative performance characteristics of different topologies, it is assumed that the basic communication delay for adjacent processors is the same in all the topologies. Thus, the relative performance just depends on the *distance* between processors. The *distance* between any pair of processors in a given topology is defined as the number of communication links a message must traverse in the most direct path between the processors. The *diameter* of a topology is defined as the largest distance between any processors in the network. In the *Line* topology of Figure 7.5 with eight processors, the diameter is 7. In general, a line topology with n processors has connectivity 2 and diameter $n - 1$. The distance between any two processors i and j is always $|i - j|$. If the basic communication delay for adjacent processors is T, the time to send a message from processor i to j is simply $T|i - j|$.

Without increasing the cost, the performance of a Line topology can be greatly improved by simply adding one more connecting link from the first to the last processor in the line. This is called a *Ring* topology, as illustrated in Figure 7.6. This one additional connection reduces the average distance between processors by a factor of two. An n processor Ring topology has a diameter of $n/2$, compared to $n - 1$ for the n processor Line topology. In Figure 7.6, the maximum distance is between processors that are directly opposite in the Ring. Thus, at most only half the distance around the Ring must be traveled by a message, whereas, in the Line topology of Figure 7.5, a message traveling from 0 to 7 must pass through all the connecting links in the entire network.

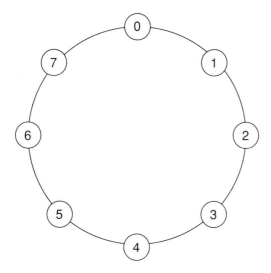

FIGURE 7.6   Ring topology.

7.2.2 Mesh Topology

By increasing the number of communication links connected to each processor, it is possible to reduce the diameter of the network and the average communication delay. One such topology is the two-dimensional *Mesh*, as illustrated in Figure 7.7. This multicomputer topology consists of processors arranged in a two-dimensional array. A given processor at row i and column j is connected to its four immediate neighboring processors to the left, right, above, and below: at locations $(i-1, j)$, $(i+1, j)$, $(i, j-1)$, $(i, j+1)$. All connections are horizontal between adjacent columns, or vertical between adjacent rows, as shown in

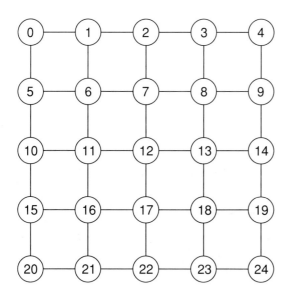

FIGURE 7.7   Two-dimensional mesh topology.

Figure 7.7. There are no diagonal connections. Boundary processors have only two or three immediate neighbors.

In the processor numbering scheme of Figure 7.7, the processors are numbered sequentially by rows, with processor 0 in the upper left corner. This numbering scheme is called *row-major order*. Messages traveling between distant processors must travel along horizontal or vertical paths between intermediate processors. For example, a message traveling from processor 6 to 13 will first travel to processor 11, then to 12, and finally to 13: a total of three steps. The message might also take alternate paths 6–7–8–13 or 6–7–12–13, but the number of steps is still 3. Every pair of processors will have a minimum *path-length* between them, measured by the sum of the row distance and the column distance. If the basic communication delay for adjacent processors is T, then the interprocessor communication time for any pair of processors is just this *path-length* multiplied by T. For an m by m Mesh, the diameter of the network is simply the path-length between processors at opposite corners of the Mesh. This is always $2(m - 1)$.

In a Mesh topology, each row and column is similar to a Line topology. Just as the Line topology was improved by adding an end-around connection to turn it into a Ring, the performance of the Mesh can be improved by adding such connections to each row and column. This will change each row and column from a Line to a Ring. This is illustrated in Figure 7.8. Each processor at the left boundary is connected to its counterpart on the right boundary. Similarly, each processor along the upper boundary is directly connected to its counterpart along the lower boundary. This is called a *Torus* topology. The connectivity of any such Torus topology is always 4, since every processor now has exactly four connecting links. Just as when the Line topology is changed into a Ring, thereby reducing the diameter by a factor of two, this same performance improvement results when a Mesh is changed into a Torus by adding all the wraparound connections. Processors at opposite corners are now separated only by distance 2. The maximum distance in the Torus is

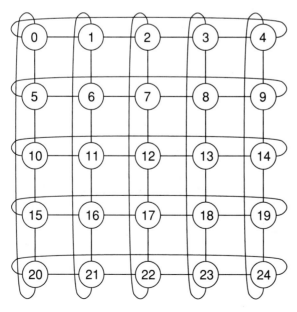

FIGURE 7.8   Torus topology.

between the corner and the center processor. Thus, an *m* by *m* Torus topology will have diameter *m*.

This Mesh pattern may be extended to three dimensions, as illustrated in Figure 7.9. A three-dimensional *Mesh* topology may be visualized as a series of two-dimensional meshes, one behind the other, with connections between the corresponding processors in adjacent 2-D meshes. For subsequent discussion, each of the 2-D meshes is called a *plane*. Each processor position in the three-dimensional Mesh will have three coordinates (i, j, k), where *i* is the row number, *j* is the column number, and *k* is the plane number. As with the two-dimensional mesh topology, each processor has direct connections to its four immediate neighbors in the same plane. In addition, each processor is connected directly to the corresponding processor in the plane in front and behind. For example, a processor with coordinates (i, j, k) has six direct connections to the following processors: $(i - 1, j, k)$, $(i + 1, j, k)$, $(i, j - 1, k)$, $(i, j + 1, k)$, $(i, j, k - 1)$, $(i, j, k + 1)$. Processors at the boundaries will have fewer than six direct connections (either four or five). A 3-D Mesh with m^3 processors has a diameter $3(m - 1)$.

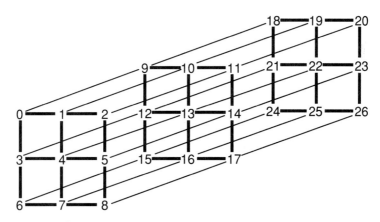

FIGURE 7.9   Three-dimensional mesh topology.

7.2.3 Hypercube Topology

In a Hypercube interconnection topology, the number of processors is always an exact power of 2. If the number of processors is 2^d, then *d* is called the *dimension* of the hypercube. Each processor will have a number whose binary representation has *d* bits. The definition of the Hypercube interconnection scheme is simple: any given processor with binary number *i* will have direct connections to all processors with binary number *j*, such that *j* differs from *i* in exactly one binary digit. For example, a hypercube with $d = 3$ will have eight processors numbered 000, 001, 010, 011, 100, 101, 110, 111. Processor 000 will have direct connections to the following processors: 001, 010, 100. Processor 011 will have connections to the following processors: 111, 001, 010.

Figure 7.10 shows a Hypercube with dimension $d = 3$. For this low dimension, the hypercube appears similar to the 3-D Mesh topology. However, with higher dimensional Hypercubes, the structure is quite different. In a Mesh, each processor has a fixed number of connections, independent of the size of the Mesh. In a Hypercube, the number of

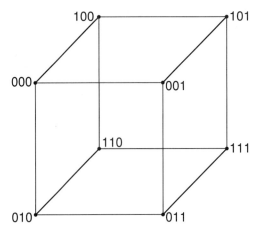

FIGURE 7.10   Hypercube topology with dimension 3.

connections to each processor grows as the number of processors grows. The number of direct connections for each processor in a hypercube is always equal to the dimension of the Hypercube. Figure 7.11 shows a Hypercube topology with 16 processors and dimension 4. Notice that each processor has four direct connections to other processors, as compared to Figure 7.10, which has only three direct connections per processor. A Hypercube with 128 processors has dimension 7, and therefore each processor will have seven direct connections. The additional connections in the higher-dimensional Hypercubes will reduce the average communication delay as compared to the Mesh topology.

The distance between processors in a Hypercube is clearly equal to the number of bit positions in which their processor numbers differ. For example, in Figure 7.10, processor 000 is two steps from processor 011. For processor 000 to communicate with 011, it will first send the message to its immediate neighbor 001, which will forward the message to its immediate neighbor 011. Thus, the total communication from 000 to 011 takes two steps. For $d = 3$, each processor will have three immediate neighbors, and the maximum distance between processors is three steps. In general, for a Hypercube of dimension d, the

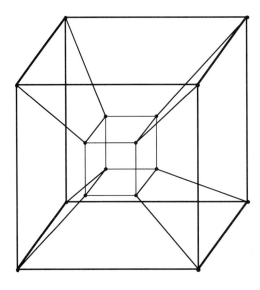

FIGURE 7.11   Hypercube topology with dimension 4.

processors will each have d immediate neighbors and a maximum distance of d steps between processors. Thus, the connectivity of the network is d, and the diameter of the network is d.

A Hypercube topology may be defined with a simple recursive construction rule. A Hypercube of dimension 1 is defined as having two processors, numbered 0 and 1 with a single direct connection between them. A Hypercube of dimension $d + 1$ is defined recursively by the following construction procedure:

1. Create an exact duplicate of the Hypercube with dimension d, including processor numbers.

2. Create a direct connection between processors with the same number in the original and duplicate.

3. Append a binary 1 to the left of each processor number in the duplicate, and a binary 0 to left of each processor number in the original.

This recursive construction is illustrated for dimension 1-3 in Figure 7.12. To create a Hypercube of dimension 4, the rules say to duplicate the pattern for dimension 3, and connect the corresponding positions in the original and duplicate. This was already shown in Figure 7.11. This recursive construction rule gives some insight into the Hypercube structure and will be useful later as an aid in designing efficient algorithms for execution on Hypercube multicomputers.

Dimension 1:
0   1

Dimension 2:

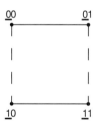

Dimension 3:

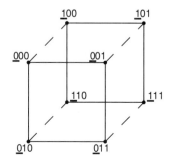

FIGURE 7.12   Recursive hypercube construction.

The following chart summarizes and compares the characteristics of each of topologies by considering the *connectivity* and the *diameter*. The connectivity is a measure of the relative cost of the topologies, and the diameter is a measure of the relative performance. For comparison purposes, it is assumed that each topology has a total of n processors. The topologies are listed in order of increasing cost and improving performance:

Topology	Connectivity	Diameter
Line	2	$n-1$
Ring	2	$n/2$
2D-Mesh	2–4	$2(n^{1/2}-1)$
Torus	4	$n^{1/2}$
3D-Mesh	3–6	$3(n^{1/3}-1)$
Hypercube	$\log n$	$\log n$

7.3 BROADCASTING AND AGGREGATION

To gain a deeper understanding of the structure and relationship of the various multicomputer topologies, it will be useful to consider the implementation of two important operations that occur frequently in a wide variety of parallel algorithms: broadcasting and aggregation. These operations were already discussed in Chapter 6 with respect to one of the major organizational techniques for parallel programs: Compute, Aggregate, and Broadcast. Iterative numerical algorithms, such as the Jacobi Relaxation method, usually require a periodic convergence test to determine if the program should terminate. This involves collecting or "aggregating" a local convergence test from each processor, and then broadcasting the collective result back to each processor.

For purposes of this section, a *broadcast* is defined as the operation of distributing a copy of a data item from processor 0 to all the other processors in the multicomputer. An *aggregation* is defined as collecting a data item from each processor, and combining these into a single data item by successive application of an operation that combines a pair of data items into a single data item. It is assumed that the combining operation has the "associative" property, which means that the final result is independent of the order of combining the data items. The following are examples of such combining operations: +, *, *AND, OR, max, min*. Recall that in the Jacobi Relaxation program, the convergence testing was done by applying the combining operation "AND" to the Boolean *mydone* produced by each process. The result was a global Boolean indicating whether the whole program should terminate.

It is interesting that broadcasting and aggregation are very similar operations, except that they go in the opposite direction. Broadcasting spreads a single value to all the processors, and aggregation collects a value from each processor and combines them into a single value. Broadcasting moves out from processor 0 to all the other processors, and aggregation moves in from all the processors to processor 0. In a multicomputer, the overall computational method and the computing time are almost identical for broadcasting and aggregation, except that the data flows in opposite directions in the two operations.

With broadcasting the data value flows out from processor 0 to neighboring processors, where it is copied and passed on to their neighbors, and so on, until every processor receives a copy. An aggregation is like a broadcast running backwards in time, with values flowing toward processor 0 instead of away.

This property is illustrated in Figures 7.13 and 7.14. Figure 7.13 shows the successive stages of a broadcast operation on a Line multicomputer topology. The data value is first sent from processor 0 to processor 1. Processor 1 keeps a copy and sends a copy on to processor 2, and so on, until the data value finally reaches processor n at the far right end of the Line. Assume that the communication delay between neighboring processors is T time units. Also, assume that the computation time required at each processor to copy the data value is negligible compared to the communication delay. Then the total execution time for this broadcast operation on a Line topology with $n + 1$ processors is nT.

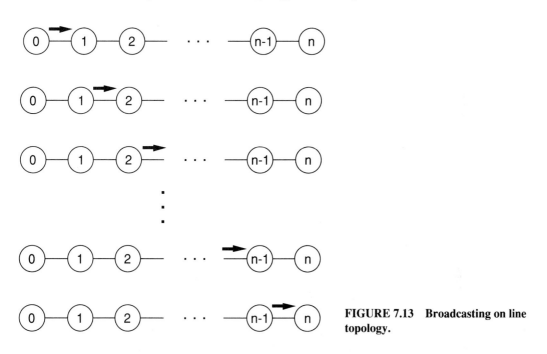

FIGURE 7.13 Broadcasting on line topology.

The aggregation operation is shown in Figure 7.14. Each processor has its own data value initially. For illustrative purposes, assume that it is a Boolean data value, and the combining operation is logical *AND*. During the first step, processor n will send its Boolean value to processor $n - 1$. Processor $n - 1$ will then combine this incoming Boolean with its own Boolean value by applying a logical *AND*. The resultant Boolean value will be sent by processor $n - 1$ to its left neighbor. This communication and *AND* operation continues at each successive processor, until the final result reaches processor 0. If we assume that the execution time of the *AND* operation is negligible compared to the communication time, the total execution for this aggregation operation is exactly the same as the broadcast operation: nT.

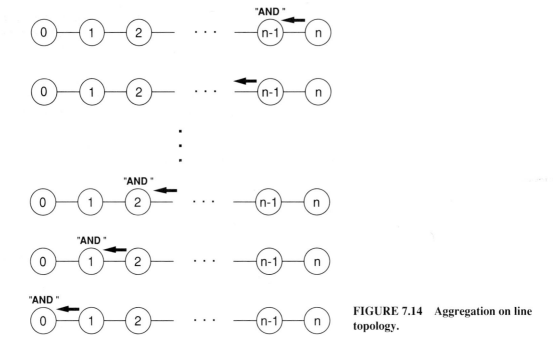

FIGURE 7.14   Aggregation on line topology.

For a Ring topology the broadcast operation can be performed in half the time, as illustrated in Figure 7.15. Processor 0 sends a copy of the data value in opposite directions around the Ring. Thus, the total number of communication steps required for an n processor Ring is only $n/2$. As in the Line topology, the aggregation operation is the opposite of the broadcast. In Figure 7.15, processors 4 and 5 both begin the aggregation by sending their own data value to their immediate neighbor, in the direction of processor 0. Both sides of the Ring are computing in parallel, and therefore the total time is half of what it was in the Line topology.

For the 2-D Mesh topology, a broadcast is done by sending the data value across the top row of processors, thereby reaching the top of each column. Then the data travels down each column in parallel. This is illustrated in Figure 7.16. The dark arrows show the direction in which the data value flows. The total time required for the broadcast is proportional to the length of the path from the source processor 0 in the upper left corner of the Mesh, to the processor in the lower right corner. In an m by m Mesh, this path length is $2(m-1)$, which is exactly equal to the diameter of the network. This same property has been true of the broadcast time in the Line and Ring, also. In the Line, Ring, and 2-D Mesh topologies, the broadcast and aggregation execution times are just the diameter of the topology times the communication delay along a single link. From the definition of the diameter, it is clear that this will determine the theoretical minimum time required for a broadcast or aggregation. For all of the topologies, it is possible to actually achieve this optimal execution time.

For an aggregation on a 2-D Mesh, just reverse the direction of the arrows shown for the broadcast in Figure 7.16. For a Torus topology of the same dimension, both the broadcast and aggregation can be done in half the time. The technique used is similar to the

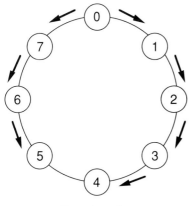

Broadcasting

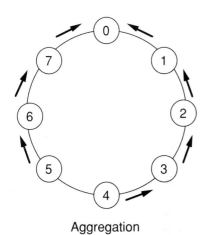

Aggregation

FIGURE 7.15 Broadcasting and aggregation on ring topology.

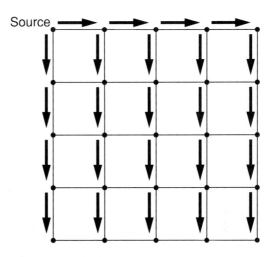

Source

FIGURE 7.16 Broadcasting on 2-D mesh.

2-D Mesh: send the data across the top row, and then down all the columns simultaneously. In a 2-D Mesh, each row or column is a "line" structure. However, the addition of wraparound connections in the Torus converts each row and column into a "ring" structure. Thus, the time to traverse each row or column is half as much in the Torus by using the same technique as in the Ring topology (see Figure 7.15). For an m by m Torus, the number of communication steps to transmit data across the top row is $m/2$, and similarly for a column. If the communication delay for a single link is T time units, then both the broadcast and aggregation on a Torus require execution time $Tm/2$. Just as with the Line, Ring, and 2-D Mesh, this time is T multiplied by the diameter of the topology.

For a broadcast on a 3-D Mesh, the source processor 0 sends a copy of the data item to the upper left corner of each plane. Then the broadcast throughout each plane takes place in parallel with all the other planes. The procedure used on each plane is just the same as the 2-D Mesh, since each plane is essentially a 2-D Mesh with some additional connections. For a $3 \times 3 \times 3$ Mesh, the broadcast operation is illustrated in Figure 7.17. The operation has a considerable amount of parallelism, reducing the overall execution time to the cube root of the total number of processors. For an $m \times m \times m$ 3-D Mesh, the broadcast operation has execution time $3T(m - 1)$. The aggregation time is the same.

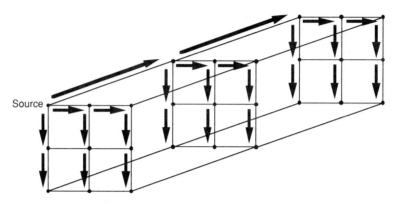

FIGURE 7.17   Broadcasting on 3-D mesh.

In a Hypercube topology with dimension d, the theoretical minimum for the broadcast or aggregation time is Td. To achieve this minimum requires an algorithm based on the recursive definition of the Hypercube structure given in the previous section on Hypercube topology. Referring back to Figure 7.12, we see that the basis of the recursive Hypercube definition is the duplication of the previous structure at each stage. To move from stage n to $n + 1$, create a copy of the entire structure of stage n, and then connect the corresponding points in the original and the duplicate. This can be used as the basis of a recursive broadcast algorithm. The recursive Hypercube definition can actually be viewed as a "construction" algorithm, where the Hypercube is actually being built up by adding new processors and connections at each stage. To change this construction algorithm into a broadcast algorithm, the addition of a connection between corresponding processors in the original and duplicate is replaced by a "communication" from the original to its corresponding processor in the duplicate.

The successive stages of this recursive broadcast algorithm are illustrated in Figure 7.18. In step 1, the source processor 0 sends a copy of the data item to processor 1. In the next step, both processor 0 and 1 send to their corresponding processors in the "duplicate." Each processor can find its corresponding duplicate by simply appending a binary "1" to the left of its own processor number. In step 3, each of these four processors that now already has a copy of the data item sends a copy to its "duplicate," which is chosen by again appending a binary "1" to left of the processor number (see Figure 7.18). All four of these communications in step 3 occur in parallel. Now in the next step 4, each processor that has the data value sends a copy to its corresponding "duplicate," again chosen by appending a binary 1 to the processor number. If the Hypercube has dimension d, it is clear that this recursive algorithm will require d steps to reach all the processors in the Hypercube.

Since the Hypercube has dimensions d, there are a total of d bit positions in each processor number. These bit positions can be numbered from right to left. From the

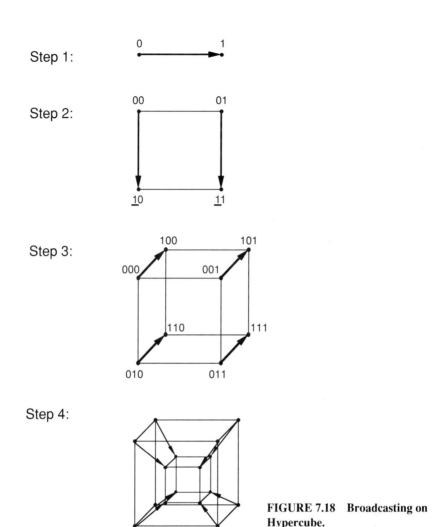

Step 1:

Step 2:

Step 3:

Step 4:

FIGURE 7.18   Broadcasting on Hypercube.

recursive broadcast algorithm illustrated in Figure 7.18, it is clear that the processors involved in communication during each stage i are just those with a processor number having 0 in bit positions $i + 1$ to d. Of the processors that do communicate during stage i, those with a 0 in bit position i are senders, and those with a 1 in bit position i are receivers. In light of these simple observations, it is possible to write a simple iterative procedure to be executed at each processor for implementing the broadcast. This is considered in one of the exercises at the end of this chapter.

Just as in all the previous topologies, the aggregation algorithm can be defined by simply viewing the broadcast backward in time, with all the communication directions reversed. For a Hypercube with n processors, both the broadcast and aggregation algorithms have execution time $O(\log n)$, which is the dimension of the Hypercube. It is interesting that these algorithms described in Figure 7.18 are very similar to the tournament algorithm described in Chapter 6. This tournament algorithm performs an aggregation followed by a broadcast in time $O(\log n)$. This tournament method can also be adapted to perform an aggregation or broadcast on a Hypercube. This is considered in the exercises of this chapter. The following chart summarizes the execution time required for broadcasting or aggregation on each of the topologies with n processors:

Topology	Broadcast Time
Line	$O(n)$
Ring	$O(n)$
2-D Mesh	$O(n^{1/2})$
Torus	$O(n^{1/2})$
3-D Mesh	$O(n^{1/3})$
Hypercube	$O(\log n)$

7.4 HYPERCUBE EMBEDDINGS

Each parallel algorithm will have its own natural communication structure when executed on a multicomputer. If the *logical* communication structure used in the algorithm matches the *physical* communication structure of the multicomputer topology, then performance is enhanced. For example, consider the *pipeline* algorithms described in Chapter 4, including Back Substitution. In these pipeline algorithms, the processes are conceptually viewed as being arranged in a straight line, with communication only between immediate neighbors in this line. This *logical* pipeline process structure is easily mapped onto a *physical* Line multicomputer topology—the two structures are essentially identical. With this mapping, processes that communicate directly in the algorithm will always find a direct communication link between the physical processors where they are executing. There will never be any need for intermediate processors to forward messages.

The Ring topology is also equally suitable for executing pipeline algorithms. The process pipeline is arranged around the Ring just as it is in the Line topology. With respect to the 2-D Mesh topology, the process pipeline does not physically match the Mesh structure. However, the pipeline can be embedded in the 2-D Mesh so that adjacent processes in the pipeline have a direct communication link in the Mesh. This is illustrated in Figure 7.19, where the arrows show the adjacent processors in the pipeline. This linear ordering of the processors in a 2-D Mesh is sometimes called a *snake-like* ordering, as opposed to the *row-major* ordering originally shown in Figure 7.7. By using a similar ordering technique, it is also possible to embed a Ring structure in a Mesh, provided that the number of processors is even.

This embedding of a Line in a Mesh is a specific example of an important concept in multicomputer programming called *topological embedding*. A topology X can be *embedded* in a topology Y if there is some specific mapping of processors in X to processors in Y, such that every communication link in topology X has a corresponding communication link in Y. A topological embedding also requires that the number of processors in the two topologies be the same. Among the topologies discussed here, it is generally true that the topologies of lower connectivity can be embedded in the topologies with higher connectivity. The most notable exception is the 3-D Mesh, which may not accept embedding of Torus or 2-D Mesh topologies. The most interesting topology with respect to embeddings

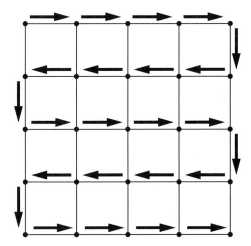

FIGURE 7.19   Line embedded in a mesh.

is the Hypercube, because it has the highest connectivity. The Hypercube has the important property that any of the topologies discussed in this chapter can be embedded in a Hypercube, provided that the number of processors is an exact power of two. This "power of two" requirement is necessary because Hypercubes always have a number of processors that is an exact power of two.

Recall that in a Hyercube, each processor has direct connections to all processors whose number differs in exactly one binary digit. A useful concept with respect to Hypercube embeddings is the *Gray Code*. A Gray Code is a sequence of numbers such that each successive number differs from the previous one in only one binary digit. For example, the following is a Gray Code for the numbers 0 to 7:

```
000 001 011 010 110 111 101 100
```

This Gray Code can be used for embedding a Line topology with eight processors into a Hypercube with eight processors. Since each of the binary processor numbers in the above Gray Code sequence differs from its left and right neighbors in only one bit position, there is a direct connection in the Hypercube between every adjacent pair of processors in the above Gray Code ordering. Thus, they form a Line topology. Notice that the last number in the above sequence differs from the first number in only one binary digit. Therefore, there is also a direct connection in the Hypercube between the two endpoints of this line of processors, and they define a Ring topology, as well as a Line topology.

The above sequence is called a 3-bit Gray Code because each number in the sequence has three binary digits. In general, the k-bit Gray Code G_k is defined recursively as follows:

$$G_1 \text{ is the sequence: } 0 \quad 1$$

For all $k > 1$, G_k is the sequence constructed by the following rules:

1. Construct a new sequence by appending a 0 to the left of all members of G_{k-1}.
2. Construct a new sequence by reversing G_{k-1} and then appending a 1 to the left of all members of the sequence.

3. G_k is the concatentation of the sequences defined in steps 1 and 2.

Applying these rules to the 3-bit Gray Code shown previously, step 1 results in the following sequence:

$$0000 \quad 0001 \quad 0011 \quad 0010 \quad 0110 \quad 0111 \quad 0101 \quad 0100$$

Step 2 results in the following sequence:

$$1100 \quad 1101 \quad 1111 \quad 1110 \quad 1010 \quad 1011 \quad 1001 \quad 1000$$

Concatenating these two sequences gives a 4-bit Gray Code. Notice that each number in the sequence differs from its neighbors by exactly one bit. Therefore, this Gray Code can be used to embed a 16 processor Line or Ring in a Hypercube of dimension 4 as follows:

$$0000 — 0001 — 0011 — 0010 — 0110 — 0111 — 0101 — 0100$$

$$1000 — 1001 — 1011 — 1010 — 1110 — 1111 — 1101 — 1100$$

Notice in the above arrangement that there is also a vertical relationship between the processor numbers. All the pairs of processors that are directly above and below each other in this arrangement also differ in exactly one bit position, and are therefore directly connected in the underlying Hypercube topology. By arranging the same 4-bit Gray Code in four rows and four columns, it is possible to create a 2-D Mesh topology, as shown in Figure 7.20. The connecting arrows in the figure identify the Gray Code sequence. Notice that each processor in this arrangement differs from all its immediate neighbors by exactly one bit. Therefore, each processor has direct physical connections in the Hypercube to all its immediate neighbors in the mesh. This *snake-like* arrangement of the Gray Code sequence can be used to embed any 2-D Mesh in a Hypercube topology with the same number of processors. For an m by m Mesh, the number of processors is m^2, and therefore the dimension of required Hypercube is $2 \log m$.

The processor arrangement of Figure 7.20 also defines a 4 by 4 Torus, because all the boundary processors differ from the opposite boundary by exactly one bit. By applying this

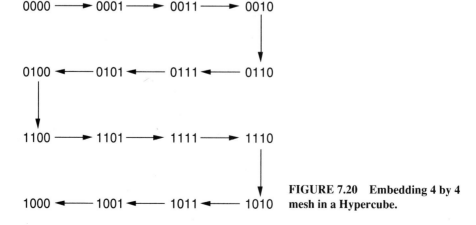

FIGURE 7.20   Embedding 4 by 4 mesh in a Hypercube.

snake-like ordering of the Gray Code, it is possible to embed any 2-D Mesh or Torus in a Hypercube topology with the same number of processors, provided that the number of processors is an exact power of two. To create the embedding, first compute a Gray Code ordering for all the processors in the Hypercube. Then wind the Gray Code sequence into a two-dimensional snake-like order that gives an equal number of rows and columns. The result has all the connections necessary for a 2-D Mesh or Torus.

The success of this embedding method lies with the recursive definition of the Gray Code. The code is created by continuing to reverse and duplicate the same pattern, and then adding a single 0 or 1 bit to differentiate the original and its duplicate. Thus, a Gray Code sequence $p_1, p_2, \ldots, p_n$ will define the next Gray Code sequence with twice the length as follows:

$$0p_1, 0p_2, \ldots, 0p_n, 1p_n, 1p_{n-1}, \ldots, 1p_1$$

If this sequence is folded over on itself with a snake-like pattern, the following is the result:

$$0p_1 — 0p_2 — 0p_3 — \ldots — 0p_n$$

$$1p_1 — 1p_2 — 1p_3 — \ldots — 1p_n$$

Notice in the above that this snake-like folding reverses the order of the second half of the sequence and therefore places each number directly below its corresponding number in the first half of the sequence. Thus, each pair of vertically opposite numbers differs in exactly one binary digit. If we now again fold each of the top and bottom sequences to get a snake with four rows, the same correspondence will result for all vertically adjacent numbers. Further confirmation of this interesting property of Gray Codes is considered in one of the exercises at the end of this chapter.

This snake-like Gray Code ordering can also be used to embed any 3-D Mesh into a Hypercube with the same number of processors. The "snake" moves down the front plane of the 3-D Mesh just as it would for a 2-D Mesh; then it moves up the second plane using the same snake-like pattern, but moving in the opposite direction. After reaching the top of the second plane, it snakes down the third plane, up the fourth plane, and so on. In this way, a single Gray Code ordering of all the processors in any Hypercube can be used to embed a 3-D Mesh with the same number of processors. This technique is illustrated in Figure 7.21, which shows a $4 \times 4 \times 4$ 3-D Mesh embedded in a Hypercube of dimension 6.

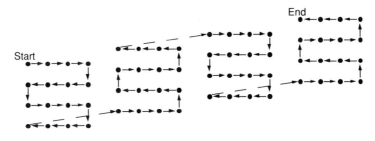

FIGURE 7.21   3-D mesh embedded in Hypercube.

This section has shown that the Gray Code ordering technique allows any of the topologies discussed in this chapter to be embedded in the Hypercube topology. This includes Line, Ring, 2-D Mesh, Torus, and 3-D Mesh. Therefore, any algorithm having a logical communication structure that corresponds to any of the other topologies will run just as efficiently on a Hypercube with the same number of processors. If the algorithm contains some global communication operations, such as broadcast or aggregation, then the additional connections of the Hypercube will allow it to run even more efficiently than on the other topologies. The disadvantage of the Hypercube is that the cost of the communication network grows as the logarithm of the number of processors, whereas in all the other topologies, the cost grows linearly with the number of processors.

7.5 SUMMARY

The purpose of this chapter has been to provide an overview of the architecture of a major class of parallel computers called *multicomputers*. Multicomputers are distinguished by the property that each processor has its own local memory, and there is no shared memory. Each processor computes with its own local memory very much in the way the processor of a sequential computer interacts with the memory. This is the origin of the term "multi"computer. In a multicomputer, there is also a communication network connecting the processors and allowing them to exchange data while computing. This communication provides the means for the processors to interact and work together on a single computational problem, and thereby to reduce the overall execution time of the computation.

From the point of view of a programmer, the most important property of the interprocessor communication network is that a significant amount of time is required for data communication. The implications of this communication delay with respect to program design and organization are considered in the following two chapters. The communication between processors is facilitated through a hardware communication interface attached to each processor. The interfaces are connected to each other with communication links capable of electronically transmitting a sequence of bits between two interfaces. In addition to the actual physical transmission, a mechanism for error detection and correction is required. Interfaces that are not physically connected by a link can also communicate by having intermediate interfaces forward the message. In a complex interconnection network, this also requires the interface (in conjunction with the processor) to make routing decisions for the messages. All of these activities—physical transmission, error detection, and routing—require some time and result in a communication delay for sending data between processors during a computation.

To try to balance cost against performance, a variety of interconnection topologies have been devised for the communication network. The goal is to minimize the number of connecting links per processor, while also keeping the communication time between processors as short as possible. There is a hierarchy of multicomputer topologies with increasing cost and improving performance: Line, Ring, 2-D Mesh, Torus, 3-D Mesh, Hypercube. All of the topologies have a very regular interconnection pattern to help simplify the programming process. All of the topologies except the Hypercube have a connectivity that is constant and not dependent on the total number of processors. In the Line and Ring topologies, the diameter of the network grows linearly with the number of processors. In the 2-D Mesh and Torus, the diameter grows as the square root of the number of processors, and in the 3-D Mesh, grows as the cube root of the number of processors. In the Hypercube, both the connectivity and diameter grow as the logarithm of the number of processors, making it the most costly but also giving it the best performance.

To help compare the use and relative performance of these topologies, two important operations were considered: broadcasting and aggregation. These are good measures of the overall quality of a topology because they are both "global" operations that involve bringing all the processors together through collective communication. The execution time required for broadcasting and aggregation is proportional to the diameter of the topology.

The final topic considered in this chapter is topological embedding. The Hypercube topology is important in this regard because it will accept an embedding of any of the other topologies described in the chapter. This means that any parallel program that performs at a certain level on one of the other topologies will perform at least as well on a Hypercube. Informally, one could say that the Hypercube "contains" all of the other topologies, plus some additional connections to further improve the performance. The Hypercube embedding is done with the help of Gray Code ordering of the binary processor numbers, in which successive numbers differ in only one binary digit.

Now that some understanding of multicomputer architecture has been gained through this chapter, the next chapter can begin to describe general programming techniques for multicomputers. The primary concern in multicomputer programs is to limit the performance degradation caused by the communication delays.

REFERENCES

The various technical issues arising in computer communication networks are thoroughly discussed in Tanenbaum [1989], including physical data transmission, error detection and correction, routing, and congestion. The texts by Siegel [1984] and Ullman [1984] both contain extensive coverage of processor interconnection networks and multicomputer topology.

The Hypercube broadcasing algorithm described in this chapter is from Fox, et al. [1988]. The Gray Code Hypercube embedding technique can be found in Chan and Saad [1986] and in Ranka and Sahni [1989].

EXERCISES

1. In a communication network, assume that two processors X and Y are separated by m communication links. This means that a message traveling from X to Y must traverse m links along the way. Assume also that the time to transmit a given message through a single link is T time units. Clearly, the minimum communication time for a message to be sent from X to Y is mT time units. However, sometimes during the running of a program, the actual communication time is much longer than this minimum. Explain all the possible causes of the additional time.

2. Consider a routing technique to help reduce congestion in a communication network. In this technique, a given communication interface will first select all connecting links with the following properties:

(a) Sending the message through the link will move it closer to its goal.

(b) The communication interface at the other side of the link is not "congested"—it does not have a long queue of messages waiting to be sent.

If there is more than one such link, then a random choice is made between them. If there are no links that have the above two properties, then a random choice is made from among all links that have property (b). If there are no links with property (a), then a random choice is made among all links with property (a).

This routing algorithm does help avoid and reduce congestion in the network. However, it has the undesirable property that arbitrarily long delays may result during communication. There is no limit to the number of link traversals that a message may encounter in traveling between its source and goal. Explain in detail the reasons for this "arbitrarily long delay" property. Describe a simple scenario which shows how a message might have to traverse a very large number of links before reaching its goal.

3. To help avoid congestion and to balance the flow of messages in a communications network, one simple routing technique is to use random selection. At each communication interface, it is determined which connecting links will move the message closer to its goal. If there is more than one such link, then a random choice is made from among them. This technique results in the undesirable property that messages sent from the same source to the same goal may arrive in a different sequence than they were sent. Explain in detail the reasons for this property. Describe a simple scenario that shows how this can happen.

4. A multicomputer communication network has links with bandwidth B. Communication is done by segmenting each message into packets of size s. The processing time per packet in each communication interface is P. The processing at each interface can be done in parallel with physical communication on any of its connecting links.

(a) Give an algebraic expression for the total time to communicate a message of length L between two processors separated by m communication links. (Assume there are no congestion delays.)

(b) Use the above expression to compute the optimal packet size to minimize the communication delay. For simplicity, assume that L is an exact multiple of s.

(c) Repeat part (a), assuming that the full attention of the communication interface is needed during transmission or reception of any packet. Therefore, processing in the interface cannot occur in parallel with either transmission or reception.

5. A computer manufacturer has just introduced a new model of its multicomputer, in which a communications coprocessor has been added to each communication interface to assist in the communication. No other changes have been made. The following two facts are observed regarding the performance of this new model:

(a) The communication delays are the same as in the previous model.

(b) The performance of programs that do a lot of communications is much better on the new model.

Give a plausible explanation for these two facts.

6. (a) The text states that the diameter of a 3-D Mesh topology with n processors is $3(n^{1/3} - 1)$. Show in detail that this is correct.

(b) Just as a 2-D Mesh can be enhanced by adding wraparound connections between processors on the opposite boundaries, a 3-D Mesh can also be enhanced in the same way. Processors along all the six outer boundary faces of the Mesh are connected to their counterparts on the opposite boundary face. This makes the connectivity of every processor exactly equal to six. What is the diameter of such an "enhanced" 3-D Mesh with n processors? Explain your answer.

7. In a *Tree* Topology, the processors are connected in a binary tree pattern with the main processor 0 at the root of the tree.
   (a) What is the connectivity of this Tree topology?
   (b) For a Tree topology with n processors, what is the diameter?
   (c) It appears that this topology achieves both low connectivity and low diameter. However, for algorithms with frequent communication, the Tree topology has a serious problem that degrades performance significantly. Describe the nature and cause of this performance degradation.

8. Assume that the time for transmitting a message through a single connecting link is always exactly T time units. In a Line topology, the communication time for sending a message from processor number i to processor number j will be $T|i - j|$. Derive a similar formula for the communication time between any two processors in each of the following topologies:
   (a) An $m \times m$ 2-D Mesh
   (b) An $m \times m \times m$ 3-D Mesh

9. Figure 7.11 shows the structure of a Hypercube with dimension 4. Complete the diagram by writing the four-bit processor number of each of the 16 processors.

10. For the Torus topology of Figure 7.8, describe an optimal broadcast algorithm for processor 0 to distribute a copy of a data item to every other processor. Draw the broadcast pattern by adding arrows to Figure 7.8, as was done for the other topologies in Figures 7.13–7.17.

11. In a *multinode broadcast*, each processor broadcasts its own data item to every other processor. Consider the problem of a multinode broadcast on a Line topology.
    (a) Assuming that each communication link can handle only one message at a time, describe an efficient multinode broadcast algorithm. What is the total execution time for this algorithm?
    (b) Repeat part (a), assuming that each communication link can send messages in opposite directions simultaneously.

12. Write a Pascal function "Delay(Source,Destination)" that will take two processor numbers in a Hypercube topology as input parameters. The function will compute the number of connecting links that a message must travel in being sent between these two processors in the Hypercube. Assume that the dimension of the Hypercube is d.

13. The concept of 2-D and 3-D Mesh can be generalized to include meshes of higher dimensions. For simplicity, assume that the size of any given mesh is always equal in all dimensions. This means for example that a 4-D Mesh will be $m \times m \times m \times m$. Answer each of the following questions with respect to an arbitrary mesh with d dimensions and a total of n processors:
    (a) What is the connectivity?
    (b) What is the diameter?
    (c) Assuming that the basic communication time for any connecting link is always T time units, what is the time required for an optimal broadcast?
    (d) Describe the structure of an optimal broadcast algorithm.

14. Figure 7.21 shows the embedding of a 3-D Mesh in a Hypercube using a snake-like arrangement of the Gray Code sequence. Determine the binary processor number for each processor in this figure and verify that they do have all the needed connections to form a 3-D Mesh.

15. Write down a 5-bit Gray Code, which is a sequence of 32 5-bit numbers.

16. Write a Pascal procedure ComputeGray(n: INTEGER), which computes the values for an n-bit Gray Code and stores the results in an array *GrayCode*. Each number can be represented in the array as an ordinary integer value, but the sequence of numbers should correspond to the Gray Code sequence. For example, the 2-bit Gray Code sequence is 0, 1, 3, 2.

Run and test the program, using the Multi-Pascal interactive system. Try to make the program as efficient as possible.

17. In this chapter, a Hypercube broadcast algorithm is described. Write a simple iterative Pascal procedure "Broadcast(i)" that can run on each processor number i to carry out this broadcast. To perform communication, use the following two operations:

Send(M, j)   sends data value M to processor number j.

Receive(M)   receives the next incoming data value and stores it in variable M.

For simplicity, assume that a single integer data value is being broadcast from processor 0 to all the other processors in the Hypercube.

18. The Tournament technique described in Chapter 6 is essentially performing an aggregation followed by a broadcast. In this technique, every pair of communicating processes always differ in their processor number by exactly one bit. Therefore, this method could be adapted to perform an aggregation or broadcast on a Hypercube topology.

  (a) Describe a simple Hypercube broadcast algorithm based on this Tournament method. Draw the structure of the broadcast on the Hypercube of Figure 7.11. (*Hint*: This method is almost the same as the broadcast algorithm given in this chapter. Only the sequence of communication partners for each processor is different.)

  (b) Compare this Tournament broadcast method to the Hypercube broadcast algorithm given in this chapter. Explain the differences.

8

Message-Passing Programs

The discussion of multicomputer architecture in the previous chapter has provided a basis for a consideration of multicomputer programming techniques. The most important characteristics of a multicomputer are the local memory attached to each processor and the processor communication network. Because of the absence of a shared memory in multicomputers, a different style of parallel programming is required. For the multicomputer programs to perform efficiently, their overall organization must reflect the overall character of multicomputer architecture.

When programming a *multiprocessor*, the programmer conceptually views his program as a collection of processes accessing a central pool of shared variables. In a *multicomputer*, the programmer must view his program as a collection of processes, each with their own private local variables, plus the ability to send and receive data from other processes through *message-passing*. In this *message-passing* style of parallel programming, processes do not have access to any common shared variables. Each process computes on its own with its local variables, and occasionally will send or receive data from other processes. The main purpose of this chapter is to introduce this *message-passing* style of multicomputer programming, and show how it is done when the Multi-Pascal language is used.

The Multi-Pascal language is easily adapted to writing programs for multicomputers. In the Multi-Pascal language, shared data values are stored in the shared variables accessible by many processes in parallel. When Multi-Pascal is implemented on a multicomputer, no shared variables are permitted. Each process has only *local* variables, as a reflection of the local physical memory attached to each physical processor. Each process computes using its own local variables. In a multicomputer implementation of Multi-Pascal, communication between processes is done through *ports* associated with each process. The usage and properties of these communication ports are almost identical to channel variables, the

183

main difference being the restriction that only one process may receive messages from a given port. The elimination of shared variables and the introduction of communication ports converts the Multi-Pascal language from a multiprocessor language to a multicomputer language. As we see in this chapter, this change in the language forces a *message-passing* style of programming, which is necessary to achieve good performance on a multicomputer.

Another important issue discussed in this chapter is the selection and specification of various multicomputer topologies when the Multi-Pascal interactive system that accompanies this text is used. All of the multicomputer topologies discussed in Chapter 7 are included in the Multi-Pascal simulation system, including Line, Ring, Mesh, Torus, and Hypercube. When running a program using the Multi-Pascal system, one can select the desired multicomputer topology with parameters to specify the number of processors and the basic communication delay for connecting links. Details are given in Appendix B. The Multi-Pascal system has a sophisticated communication model for multicomputers, including a consideration of congestion in the communication network.

Because of the long time delay involved in message passing between processors, the performance of a program will be critically dependent on the placement of data and processes with respect to the physical processors. Severe performance degradation can result if processes are required frequently to wait for messages to arrive from distant processors. The nature of these message delays is also very much dependent on the particular multicomputer topology. Therefore, the Multi-Pascal language has a special feature to allow the program to choose explicitly the processor where any given process will be executed. This gives the programmer the ability to optimize program performance for a specific multicomputer topology.

8.1 COMMUNICATION PORTS

The basic feature that distinguishes a message-passing program is the lack of centrally shared variables accessible to all the processes. In a multiprocessor, there is a physically shared memory, which can be directly read or written by any physical processor. This *physical* architecture of the machine is reflected in a *conceptual* software structure, in which software processes share access to a central pool of *shared variables*. Any software process is free to read or write any shared variable at any time, subject to possible delays due to memory contention on the physical level. This conceptual parallel programming model is the one used in all the previous chapters of this text, which dealt with multiprocessor programming.

When one is programming a multicomputer, a completely different conceptual software model is needed because of the lack of a shared physical memory. In a multicomputer, each physical processor has its own private local memory for reading and writing data values. The processors are physically connected by a network, which can transmit blocks of data from one process to another. All physical interaction between processors is by sending messages through this interconnection network. No processor has direct access to any local memory except its own. If a processor wants to use some data stored in the local memory of a remote processor, that remote processor must read the data from the local memory and send it as a message through the network.

To help the programmer write efficient programs for these multicomputers, it is useful to have a conceptual software model that reflects the physical architecture. For this reason, the Multi-Pascal language does not have shared variables when implemented on a multicomputer. In previous chapters dealing with multiprocessors, any variables declared at the beginning of the main program were shared by all the processes, and could be directly accessed by any process. With multicomputers, these variables at the start of the main program are *local* to the main process, and are not directly accessible by any other process.

8.1.1 Communication Channels

Even though there are no shared variables, there must be some mechanism in the language that permits processes to interact while they are executing. In the hardware of the multicomputer, the physical processors interact by sending messages through the communication links that connect them. In Multi-Pascal, the "process" is the software abstraction of the physical processor. Therefore, a natural software abstraction of the physical communication links would be some kind of communication channels between the software processes. For this purpose in Multi-Pascal, channel variables are used. A physical processor can communicate with another processor by sending a message through the connecting communication link. Similarly, a Multi-Pascal process can communicate with another process by sending a message through a channel variable.

To adapt channel variables to usage in multicomputer programs, their usage and semantics must be somewhat modified from that of multiprocessors. In multiprocessors, the channels are like *shared variables*—they reside in the shared memory and can be freely read or written by any process at any time. In this way, they are unlike the communication links of a multicomputer, which physically connect two specific processors. To allow channel variables to more closely reflect the properties of communication links, the "receiving" end of each channel variable is directly connected to a specific process.

This is illustrated in Figure 8.1. Channel variable $Com[i]$ is connected to Process i at the receiving end. Therefore, Process i is the only one that can receive messages from this channel. However, any other process may send a message to Process i by writing it into channel variable $Com[i]$. In the figure, Processes X, Y, Z, all are sending messages to Process i. Each of these Processes X, Y, Z also has its own input channel variable for receiving return messages from Process i, or messages from any other process. This requirement that every channel variable be connected at the receiving end to a specific process is a useful abstraction of the property of communication links in multicomputers, which are directly connected at both the sending and receiving ends to specific physical processors.

In Figure 8.1, the processes may be running on any of the physical processors in the multicomputer. When Processes X, Y, Z write a message into channel variable $Com[i]$, it is automatically routed through the communication network of the underlying multicomputer topology to its destination at Process i. The message forwarding and routing are done by the communication interface hardware working in conjunction with the Multi-Pascal implementation. The routing and forwarding are hidden from the Multi-Pascal program-

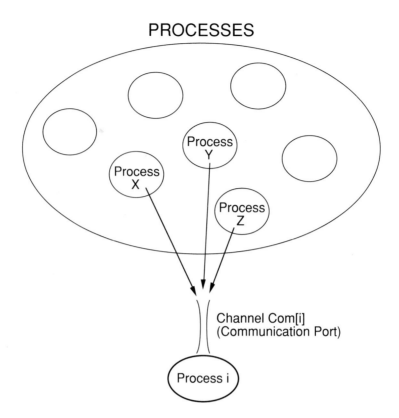

FIGURE 8.1 **Communication channels in Multi-Pascal.**

mer, thus simplifying the programming process. However, the movement of the message through the communication network is reflected in the *performance* of the program. In Figure 8.1 when Process X writes into channel $Com[i]$, there is a time delay before it actually arrives at Process i. The size of this communication delay depends on the topology and performance characteristics of the underlying multicomputer.

One important characteristic of the communication, which is guaranteed by the Multi-Pascal implementation, is that messages sent from a single source to the same destination will arrive in the same order as they are sent. In Figure 8.1 this property means that a sequence of messages sent from Process X to Process i will arrive in the same order. The messages may experience arbitrary routing or congestion delays in the communication network, but the Multi-Pascal implementation will ensure that the messages are delivered to Process i in the proper order. This maintenance of message sequence is necessary and important in certain types of programs, and therefore is part of the definition of the Multi-Pascal language. This property is not concerned with the relative ordering of messages sent from *different* sources. For example, a message may be sent from Process X to Process i, and then another message may be sent at a much later time from Process Z to Process i. Yet it is possible that the communication delays may cause the message from Process Z to arrive at Process i first. Also, the ordering property is not concerned with messages sent to different destinations.

8.1.2 Port Declarations

When channel variables are assigned to specific processes in multicomputers, their properties are slightly different from ordinary channel variables in multiprocessors. For this reason, a new name is used in the Multi-Pascal language: *communication port*. A *communication port* in Multi-Pascal is simply a channel variable that has been assigned to a specific process, for the purpose of receiving messages. There are two parts to the declaration of every communication port. The first part is its declaration as an ordinary channel variable at the beginning of the main program. The second part is a *PORT* declaration that appears with the process creation statement. The channel declaration at the beginning of the main program defines the name and component type, while the *PORT* declaration assigns it to a specific process.

The general structure of a message-passing program in Multi-Pascal is illustrated in Figure 8.2. An array of channels *Com* is declared at the beginning of the program. Each of these channels will act as the communication port for a specific process to receive messages from other processes. When the processes are created in the body of the main program with a *FORALL* statement, each channel of the array is assigned to its process with the Multi-Pascal keyword *PORT*. This expression (*PORT Com*[*i*]) is considered as a Multi-Pascal declaration indicating that the receiving end of channel *Com*[*i*] is "connected" to Process *i*. The reading and writing of ports uses the ordinary syntax of reading and writing channels. Inside a given Process *i*, the process may read values from its own port *Com*[*i*]. These are the values sent by other processes. Process *i* may send a value to another Process *k* by simply writing into *Com*[*k*], which is the channel assigned as the communication port of Process *k*.

This use of an array of channels for process communication has appeared several times in the multiprocessor programs of previous chapters. The syntax of the channel declaration and the read or write channel statements are the same in the multicomputer case. However, there are several important differences in the multicomputer implementation. Each channel of the array can be read by only one process, and that is the process to which it is assigned as a port by the *PORT* declaration. Thus, each channel may have multiple writers, but only one reader. Each channel is physically stored in the same local memory as the process for which it is acting as a communication port. If Process *i* is being executed on physical processor *i*, then channel *Com*[*i*] is stored in the local memory of processor *i*.

When a process performs a *write* operation to a channel, it appears to happen in the same way as it did in multiprocessors, with one important exception: there is a time delay before the value actually arrives at its destination channel. The *write* operation itself is *nonblocking* to the writer process—the writer is not delayed by the write operation. However, there is a time delay while the automatically generated *write* message is traveling through the processor interconnection network. The duration of this delay depends on the characteristics of the multicomputer topology, and the relative location of the destination channel. The writer process may continue execution while the message is still traveling.

This kind of *delayed* write operation is not possible in a multiprocessor, because each process reads and writes all shared variables directly. If a process contains a *write* operation to a channel, it is always sure that once it completes execution of that operation,

```
PROGRAM Sample;

VAR Com: ARRAY [1..30] OF CHANNEL OF INTEGER; (*Communication channels*)
    ...


  PROCEDURE Process(i: INTEGER);
  VAR invalue, outvalue, k: INTEGER;
     ...
  BEGIN
    ...

    invalue := Com[i];  (*read from my own communication port*)
    ...

    Com[k] := outvalue;  (*send "outvalue" to Process k*)
    ...

  END;


BEGIN
  ...

  FORALL i := 1 TO 30 DO
    (PORT Com[i]) Process(i);
  ...

END.
```

FIGURE 8.2   Use of communication channels.

the write has actually taken place. Consider executing the program of Figure 8.2 on a multiprocessor. When Process i executes the statement "Com[k] := outvalue", the value is actually physically written into the channel at that time. However, in a multicomputer something different occurs. Assume for example that "k" is 5 and "outvalue" is 150. The Multi-Pascal implementation will automatically generate a "write 150 to Com[5]" message, and send it through the interconnection network to processor 5. Process i will continue execution at the next statement immediately, while the message is still traveling to its destination. Thus, the write-channel operation happens just as it did in the multiprocessor case, except in a *delayed* fashion.

This delay in the occurrence of write operations to channels has important implications with respect to the program performance. In most multicomputers, the message communication delay through the interconnection network will be 50–100 times the processor instruction cycle time. If processes are frequently required to wait for data being sent from remote locations, then severe performance degradation may result. When creating a multicomputer program, the programmer must be aware of these communication delays in the underlying architecture, and seek to structure the program to minimize the impact of these delays. This issue is considered in more detail in the next chapter.

8.1.3 Comparison with Other Languages

As in the Multi-Pascal language, the most common communication technique in other multicomputer programming languages requires the writer process to execute some kind of "send message" operation and the reader process to execute a "receive message" operation. The exact syntax and semantics of these communication operations vary considerably in different languages. However, these communication primitives can be divided into two general categories called *asynchronous* and *synchronous*. *Asynchronous* communication is *nonblocking* for the writer process; the writer does not have to wait for the reader to actually receive the message. Asynchronous communication is also usually *buffered*, which means that messages are stored in buffers until the reader process decides to actually receive them.

In *synchronous* communication, both the writer and reader are blocked until the communication is complete. The writer and reader actually come together at the same time to exchange the message. This type of communication is sometimes called a *rendezvous*. Synchronous communication is usually *unbuffered*—there is no need to buffer any messages, since each message goes directly from the writer to reader. Thus, *asynchronous* communication is *buffered* and *nonblocking* for the writer, whereas *synchronous* communication is *unbuffered* and *blocking* for the writer. Both types of communication are blocking for the reader. The channel communication used in the Multi-Pascal language is of the asynchronous type.

A typical syntax for asynchronous communication in other multicomputer languages is as follows:

```
Writer Process executes:
    Send(processor_number, process_number, message_pointer);

Reader Process executes:
    Receive(message_pointer);
```

In the above "Send" operation, the writer identifies the destination process using the physical processor number where the process is running. In case there are many processes running on the destination processor, a local "process number" is also included. Together the pair "(processor_number, process_number)" represents a unique process identifier that determines the destination for the message. The "message_pointer" parameter simply points to the block of data to be transmitted. The reader process needs only a "message_pointer" parameter to receive the transmitted data. In some languages there are also mechanisms by which the reader can select a particular sender from whom to receive a message.

In Multi-Pascal, the destination for each message is determined by the array index of the array of communication ports. The above Send and Receive primitives are replaced in Multi-Pascal by the following:

```
Writer Process:
    Com[i] := message;   (*Send to Process i*)

Reader Process i:
    message := Com[i];   (*Receive message*)
```

The array index *i* serves as a kind of process identification number to replace the pair "(processor_number, process_number)" used with the Send and Receive primitives. This is the reason that the *PORT* declaration is necessary in Multi-Pascal. This binds the channel *Com*[*i*] to Process *i*, so that the system knows where to find *Com*[*i*] when a process writes to it.

The other major category of communication primitives, *synchronous communication*, may also use a general syntax like the "Send" and "Receive" shown above. Often with synchronous communication, instead of identifying the destination process, the writer process will specify a physical communication link through which the communication is to take place. The physical link will connect to a neighboring physical processor. The reader process must reside on the destination processor and also specify the physical link, as follows:

```
Writer Process executes:
    Send(link_number, message_pointer);

Reader Process executes:
    Receive(link_number, message_pointer);
```

Since these are synchronous communication primitives, they will both execute at the same time on opposite ends of the specified physical communication link. If either the writer or reader process arrives early, it will be forced to wait for the other. This type of mutually blocking communication on a physical link is more primitive than the asynchronous communication described above. In some languages, the physical link number may be replaced by a logical or "virtual" communication link that does not necessarily correspond to a physical link in the multicomputer hardware. The link number may also be replaced by the name of a "communication channel" defined in the program, which is bound to some specific physical link. This is the approach in the OCCAM parallel programming language used with the INMOS Transputer (Inmos 85).

8.2 LANGUAGE SUPPORT FOR MESSAGE-PASSING

Multi-Pascal has a few special features designed to support the message-passage programming style required for multicomputers. These additional features are needed because of the lack of shared variables in the multicomputer implementations of Multi-Pascal. One of these features is the *PORT* declaration, used to bind a channel to a process for purposes of receiving communication from other processes. This section will present the detailed syntax and semantics of the *PORT* declaration. Another aspect of communication is the interaction between the main program and the child processes. Multi-Pascal has special features that allow convenient transfer of initial data and final results between the main program and the processes. This is done with the procedure parameters of the procedure call that creates each process. Also presented in this section is the @ primitive for controlling the assignment of processes to physical processors. This is necessary to help optimize program performance for specific multicomputer topologies.

One additional modification to Multi-Pascal for multicomputers is the elimination of the *spinlock* feature. Because of the absence of shared variables, the concept of atomic operations is not useful in multicomputer programming. In multiprocessor implementations, the Multi-Pascal language has *spinlocks* to help facilitate the modification of shared data by many processes. This is not necessary in message-passing programming style, and would be highly inefficient if implemented on a multicomputer. Thus, the *spinlock* feature is eliminated.

8.2.1 The PORT Declaration

A *PORT* declaration is used to assign a channel variable to a specific process, so that the process can receive messages from other processes through the channel. Any process may write values to any channel, but each process may read values only from its own assigned channel. All of the channel variables must be declared at the beginning of the main program as usual. When any process is created with any of the usual Multi-Pascal methods (*FORALL* or *FORK*), a *PORT* declaration may be included to assign one or more of the channels to the created process. The general syntax of the *PORT* declaration is as follows:

```
( PORT <channel-list> ) <statement>;
```

The <statement> forms the body of the process being created, which is almost always a procedure call in multicomputer programs. The <channel-list> is a list of program channel references separated by semicolons. In this context, a *channel reference* is defined as being a member of one the following categories:

1. a channel variable
2. an array of channels

Category 1 is any ordinary channel variable reference that could appear in an expression at that position in the program. The validity of the channel reference is determined by the declarations at the beginning of the main program. The channel variable reference identifies a particular channel to be assigned to the created process. Category 2 is any valid array reference, possibly a multidimensional array, in which the primitive component of the array is a channel. In this case, the *PORT* declaration will assign the entire array of channels to the created process. Any channel in the array may then be used by that process to receive messages.

The syntax of assignment statements to read or write channels is the same as it was in multiprocessors: channels are written by using their name on the left side of an assignment statement, and are read by using their name on the right side of an assignment statement. The only difference is the restriction that only one process is allowed to execute a read operation on a given channel, and that is the process to which that channel has been connected by a *PORT* declaration.

As an example, consider the following channel declarations appearing at the beginning of the main program:

```
VAR C: CHANNEL OF CHAR;
    archan: ARRAY[1..10] OF CHANNEL OF INTEGER;
```

For these declarations, the following are valid *PORT* declarations:

```
( PORT C )
( PORT archan[2] )
( PORT archan )
```

In the above list, the first *PORT* declaration assigns the channel *C* to the newly created process. The second *PORT* declaration assigns the channel *archan*[2] to the new process: all of the other nine channels in the array *archan* are not affected by this declaration. The third *PORT* declaration assigns all the channels in the array *archan* to the new process.

The *PORT* channel-reference list may specify individual components of any array of channels that is declared at the beginning of the main program, including multidimensional arrays. For an example consider a two-dimensional array *A* declared as follows:

```
VAR  A:  ARRAY [1..10, 1..20] OF CHANNEL OF REAL;
```

For this array, the following are all legal *PORT* declarations:

```
( PORT A[3,4] )
( PORT A[1,1]; A[2,3] )
( PORT A )
( PORT A[2] )
```

The first two *PORT* declarations in the above list assign specific channels in array *A* to the new process. The third *PORT* declaration in the list assigns the entire two-dimensional array to the new process. The final example in the list assigns the second row of the array. It is important to understand that the use of *PORT* declarations does not change the way the channel variables are referenced in the program. In the above example, all the processes still have access to *A* as an array of channel variables, and can still reference any element of *A* in the usual way with ordinary subscripting. The only change is the restriction regarding reading each channel by only the assigned process.

Any valid Multi-Pascal expression may also be used to identify subscripts in a *PORT* declaration channel-reference list. The subscript expressions are evaluated dynamically at runtime in the ordinary way to select the specific array elements. If we assume that variables i, j, k are all declared as *INTEGER*, the following are valid *PORT* declarations:

```
( PORT A[1,j] )
( PORT A[i+1,j] )
( PORT A[i, j] )
( PORT A[k, j+2*k] )
```

Any channels declared at the beginning of the main program, which are not included in any *PORT* declarations, are assigned by default to be communication ports for the main process. The purpose of each *PORT* declaration is to assign a channel to a process. One implementation technique for *PORT* declarations is to have the main process build a "Port Table" from all the *PORT* declarations, with each table entry consisting of a channel identification number, process identification number, and the processor number on which the process is running. This Port Table can then be broadcast to all the processes, so that each process knows where to send its messages.

8.2.2 Communication with the Main Program

In multicomputer programs, the main program serves a special function. It interacts with the user and reads in the initial data arrays from the disk. The main program also creates the child processes to perform the parallel computation, then collects the final computed results, and reports them to the user or writes them to the disk. Because of this special role, it is useful to have some Multi-Pascal language features designed to facilitate the interaction of the main program with the child processes. The main focus of these features is on distributing the initial data to the processes, and collecting the final computed results.

In multiprocessor programs, the initial data is usually put into shared data arrays that reside in the shared physical memory. From there it can be accessed directly by all the processes. However, in a multicomputer the lack of this shared physical memory necessitates another mechanism. The method used in multicomputers is to pass the required initial data to each process using the parameters of the procedure call that creates each process. Generally, the initial data can be *partitioned*, so that only a portion of the data need be given to each created process. Since the creation of each process is almost always done with a procedure call in multicomputer programs, the "value" parameters of the procedure provide a convenient language mechanism for data to be copied from the main program to the child process. When the first statement of a process is a procedure call in Multi-Pascal, the evaluation of the procedure parameters is done by the main program, thus allowing local data of the main program to be *copied* into "value" parameters and passed to the child.

A typical program structure is illustrated in Figure 8.3. The initial data is put by the main program into a two-dimensional array *inputdata*. When each process *i* is created, it uses a "value" parameter to copy the *i*th row of this array. The two parameters *i* and *inputdata*[*i*] are evaluated by the main program. These variables are both *local* to the main program, and therefore can be read and copied during this parameter evaluation. These parameter evaluations are then bundled with the process creation message and sent off to the destination physical processor. When the process starts running on the destination processor, it will be executing within Procedure "Process". The procedure parameter called *mydata* will contain a copy of *inputdata*[*i*]. This parameter is a local variable of the process, and therefore can be conveniently accessed during process execution.

After each process completes its execution, it will often have to return a final computed result to the main program. These final results from all the processes will be collected by the main program, and reported to the user or written to a disk file. A convenient language mechanism for returning these final results is *VAR* parameters in the process definition procedure. Unlike *value* parameters, which pass a complete copy of the argument to the procedure, *VAR* parameters pass only the address of the argument. This address is then used in the procedure to read and write the argument variable directly.

```
PROGRAM Message-Passing;
CONST n = ... ;  (*number of processes*)
TYPE datatype = ARRAY [1..m] OF REAL;
VAR  inchan:  ARRAY OF CHANNEL OF INTEGER;
     i: INTEGER;
     inputdata: ARRAY [1..n] OF datatype; (*master data array*)
       ...


  PROCEDURE Process(i: INTEGER; mydata: datatype);
  VAR ... (*local variables for the process*)
  BEGIN
     ...

  END;


BEGIN (*Main*)

  ... (*Read initial values for "inputdata" array*)

  FORALL i := 1 TO n DO  (*Create the Processes*)
    (PORT inchan[i]) Process(i, inputdata[i]);
  ...

END.
```

FIGURE 8.3   Distributing initial data to processes.

When *VAR* parameters occur in the process definition procedure in Multi-Pascal, they are called *Remote-VAR* parameters and have some special properties. *Remote-VAR* parameters are *write-only* within the created process. They may not be read in any way within the process. Therefore, they cannot occur on the right side of an assignment statement or in any expression that is evaluated by the process. However, *Remote-VAR* parameters may occur on the left side of assignment statements. In this case, the assigned value is automatically sent through the communication network back to the main program, where it is written to the original variable. This semantics is essentially the same as ordinary *VAR* parameters—a write operation to a *VAR* parameter will always modify the original variable in this way. The only difference with *Remote-VAR* parameters is that the target variable happens to be located in the local memory of a remote processor.

This use of *Remote-VAR* parameters to pass final results back to the main program is illustrated in Figure 8.4. The array *outputdata* is a local variable of the main program, and is used to collect the final results from all the processes. As each process *i* is created, it has *outputdata*[*i*] as a *Remote-VAR* parameter. Assume now that a final result "x = 45.6" is computed by Process 3. This result is written to the *Remote-VAR* parameter with the assignment statement "out := x". Since parameter *out* is connected to *outputdata*[3] in the main program, this assignment to *out* will automatically generate a message "write 45.6 to outputdata[3]", which will be sent through the communication network to processor 0, where the main program is running. In this way the array *outputdata*, which is local to the main program, will collect the final results from all the processes.

This use of *value* and *VAR* parameters for communication with the main program in Multi-Pascal closely resembles an important language feature called *Remote Procedure Call* (RPC). The RPC feature is common in programming languages for distributed systems based on computer networks. An RPC is essentially a request by one computer to have a specific procedure executed on another computer in the network. The RPC has two types of parameters: "in" parameters pass initial values to the target computer, and "out" parameters pass computed results back to the caller. This closely parallels the use of *value* and *VAR* parameters in Multi-Pascal. This adaptation of the RPC mechanism to Multi-Pascal programs on multicomputers provides a simple and convenient language feature for the special type of communication that usually occurs between the main program and the child processes.

```
PROGRAM Message-Passing;
CONST n = ... ;  (*number of processes*)
TYPE datatype = ARRAY [1..m] OF REAL;
VAR  inchan:  ARRAY OF CHANNEL OF INTEGER;
     i: INTEGER;
     inputdata: ARRAY [1..n] OF datatype; (*master data array*)
     outputdata: ARRAY [1..n] of REAL;  (*final computed results*)
       ...


  PROCEDURE Process(i: INTEGER; in: datatype; VAR out: REAL);
  VAR x: REAL;
       ... (*other local variables for the process*)

  BEGIN
     ...  (*compute final result "x"*)

     out := x;  (*copy final result back to main program*)

  END;


BEGIN (*Main*)

   ... (*Read initial values for "inputdata" array*)

   FORALL i := 1 TO n DO  (*Create the Processes*)
     (PORT inchan[i]) Process(i, inputdata[i], outputdata[i]);
   ...

END.
```

FIGURE 8.4   Communication with the main program.

8.2.3 The @ Primitive for Processor Allocation

In most multicomputer topologies, the communication delay between processors varies considerably, depending on the relative location of the processors. Distant processors may require a communication delay that is 10 or even 100 times longer than nearby processors. For example, a 10 by 10 two-dimensional mesh may have a communication delay of 50 time units for adjacent processors, but this means that processors 0 and 99 have a delay of 900 time units. To minimize the communication delays in a parallel program, it is important to place communicating processes in nearby processors. For this reason, the Multi-Pascal language has a special primitive to allow the programmer to override the default allocation rules for processors. By preceding the process definition in the Multi-Pascal program with an @ and the desired processor number, a process may be assigned to run on any processor. The general syntax of the @ primitive is as follows:

```
( @ <expression> ) <statement>;
```

The <statement> defines the body of the process being created. The <expression> is any valid Multi-Pascal expression that evaluates to an integer value. The expression is evaluated at runtime, and is used as the processor number to assign the newly created process defined by <statement>. The following examples illustrate the use of @ with the *FORK* operator:

```
FORK ( @ 3 ) Expand;
FORK ( @ i ) Filter(outchan);
FORK ( @ i*10+j ) Compute(i);
```

The @ may also be used in conjunction with *FORALL* statements, as illustrated in the following examples:

```
FORALL i := 1 TO 50 DO
  (@ i-1 ) Compute(i);

FORALL j := 1 TO 10 DO
  ( @ j ) Process(j, A[j] );
```

In some programs it is useful for a process to know its own processor number as a reference point for placing newly created processes. Multi-Pascal has a built-in function *%Self* that can be used in any expression, and evaluates to the processor number on which it is executed. This function is especially useful as part of the @ expression, as in the following examples:

```
FORK ( @ %Self+1 ) Filter(outchan);
FORK ( @ 2*%Self+10 ) Point(i,j);
```

When the @ is not present in front of a process definition, then the Multi-Pascal implementation will use the default processor allocation rule, as explained in Appendix B, to try to balance the load on all processors. The default rule is mainly suited to shared-memory multiprocessors and also the Fully Connected multicomputer topology, in which there is a communication link between every pair of processors. For other architectures, it is advisable to use the @ primitive to place communicating processes near to each other. When both the @ and *PORT* primitives are used in front of the same process definition, the @ comes first and only one set of parentheses is used. The general syntax is as follows:

```
( @ <expression>  PORT <channel-list> )  <statement>;
```

8.3 PIPELINE PROGRAMS ON MULTICOMPUTERS

Now that all the Multi-Pascal language features have been described for supporting the message-passing programming style on multicomputers, it will be useful to consider a few example programs. The pipeline programs described in Chapter 4 already use a message-passing style, although they were written for multiprocessor execution. In these programs, the processes interact entirely by sending data into each other's channels. This communication is implemented with an array of channels declared at the beginning of the main program. Process i in the pipeline receives messages from channel i of the array, and sends data to its right neighbor via channel $i + 1$. This general structure of a pipeline program was illustrated in Figure 4.5.

Any of these pipeline programs is easily converted to complete message-passing style, suitable for multicomputer execution. Three pipeline programs are considered in this chapter: an Insertion Sort in this section, an Exchange Sort in the programming projects, and a Back Substitution program in the exercises. In a pipeline Insertion Sort program, the main process sends the data values one at a time into the pipeline. As each process receives data values from its left neighbor, it always retains the smallest value it has received so far, and sends all other data values on to its right neighbor. Using an initial list of n data values and n processes, this algorithm will result in a sorted list with each process i holding the ith data value in the fully sorted list.

The Insertion Sort program for a Fully Connected multicomputer topology is shown in Figure 8.5. Since a Fully Connected topology has a direct communication link between every pair of processors, it is not practical for real multicomputers. However, it is useful as a conceptual tool to help evaluate program performance properties. As described in Appendix B, the specific target architecture is specified with the keyword *ARCHITEC-TURE* at the very beginning of the program. In this case, it is a Fully Connected multicomputer with 101 processors.

In Figure 8.5, notice the *PORT* declaration for the channels forming the pipeline. Each process j uses *pipechan*[j] as its input channel for receiving data values. Therefore, *pipechan*[j] must be declared as a port for process j. To allow the processes to return the final sorted values back to the array *sorted* in the main program, a *Remote-VAR* parameter *sorteditem* is used in the process creation statement. After creating all the pipeline processes with a *FORK* operator, the main program sends the list of values into the pipeline. This is necessary because the *list* array that is being sent into the pipeline is a local variable of the main program, and therefore not directly accessible to any other process.

```
PROGRAM InsertionSort;
ARCHITECTURE  FULLCONNECT(101); (*Fully Connected topology*)
CONST n = 100;
VAR list,sorted: ARRAY [1..n] OF INTEGER;
    pipechan: ARRAY [1..n] OF CHANNEL OF INTEGER;
    j,k: INTEGER;

PROCEDURE Pipeprocess(me: INTEGER; VAR sorteditem: INTEGER);
VAR internal,newitem,i: INTEGER;
BEGIN
  internal := pipechan[me]; (*Read first item from the left*)
  FOR i := 1 TO n-me DO
    BEGIN
      newitem := pipechan[me]; (*Read new item from the left*)
      IF newitem < internal THEN
        BEGIN
          pipechan[me+1] := internal; (*Send "internal" to the right*)
          internal := newitem;
        END
      ELSE pipechan[me+1] := newitem; (*Send "newitem" to the right*)
    END;
  sorteditem := internal;  (*Return my final sorted list item*)
END;


BEGIN
  ... (*Initialize items to be sorted in "List" array*)

FOR j := 1 TO n DO (*Create the pipeline processes*)
  FORK ( PORT pipechan[j] ) Pipeprocess(j, sorted[j]);
FOR k := 1 TO n DO
  pipechan[1] := list[k]; (*Send list into start of pipeline*)

  ...

END.
```

FIGURE 8.5   Insertion sort on multicomputer.

To illustrate the use of the @ primitive, consider running the Insertion Sort program of Figure 8.5 on a *LINE* architecture. The most efficient arrangement of processes is to map the process pipeline directly onto the *LINE* architecture processor pipeline. Then each processor will be sending messages to a neighbor processor, and no messages will have to be forwarded to distant processors. Recall that the processors in a *LINE* topology are numbered sequentially down the line. To map the Insertion Sort process pipeline onto this processor pipeline, simply assign process *j* to physical processor *j*. This is shown in Figure 8.6. With this process arrangement, each pair of communicating processes is running on neighboring physical processors, thus minimizing communication delays.

```
PROGRAM InsertionSort;
ARCHITECTURE  LINE(101); (*Line topology with 101 processors*)
CONST n = 100;
VAR list,sorted: ARRAY [1..n] OF INTEGER;
    pipechan: ARRAY [1..n] OF CHANNEL OF INTEGER;
    j,k: INTEGER;

PROCEDURE Pipeprocess(me: INTEGER);
  ... (*same as Figure 8.5*)

END;

BEGIN
  ... (*Initialize items to be sorted in "List" array*)

FOR j := 1 TO n DO (*Create the pipeline processes*)
  FORK (@j PORT pipechan[j]) Pipeprocess(j, sorted[j]);
FOR k := 1 TO n DO
  pipechan[1] := list[k]; (*Send list into start of pipeline*)

  ...

END.
```

FIGURE 8.6   Insertion sort on LINE topology.

8.4 COMMUNICATION DELAY

There are four types of events in the execution of a Multi-Pascal program which will cause a message to be sent through the communication network:

> Writing to a communication port
> Creating a new process
> Writing to a *remote-var* parameter
> Process termination

Writing to a communication port has already been discussed extensively in this chapter. This event causes a message to be sent from the "Writer" process to the process that owns the communication port. If we assume that these processes are running on different processors, this will result in a message being sent through the multicomputer communication network. The execution of a process creation statement will also generate a message—a "create process" message will be sent to the processor on which the new process will be executed. This "create process" message will also contain the initial data from the parameters of the process creation procedure, as discussed in the previous section of this chapter.

When any running process writes to a *remote-var* parameter to return some data to the main program, this operation also causes the data to be sent in a message through the communication network to the processor where the main program is located. When any process finally terminates, the parent process must be notified, because the parent waits for termination of its children. This notification is done through a "termination" message that is sent through the communication network from child to parent.

In the Multi-Pascal simulation software that accompanies this text, the communication delay is determined for each of the above four categories of messages. This delay is based on the chosen multicomputer topology, the physical characteristics of the communication network, and the current message traffic in the network. The communication delay is taken into account in the simulation of the program execution and the reported performance statistics. The purpose of this section is to explain the communication model used in the simulation software to determine the communication delay. This same communication model is also used in the performance analysis of multicomputer programs in subsequent chapters.

8.4.1 Basic Communication Model

When any message is generated, it is first divided into packets. Data values are bundled into packets with three values per packet. In this context a "data value" is any of the basic Pascal data types: *Integer, Real, Boolean*, or *Char*. If the total number of data values in the message is not evenly divisible by three, the last packet will contain only one or two values. For example, an array with 10 values will generate a message with 4 packets. A process termination message is assumed to consist of one single packet. Similarly, a process creation message consists of one packet, plus whatever additional number of packets is needed to contain the initial parameter data for the process. The process creation message does not contain the program code for the process—it is assumed that the program code is already stored in the local memory of every processor. Most multicomputers have a special high-speed mechanism for broadcasting the program code to every processor before program execution begins.

One important parameter that determines the speed of communications in a multicomputer is the time T to transmit a packet through a single physical communication link. Another important parameter is the processing time P for each packet in the communication interface. If we assume that the processing time is negligible, the previous chapter developed the following formula for the communication time of a message with k packets along a path with m communication links:

$$\text{Communication Delay:} \quad (m + k - 1)T$$

This formula was computed by adding two terms: the time for the lead packet to reach the destination (mT), and the time for the remaining packets to follow ($[k - 1]T$). If the processing time P is not negligible it may effect both of these components. It is assumed that processing in each communication interface can be fully overlapped with transmission on connecting communication links. Thus, any communication interface may be processing one packet while other packets are being transmitted or received on its connecting links. Under this assumption, the time for the lead packet of a message to reach its destination will be $m(T + P)$. The remaining packets will then follow at regular intervals, whose duration is determined by $\max(T, P)$. Therefore, the total communication delay for a message is as follows:

Communication Delay: $m(T + P) + (k - 1)\max(T, P)$

In the Multi-Pascal simulation software, the user may specify what is called the *basic communication delay*, which is the sum $T + P$. For simplicity, it is assumed that $T = P$. Denoting the basic communication delay as D, we have $T = P = D/2$. The above formula then simplifies to the following:

$$\text{Communication Delay: } \left(m + \frac{k - 1}{2}\right)D$$

For a message with only one packet, this formula gives the communication delay mD. Thus, the parameter D can be understood as the basic time to communicate a single packet between two processors with a direct physical communication link. To send a packet along a path with m links, the communication delay is mD. The application of this formula is illustrated in Figure 8.7, showing the successive steps in the transmission of a three-packet message ($k = 3$) along a path with three communication links ($m = 3$). In this case the formula predicts a communication time $4D$.

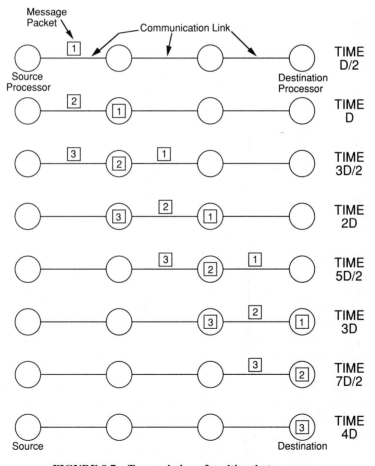

FIGURE 8.7   Transmission of multipacket message.

Figure 8.7 shows a snapshot of the situation after every $D/2$ time units, with time flowing vertically from top to bottom in the figure. The circles represent the processors, each with its own communication interface, and the connecting lines represent the communication links. The three packets of the message are represented by the the three small rectangles, numbered 1–3. When a message packet is above a communication link in the figure, then it is being transmitted by that link. A message packet inside a processor circle means that the packet is being processed by the communication interface of that processor. Since the processing time in each interface and the transmission time along each link are all equal to $D/2$, the message packets move in tandem along the communication path, as illustrated in the figure.

The above formula for the communication delay is adequate when the message traffic is low enough that there is no interference between messages that might result in congestion delays. This is actually the case for most of the example multicomputer programs presented in this text. Multicomputer programs are usually designed to minimize the communication delays by having all communication between neighboring processors only. The communication often has a global organization in which all processors communicate at the same time, but along different communication links. For such communication, the above formula is adequate.

Some programs have more frequent communication that travels longer paths in the network, resulting in the potential for message congestion and resultant delays that may degrade program performance. For simulating the execution of such programs, the Multi-Pascal software system has a "congestion" option, in which every individual message packet is followed as it moves through the communication network. The system keeps track of which communication links and interfaces are busy at various times. When a packet requires use of a link or interface that is currently busy, the movement of the packet is delayed. Details on the congestion option can be found in section 10.2 of Appendix B.

8.4.2 Software Overhead

The preceding discussion of the communication delay refers to the time for messages to travel through the communication network from source to destination. It will be useful to briefly consider the role of the processor in this communication. All communication is initiated by some operation in the Multi-Pascal program, such as a write operation to a communication port. The Multi-Pascal system will charge a small software overhead for the execution time of these operations, as is the case for all instructions in the Multi-Pascal program. Also, there will be some additional software overhead charged at the destination, where a Multi-Pascal instruction is executed to receive the message, such as the reading of a communication port. Thus, the total communication time will be the sum of this fixed software overhead at the source and destination processor, plus the delay in the communication network, computed as described above.

The software overhead will usually be about 10 time units at the source and also at the destination, depending on the complexity of the Multi-Pascal instruction that causes the communication. Aside from the time required to execute these instructions at the source and destination processors, no additional processor overhead is incurred by communication. It is assumed that the communication network can operate independently once the message is delivered to it by the source processor. Even while the message is traveling through the network, all the processors can continue to execute normally with no performance degradation. Although this is not the case in all multicomputer systems, it is true of many of the more recent models with sophisticated communication networks. This important property of the communication network leads to the possibility of *overlapping* communication with computation—an issue that is discussed more thoroughly in Chapter 9.

To illustrate the use of the Multi-Pascal simulation system for analyzing the performance of multicomputer programs, consider the pipeline program given in the previous section. The Insertion Sort was run on the Multi-Pascal system using a Fully Connected topology and a Line topology, each with 101 processors. The results are shown in Figure 8.8. The vertical axis is the program execution time, and the horizontal axis gives the value of the basic communication delay. In the Multi-Pascal simulation system, there is a command that allows the user to vary the value of the basic communication delay (the parameter D in the formula discussed earlier), in order to evaluate the influence of communication delays on program performance.

In Figure 8.8, performance curves are shown for the following three topologies: Fully Connected topology, Line topology with the congestion option off, and Line topology with the congestion option on. For the Fully Connected topology, the execution time increases linearly with the basic communication delay. This performance pattern is typical of pipeline programs. The two Line topology curves show that congestion in the communication network starts to become a problem when the basic communication delay is larger than 40 time units, although not a severe problem.

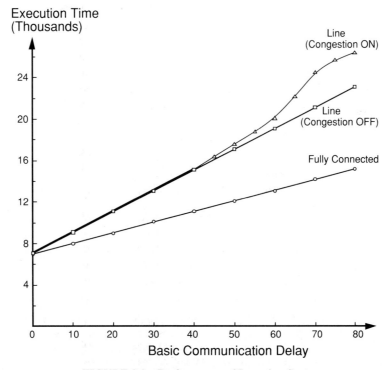

FIGURE 8.8 **Performance of Insertion Sort.**

8.5 MULTIPLE PORT COMMUNICATIONS

In all of the example programs presented so far in this chapter, each process had only one communication port for receiving data from other processes. Although one port is sufficient in principle for any program, there are some programs in which it is more convenient to have multiple communication ports for each process. This is especially useful when each process is receiving messages from several other processes. In this case the multiple communication ports can be used to distinguish the source of each message, by having each sender write to different ports. One example of such a program is the Bitonic Merge Sort presented in Chapter 4. In this program, each process must have an array of channels for receiving values from its partner processes. This is an example of what is called "multiple port" communications.

8.5.1 Multiple Aggregation

Another interesting example of multiple port communications occurs in the context of an efficient aggregation and broadcasting algorithm for a Hypercube multicomputer. It was seen in Chapter 6 that such an operation was useful for convergence testing during the execution of many iterative numerical programs. In such programs, an iterative computational procedure gradually moves an approximate solution closer to the actual solution. During the early iterations, large changes in the approximate solution occur. The size of the changes gradually decreases until eventually the change becomes smaller than the desired tolerance in the solution. At this point the program terminates.

In Chapter 6, it was shown how this convergence testing can be done in parallel programs by having each process apply the test locally to generate a Boolean value. The Booleans from all the processes are then aggregated to determine if global convergence has been achieved, and the result is broadcast back to all the processes. For a Hypercube topology, the Tournament technique described in Chapter 6 is especially useful because all direct communication occurs between processes whose binary number differs in only one bit. Therefore, if this Tournament algorithm is executed on a Hypercube, each message need traverse only a single communication link to reach its destination.

In this Tournament algorithm, all the Boolean values from all the processes gradually converge through a binary tree to process 0, which is at the root of the tree. Process 0 will then broadcast the final aggregated value back to all the processes down through the same binary tree structure (see Figures 6.8 and 6.9). For a Hypercube with n processors and basic communication delay D, the amount of communication time overhead required for this algorithm is $2D \log n$. The multiplier of 2 in this formula results from the fact that the binary tree is traversed twice. By using a slightly different algorithm, it is possible to traverse the tree only once and thus reduce the communication overhead by a factor of two.

In this new algorithm, called a *Multiple Aggregation*, many binary trees are built simultaneously, such that each processor lies at the root of one these trees. In this way, the tree traversal takes place only once. In this new Aggregation algorithm, each processor chooses its communication partner at each stage by examining the bits of its own number. For a Hypercube with dimension d, each processor number has d bits. These bits can be numbered from right to left, 1 through d. The Aggregation algorithm has d stages. At stage i, each processor determines its communication partner by reversing the ith bit in its own processor number. Each processor maintains its own internal Boolean value. During stage *i* it sends its own Boolean to its communication partner, and receives a copy of its partner's Boolean. The received Boolean is then merged into its own internal Boolean by using an *AND* operation.

The following is a high-level description of this Multiple Aggregation algorithm. Each processor will run this code:

```
FOR i := 1 TO d DO
  BEGIN
    Compute "partner" by reversing ith bit of my number;
    Send "myboolean" to partner;
    Receive "hisboolean" from partner;
    myboolean:= myboolean AND hisboolean;
  END;
final result is in "myboolean";
```

For a Hypercube with dimension 3, Figure 8.9 shows the overall structure of this Mutiple Aggregation algorithm. Each thick vertical line represents one of the eight processors. The diagonal lines with arrowheads show the communication that takes place at each stage of the algorithm. Notice that the communication partners at each successive stage are twice as far away as in the previous stage. This is because the bits of the processor numbers are being examined from right to left in order to determine the communication partner. This is essentially the same pattern as used in the *butterfly* interconnection network, as illustrated in Figure 3.7. This "butterfly" pattern is useful in many different algorithms, especially when one is dealing with Hypercube topologies.

Through careful examination of the diagram in Figure 8.9, it can be seen that every processor lies at the root of its own binary tree, with all the processors at the leaves of that

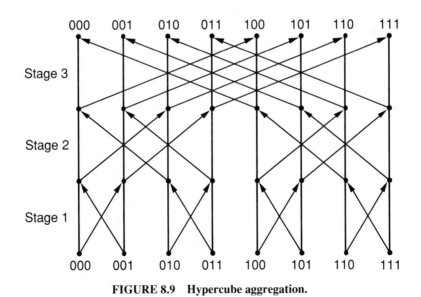

FIGURE 8.9 Hypercube aggregation.

tree. This is explicitly shown for processor 010 in Figure 8.10. The binary tree rooted at 010 is indicated by the thicker darker lines in the butterfly pattern. At each node in this binary tree structure, the algorithm is performing a logical *AND* operation. Therefore, processor 010 will receive the combined logical *AND* of all the initial Boolean values of all the processors. Since each processor is the root of its own binary tree, each processor will also receive the same combined logical *AND* of all the initial Booleans. Building all these binary trees in parallel eliminates the necessity of traversing the tree twice, as in the Tournament algorithm of Chapter 6. For a Hypercube with n processors and basic communication delay D, this Multiple Aggregation algorithm has a communication overhead $D \log n$, provided that each physical communication link can transmit messages in both directions simultaneously.

To implement this Multiple Aggregation algorithm in Multi-Pascal, each process must have a separate communication port for each partner. For the algorithm to work correctly, it is necessary for the communication from each partner to be processed in the proper sequence. One of the homework exercises at the end of this chapter deals with the nature of the errors that occur if communication is not processed in the proper order. Since all of its partners may be executing at different speeds, the communications may be actually physically received in any order. Therefore, each process requires a separate communication port to receive from each partner. This is done in Multi-Pascal with a two-dimensional array of channels:

```
inchan: ARRAY [0..n,1..d] OF CHANNEL OF BOOLEAN;
```

The first index ranges over all the processes, and the second index over all the communication partners for each process. When each process i is created, it is assigned *inchan[i]* as its array of communication ports. During stage k of the algorithm, process i will receive communication from port *inchan[i, k]*. This use of an array of ports at each process allows it to consider the communications in the required sequence. The complete

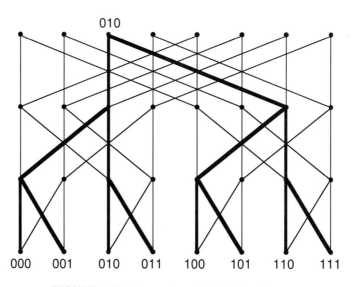

010

000   001   010   011   100   101   110   111

FIGURE 8.10   Binary tree in butterfly pattern.

Multi-Pascal code is shown in Figure 8.11. The Function "Aggregate" receives a Boolean value *mydone* from each process, and then returns the final aggregation of the Boolean values all as the result of the function.

```
PROGRAM MultipleAggregate;
ARCHITECTURE HYPERCUBE(6); (*Hypercube topology with dimension 6*)
CONST d = 6; (*Dimension of Hypercube*)
      n = 63;
VAR inchan: ARRAY [0..n,1..d] OF CHANNEL OF BOOLEAN; (*Comm. Ports*)
    i: INTEGER;

FUNCTION Aggregate(mydone: BOOLEAN): BOOLEAN;
VAR mynum,partner,bitvalue,stage: INTEGER;
    hisdone: BOOLEAN;
BEGIN
  mynum := %SELF; (*Get my processor number*)
  bitvalue := 1;
  FOR stage := 1 TO d DO
    BEGIN
      IF mynum DIV bitvalue MOD 2 = 0     (*Compute partner*)
        THEN partner := mynum + bitvalue
        ELSE partner := mynum - bitvalue;
      inchan[partner,stage] := mydone;   (*Send mydone to partner*)
      hisdone := inchan[mynum,stage];    (*Receive hisdone from partner*)
      mydone := mydone AND hisdone;
      bitvalue := 2 * bitvalue;          (*Move to next bit position*)
    END;
  Aggregate := mydone;
END;

PROCEDURE Process(i: INTEGER);
VAR mydone,done: BOOLEAN;
BEGIN
  REPEAT
    ... (*Perform iteration and compute "mydone"*)

    done := Aggregate(mydone);

  UNTIL done;
END;


BEGIN (*Main*)
  ...

FORALL i := 0 TO n DO
  (@i PORT inchan[i]) Process(i); (*Create processes*)

END.
```

FIGURE 8.11   Multiple aggregation function.

8.5.2 Multiple Broadcast

The Multiple Aggregation algorithm is easily converted into what is called a *Multiple Broadcast* algorithm. In an ordinary broadcast, a single process is broadcasting a copy of its data value to every other process. In a multiple broadcast, every process is performing a broadcast at the same time. If there are n processes, a multiple broadcast will cause each process to receive n data values. The Multiple Aggregation algorithm can be converted into a Multiple Broadcast by replacing the logical *AND* operation by a "list concatenate" operation. This means that the internal *mydone* variable in each process would become a list of all received values *mylist*. When *mylist* is sent to the partner process at each stage, the entire list is sent. When a list is received from the partner at each stage, this entire list is simply concatenated onto the internal *mylist*. When the algorithm finishes, the internal *mylist* of each process will contain a copy of each of the original values from the n processes.

The Multi-Pascal code is shown in Figure 8.12. The Procedure "Broadcast" receives a single integer value *myvalue* from each process, and returns a list of n integer values in array parameter *mylist*. It is interesting to analyze the size of *mylist* at each stage of the broadcast. During each stage every process will receive the whole list of its partner and concatentate it to *mylist*. Thus, the size of *mylist* will double during each stage. The number of communication operations performed by a process during each stage is just twice the list size, since a list is both sent and received during each stage. For a Hypercube with n processors and dimension d, the total number of communication operations performed by each process during the d stages of the broadcast is as follows:

$$2^1 + 2^2 + 2^3 + \cdots + 2^d = 2(2^d - 1) = 2(n - 1)$$

Since the communication operations are the most time-consuming, the entire Multiple Broadcast algorithm will have an execution time that is $O(n)$. This is in contrast to the Multiple Aggregation algorithm, which is $O(\log n)$. Even though the number of stages in the Multiple Broadcast is $\log n$, the doubling of the list size at each stage results in an $O(n)$ execution time.

It will be revealing to compare this algorithm to another Multiple Broadcast algorithm, in which each process simply sends a copy of its internal value directly to every other process. This can be done with a *FOR* loop in each process that iterates through the n processes, sending them each a copy of the value. This is shown in the Broadcast procedure of Figure 8.13. The number of communication operations in this more naive approach to multiple broadcasting is $2n$, the same as the previous algorithm. Thus, the same software overhead is incurred. Also, the automatic Hypercube message routing algorithm will ensure that all messages take a minimum distance path to their destination. However, this new method suffers from the possibility of severe congestion in the communication network, which may seriously degrade performance. In the subsequent discussion, this new multiple broadcast method will be called the "Direct" method, and the previous method will be called the "Butterfly" method.

```
PROGRAM MultipleBroadcast;
ARCHITECTURE HYPERCUBE(6); (*Hypercube topology with dimension 6*)
CONST d = 6;
      n = 63;
TYPE listtype = ARRAY [0..n] OF INTEGER;
VAR inchan: ARRAY [0..n,1..d] OF CHANNEL OF INTEGER; (*Comm. ports*)
    i: INTEGER;

PROCEDURE Broadcast(myvalue: INTEGER; VAR mylist: listtype);
VAR mynum,partner,bitvalue,stage,j: INTEGER;
    hisdone: BOOLEAN;
BEGIN
  mynum := %SELF;
  mylist[0] := myvalue;
  bitvalue := 1;
  FOR stage := 1 TO d DO
    BEGIN
      IF mynum DIV bitvalue MOD 2 = 0      (*Compute partner*)
        THEN partner := mynum + bitvalue
        ELSE partner := mynum - bitvalue;
      FOR j := 0 TO bitvalue-1 DO          (*Send mylist to partner*)
        inchan[partner,stage] := mylist[j];
      FOR j := bitvalue TO 2*bitvalue-1 DO
        mylist[j] := inchan[mynum,stage]; (*Receive partner's list*)
      bitvalue := 2 * bitvalue;           (*Go to next bit position*)
    END;
END;

PROCEDURE Process(i: INTEGER);
VAR values: listtype;
    myvalue: INTEGER;
BEGIN
  ...

  Broadcast(myvalue, values); (*Send myvalue to all processes*)
                             (*Receive in array "values"*)
END;


BEGIN (*Main*)
  ...

FORALL i := 0 TO n DO
  (@i PORT inchan[i]) Process(i); (*Create processes*)

END.
```

FIGURE 8.12   Multiple broadcast on Hypercube.

```
PROGRAM DirectBroadcast;
ARCHITECTURE HYPERCUBE(6);
CONST d = 6;
      n = 63;
TYPE listtype = ARRAY [0..n] OF INTEGER;
VAR inchan: ARRAY [0..n] OF CHANNEL OF INTEGER;
   ...

PROCEDURE Broadcast(myvalue: INTEGER; VAR values: listtype);
VAR mynum,partner,bitvalue,stage,i: INTEGER;
    hisdone: BOOLEAN;
BEGIN
  mynum := %SELF;
  FOR i := 0 TO n DO  (*Send a copy of "myvalue" to every process*)
    inchan[i] := myvalue;
  FOR i := 0 TO n DO  (*Receive broadcasted values from others*)
    values[i] := inchan[mynum];
END;


   ...
```

FIGURE 8.13   Multiple broadcast with congestion.

In the Direct method, each of the n processes sends n messages into the communication network. These n^2 messages can cause considerable congestion. However, the Butterfly method is designed to completely eliminate the possibility of congestion. At each stage, every processor communicates with its own partner along a direct communication link connecting them. Thus, no interference can be created among the messages. Using the Multi-Pascal simulation system, the performance of these two Multiple Broadcast algorithms was compared for various values of the basic communication delay from 0 to 100, using a Hypercube topology with $n = 32$ processors. The results are shown in the graph of Figure 8.14. Since the Direct Method has a slightly lower software overhead, it actually has superior performance for small values of the basic delay. However, as the basic delay increases, the congestion in the Direct Method causes the execution time to increase sharply. The increase in basic delay does cause the Butterfly Method to increase also, but much more gradually.

The crossover point for the two curves in Figure 8.14 is basic delay 22. Thus, for delay greater than 22, the Butterfly Method has superior performance. This is with reference to a Hypercube multicomputer with $n = 32$ processors. It is instructive to look at how this "crossover point" changes for various values of n. This is shown in Figure 8.15 for $n = 4, 8, 16, 32, 64$. The solid line in the graph connects the crossover points for the various values of n. To the right of this solid line is the region in which the Butterfly Multiple Broadcast method shows superior performance compared to the Direct Multiple Broadcast method. To the left of the solid line, the Direct Method has superior performance. The shape of this graph shows that for smaller numbers of processors, the communication delay must increase to a higher value before the congestion in the Direct Method becomes a serious problem.

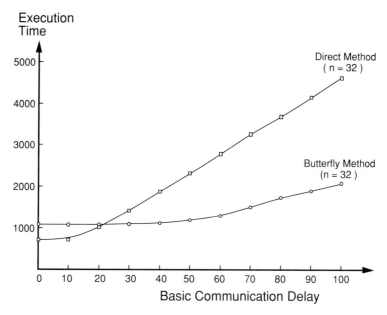

FIGURE 8.14   **Comparison of multiple broadcast methods.**

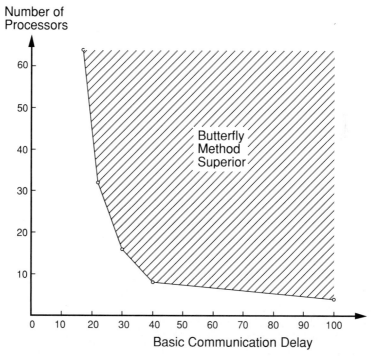

FIGURE 8.15   **Region of superior performance for butterfly multiple broadcast method.**

8.6 SUMMARY

Programming of multicomputers involves an additional level of complexity as compared to multiprocessor programming. Because of the time-consuming interprocessor communication delays in multicomputers, programmers must be aware of the machine architecture and plan their programs to minimize the amount of communication overhead. Simply taking a parallel program that performs well on a shared-memory multiprocessor and moving it to a multicomputer will almost always result in very poor performance. The distributed nature of the local memories in multicomputers requires that the programs be organized in a more distributed fashion, with each process relying mainly on its own local variables.

The *message-passing style* of parallel programming is designed to provide greater efficiency for execution on multicomputers. In the message-passing style, the organization of the program reflects the underlying organization of the multicomputer. Each process is created by a procedure call with all needed shared data being passed as value parameters to the procedure. Once created, each process relies mainly on its own local variables, which are stored in the local memory of that processor. All process interaction is done via message-passing using communication ports, which are channel variables that have been assigned to receive messages for a particular process. Communication ports are created with a two-part declaration—the channel variable declaration at the beginning of the main program, and the *PORT* declaration at the process creation statement.

When any process writes a data value to the communication port of another process, the data is automatically sent through the processor communication network to the destination process, where it arrives after some communication delay that depends on the multicomputer topology. The Multi-Pascal simulation system that accompanies this text includes options for the following multicomputer topologies: Line, Ring, 2-D Mesh, Torus, 3-D Mesh, and Hypercube. The simulation system will determine the communication delay for every message sent through the communication network, including process creation and termination messages. The delay for each message is computed by using the basic communication delay along each physical link in the network, which may be specified by the user. The user may also choose a "congestion" option, in which the flow of individual messages is tracked through the network in detail.

The "@" feature allows the program to override the default processor allocation policy, and place processes in any physical processor. By being aware of the underlying multicomputer topology and the process communication pattern of the program, the programmer can optimize program performance by locating processes in a judicious manner. As seen in the Insertion Sort program in this chapter, the communication structure of the program can often be mapped directly onto the communication topology of the multicomputer. With this program, the process pipeline was mapped onto a *LINE* topology, so that all communication is with immediate neighbors only.

The chapter concludes with a discussion of multiple port programs, in which each process requires several communication ports for receiving data from different sources. Two important examples of such programs are presented: a Multiple Aggregation algorithm and a Multiple Broadcast algorithm for a Hypercube. Both of these algorithms are based on a butterfly communication pattern, in which processes select a communication partner at each stage by reversing the corresponding bit in its own processor number. Both of these algorithms are useful for a wide variety of iterative numerical programs, of the type studied in Chapter 6. The next chapter gives further examples of multicomputer programs, with special emphasis on the issue of partitioning the central data structures among the processors.

REFERENCES

The use of @ and *%SELF* primitives for assigning processes to processors has appeared in several parallel programming languages (see for example, Halstead, 1985 and Hudak, 1986). In the context of the Multi-Pascal language, these primitives were first introduced in Lester and Guthrie [1987], along with the basic concepts of communication ports.

A critical evaluation of the status and future of multicomputer architectures and programming is presented in Athas and Seitz [1988]. The multiple aggregation and multiple broadcasting algorithms are from Fox, et al. [1988], which also has a comprehensive discussion of many aspects of Hypercube communications.

PROGRAMMING PROJECTS

1. SORTING ON A LINE TOPOLOGY

An Exchange Sort is a pipeline-style algorithm in which data values flow in both directions through the process pipeline. Small values flow to the left and large values to the right, eventually resulting in a sorted arrangement of the values. Initially, each process is assigned a whole group of values from the original unsorted list. Each process iteratively repeats two computational phases—a *left-moving* phase and a *right-moving* phase. During the left-moving phase, each process sends the smallest value from its own group to the left neighbor, and then receives the incoming value from its right neighbor. During the right-moving phase, each process sends the largest value from its own group to the right neighbor, and then receives the incoming value from its left neighbor.

For increased efficiency, it is useful for each process to maintain its own group of items in sorted order throughout the algorithm. After each process receives a new value from either neighbor, it should be integrated into its internal sorted group. If there are n values in the original list, then $n/2$ iterations of the left-moving and right-moving phases are required to sort the list. Your job is to write this Parallel Exchange Sort algorithm. The size of each local group will be specified in your program by a constant *groupsize*, defined at the beginning. You may assume that the size of the master list n is evenly divisible by *groupsize* so that all processes have equal size groups.

Write a program for this sorting algorithm on a *LINE* multicomputer topology. Run the program to determine the speedup and execution time for various values of the basic communication delay in the *LINE* architecture. Draw a performance graph of the program execution time versus the basic communication delay.

2. NUMERICAL INTEGRATION ON A MESH

Convert the numerical integration program given in Figure 5.8 to run on a 2-D Mesh multicomputer topology. A new technique for adding the local sums will be required, which is more suited to multicomputers. Try to design the program so that it specifically performs well on a 2-D Mesh.

To test your program, use the following function for integration:

```
FUNCTION f(t: REAL): REAL;
BEGIN
  f := Sqrt(4 - t*t);
END;
```

Perform the integration between the boundary points $a = 0$ and $b = 2$. The result of this integration program should be a good approximation to the value of *pi*.

3. SOLVING LINEAR EQUATIONS ON A HYPERCUBE

Consider a system of n linear equations defined by an n by n array of coefficients A and an array B. Each equation i of this system has the following form:

$$A[i, 1]x[1] + A[i, 2]x[2] + ... + A[i, n]x[n] = B[i]$$

The goal is to determine values for the array x that satisfy all the equations. If all the values of x are known except $x[i]$, then the above equation can be used to compute $x[i]$ as follows:

$$x[i] := \frac{-1}{A[i, i]} \left(\sum_{j <> i} A[i, j]x[j] - B[i] \right)$$

If only some approximate estimates for the other values of x are known, then the above equation can be used to compute an estimate for the value of $x[i]$. Given a complete set of approximate values for x, the above technique can be applied to each component of x simultaneously to compute a new set of values for x. For a large variety of linear systems, the repeated application of this procedure will actually converge to a solution.

Your job in this programming project is to write a Hypercube program that solves a system of linear equations using this iterative method. One equation will be assigned to each processor, which will be responsible for iteratively computing the succesive values of that $x[i]$. After each processor computes a new value for its assigned component of x, each processor must receive a copy of all the new values from the other processors before proceeding to the next iteration. This exchange of values is essentially a multiple broadcast operation.

To determine when the program should terminate, a desired accuracy in the solution is specified as an input. After each processor computes a new value for its assigned $x[i]$, it compares the magnitude of the change in $x[i]$ with the desired accuracy. The result of the comparison at all the processors must then be aggregated to determine if the program should terminate. To save computing time, this aggregation can be combined with the multiple broadcast by including one additional value in the broadcast that aggregates the results of all the termination tests. Therefore, at each stage k of the multiple broadcast, instead of sending only 2^{k-1} values to its partner, each process will send $2^{k-1} + 1$ values.

When testing your program, it is necessary to choose a sample system of equations that does eventually converge to a solution. One condition on the matrix A that will guarantee convergence is called *row diagonal dominance* (see Bertsekas and Tsitsiklis, 1989):

$$\text{For each row } i, \qquad A[i, i] > \sum_{j <> i} |A[i, j]|$$

EXERCISES

1. For each of the following multicomputer topologies, compute the communication delay for sending a message with five packets from processor 3 to processor 20. Use the communication model described in section 8.4.1, and assume that the basic communication delay is 10 time units.
   (a) SHARED(50)
   (b) FULLCONNECT(50)
   (c) LINE(50)
   (d) RING(50)
   (e) MESH2(7)
   (f) MESH3(4)
   (g) TORUS(7)
   (h) HYPERCUBE(5)

2. When message-passing programming style is used, atomic operations are no longer required. Explain in detail the reasons for this. Give a specific example of the use of atomic operations on a multiprocessor, and explain why this should not be done on a multicomputer.

3. In some multicomputer systems, the language mechanism for communication between processors is two functions:

   Send(M, i)   sends the value contained in variable M to processor i

   Receive(M)   receives the next incoming communication and stores it in variable M.

   Compare and contrast this language mechanism to the communication ports of Multi-Pascal. What are the advantages and disadvantages of each?

4. Give an overview of an implementation technique for Port Tables, as part of the Multi-Pascal language implementation of communication ports. Discuss each of the following issues in detail:
   (a) What information is contained in the Port Table?
   (b) When and how is the Port Table created?
   (c) When and how is the Port Table distributed to the processes?
   (d) How is the Port Table used during writing and reading of communication ports by processes? Describe the detailed steps that occur when a process executes a "write" operation to a port.
   (e) What happens if a process attempts to write to a port that is not yet assigned to its designated process? (Be sure that your implementation handles this possibility without error.)

5. For sending a message with k packets through a path with m links, the following formula is given in this chapter for the communication delay:

$$m(T + P) + (k - 1) \max(T, P)$$

   Give a detailed derivation and justification of this formula, with special emphasis on the "max" term.

6. For a *LINE* architecture, the following function will compute the communication delay for a message with one packet, between any source and destination processor:

```
FUNCTION Delay( Source, Destination: INTEGER): INTEGER;
CONST D = 10; (*Basic Delay to an adjacent processor*)
BEGIN
  Delay := D * ABS(Destination - Source);
END;
```

For each of the following architectures, write a corresponding function to compute the communication delay for one packet between any source and destination processor:
(a) RING(100)
(b) FULLCONNECT(100)
(c) MESH2(10)
(d) HYPERCUBE(7)

7. Consider a new multicomputer topology with a connection structure in the form of a binary tree. Processor number 0 at the root is directly connected to two processors. Each of these processors is in turn connected to two additional processors. This TREE topology is in the form of a complete binary tree with one processor at each node and leaf of the tree. The topology is characterized by a parameter giving the depth of the tree. For this tree topology, write a "Delay" function as described in exercise 6.

8. When dealing with Mesh topologies, one useful aid is a function to translate between processor numbers and processor coordinates in the mesh. In a *MESH2* topology, each processor has a row and column coordinate in the mesh. In a *MESH3* topology, each processor has three coordinates to locate it in the three-dimensional array: row, column, and plane (depth).
(a) For a *MESH2(m)* topology, write the following Multi-Pascal functions:
    FUNCTION Procnum   converts coordinate position to processor number
    FUNCTION Position   converts processor number to coordinates
(b) For a *MESH3(m)* topology, write the following Multi-Pascal functions:
    FUNCTION Procnum   converts coordinate position to processor number
    FUNCTION Position   converts processor number to coordinates

9. In section 10.1 of Appendix B, a standard Hypercube routing algorithm is described.
(a) Show that this algorithm always leads to a minimum length path from source to destination.
(b) Describe an alternative algorithm in which messages take a different route, but still have the minimum length.

10. The following is a Parallel Factorial program for a multiprocessor:

```
PROGRAM Factorial;
VAR i,j,n,middle: INTEGER;
    prod, fact: REAL;
BEGIN
  Write('Input number: ');
  Readln(n);
  middle := n DIV 2;
  FORK
    BEGIN
      prod := 1;
      FOR i := n DOWNTO middle DO prod := prod * i;
    END;

  FORK
    BEGIN
      fact := 1;
      FOR j := middle-1 DOWNTO 2 DO fact := fact * j;
```

```
      END;
   JOIN; JOIN;
   Writeln('Factorial is ', fact*prod:1);
END.
```

(a) Run this program on the Multi-Pascal system to determine the execution time and speedup.

(b) Modify the program to conform to the message-passing style. Run the modified program using a *FULLCONNECT* architecture to determine the execution time and speedup.

11. Suppose the multicomputer implementation of Multi-Pascal allowed channel variables to be read or written freely by any process, just as in multiprocessors. Explain why frequent use of such operations would result in severe performance problems in many programs. Give a detailed example of a program structure that performs well on a multiprocessor, but would perform poorly on a multicomputer because of the channel operations.

12. Run the following program on the Multi-Pascal system to determine the execution time and speedup:

```
PROGRAM Pipeline;
TYPE pipetype = CHANNEL OF INTEGER;
VAR pipe: ARRAY [1..3] OF pipetype;
    i: INTEGER;

   PROCEDURE Process(VAR in, out: INTEGER);
   VAR value: INTEGER;
   BEGIN
     REPEAT
       value := pipe[in];
       pipe[out] := value;
     UNTIL value = -1;
   END;

BEGIN
FORK Process(1,2);
FORK Process(2,3);
FOR i := 1 TO 100 DO
   pipe[1] := i;
pipe[1] := -1;
END.
```

Change the architecture in the above program to *RING*(10). Without changing any other aspects of the program, add *PORT* and @ primitives to the program to optimize performance on the *RING* topology. Run the program again to determine the execution time and speedup.

13. To achieve good speedup in multicomputer programs, the process granularity must generally be much larger than in multiprocessor programs. Explain the reasons for this.

14. In the Multiple Aggregation function of Figure 8.11, each process has a separate communication port for each stage of the algorithm. Consider replacing these multiple ports with one single port that is reused at each stage. If no other changes are made to the algorithm, show that an error might occur if the processes are running at different speeds. Give a detailed description of how and when the error occurs. Explain how this error is avoided in the multiple port version.

15. Chapter 6 presented three Barrier implementation techniques: Counting Variable method, Tournament technique, and Local-Barrier method. Which of these techniques is suitable for multicomputer implementation? Justify your answer.

16. Give a detailed discussion showing that the "Butterfly" Multiple Broadcast method described in section 8.5.2 actually works correctly.

17. In Chapter 6 it was explained that some iterative numerical algorithms require global synchronization, while some can use the more efficient local synchronization method. With multiprocessors, the local synchronization method is faster than the global synchronization. However, the disparity between these two methods is much more pronounced in multicomputers. Explain in detail the reason for this.

18. In Chapter 2 a simple parallel matrix multiplication program is presented. Convert this program to message-passing style so that it will run on a multicomputer.

19. In Chapter 4 a parallel Back Substitution program is given. Convert this program to run on a Ring multicomputer topology.

9

Data Partitioning

The principle of *data parallelism* was presented in Chapter 2 and has been illustrated in the many examples presented throughout the text. *Data parallelism* simply means that the database is used as a basis for creating parallel activity: different parts of the database are processed in parallel. Parallel application programs almost always involve large multidimensional arrays of numbers, which form the basis for the data parallelism. This principle of data parallelism is central to both multiprocessor and multicomputer programming. However, when this principle is applied to multicomputers, the distributed nature of the physical memory requires that a special type of data parallelism is used, called *data partitioning*.

In *data partitioning* the shared database is "partitioned" into separate portions, which are distributed across the local memories of the multicomputer. A single parallel process is assigned to operate on each individual portion of the database. The process resides in the same local memory as its assigned portion of the database, and therefore can access this data locally. To achieve good performance, each process must rely mainly on its own local variables and its own local portion of the shared database. When a process needs to gain access to data stored in remote memories, this can be done through the message-passing network that connects the processors. However, because of the long time delay involved in this interprocessor communication, the message passing must be relatively infrequent.

This chapter describes the various techniques of data partitioning and illustrates them with example programs. Several important organizational issues will be discussed for multicomputer programs that use data partitioning. It is usually not possible to completely limit each process to its own local portion of the database. The parallel algorithm can be organized so that most of the computing is done with the local data. However, processes will periodically need to access data in nonlocal portions of the database. This is achieved through periodic interprocess communication using orderly connection patterns between the processes.

The first example presented in this chapter is the N-Body problem from astrophysics, in which the mutual gravitational influence is calculated for a group of massive objects. In this program, the data array describing the mass and position of each object can be partitioned among the processes, but each process still needs eventually to access all the data in the array. This is accomplished through a virtual "ring" communication topology, around which all the data circulates, eventually reaching every process. An iterative algorithm alternates local computation with communication around the ring. As long as the granularity of the computation phase is sufficiently large compared to the communication delays in the underlying multicomputer, the algorithm can achieve good performance.

The next example in this chapter is Parallel Matrix Multiplication on a *TORUS* multicomputer topology. The two arrays to be multiplied are partitioned among the processors in the two-dimensional torus. Each processor performs a local matrix multiplication, using its local portions of the master arrays. Then a communication phase follows, in which each processor sends its local portions to other processors, and receives new portions. The iterative algorithm alternates local matrix multiplication with communication, and eventually arrives at the final total matrix product. The parallel algorithm makes full use of the *TORUS* topology by communicating both in the vertical and horizontal direction.

The final example is a multicomputer version of the Parallel Jacobi Relaxation program described in Chapter 6 for solving a differential equation. The master data array is easily partitioned in this algorithm. However, each process needs data not only in its own partition, but also from its immediate neighboring partitions. Therefore, after each iteration, each process must send a copy of its local data partition to all neighboring processes. This must be done after each iteration, because the data values change, and the neighboring processes need the new values on the next iteration.

The purpose of this chapter is to illustrate how all the parallel programming techniques presented in earlier chapters can be adapted to the particular needs of multicomputers. Most of the principles and organization techniques presented earlier in the context of multiprocessors are also valid for multicomputers. However, as we see in this chapter, some reorganization of the parallel algorithms is required. This chapter also serves to illustrate the use of the message-passing style of parallel programming discussed in Chapter 8.

9.1 COMMUNICATION OVERHEAD

One of the major themes of this chapter is general organizational techniques for multicomputer programs that minimize the impact of communication delays on performance. Through a series of examples, it will be seen that the communication overhead can be reduced to an acceptable level through proper organization of the program. Before we enter into specific examples, it will be useful to briefly present a general algebraic analysis of communication overhead in multicomputer programs. This will lead to some important insights into the performance of multicomputer programs, and also will provide the basis for more detailed performance analysis of the subsequent examples of this chapter.

Multicomputer programs are often organized as iterative computations, with each iteration having two phases: a computation phase and a communication phase. During the computation phase, each processor performs a local computation using its own assigned data partition. Then during the communication phase, all or part of these locally computed results are transmitted to one or more neighboring processors. Let the size of the data partition assigned to each processor be denoted by k. The duration of the computation phase generally is proportional to a power of the partition size, as expressed in the following:

$$\text{Computation phase: } Sk^b$$

Both S and b will vary between different algorithms, but will be constant for each particular algorithm. The value of the exponent b is very important in determining the performance characteristics of the program. Among the three example programs presented in this chapter, the following are the values of the exponent b:

N-Body Problem:	$b = 2$
Matrix Multiplication:	$b = 3/2$
Jacobi Relaxation:	$b = 1$

The communication phase involves sending some of the results of the computation phase to neighboring processors. Therefore, the amount of data sent is usually proportional to the size of the data partition k. In the analysis of communication delays in the previous chapter, it was seen that the communication delay between nearby processors has two terms: a term proportional to the amount of data being transmitted, and a constant term. Thus, the duration of the communication phase has the following general form:

$$\text{Communication phase: } Vk + F$$

The total duration of each iteration is the sum of the computation and communication phases, and therefore has the following form:

$$\text{Duration of iteration: } Sk^b + Vk + F$$

The *communication overhead* is defined as the percentage of the total execution time consumed by communication operations. By using the above expressions, the communication overhead can be determined by dividing the duration of the communication phase by the duration of the iteration:

$$\text{Communication overhead: } \frac{Vk + F}{Sk^b + Vk + F}$$

The above expression ignores process creation and initial data distribution times. A consideration of these items is postponed to later in the chapter. Using this expression for the communication overhead, we can gain some interesting insights into the nature of the performance degradation that results from communication delays. The value of the exponent b is very important. If $b > 1$, which is the case for a wide range of algorithms, then the communication overhead gradually vanishes as k increases. This means that communication delays, no matter how large, can be overcome by using larger data sets that will increase the size of the data partition assigned to each processor. This is because the communication delays grow linearly with the k, while the computation time grows as a higher power of k. This result is encouraging for the application of multicomputers.

In some algorithms the exponent $b = 1$. In this case, the communication overhead will approach a constant as the size of the data partition k is increased:

$$\lim_{k \to \infty} \text{Comm. overhead} = \frac{V}{S + V}$$

Although this is not as good as the previous case, in which the communication overhead vanished for large k, it is an acceptable performance overhead because the speedup will still grow linearly with the number of processors. For p processors, the speedup for increasing k approaches the following limit:

$$\frac{pS}{S + V}$$

This analysis has shown that even large communication delays in multicomputers can be overcome by increasing process granularity through larger data sets. However, for specific problems that may require small data sets, the performance may not be good. Thus, the size of the communication delays in specific machines may place limitations on the problems that can be efficiently solved on that machine. This short general discussion of communication overhead in multicomputer programs provides the basis for more detailed performance analysis of the sample programs presented in the subsequent sections of this chapter.

9.2 N-BODY PROBLEM IN ASTROPHYSICS

The N-Body problem is an example of an important class of parallel algorithms that exhibit *long-range* data interactions. This results from the long-range nature of the gravitational force. To compute the force on a single mass, all of the other masses must be considered. Therefore, a computation must be performed on every pair of masses. This consideration of all possible pairs is mathematically called a *cross-product*. The amount of computation required for these cross-product calculations is proportional to the square of the number of data items.

This type of cross-product algorithm is common in particle simulations, such as the molecular dynamics calculations done in physics and chemistry, where each molecule is acted upon by a long-range force from every other molecule. With the advent of high-speed supercomputers, these types of particle system simulations have grown in popularity. These simulations are so computationally intensive that previous generations of computers could practically solve systems with only relatively small numbers of particles. Scientists had to resort to other simpler approximate mathematical techniques for understanding the behavior of large particle systems. Especially with the growing availability of powerful parallel computers, it is now becoming feasible to gain insights into the behavior of these types of physical systems through direct simulation of the interactions of individual particles. In most such particle simulations, there will be some long-range component to the interparticle forces that requires a cross-product type computation.

9.2.1 Shared Memory Version

The *N-Body* problem is used in astrophysics to calculate the dynamics of the solar system and galaxies. Each mass in this problem experiences a gravitational attraction by every other mass, in proportion to the inverse square of the distance between the objects. Newton's universal law of gravitation gives the force between any two objects with masses m_1 and m_2, separated by a distance d:

$$\text{Force} = \frac{G m_1 m_2}{d^2}$$

where G is the gravitation constant.

Usually the N-Body problem involves computing the trajectories of the masses over a period of time, based on their initial velocity and the gravitational interaction. The problem is solved iteratively in small time increments by computing the gravitational force on each mass, and then computing the movement of each mass during that short time interval. For simplicity, we will consider only the computation of the gravitational force on each mass based on the attraction by every other mass. An example using six bodies is shown in Figure 9.1. Mass m_1 in the center of the figure experiences a gravitational force pulling it toward each of the other masses. The arrows indicate the direction of these forces. The magnitude of each force is computed, using Newton's law. The figure shows only the forces acting on mass m_1.

To focus attention on the overall organization of the cross-product algorithm, the calculations will be simplified by using only two spatial dimensions, rather than three. The calculation for each pair of objects is illustrated in Figure 9.2. Mass 1 is at position (x_1, y_1) and Mass 2 at (x_2, y_2). From these two-dimensional coordinates, the *xdist, ydist,* and *dist* are easily computed. By using this computed distance between the bodies and Newton's law, the magnitude of the gravitational force f can then be directly computed. This force f can be reduced to its x and y components as follows:

$$\text{force in } x \text{ direction} = f * \text{xdist/dist}$$
$$\text{force in } y \text{ direction} = f * \text{ydist/dist}$$

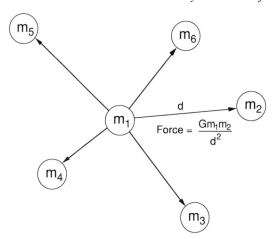

FIGURE 9.1 Gravitational forces.

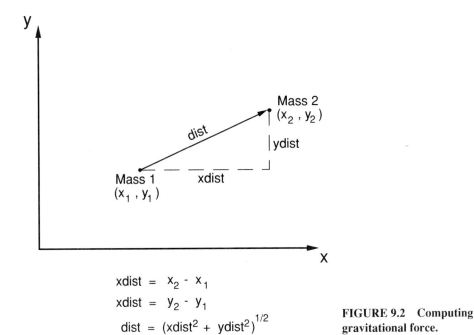

$$xdist = x_2 - x_1$$
$$xdist = y_2 - y_1$$
$$dist = (xdist^2 + ydist^2)^{1/2}$$

FIGURE 9.2   Computing gravitational force.

Figure 9.3 shows the Multi-Pascal program for the N-Body problem on a shared-memory multiprocessor. The cross-product of all pairs of bodies is created by the two nested loops. The outer *FORALL* statement ranges over all bodies *i*, and the inner *FOR* loop within each process ranges over all bodies *j*. The code inside the FindForce procedure uses Newton's law of gravitation to compute the force exerted by body *j* on body *i*. The variable *force*[*i*] is used to accumulate the sum of forces on body *i* by all the other bodies.

9.2.2 Partitioning the Data Array

To create a multicomputer program for this N-Body problem, the data array containing the mass and position of the bodies can be partitioned among the local memories of the processors. If there are *n* bodies and *p* processors, each processor is assigned $k = n/p$ bodies. However, to compute the force on its assigned bodies, each processor will still need to have access to information on all the other bodies. One obvious solution to this problem is to duplicate the master data array in every local memory, so that each processor has its own complete local copy of the array. For a large array, this will produce a very long initialization time for copying the entire array to each local memory.

In another more efficient solution, the master data array is fully partitioned among the local memories. The processes are organized into a virtual "ring" communication structure. Each process sends a copy of its partition to its nearest neighbor in the communication ring. After receiving the partition from its neighbor, each process uses this for internal computing purposes and then sends it on to the next process in the ring. In this way, all the partitions gradually circulate around the ring, eventually reaching every process. Each process will see all the partitions and use them all for internal computing.

```
PROGRAM NBody;
CONST  n = 100;    (*Number of bodies*)
       G =  ... ; (*Gravitational constant*)
TYPE bodytype = RECORD
                  mass,x,y: REAL; (*Mass and position*)
               END;
     forcetype = RECORD
                   x,y: REAL;      (*Force in x and y direction*)
               END;
VAR  body:  ARRAY [1..n] OF bodytype; (*master data array*)
     force: ARRAY [1..n] OF forcetype; (*resultant forces*)
     i: INTEGER;

PROCEDURE FindForce(me: INTEGER);
VAR  j: INTEGER;
     xdist,ydist,dist,distsq,pull: REAL;
BEGIN
   force[me].x := 0; force[me].y := 0;
   FOR j := 1 TO n DO (*Consider every other body*)
     IF j <> me DO
       BEGIN
         xdist := body[j].x - body[me].x;
         ydist := body[j].y - body[me].y;
         distsq := xdist*xdist + ydist*ydist;
         dist := Sqrt(distsq);    (*Distance between the bodies*)
         pull := G * body[me].mass * body[j].mass / distsq;
         force[me].x := force[me].x + pull*xdist/dist; (*x force*)
         force[me].y := force[me].y + pull*ydist/dist; (*y force*)
       END;
END;

BEGIN

  ... (*Initialize master array "body"*)

FORALL  i := 1 TO n DO (*Create processes*)
   FindForce(i);

END.
```

FIGURE 9.3   N-Body problem for multiprocessor.

However, at any given time, each process has only two partitions—its own permanent local partition and one other circulating partition. Considering all the local memories, there will be exactly two complete copies of the master data array, both of which are partitioned. One copy will be fixed in location, with each partition permanently assigned to a specific local memory. A second copy of the array will be circulating around the ring, with each partition gradually moving from one local memory to the next.

Initially, the master data array is partitioned equally among the processes in the ring. This forms the *permanent partition* for each process. Then each process copies its permanent partition into its *circulating partition*. The following iterative procedure is then carried out by each process:

```
For each body i in my "permanent partition" do
 For each body j in the "circulating partition" do
  Compute force exerted by body j on body i;
Send circulating partition to right-neighbor process;
Receive new circulating partition from left-neighbor process;
```

The above procedure is repeated by each process until all the processes have seen a copy of all the circulating partitions. To illustrate the movement of the circulating partitions, consider a master data array with five partitions: *A*, B, C, D, E. The following table shows the partitions held by each process during the successive iterations of the algorithm. Initially, each process is given its permanent partition, which is copied into its circulating partition. For each process in this table, the permanent partition is on the left and the circulating partition on the right:

Process 1 $\longrightarrow$		Process 2 $\longrightarrow$		Process 3 $\longrightarrow$		Process 4 $\longrightarrow$		Process 5 $\longrightarrow$ to 1	
A	A	B	B	C	C	D	D	E	E
A	E	B	A	C	B	D	C	E	D
A	D	B	E	C	A	D	B	E	C
A	C	B	D	C	E	D	A	E	B
A	B	B	C	C	D	D	E	E	A

After the first iteration, each process sends its circulating partition to the right neighbor. Since the processes form a virtual ring, Process 5 sends to Process 1. During each successive iteration, it can be seen in this table how the circulating partitions gradually move around the ring until they have reached every process. By the end of the five iterations, each process has seen the entire data array, and therefore has computed the total force on every one of the bodies in its own permanent partition.

9.2.3 N-Body Program on Ring Topology

Figure 9.4 shows the complete N-Body program for a *RING* multicomputer topology with 25 processors. For programming convenience, the master data array *bodies* is organized as an array of partitions, each containing four data elements. For process communication, there is an array of channels *inchan* with one channel assigned to each of the 25 processes. The PROCEDURE FindForce runs on each processor. The heart of the procedure is three nested *FOR* loops. The outer loop with index k controls the circulation of partitions: each time around this loop, the partitions are circulated by one step around the ring. The inner loops with indices i, j compare each element of the permanent partition (*body*) with each element of the circulating partition (*circ*).

After completing these two inner loops, each process sends a partition to its right neighbor by writing into the *inchan* assigned to the right neighbor. Each process receives its new circulating partition by reading its own *inchan,* using its process number *me* as an index. By the time these three nested *FOR* loops are finished, the process will have computed the forces on all the bodies in its permanent partition. The last step in procedure FindForce is for the process to write the computed force for the elements of its partition back to the main process, using the *VAR* parameter technique described in Chapter 8.

One interesting feature of this N-Body program is the method used for assigning processes to the *RING* and distributing to each process its initial partition. This is all done simply inside the *FORALL* statement that creates the processes in the main program. The procedure call to FindForce creates each process. This procedure call passes each process its permanent partition as a parameter *bodies*[*i*]. Since the *bodies* array is organized as an array of partitions, a single index is enough to select the proper partition for each created process.

```
PROGRAM NBody;
ARCHITECTURE RING(25);
CONST n = 100;     (*Number of bodies*)
    numproc = 25;  (*Number of processes*)
    partsize = 4;  (*Size of each partition*)
    G = ... ;      (*Gravitational constant*)
TYPE bodytype = RECORD
          m,x,y: REAL;    (*Mass and position*)
        END;
    forcetype = RECORD
          x,y: REAL;    (*Force in x and y direction*)
        END;
    parttype = ARRAY [1..partsize] OF bodytype;
    resulttype = ARRAY [1..partsize] OF forcetype;
VAR bodies: ARRAY [1..numproc] OF parttype;     (*master data array*)
    finalforce: ARRAY [1..numproc] OF resulttype; (*resultant forces*)
    i,j: INTEGER;
    inchan: ARRAY [1..numproc] OF CHANNEL OF parttype; (*communication*)


PROCEDURE FindForce(me: INTEGER;
          body: parttype;     (*my permanent partition*)
          VAR result: resulttype); (*to send result back*)
VAR i,j,k: INTEGER;
   circ: parttype;   (*circulating partition*)
   force: resulttype; (*for accumulating force on my bodies*)
   xdist,ydist,dist,distsq,pull: REAL;
BEGIN
 circ := body;   (*copy permanent partition into circulating*)
 FOR i := 1 TO partsize DO
  BEGIN force[i].x := 0; force[i].y := 0; END;
  FOR k := 1 TO numproc DO
  BEGIN
   FOR i := 1 TO partsize DO
```

FIGURE 9.4 N-Body problem on a ring multicomputer.

```
FOR j := 1 TO partsize DO
  BEGIN (*Compute force exerted by body j on body i*)
    xdist := circ[j].x - body[i].x;
    ydist := circ[j].y - body[i].y;
    distsq := xdist*xdist + ydist*ydist;
    dist := Sqrt(distsq);
        IF dist <> 0 THEN
            BEGIN
                pull := G * body[i].m * circ[j].m / distsq;
                force[i].x := force[i].x + pull*xdist/dist;
                force[i].y := force[i].y + pull*ydist/dist;
            END;
        END;
    inchan[me MOD numproc + 1] := circ; (*send to right*)
    circ := inchan[me];  (*receive from left neighbor*)
  END;
  result := force;        (*final answer back to main process*)
END;

BEGIN  (*Main*)

  ... (*Initialize master data array "bodies"*)

FORALL  i := 1 TO numproc DO (*Create processes*)
   (@i-1 PORT inchan[i]) FindForce(i,bodies[i],finalforce[i]);

END.
```

FIGURE 9.4   (continued)

9.2.4 Performance Analysis

This N-Body program conforms to the general properties presented in the first section of this chapter: each iteration has a computation and a communication phase. During the computation phase, each process computes the force on each of the bodies in its permanent partition exerted by each of the bodies in the circulating partition. If we let k denote the partition size, the total duration of the computation phase during each iteration will have the form Sk^2.

During the communication phase, the k data items of the circulating partition are transmitted to the neighboring processor in the Ring topology. Using the communication model described in Chapter 8 (section 8.4.1), the hardware communication delay for transmitting r packets, assuming a basic communication delay D, is as follows:

$$\left(1 + \frac{r-1}{2}\right)D$$

In this communication model, the number of packets r is just $k/3$. Substituting in the above expression results in the following:

$$\frac{D}{6}k + \frac{D}{2}$$

In addition to this, there is also a software overhead associated with the writing and reading of the communication port. This overhead also has two terms, a term proportional to k and a constant term. Therefore, this complete communication delay, including both hardware and software overheads, has the following general form:

$$Vk + F$$

Adding together this communication time and the computation time results in the same formula already given in section 9.1 of this chapter. The execution time of each iteration is as follows:

$$Sk^2 + Vk + F$$

The total number of iterations in the N-Body program is equal to the number of processors p. Therefore, the total execution time for the whole program (excluding process creation) is as follows:

$$p(Sk^2 + Vk + F)$$

Letting n denote the total number of bodies, we can substitute $k = n/p$ in the above expression, resulting in the following:

$$\frac{Sn^2}{p} + Vn + Fp$$

The n^2 term in the above execution time results from the basic properties of the sequential N-Body algorithm, which is $O(n^2)$. Since there are p processors running in parallel, the n^2 term is divided by p. The second term (Vn) in the execution time is the communication overhead required to circulate the n bodies around the Ring. The third term Fp results from the fact that the communication is done in p discrete stages, one stage during each of the p iterations.

Intuitively, it is expected that an increase in the number of processors will decrease the total execution time for a parallel program. This property is expressed in the first term of the execution time Sn^2/p, which decreases with increasing values of p. However, the third term increases with p—the communication overhead grows in proportion to the number of processors. Since there are these two opposing tendencies as the number of processors is increased, there will be some optimal number of processors to produce the minimum program execution time for a given value of n. This optimum can be determined by taking the derivative of the execution time with respect to p and setting it equal to 0 (assuming n is held constant):

$$\frac{dT}{dp} = 0 = -\frac{Sn^2}{p^2} + F$$

Solving this equation yields the following optimal value for the number of processors in the Ring:

$$\text{optimal } p = n\sqrt{\frac{S}{F}}$$

This performance analysis has uncovered an important property of the parallel N-Body program: the optimal performance does not necessarily utilize all the available processors. Because of the nature of the communication overheads, performance may be improved by decreasing the number of processors and thereby increasing the partition size and granularity of each process. From the above formula for the optimal p, it is seen that increasing the basic communication delay D, which will increase F, should decrease the optimal number of processors.

Figure 9.5 shows a graph of the total execution time of the N-Body program for various values of k, the partition size. The vertical axis is the execution time of the N-Body program, and the horizontal axis is the basic communication delay D. The total number of bodies n is held constant as k is varied. The number of processors used for each value of k is of course $p = n/k$. In Figure 9.5, it can be seen that the best choice of k depends on the specific value of D. For $D < 135$, $k = 1$ and $p = 100$ produce the best performance. For $135 < D < 230$, $k = 2$ and $p = 50$ produce the best performance. For $D > 230$, $k = 3$ and $p = 34$ are optimal. Although it is not shown in the figure, as D is increased still further, $k = 4$ and then $k = 5$ will eventually become superior.

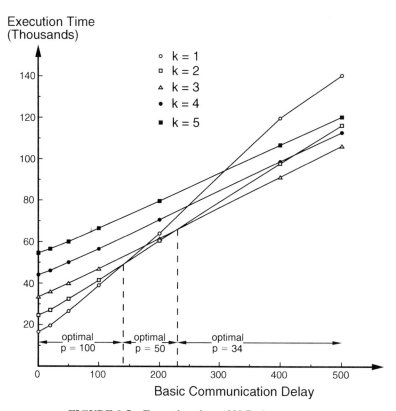

FIGURE 9.5   **Execution time of N-Body program.**

9.2.5 Overlapping Communication with Computation

It is possible to improve the performance of the N-Body program of Figure 9.4 by a simple modification that allows computing to continue even during the processor communication. As the program is now, each process performs the following sequence of activities during each iteration:

1. Compute force exerted by all bodies in the circulating partition on all bodies in the permanent partition.
2. Send current circulating partition to right neighbor.
3. Receive new circulating partition from left neighbor.

Each process will experience a communication delay between steps 2 and 3, while it is waiting for the new partition to arrive. During this waiting phase, the process is idle. This waiting time can be eliminated by having each process execute the send operation *before* the compute phase. In this way, all the processes can enter their compute phase while the new partitions are in transit between processors. When each process finishes its compute phase, it will find that the new partition has already arrived from the left neighbor, and can read it without experiencing any additional delay. In this way the impact of the communication overhead is completely eliminated, provided, of course, that the compute phase is longer than the communication delay.

Figure 9.6 shows the new FindForce procedure with the needed modification. The only change is the moving of the "send" instruction from below the "compute" phase to above the compute phase. Since all processes follow this procedure, they will find that when they reach the "receive" operation, the required data from the left neighbor will have already been received. Actually, if the communication delay in the hardware is longer than the duration of the compute phase, then the process will experience some delay when reaching the "receive" operation. In the performance analysis for the original nonoverlapped program of Figure 9.4, the total time for each iteration is derived by adding the duration of the compute and communicate phases. In the overlapped version, the time for each iteration is the maximum of the compute and communication phases. A more detailed performance analysis of the overlapped version is considered in one of the exercises at the end of this chapter.

9.2.6 Virtual Vs. Physical Topology

Each algorithm will have its own natural process communication topology. In the case of the N-Body program, the "Ring" is the natural topology—each process communicates only with its left and right neighbors in the Ring. Because of this *virtual* Ring topology in the algorithm, a physical *RING* multicomputer topology has been chosen. However, this same virtual Ring can be embedded in the more highly connected physical topologies, including the Mesh, Torus, and Hypercube, as discussed in Chapter 7. The additional physical communication links in the more highly connected topologies will not be used during the iterative execution of the processes. However, these extra connections will help to reduce the time to create the processes and distribute them along with their initial partitions to the processors. The lower diameter of the highly connected topologies will

```
PROCEDURE FindForce(me: INTEGER;
                    body: parttype;              (*my permanent partition*)
                    VAR result: resulttype); (*to send result back*)
VAR  i,j,k: INTEGER;
     circ: parttype;     (*circulating partition*)
     force: resulttype; (*for accumulating force on my bodies*)
     xdist,ydist,dist,distsq,pull: REAL;
BEGIN
  circ := body;      (*copy permanent partition into circulating*)
  FOR i := 1 TO partsize DO
    BEGIN force[i].x := 0; force[i].y := 0; END;
   FOR k := 1 TO numproc DO
    BEGIN

      inchan[me MOD numproc + 1] := circ; (*send to right*)

      (*Compute Phase*)
      FOR i := 1 TO partsize DO
        FOR j := 1 TO partsize DO
          BEGIN (*Compute force exerted by body j on body i*)
            xdist := circ[j].x - body[i].x;
            ydist := circ[j].y - body[i].y;
            distsq := xdist*xdist + ydist*ydist;
            dist := Sqrt(distsq);
            IF dist <> 0 THEN
              BEGIN
                pull := G * body[i].m * circ[j].m / distsq;
                force[i].x := force[i].x + pull*xdist/dist;
                force[i].y := force[i].y + pull*ydist/dist;
              END;
          END;

      circ := inchan[me];  (*receive from left neighbor*)

    END;
  result := force;           (*final answer back to main process*)
END;
```

FIGURE 9.6   Overlapping computation and communication in N-Body program.

reduce the time for this process creation and initialization step, as well as the process termination step.

It is often the case that topologies with lower connectivity can be embedded in topologies with higher connectivity. For the multicomputer topologies presented in Chapter 7, the following list is ordered by increasing connectivity:

1. Line

2. Ring

3. 2-D Mesh

4. Torus

5. 3-D Mesh

6. Hypercube

7. Fully connected

In general, all the lower-numbered topologies in the above list can be embedded in the higher-numbered topologies. In some cases, however, the embedding requires that some processors remain unused. For example, embedding a 25-processor *Ring* in a Hypercube requires a 5-dimensional Hypercube with 32 processors. Of course, any vitual communication structure can be implemented in any physical topology, provided that one is willing to bear the additional time delays of communication between processors with no direct physical connection.

Mapping a virtual topology in a parallel program to a specific physical multicomputer topology is very easy in Multi-Pascal. Actually, the physical topology is transparent to the program and affects the communication delays only when messages are sent between processes. The only time the programmer needs to refer directly to the physical topology is when using the @-feature, because it refers to real physical processor numbers. Referring back to the N-Body program of Figure 9.4, the @-feature appears only in the process creation statement. For convenience, this statement is repeated here:

```
FORALL  i := 1 TO numproc DO (*Create processes*)
  (@i-1 PORT inchan[i]) FindForce(i,bodies[i],finalforce[i]);
```

The "@i-1" primitive assigns each process to its proper physical processor in the underlying *RING* multicomputer topology. To implement this program on a Hypercube multicomputer, only a few changes are needed. Recall that in a Hypercube, each processor has direct connections to all processors whose number differs in exactly one binary digit. A virtual ring communication structure can be embedded into a physical Hypercube topology by using a *Gray Code,* as discussed in Chapter 7. A Gray Code is a sequence of numbers such that each successive number differs from the previous in only one binary digit.

In the program, an array *Gray* must be created that contains the Gray Code numbering to embed a virtual Ring in the Hypercube. The sequence of numbers in the array *Gray* is simply the Gray Code sequence. For example, if the program creates eight processes (*numproc* = 8), then the array *Gray* must contain the following numbers:

Gray[1] = 0 (binary 000)

Gray[2] = 1 (binary 001)

Gray[3] = 3 (binary 011)

Gray[4] = 2 (binary 010)

Gray[5] = 6 (binary 110)

Gray[6] = 7 (binary 111)

Gray[7] = 5 (binary 101)

Gray[8] = 4 (binary 100)

This sequence of numbers in array *Gray* gives the physical processor sequence in the Hypercube that forms a virtual Ring. The values for this array can be read into the program or computed internally, using the definition for Gray Codes presented in Chapter 7. The only other change to the original N-Body program of Figure 9.4 is to modify the expression following the @ in the process creation statement as follows:

```
FORALL  i := 1 TO numproc DO (*Create processes*)
  (@Gray[i] PORT inchan[i]) FindForce(i,bodies[i],finalforce[i]);
```

This "@Gray[i]" primitive will assign the processes to the proper physical processors in the Hypercube, so that communicating processes will always have a direct physical connection in the Hypercube. By using a similar programming technique, the N-Body program can be run on any of the multicomputer topologies. All that is needed is an array that contains the physical processor sequence needed to create a virtual Ring from the underlying multicomputer topology.

9.3 MATRIX MULTIPLICATION

Numerical computing in science and engineering usually deals with large multidimensional arrays of numbers, sometimes called *matrices*. The problem of multiplying two matrices is common in such applications. Matrix multiplication can be expressed with a simple computational procedure, and has a good potential for parallelization. Therefore, it has become an important standard example and benchmark for parallel programming. This section develops a parallel matrix multiplication program on a Torus multicomputer topology. The purpose is to illustrate general techniques for data partitioning and interprocess communication to achieve good performance on multicomputers. The parallel matrix multiplication program will be somewhat more complex than the N-Body program, because it requires a two-dimensional process communication pattern. This is why a Torus topology has been chosen for this example rather than a Ring, as was used for the N-Body program.

To define matrix multiplication, let us first define an operation called the *dot product* of two vectors (a vector is just a one-dimensional array). For two vectors $X = (x_1, x_2, \ldots, x_n)$ and $Y = (y_1, y_2, \ldots, y_n)$, the dot product is as follows:

$$X \cdot Y = x_1 y_1 + x_2 y_2 + \cdots + x_n y_n$$

The dot product is computed by multiplying the corresponding elements of the two vectors and adding the results.

Now let us define *matrix multiplication* of two matrices A and B to form a product matrix C. A, B, C can all be represented as two-dimensional arrays. For simplicity, assume that A and B are square matrices, both with dimension n by n. Then the product matrix C will also be n by n. Each element C_{ij} of the matrix product is defined as follows:

$$C_{ij} = \text{dot product of row } i \text{ of } A \text{ with column } j \text{ of } B$$

Thus, the computation of each single element in the matrix product requires the use of an entire row of matrix A and an entire column of matrix B. From this definition of matrix multiplication, the following sequential algorithm is easily derived:

```
FOR i := 1 TO n DO      (*i is row index*)
  FOR j := 1 TO n DO    (*j is column index*)
    BEGIN
      C[i,j] := 0;
      FOR k := 1 TO n DO
        (*dot product of row i of A with column j of B*)
        C[i,j] := C[i,j] + A[i,k]*B[j,k];
    END;
```

9.3.1 Partitioning the Matrices

Since so many values from the two matrices A and B are required to compute each element of C, the partitioning must be done carefully on a multicomputer. A bad partitioning method will lead to excessive data requirements at the processors. For example, if each processor computes only a single row of the product matrix C, then each processor will need a full copy of the matrix B. If each processor computes a single row and single column of C, then each processor will need full copies of both A and B!

To minimize the amount of data needed at each processor in the multicomputer, the best technique is to partition C into a two-dimensional array of square partitions, as shown in Figure 9.7. The n by n matrix is divided into an m by m array of square partitions, each having n^2/m^2 elements. The rows and columns of the partitions are labeled as shown in Figure 9.7. The partition in row i and column j is denoted C_{ij}. This partitioning pattern is easily mapped onto a Torus multicomputer topology, with each partition assigned to a different processor. A processor assigned a given partition C_{ij} is responsible for computing

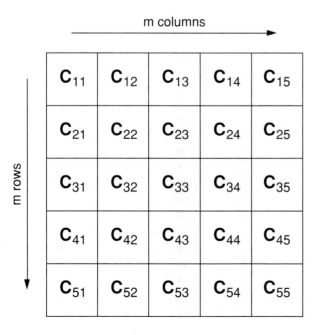

m columns

m rows

C_{11}	C_{12}	C_{13}	C_{14}	C_{15}
C_{21}	C_{22}	C_{23}	C_{24}	C_{25}
C_{31}	C_{32}	C_{33}	C_{34}	C_{35}
C_{41}	C_{42}	C_{43}	C_{44}	C_{45}
C_{51}	C_{52}	C_{53}	C_{54}	C_{55}

FIGURE 9.7 Partitioning for matrix multiplication.

all the values in that partition. This will require access to the corresponding rows and columns of the matrices A and B.

To identify the needed portions of A and B, let us also partition A and B into an m by m array of square partitions. From the definition of matrix multiplication, it is easy to show that the computation of a product partition C_{ij} requires all partitions in row i of A and column j of B. This is illustrated in Figure 9.8. The computation of partition C_{42} requires partition row 4 of matrix A and partition column 2 of B. Thus, each processor in the Torus multicomputer must have access to an entire partition row from A and an entire partition column from B.

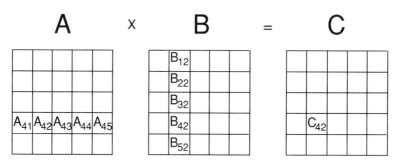

FIGURE 9.8 **Partitions needed for multiplication.**

Instead of duplicating data in matrices A and B, the partitions will be split among the processors of the Torus in the same way as matrix C. For the 5 by 5 partitioning shown in Figures 9.7 and 9.8, a 5 by 5 Torus topology is needed. Processor P_{ij} in the Torus will be assigned partitions A_{ij}, B_{ij}, and C_{ij}. With this division of the partitions, each processor initially has only part of the data it needs to compute its portion of the product matrix C. Looking at Figure 9.8, one can see that each processor P_{ij} will need access to all the A partitions assigned to row i of the Torus, and all the B partitions assigned to column j of the Torus. In Figure 9.8, processor P_{42} computes C_{42} and therefore needs access to all A partitions in row 4 and all B partitions in column 2.

The needed data is supplied to each processor through row and column rotations of the partitions of A and B. The partitions of A are rotated horizontally through all the processors in that row. Similarly, the partitions of B are rotated vertically through all the processors in that column. In Figure 9.8, the horizontal rotation of A means that processor P_{42} will eventually gain access to $A_{41}, A_{42}, A_{43}, A_{44}, A_{45}$. Similarly, the vertical rotation of B means that processor P_{42} will gain access to $B_{12}, B_{22}, B_{32}, B_{42}, B_{52}$. This rotation of partitions is similar to the circulation of partitions used in the N-Body program to ensure that each processor eventually receives all the partitions. The data movement in the Matrix Multiplication is somewhat more complex and requires a two-dimensional rotation pattern with A partitions rotating horizontally, and B partitions rotating vertically.

9.3.2 The Algorithm

To make the program simpler, first consider the multiplication of 3 by 3 matrices using a partition size of 1. A 3 by 3 Torus multicomputer topology will be used. For convenience, the processor in row i and column j of the Torus will be denoted "Processor ij." Similarly, the corresponding elements of arrays A, B, C will be denoted A_{ij}, B_{ij}, C_{ij}. The initial assignment of data to the Torus processors is shown below:

Processor 11	Processor 12	Processor 13
A_{11}, B_{11}, C_{11}	A_{12}, B_{12}, C_{12}	A_{13}, B_{13}, C_{13}
Processor 21	Processor 22	Processor 23
A_{21}, B_{21}, C_{21}	A_{22}, B_{22}, C_{22}	A_{23}, B_{23}, C_{23}
Processor 31	Processor 32	Processor 33
A_{31}, B_{31}, C_{31}	A_{32}, B_{32}, C_{32}	A_{33}, B_{33}, C_{33}

Focusing on Processor 11, the computation of C_{11} requires all the A values in row 1 and B values in column 1 as follows:

$$C_{11} = A_{11}B_{11} + A_{12}B_{21} + A_{13}B_{31}$$

The ideal structure for the program is to alternate computation with communication, as in the N-Body program. In this way, the data storage needed at each processor is minimized, and it becomes possible to overlap computation with communication for greater efficiency. Notice that Processor 11 initially contains values A_{11} and B_{11}, and therefore can begin to compute C_{11} immediately by multiplying $A_{11}B_{11}$ and saving the result. If the A values are rotated left and the B values rotated up, then Processor 11 will have values A_{12} and B_{21}, which can be multiplied and added to the previous result to get the partial sum: $A_{11}B_{11} + A_{12}B_{21}$. After one more left rotation of A and upward rotation of B, Processor 11 will have A_{13} and B_{31}, which can be multiplied and then added to the partial sum to give the final value of C_{11}.

With the initial allocation of values as shown above, this same nice behavior will also be true of Processors 22 and 33. However, consider the situation at Processor 12. The computation of C_{12} at that processor is as follows:

$$C_{12} = A_{11}B_{12} + A_{12}B_{22} + A_{13}B_{32}$$

Initially, this Processor 12 has A_{12} and B_{12}, which both appear in the computation, but in different places. Thus, Processor 12 has nothing to do, and must wait for a data rotation before it can compute anything. All the needed values of A and B will eventually be rotated into Processor 12, but there will be some delays, and the processor will also have to store some of the values temporarily. This same problem arises in all the processors that are not on the main diagonal, that is, all processors except 11, 22, 33.

To correct this problem, there is a very simple but clever adjustment that can be made to the initial assignment of values to the processors. Instead of assigning each member of A to the corresponding processor in the Torus, the elements of A are initially assigned using a leftward rotation as follows: for row i of matrix A, all values are initially rotated left by $i - 1$ steps. Similarly, all elements of B are initially assigned using an upward rotation as follows: for column j of B, all values are initially rotated upward by $j - 1$ steps. This rotation rule will result in the following initial assignment of data to the processors of the Torus:

Processor 11	Processor 12	Processor 13
A_{11}, B_{11}, C_{11}	A_{12}, B_{22}, C_{12}	A_{13}, B_{33}, C_{13}
Processor 21	Processor 22	Processor 23
A_{22}, B_{21}, C_{21}	A_{23}, B_{32}, C_{22}	A_{21}, B_{13}, C_{23}
Processor 31	Processor 32	Processor 33
A_{33}, B_{31}, C_{31}	A_{31}, B_{12}, C_{32}	A_{32}, B_{23}, C_{33}

With a little study, the reader can ascertain that now each processor has values of A and B that it can use immediately. In fact, the algorithm now becomes exceedingly simple. Each processor multiplies its current values of A and B and saves the result. Then all A values are rotated left, and B values are rotated up. Then each processor multiplies the newly received values of A and B, and adds this product to the partial sum. After one more rotation and computation step, the final values of C will all be computed. The procedure used at each processor is as follows:

```
VAR myA, myB, myC: REAL;
    i: INTEGER;
BEGIN
  myC := 0;
  FOR i := 1 TO 3 DO
    BEGIN
      myC := myC + myA*myB;
      send myA to neighbor processor in leftward rotation;
      send myB to neighbor processor in upward rotation;
      receive new myA;
      receive new myB;
    END;
  write myC back to master product array;
END;
```

9.3.3 Simplified Version

To make the program easier to understand, let us first present a Multi-Pascal program with a partition size of 1. The program is shown in Figure 9.9. The multicomputer architecture used is a 3 by 3 Torus. For communication purposes, each processor will be assigned two ports for receiving communication. The arrays *Achan* and *Bchan* are used for this purpose.

The procedure Multiply is essentially the same as the algorithm presented in the previous section. The procedure initially receives its own location (*row, col*) in the Torus, and its initial values for *myA, myB*. To prepare for the subsequent rotations of values, the Multiply procedure first computes the location of its neighbors in the leftward and upward rotations. Since the Torus topology has wraparound connections between opposite boundaries, it is ideally suited for the two-dimensional rotations performed in this program. In the main body of the Multiply procedure, communication is alternated with computation during each iteration by using a technique similar to the N-Body program. The main difference is that communication goes in two directions in this Matrix Multiplication. Notice in Figure 9.9 that the computation step is sandwiched between the sending and receiving communication steps. This allows an overlap between communication and computation, as explained in detail for the N-Body program.

In the body of the main program, one process is created to run on each processor of the 3 by 3 Torus. In the nested *FOR* loops, index *i* is the row index and index *j* is the column index. Since the processors in the Torus are numbered sequentially in row-major order (see Figure 7.8), the expression "@i*n+j" is needed to assign each process to the appropriate processor number. For each created processs, a *PORT* declaration is used to assign the corresponding channels from the *Achan* and *Bchan* arrays. The processes are actually created by the call to the Multiply procedure following the *FORK* primitive.

```
PROGRAM Matrixmult;
ARCHITECTURE TORUS(3);
CONST n = 3;
VAR A,B,C: ARRAY [0..n-1,0..n-1] OF REAL; (*master data arrays*)
    Achan,Bchan:  ARRAY [0..n-1,0..n-1] OF CHANNEL OF REAL;
    i,j: INTEGER;

PROCEDURE Multiply(row,col: INTEGER; myA,myB: REAL; VAR mainC: REAL);
VAR iter,above,left: INTEGER;
    myC: REAL;
BEGIN
  IF row > 0 THEN above := row-1 ELSE above := n-1; (*up neighbor*)
  IF col > 0 THEN left := col-1 ELSE left := n-1;   (*left neighbor*)
  myC := 0;
  FOR iter := 1 TO n DO
    BEGIN
      Achan[row,left] := myA;  (*Send myA in leftward rotation*)
      Bchan[above,col] := myB; (*Send myB in upward rotation*)
      myC := myC + myA*myB;
      myA := Achan[row,col];   (*Receive new myA*)
      myB := Bchan[row,col];   (*Receive new myB*)
    END;
  mainC := myC; (*Send final value to main process*)
END;

BEGIN
  ... (*Initialize values of A and B matrices*)

 FOR i := 0 TO n-1 DO
  FOR j := 0 TO n-1 DO
     FORK (@i*n+j PORT Achan[i,j];Bchan[i,j])
       Multiply(i, j, A[i, (j+i) MOD n], B[(i+j) MOD n, j], C[i,j]);
END.
```

FIGURE 9.9 Simplified matrix multiplication.

The four parameters of Multiply are the row and column numbers, followed by the initial values for *myA* and *myB*. Recall that the initial values of *A* are rotated left: row *i* is rotated *i* − 1 positions. This initial assignment of rotated values is accomplished with the parameter $A[i, (j + i) \; MOD \; n]$. The initial values of *B* must be rotated upward: column *j* is rotated *j* − 1 positions. This is accomplished with the parameter $B[(i + j) \; MOD \; n, j]$.

9.3.4 Complete Program

The simplified Matrix Multiplication program with partition size 1 does not produce good performance because the process granularity is too small. To overcome the process creation and communication overheads, the amount of computation performed in each process must be increased. This is accomplished by using larger matrices and increasing the partition size. The resultant Multi-Pascal program is very similar in structure to the simplified program of Figure 9.9. However, the coding in somewhat more complex because each partition is now a two-dimensional array rather than a single real number. The complete program is shown in Figure 9.10.

To facilitate the partitioning, each of the arrays *A, B, C* is structured as a two-dimensional array of partitions, with each partition being a two-dimensional array of real numbers. Refer to the constant, type, and variable declarations at the beginning of the main program in Figure 9.10. Each of the master arrays *A, B, C* is an *m* by *m* array of partitions, with each partition being a *p* by *p* array of real numbers. The communication channels *Achan* and *Bchan* must also be channels whose component type is a partition. Every effort has been made in the program to handle each partition as a single entity, thus avoiding time-consuming nested loops.

This program of Figure 9.10 is remarkably similar to the simplified one of Figure 9.9. The major difference is in the computational portion of the Multiply procedure. For partition size 1, the computation consisted of a single multiplication and addition:

```
myC := myC + myA*myB;
```

For larger partition sizes, this multiplication and addition of single real numbers must be replaced by *matrix* multiplication and addition. Each partition is a *p* by *p* matrix of real numbers. In the computational portion of the Multiply procedure, the partitions *myA* and *myB* must be multiplied using matrix multiplication, and the result added to the partition *myC*, using matrix addition. It is a standard property of matrix multiplication that the matrices can be partitioned and multiplied in this way. The same matrix multiplication algorithm can be applied to the partitions, as if each were simply a single number. The only difference is that the ordinary operations of multiplication and addition of single numbers are replaced by matrix multiplication and addition of the partitions. This important property of matrix multiplication is further analyzed in the exercises for this chapter.

One interesting feature of this program is the use of the *FORK* operator for creating the processes. One might be tempted to use the following nested *FORALL* instead:

```
FORALL i := 0 TO m-1 DO
  FORALL j := 0 TO m-1 DO
    (@... PORT ...)
      Multiply(i,j,A[...],B[...],C[...] );
```

```
PROGRAM Matrixmult;
ARCHITECTURE TORUS(7);
CONST m = 7; (*Torus has m by m processors*)
      p = 5; (*Partition size is p by p*)
TYPE partition = ARRAY [1..p,1..p] OF REAL;
     chantype = CHANNEL OF partition;
VAR A,B,C: ARRAY [0..m-1,0..m-1] OF partition; (*master data arrays*)
    Achan,Bchan:  ARRAY [0..m-1,0..m-1] OF chantype; (*Communication*)
    i,j: INTEGER;


PROCEDURE Multiply(row,col: INTEGER; myA,myB: partition;
                     VAR mainC: partition);
var i,j,k,iter,above,left: INTEGER;
    myC: partition;
BEGIN
  IF row > 0 THEN above := row-1 ELSE above := m-1;
  IF col > 0 THEN left := col-1 ELSE left := m-1;
  FOR i := 1 TO p DO
    FOR j := 1 TO p DO
      myC[i,j] := 0;
  FOR iter := 1 TO m DO
    BEGIN
      Achan[row,left] := myA;  (*Send myA in leftward rotation*)
      Bchan[above,col] := myB; (*Send myB in upward rotation*)
      FOR i := 1 TO p DO  (*Multiply the A and B partitions*)
        FOR j := 1 TO p DO
          FOR k := 1 TO p DO
            myC[i,j] := myC[i,j] + myA[i,k]*myB[k,j];
      myA := Achan[row,col];   (*Receive new myA*)
      myB := Bchan[row,col];   (*Receive new myB*)
    END;
  mainC := myC;  (*Write product back to master C*)
END;

BEGIN
  ... (*Initialize values for A and B matrices*)

FOR i := 0 TO m-1 DO
  FOR j := 0 TO m-1 DO
     FORK (@i*m+j PORT Achan[i,j];Bchan[i,j])
       Multiply(i, j, A[i, (j+i) MOD m], B[(i+j) MOD m, j], C[i,j]);
END.
```

FIGURE 9.10   Matrix multiplication on a Torus.

This nested *FORALL* structure will not produce the desired effect because of the dynamics of the *FORALL* statement. The outer *FORALL* with index *i* will create *m* processes, each of which will consist of the inner *FORALL*. This first set of *m* processes will each create *m* additional processes by calling the procedure Multiply. The problem is that the first set of m processes based on index i will all be assigned to new processors for execution. However, the master matrices A and B are local to process 0. Therefore, when the A and B matrices are referenced in the call to the Multiply procedure, a illegal nonlocal reference back to arrays A and B will result. It is generally recommended that Multi-Pascal programmers avoid nested *FORALL* statements when writing multicomputer programs with data partitioning. However, as is illustrated in the N-Body program of Figure 9.4, single unnested *FORALL* statements are quite useful.

9.3.5 Performance Analysis

To develop a general algebraic expression for the overall program execution time, let us define the following symbols:

n dimension of the matrices
m number of rows and columns in the Torus
k number of rows and columns in each partition
D basic communication delay in the Torus
C process creation time

The general analysis of the program performance is similar to the analysis of the N-Body program. Each iteration has a computation and a communication phase. The computation phase is dominated by the matrix multiplication of the A and B partitions. This is done with three nested loops that each repeat k times. Thus, the duration of the computation phase during each iteration has the following form:

Computation phase: Sk^3

During the communication phase, the current A and B partitions are sent to the neighbor, and the new partitions are read. Because the send operation occurs before the computation phase, and the receive operation after the computation, the actual hardware transmission of the data overlaps with the computation. Therefore, if the hardware communication delay is less than the duration of the computation phase, then it will not affect the execution time. By using the communication model described in Chapter 8, the communication time for a message with r packets is as follows:

$$\left(1 + \frac{r-1}{2}\right)D$$

Since each partition contains k^2 data values, and they are grouped with three in each packet, the communication time is as follows:

$$\left(1 + \frac{\frac{k^2}{3} - 1}{2}\right)D = \left(\frac{1}{2} + \frac{k^2}{6}\right)D$$

Comparing this to the computation time shows that the communication time will have no influence if it satisfies the following:

$$D < \frac{6Sk^3}{3 + k^2}$$

Using the Multi-Pascal system, we can determine that the constant S has value 30. Substituting this in the above inequality yields the following:

$$k = 1: \qquad D < 45$$
$$k = 2: \qquad D < 205$$
$$k = 3: \qquad D < 405$$
$$k = 4: \qquad D < 606$$
$$k = 5: \qquad D < 800$$

This analysis shows that for all except the smallest partition sizes, the hardware communication delay can be essentially ignored in the performance analysis of this program (unless the basic communication delay D is extremely large). Therefore the total duration of the computational portion of the program can be determined by multiplying the duration of the computation phase of each iteration (Sk^3) times the total number of iterations m:

$$\text{Computation execution time: } Sk^3m = \frac{Sn^3}{m^2}$$

This total execution time is just the sequential execution time required for the matrix multiplication (Sn^3) divided among the number of processors in the Torus topology (m^2). The major overhead that may reduce the speedup below this ideal value comes from the process creation and data distribution that occurs at the beginning of the program. It will be interesting to analyze this initial phase of the program in more detail. Since there are m^2 processes, the time to create them all is as follows:

$$\text{Process creation time: } Cm^2$$

As these processes are created, they are dispatched along with their initial data partitions to the physical processors. The time required for this communication in the Torus topology is difficult to calculate analytically. However, using an oversimplified view, we can develop an approximation. Since both the A and B arrays are distributed to the processors, the total amount of data distributed is $2n^2$, which results in $2n^2/3$ communication packets. The main bottleneck in this distribution is getting them out of processor 0, which has only four connecting links. In the routing method used in the Multi-Pascal system, the packets always move horizontally first. Therefore, the vast majority of packets will be concentrated along the two horizontal links from processor 0. Each packet keeps a link busy for time $D/2$. Therefore, the total time to move all the packets through the two horizontal links is as follows:

$$\frac{D}{2} \frac{1}{2} \frac{2n^2}{3} = \frac{Dn^2}{6}$$

All of this data is gradually sent into the communication network as the processes are created. Each procedure call that creates a process also sends it assigned data partitions into the network. Therefore, this data distribution overlaps with the process creation. The total duration of this initial phase will thus be the maximum of these times:

$$\text{Initial phase:} \quad \max\left(Cm^2, \frac{Dn^2}{6}\right)$$

When the basic communication delay D is small, the process creation term will dominate. As the value of D grows, a transition point will be reached, after which the data distribution time will dominate. The transition point can be calculated by equating the two times and solving for D as follows:

$$Cm^2 = \frac{Dn^2}{6}$$

Thus,
$$D = 6C\left(\frac{m}{n}\right)^2$$

Substituting $n = mk$ results in the following for the transition point:

$$D = \frac{6C}{k^2}$$

Figure 9.11 shows a graph of the actual performance of this Matrix Multiplication program for a range of values of k, the dimension of the partition. As with all the performance graphs in this chapter, this graph was generated by using the Multi-Pascal simulation software with the Congestion option turned on. The vertical axis is the speedup

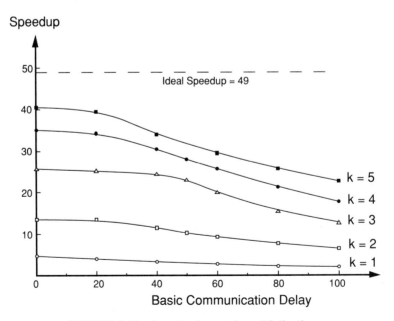

FIGURE 9.11   Speedup in matrix multiplication.

Data Partitioning   Chap. 9

achieved by the program. The number of processors in the Torus topology is held constant at 49 for all the values of k. Therefore, the upper limit on the achievable speedup is 49. The horizontal axis is the basic communication delay D. Two important properties of the program performance can be observed in this graph. First, for each value of k, the graph is relatively flat at the far left side. Second, as D increases, some transition point is reached, after which the speedup gradually decreases. This confirms the correctness of our analytical analysis above that located this transition point.

In the far left region of each graph, the process creation time is the dominant overhead. In the right portion of the graph, the communication delay for data distribution is the dominant overhead. However, it is interesting that in both regions, the achieved speedup increases as k increases. This is because the computational portion of the program has execution time $O(k^3)$, whereas the process creation time is constant for all values of k, and the data distribution time is $O(k^2)$. Thus, increasing k will reduce the impact of the overhead in both the left and right regions. This is an a specific example of the general property discussed in earlier chapters that initialization and process creation overheads can be overcome by increasing the data size for the same number of processors.

9.4 JACOBI RELAXATION

The Jacobi Relaxation algorithm solves an important differential equation called Laplace's equation. The algorithm uses computational techniques typical of a wide class of numerical algorithms. The Relaxation begins with initial values for a two-dimensional array. These numbers will reflect some physical quantity in the physical system being modeled, such as voltage, temperature, or pressure. The algorithm iteratively recomputes the value at each point in the array as the average of the four surrounding points. The term "relaxation" is used because the values gradually average out or "relax" across the entire array. Typically, the boundary points will be held at some fixed constant value.

Within each iteration, there is a large potential for parallelism in Jacobi Relaxation. Chapter 6 presented several highly parallel versions for execution on shared-memory multiprocessors. It is recommended that the reader briefly review the discussion of Jacobi Relaxation at the beginning of Chapter 6. This section will describe the implementation of parallel Jacobi Relaxation on a Hypercube multicomputer. The main focus will be on the data partitioning method and the resultant iterative communication patterns in the Hypercube. For reference, Figure 9.12 is the sequential Jacobi Relaxation program from Chapter 6.

9.4.1 Multicomputer Algorithm

The central issue in creating a multicomputer version of the algorithm is to decide how to partition the data array. Once the partitioning is decided, the rest of the algorithm follows easily. In the multiprocessor version of Chapter 6, each processor is assigned a single row of the main array A. Although this row-based partitioning is not optimal, it leads to the simplest program, and will be sufficient for our purposes here. To implement the Jacobi

```
PROGRAM Jacobi;
CONST n = 32;
      tolerance = .01;
VAR A,B: ARRAY [0..n+1,0..n+1] OF REAL;
    i,j: INTEGER;
    change,maxchange: REAL;

BEGIN
    ...   (*Read in initial values for array A*)

B := A;
REPEAT (*compute new values until desired tolerance is reached*)
  BEGIN
    maxchange := 0;
    FOR i := 1 TO n DO
      FOR j := 1 TO n DO
        BEGIN (*compute new value and its change over old value*)
          B[i,j] := (A[i-1,j] + A[i+1,j] + A[i,j-1] + A[i,j+1]) / 4;
          change := ABS( B[i,j] - A[i,j] );
          IF change > maxchange THEN maxchange := change;
        END;
    A := B;
  END;
UNTIL maxchange < tolerance;
END.
```

FIGURE 9.12   Sequential Jacobi Relaxation with convergence test.

Relaxation on a multicomputer, let us use this same partitioning technique: each processor will be assigned one row of the main array A.

The computation of the new value at each array point uses the values of the four neighboring points. Therefore, each point needs values not only from its own row, but also from the neighboring rows above and below. In a shared-memory version of the parallel program, processors can access neighboring rows easily in the shared memory, which contains the entire array. However, in a multicomputer there is no shared memory, and the rows of the array are distributed across the local memories of the processors. As each processor computes the new values for its own row, it will somehow need to gain access to values in the two neigboring rows. In accordance with the message-passing programming style, the needed values will be sent by the neighboring processors.

Assume that the rows are distributed among the processors of the multicomputer, such that processor i is given row i of the array A. Then the computation performed in processor i will require copies of row $i-1$ and $i+1$, which reside with processors $i-1$ and $i+1$, respectively. During the communication phase of the algorithm, each processor will send a copy of its own row to both immediate neighbors. This will give each processor copies of three rows: its own row, the row above, and the row below. Using these three rows, each processor now has the needed data to compute new values for all the elements in its own row, using the Jacobi averaging technique. The new values for each row i will then be available only to processor *i*. The next iteration begins with each processor again sending a copy of these new values to both immediate neighbors. Each processor can then receive the new values from its two neighbors, and recompute its own row, using the new values.

The algorithm continues in this way, with each iteration consisting of a communication phase followed by a computation phase. The procedure followed by each processor can be generally expressed as follows:

```
VAR  myrow,downrow,uprow,newrow: ARRAY [0..n+1] OF REAL;
     j: INTEGER; done: BOOLEAN;
     maxchange: REAL;
BEGIN
  REPEAT
    FOR j := 1 TO n DO (*average of four neighboring points*)
      newrow[j] := (myrow[j-1]+myrow[j+1]+downrow[j]+uprow[j]) / 4;
    myrow := newrow;
    Send myrow to neighbors above and below;
    Receive new copies of "downrow" and "uprow" from neighbors;
    Compute "maxchange" in my row;
    done := Aggregate(maxchange < tolerance); (*termination test*)
  UNTIL done;
END;
```

In the above computation, the boundary points at location 0 and $n + 1$ in the arrays are held constant. That is why the inner *FOR* loop indexes only from 1 to *n*. Notice that the computation of the new value at each point requires two values from the same row, one value from the row above, and one value from the row below. At the end of each iteration, the global termination test is performed using an "Aggregate" function to compute the logical *AND* of all the local termination tests in the processes. This function for a Hypercube has already been described in detail at the end of Chapter 8.

This pattern of alternating computation with communication is similar to both the N-Body and Matrix Multiplication programs presented earlier in this chapter. There is one crucial difference, however. In the N-Body and Matrix Multiplication programs, copies of the partitions are circulated among the processes with no modification—each process receives a copy of a partition and passes on this same copy. However, in the Jacobi algorithm the communicated values are always new values. Each processor computes new values for its own row and then sends these new values to its neighbors. Because the communicated values are always new, it is not possible to overlap communication and computation, as was done in the N-Body and Matrix Multiplication programs. Recall that this overlap was accomplished during each iteration by using the following sequence of operations: send, compute, receive. In the Jacobi algorithm, new values must first be received before the "compute" phase, so the sequence must be as follows: send, receive, compute. This inability to overlap communication with computation will increase the impact of communication delays on the performance of the Jacobi algorithm, as compared to the N-Body and Matrix Multiplication programs.

The complete Parallel Jacobi Relaxation program for a Hypercube is shown in Figure 9.13. The Hypercube topology has dimension 5, and therefore contains the neces-

```
PROGRAM Jacobi;
ARCHITECTURE HYPERCUBE(5);
CONST n = 32;          (*number of processors*)
      d = 5;           (*dimension of Hypercube*)
      numiter = 2*d;   (*number of iterations before termination test*)
      tolerance = .1;
TYPE rowtype = ARRAY [0..n+1] OF REAL;
VAR A: ARRAY [0..n+1] OF rowtype;
    i: INTEGER;
    upchan,downchan: ARRAY [1..n] OF CHANNEL OF rowtype; (*Comm. ports*)
    GrayCode: ARRAY [1..n] OF INTEGER;
    inchan: ARRAY [0..n-1,1..d] OF CHANNEL OF BOOLEAN; (*for Aggregation*)

    FUNCTION Aggregate(mydone: BOOLEAN): BOOLEAN;
      ... (* Multiple Aggregation function from Figure 8.11 *)


    PROCEDURE Updaterow(me: INTEGER; myrow: rowtype; VAR out: rowtype);
    VAR j,k: INTEGER; maxchange,change: REAL;
        newrow,uprow,downrow: rowtype;
        done: BOOLEAN;
    BEGIN
      newrow[0] := myrow[0];  newrow[n+1] := myrow[n+1];
      IF me = 1 THEN downrow := downchan[me];
      IF me = n THEN uprow := upchan[me];
      REPEAT
       FOR k := 1 TO numiter DO (*Several iterations before term. test*)
         BEGIN
           IF me > 1 THEN
              upchan[me-1] := myrow;    (*Send to neighbor me-1*)
           IF me < n THEN
             BEGIN
               downchan[me+1] := myrow; (*Send to neighbor me+1*)
               uprow := upchan[me];     (*Receive new uprow*)
             END;
           IF me > 1 THEN
             downrow := downchan[me];   (*Receive new downrow*)
           maxchange := 0;
           FOR j := 1 TO n DO
             BEGIN
               (*Compute average of neighboring points*)
               newrow[j] := (myrow[j-1]+myrow[j+1]+downrow[j]+uprow[j])/4;
               change := ABS(newrow[j]-myrow[j]);
               IF change > maxchange THEN maxchange := change;
             END;
           myrow := newrow;
          END;
        done := Aggregate(maxchange < tolerance); (*termination test*)
```

FIGURE 9.13   Jacobi Relaxation on a Hypercube.

```
      UNTIL done;
      out := myrow; (*Write final answer back to F*)
   END;


BEGIN
   ... (*Initialize values for array A*)
       (*Initialize Gray Code array for the Hypercube*)

downchan[1] := A[0]; upchan[n] := A[n+1]; (*Fixed boundary values*)
FORALL i := 1 TO n DO
   ( @GrayCode[i]  PORT  upchan[i];downchan[i];inchan[GrayCode[i]] )
        Updaterow(i, A[i], A[i]);
END.
```

FIGURE 9.13   (continued)

sary 32 processors for the array *A* with 32 rows. The communication between processes is done with the arrays *upchan* and *downchan,* which allow a whole row to be communicated with a single statement. Each process has communication ports *upchan*[*me*] and *downchan*[*me*] for receiving rows of data from the neighboring processes. To minimize the communication delay, processes that work on neighboring rows should be run on physical processors with a direct connection in the Hypercube toplogy. For this purpose, a Gray Code is stored in array *GrayCode,* and each process *i* is assigned to physical processor number *GrayCode*[*i*]. To reduce the performance overhead of the termination test, several iterations are performed between termination tests. Each process in the program is created with the procedure Updaterow, having three parameters:

me   row number in the array *A* assigned to this process

myrow   copy of the assigned row from array *A*

out   for returning final values of assigned row back to main

The Update procedure is the same as the informal algorithm presented earlier, except that the detailed instructions for communication have been added. Each process sends a copy of its own row *myrow* to the appropriate receiving channel of its two neighboring processes. The use of *upchan* and *downchan* for each process is as follows: *downchan* receives the row from the neighbor with the lower row number, and *upchan* receives from the neighbor with the higher row number. To deal with boundary conditions, the tests *me* > 1 and *me* < *n* are necessary. The processes at the extreme upper and lower boundaries have only one neighbor, and therefore must communicate in one direction only.

The process creation statement in the body of the main program is similar to previous example programs. Each process is assigned to its physical processor using the @ with the Gray Code number. Process *i* is assigned communication ports *upchan*[*i*] and *downchan*[*i*]. Process *i* must also be assigned an *inchan* port for use by the Aggregate function during the termination test. Therefore, a different numbering system must be used for these *inchan* ports because the Aggregate function refers to real physical processor numbers when sending messages (see the discussion of Multiple Aggregation on a Hypercube at the end of Chapter 8). Process i is assigned $inchan[GrayCode[i]]$ because $GrayCode[i]$ is the physical processor number on which Process i runs.

9.4.2 Performance Analysis

The number of iterations required for convergence in this Jacobi Relaxation program will depend on the properties of the initial data values. This issue can be avoided in the performance analysis by focusing on the average execution time for each iteration. The analysis is similar to the N-Body and Matrix Multiplication programs. The following symbol definitions are needed:

n number of rows in array A (and number of processors)
d dimension of the Hypercube
D nearest neighbor communication delay in the Hypercube

As before, each iteration has a computation and communication phase. The computation phase in each process computes the new values for the n points in the assigned row of that process. This is done in the Update procedure with a FOR loop having index j ranging from 1 to n. The duration of this phase has the following general form:

$$\text{Computation phase: } Sn$$

During the communication phase, n values are sent to each of two neighbors. As discussed in previous sections, the total number of packets sent to each neighbor is $n/3$, and therefore the delay in the communication network is as follows:

$$\frac{nD}{6} + \frac{D}{2}$$

In addition, there is some software overhead for executing the communication statements at the beginning of each iteration in the Update procedure. This overhead does increase with n, but it is mainly dominated by a constant time that is independent of n. This can be added to the hardware delay time above, to get the following general form for the duration of the communication phase:

$$\text{Communication phase: } \frac{nD}{6} + F$$

Since there is no overlap between computation and communication, the duration of the two phases are simply added to get the duration of a single iteration:

$$\text{Iteration: } Sn + \frac{nD}{6} + F$$

With reference to the Jacobi program of Figure 9.13, it is seen that after each $2d$ iterations, a termination test is performed by calling the Aggregate function. Therefore, the execution time of the Aggregate function must be averaged over these $2d$ iterations. In Chapter 8, it was seen that the Aggregate function has log $n = d$ iterations, each with a short computation and communication phase. The computation consists of a few assignment statements, and the communication involves sending and receiving a single value from an immediate neighbor. The sum of these times will be a constant, which must be multiplied by the number of iterations to determine the duration of the Aggregate function:

$$\text{Aggregate function:} \quad dG$$

Since the Aggregate function is called after every $2d$ Jacobi iterations in the Update procedure, its execution time must be divided by $2d$ and added to the time for the Jacobi iteration:

$$Sn + \frac{nD}{6} + \left(F + \frac{G}{2}\right)$$

By combining the constants, this can be written as follows:

$$\text{Average Jacobi iteration:} \quad \left(S + \frac{D}{6}\right)n + H$$

In this analysis we have chosen to ignore the process creation and data initialization phase. Just focusing on the computational portion of the program is sufficient to reveal the important performance characteristics of the Jacobi program. Specifically, we are interested in examining the change in program performance as n is increased. The value of n in this version of the program is the dimension of the data size, and also the number of processors. Therefore, it is an important parameter. A useful measure of program performance for varying values of n is the *efficiency,* defined as the speedup divided by the number of processors.

The speedup is defined as the "sequential" execution time divided by the parallel execution time. A reasonable definition of the sequential execution time in this Jacobi program is the time required to execute the computation phase of each iteration, using only one processor. The communication time and the time for executing the Aggregate function are considered as overheads associated with parallel execution, and therefore are not included in the "sequential" time. Since each of the n processes requires time Sn for the computation phase of each iteration, the sequential execution time for each iteration is as follows:

$$\text{Sequential time:} \quad Sn^2$$

To determine the speedup achieved by the parallel program, divide this sequential time by the average parallel time for each Jacobi iteration:

$$\text{Speedup:} \quad \frac{Sn^2}{\left(S + \frac{D}{6}\right)n + H}$$

As n increases, this speedup will approach the limit:

$$\text{Maximum speedup:} \quad \left(\frac{S}{S + \dfrac{D}{6}}\right) n$$

Figure 9.14 shows a graph of the actual performance of the Jacobi Relaxation program for a range of values of n. The vertical axis shows the *efficiency,* defined as the speedup divided by n, the number of processors. The maximum achievable efficiency for any parallel program is, of course, 1. Each of the four curves in the figure shows the efficiency achieved as n is varied for a given fixed value of the basic communication delay D. The four sample values of D are 0, 20, 40, 60. These four curves are based on measurements of the average execution time of each iteration. As in the performance analysis above, the process creation and data initialization times are not included in these measurements. The performance analysis predicts that the efficiency should approach the following limit as n increases:

$$\text{Maximum efficiency:} \quad \frac{S}{S + \dfrac{D}{6}}$$

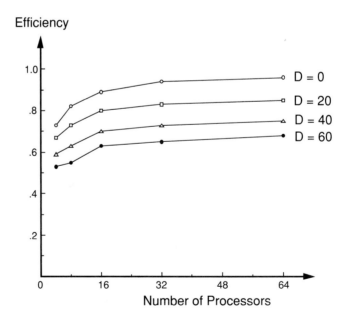

FIGURE 9.14   Performance of Jacobi Relaxation.

It is seen in this figure that each curve seems to be approaching some limiting value, in agreement with this performance prediction. The above formula predicts that the efficiency for $D = 0$ will approach the limiting value 1. The observed curve for $D = 0$ does seem to have this general property. It is also seen in Figure 9.14 that increasing the basic communication delay D to produce the other curves does gradually reduce the efficiency, which also agrees with the above theoretical prediction. The computation of the efficiency curves was done using the Multi-Pascal interactive system, with the aid of the following features: *Duration, %Seqon, Clock, Seqtime* (see Appendix B for a description of the use of these features for performance measurements).

9.4.3 Alternate Partitioning Methods

The Parallel Jacobi Relaxation program of Figure 9.13 partitions the array A by rows, with exactly one row for each processor. In a real application, the number of rows in the array may be greater than the number of available processors. If this is the case, then a similar row-partitioning technique may be used with each processor assigned a contiguous group of rows. If there are n rows and p processors, then each processor is assigned n/p rows. For this partitioning, the processors need not communicate all their rows to the neighbors during each iteration—only the boundary rows need be communicated.

The reason for the communication is to provide each point with all its neighboring values to start each new iteration. When each processor has a partition consisting of a single row only, then this row is a boundary row also, and must be sent to each neighbor. However, if there are many rows in the partition, only the first and last row of each partition need be communicated. The internal rows of each partition will not affect rows in other partitions directly. With this multiple-row partitioning, the amount of data communicated by each process during each iteration is $2n$.

To reduce the amount of communication, it is more efficient to partition the array in a two-dimensional fashion, as we did for the arrays in the Matrix Multiplication program in this chapter. This partitioning into a two-dimensional array of square partitions will minimize the number of boundary points for each partition. The number of boundary points for these different partitioning methods is illustrated in Figure 9.15. In the top part of the figure, the n by n array is partitioned by rows into p partitions. The number of boundary points is always $2n$, independent of p. With two-dimensional partitioning, each of the p partitions will be a square with n^2/p points. The partition will contain $n/\sqrt{p}$ rows and columns. The total number of boundary points in this case is $4n/\sqrt{p}$.

For large arrays, the 2-D partitioning will have fewer boundary points. For example, consider a 128 by 128 array using a multicomputer with 64 processors. Using the row-partitioning technique, each partition has $2n = 256$ boundary points. With the two-dimensional partitioning, there is an 8 by 8 array of square partitions, each of dimension 16 by 16. Therefore, the number of boundary points is 64, which is one-fourth of the amount for the row-partitioning method. One disadvantage of the two-dimensional partitioning is that it leads to a more complex program because each processor must communicate directly with four neighbors, whereas in the row-partitioning method, each processor only has to communicate with only two neighbors.

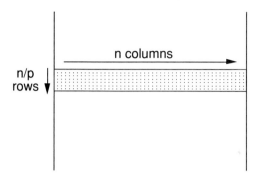

Row Partitioning: 2n boundary points per partition

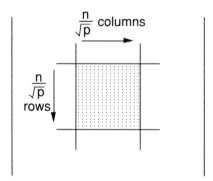

Two-dimensional Partitioning: $\dfrac{4n}{\sqrt{p}}$ boundary points per partition

FIGURE 9.15   Boundary points for partitions.

9.5 SUMMARY

The purpose of this chapter has been to describe a variety of data partitioning methods that are useful for writing efficient multicomputer programs. Writing parallel programs for multicomputers is in many ways similar to multiprocessor programming, and many of the issues and techniques are similar. The one major difference is that multiprocessors can store all the shared variables in the shared memory, where they are directly accessible to all processors, whereas in the multicomputer, the shared data must be distributed across the local memories of the processors. Access by a processor to its own local memory is fast, but access to data in remote memories requires time-consuming message-passing through the processor communication network. Therefore, efficient multicomputer programming demands that data be partitioned among the local memories in a way that minimizes the need for remote data access.

The first example presented in this chapter is the N-Body problem. This program has the undesirable property that no matter how the data is partitioned, each processor still needs to have access to all the data. However, despite this requirement, it is still possible to create an efficient multicomputer program by circulating partitions of the data around a Ring communication network, so that each processor eventually receives a copy of each partition. By overlapping communication with computation, the loss of time from the circulation of the partitions is minimized.

This virtual Ring communication structure is implemented on a Ring multicomputer topology. By embedding the virtual Ring into a more highly connected topology, the N-Body program can also be efficiently implemented on other topologies such as Mesh, Torus, or Hypercube. In general, it is often possible for topologies with lower connectivity to be embedded in more highly connected topologies. In Chapter 7, it was shown that a Gray Code numbering scheme can be used to embed Line, Ring, and Mesh virtual topologies into a physical Hypercube topology.

The second example presented in this chapter is Matrix Multiplication. Many of the issues in this program are similar to the N-Body problem, but in two dimensions instead of one. The arrays in the Matrix Multiplication are partitioned in two dimensions among the two-dimensional arrangement of processors in a Torus multicomputer. For this partitioning, each processor needs a copy of all A partitions in its own row of the Torus, and a copy of all B partitions in its own column of the Torus. To fulfill this requirement, all the A partitions are rotated through their row, and all the B partitions are rotated through their column. Since the Torus has end-around connections, it is ideal for this two-dimensional rotation of partitions. The Matrix Multiplication program also achieves a good speedup, provided that the size of the partitions is large enough to produce sufficient process granularity to overcome the process creation and initial data distribution overheads.

The final example of the chapter is the Jacobi Relaxation program implemented on a Hypercube multicomputer. The program is very similar to the multiprocessor version presented in Chapter 6. The data array is partitioned by rows, with each processor being assigned its own row, and also getting a copy of the two neighboring rows. After each iteration, the processes send the newly computed values to both their neighbors. Unlike the N-Body and Matrix Multiplication programs, the communicated data in the Jacobi Relaxation is always freshly computed data. Therefore, communication cannot be overlapped with computation in this program.

In addition to illustrating data partitioning techniques, this chapter serves to clarify the message-passing programming style for writing multicomputer programs in Multi-Pascal. All the processes are created by calling a procedure, which relies on its own local variables for computing. The data partitions assigned to each process are passed as value parameters in the procedure call. During the computing phase of the program, data is communicated between processes using their communication ports. The three example programs presented in this chapter are illustrative of general organizational techniques that can be used in a wide variety of multicomputer programs.

REFERENCES

The text by Fox, et al. [1988] is a comprehensive presentation of multicomputer data partitioning techniques for a wide variety of numerical computing problems. The N-Body program in this chapter is based on the methods for "long range interactions" described in the Fox, et al. [1988] text. Fox also has a chapter on parallel methods for solving Laplace's equation that discusses alternates to the Jacobi Relaxation scheme presented here, including an analysis of a variety of data partitioning schemes for the two-dimensional array.

Ranka, Won, and Sahni [1988] present a good overview of some of the important issues in multicomputer programming.

The Gray Code Hypercube embedding technique is from Chan and Saad [1986] and also Ranka and Sahni [1989]. The Matrix Multiplication program in this chapter is based on an algorithm presented in Quinn [1987]. Bertsekas and Tsitsiklis [1989] contains a survey of parallel matrix multiplication algorithms.

The sequential Region Growing algorithm in the programming projects is found in Ballard and Brown [1987]. Roman and Cox [1989] describe a parallel region growing method.

PROGRAMMING PROJECTS

1. REGION GROWING

Image processing is one of the most computationally intensive applications of computers because of the large amounts of data involved. With most image processing algorithms, different portions of the visual image can be processed in parallel with different processors. For this reason, image processing has become one of the major applications of parallel computers. When image processing is performed on a multicomputer, naturally the image must be partitioned among the processors. For some algorithms, there is interaction between different parts of the image, and therefore some interprocessor communication is required.

One important image processing algorithm is called *region growing,* in which a visual image is divided into contiguous regions. This region growing procedure is the first step in recognizing objects in the image. Each region will have some common characteristic, such as the same color or gray level. By grouping pixels into regions, it becomes easier to begin to identify various objects or portions of objects in the image. Your job in this project is to write a multicomputer algorithm to divide an image into regions of the same gray level.

The image will be represented as a two-dimensional array of integers. Each integer value is the "gray level" of the corresponding pixel at that position in the visual image. Each pixel is considered to have four *neighboring* pixels: above, below, left, and right. A path in the image is defined as a sequence of pixels $(x_1, x_2, \ldots, x_n)$, such that all adjacent pixels in the sequence are neighbors in the image. A region in the image is defined as a set of pixels, such that for any two pixels x and y in the region, there is a path from x to y that remains completely within the region. Intuitively, a *region* is just a "connected" group of pixels, where "connection" can move only in the horizontal and vertical direction, not diagonally.

Your program will divide the image into regions with the same gray level. For simplicity, assume that there are only two gray levels: 1 and 0. In this case, each connected "blob" of 1s or 0s is considered as a separate region. The output of your program should be a number for every pixel in the image, such that all pixels in the same region have the same number. For example, consider the following image:

$$1 \quad 1 \quad 1 \quad 0 \quad 0 \quad 0$$

$$1 \quad 1 \quad 1 \quad 0 \quad 0 \quad 0$$

$$1 \quad 0 \quad 1 \quad 1 \quad 0 \quad 0$$

$$1 \quad 0 \quad 1 \quad 0 \quad 1 \quad 1$$

$$0 \quad 0 \quad 0 \quad 0 \quad 1 \quad 1$$

$$0 \quad 0 \quad 0 \quad 1 \quad 1 \quad 1$$

The region numbering for this image is as follows (remember that diagonal pixels are not "connected"):

$$1 \quad 1 \quad 1 \quad 2 \quad 2 \quad 2$$

$$1 \quad 1 \quad 1 \quad 2 \quad 2 \quad 2$$

$$1 \quad 3 \quad 1 \quad 1 \quad 2 \quad 2$$

$$1 \quad 3 \quad 1 \quad 3 \quad 4 \quad 4$$

$$3 \quad 3 \quad 3 \quad 3 \quad 4 \quad 4$$

$$3 \quad 3 \quad 3 \quad 4 \quad 4 \quad 4$$

A sequential algorithm to achieve this "blob-coloring" is as follows:

For each pixel x, let $G(x)$ denote its gray level—either 0 or 1.

Each pixel x initially has a unique "color" number Color(x) based on its row and column position in the array.

Scan the image from left to right and top to bottom and perform the following on each pixel x:

```
For each neighbor y of pixel x,
  If G(y) = G(x) and Color(y) < Color(x),
    then Color(x) := Color(y); (*choose smaller color number*)
```

Repeat the above scanning of the whole image until no further changes take place. The final Color of each pixel is its region number.

Your job in this project is to adapt this sequential region growing algorithm to run efficiently on a Hypercube multicomputer. Naturally, the image will have to be partitioned among the processors of the Hypercube. One possible way of organizing this program is to model it after the Jacobi Relaxation program, with row-partitions and exchange of boundary values between partitions.

Try to make the program run as efficiently as possible and achieve the highest possible parallel speedup using the Multi-Pascal interactive system. Initially during testing and debugging, use small images. Then during performance testing, use larger images to increase the process granularity. Experiment with different values for the basic communication delays to see how they impact the program performance.

2. JACOBI RELAXATION ON A MESH

Red–Black Iteration is an alternate technique for parallel Jacobi Relaxation, which produces faster convergence. This method is described in Chapter 6, Programming Project 1. In this project, you will write a Jacobi Relaxation program for a 2-D Mesh topology using Red–Black Iteration. Your program should use a two-dimensional partitioning method for the data array, where each partition is in the shape of a small square, as shown at the bottom of Figure 9.15. Organize the program to minimize the communication overhead and achieve good performance. Run and test the program, using a *MESH*2 topology on the Multi-Pascal simulation system.

3. GAUSSIAN ELIMINATION

Programming Project 2 at the end of Chapter 6 describes an algorithm called Gaussian Elimination, which forms the most computationally intensive step in solving a system of linear equations. In this project, your job is to write a multicomputer version of parallel Gaussian Elimination.

The main data structure is a two-dimensional array of real numbers, which are the coefficients of the terms of the linear equations. The goal of Gaussian Elimination is to transform the array to upper-triangular form, in which all terms below the main diagonal are zero. The transformations applied during Gaussian Elimination are derived from an important property of any system of linear equations. If the coefficients of one row are multiplied by the same constant and added to another row, then the resultant system has the same solution as the original. Through a series of such transformations, the Gaussian Elimination algorithm reduces the array to upper-triangular form, which is relatively easy to solve by back substitution.

To adapt the Gaussian Elimination algorithm to a multicomputer, the array must be partitioned among the processors. Study of the algorithm reveals that a load-balancing problem may result if the array is partitioned improperly. If each processor is given a contiguous group of rows or columns, then many processors will become idle as the algorithms progresses. The best partitioning technique is for each processor to be assigned several noncontiguous columns, spaced at equal intervals across the array. If there are p processors, then columns 1 to p are assigned to processors 1 to p, respectively. Then columns $p + 1$ to $2p$ are again assigned to processors 1 to p. This is repeated throughout the entire array, so that each column number k is assigned to processor $k \, MOD \, p$. With this partitioning method, each processor will continue to have active columns as the algorithm progresses, and the load will be balanced.

Your job is to write a multicomputer version of the Gaussian Elimination algorithm, and test it on a Fully Connected multicomputer topology. For large arrays, your program should achieve a good speedup. Be careful to avoid performance bottlenecks. Vary the basic communication delay to see how it impacts the program speedup.

EXERCISES

1. The performance analysis of the N-Body program of Figure 9.4 was done with the assumption of nonoverlapping communication and computation. Modify the analysis to consider the case of overlapped communication and computation, as shown in Figure 9.6. In this analysis, you may ignore the process creation and data distribution time.
   (a) Derive a general expression for the execution time of the N-Body program of Figure 9.6.
   (b) Derive an expression that gives the "transition point" for the basic communication delay D. If D is less than this transition point, the communication delay does not affect the execution time.

2. The performance analysis of the N-Body program of Figure 9.4 ignores the time for process creation and distributing the initial data partitions to the processors. Modify the general analysis to include this time.

3. For the N-Body program of Figure 9.4, show the necessary modification to implement the program efficiently on a $TORUS(5)$ topology.

4. Write a Multi-Pascal procedure "ComputeGray(n: INTEGER)", which computes the values for an n-bit Gray Code and stores the results in an array *GrayCode*. Run and test the program, using the Multi-Pascal interactive system. Try to make the program as efficient as possible.

5. Describe the general organization of a Rank Sort multicomputer program. How is the data partitioned? What is the general form of the communication and data flow?

6. Compute the matrix product $C = A \cdot B$ of the following:

$$A = \begin{array}{cccc} 1 & 1 & 1 & 1 \\ 2 & 2 & 2 & 2 \\ 3 & 3 & 3 & 3 \\ 4 & 4 & 4 & 4 \end{array} \qquad B = \begin{array}{cccc} 4 & 4 & 4 & 4 \\ 3 & 3 & 3 & 3 \\ 2 & 2 & 2 & 2 \\ 1 & 1 & 1 & 1 \end{array}$$

   Partition each matrix into four 2 by 2 partitions as follows:

$$A = \begin{array}{cc} A_{11} & A_{12} \\ A_{21} & A_{22} \end{array} \qquad B = \begin{array}{cc} B_{11} & B_{12} \\ B_{21} & B_{22} \end{array}$$

   where each A_{ij} and B_{ij} is a 2 by 2 matrix.
   Verify that the partitions can be multiplied individually and the results added to create the matrix product, using the technique described for the general matrix multiplication algorithm of Figure 9.10.

7. Consider the multiplication of 3 by 3 matrices $A \cdot B = C$. Denote the elements of the matrices using a general row and column numbering A_{ij}, B_{ij}, C_{ij}.
   (a) For the Matrix Multiplication program of Figure 9.9, show the initial allocation of matrix elements to the processors of the Torus.
   (b) After the first communication step, show the new location of all matrix elements in the Torus.

(c) After the second communication step, show the new location of all matrix elements in the Torus.

(d) Verify that at each stage, all the processors can multiply their current A_{ij} and B_{ij} values, and add these to C_{ij}. Show that the correct final result is computed for each C_{ij} in the Torus.

8. Show what modifications are needed for the Matrix Multiplication program of Figure 9.10 for it to run efficiently on a Hypercube of dimension 6. For simplicity, assume $m = 8$ in the program.

9. The performance analysis of the Matrix Multiplication program of Figure 9.10 did not include the process termination and the communication of the final results back to the main process. Develop a general algebraic expression for the duration of this final phase of the program.

10. Give a general algebraic expression for the speedup in the Matrix Multiplication program of Figure 9.10.

11. Assume that a new version of the Matrix Multiplication program of Figure 9.10 is written with no overlap between computation and communication. Develop a general algebraic expression for the execution time of this program.

12. In Figure 9.11, the speedup increases as the parameter k is increased. However, these increases in speedup for increasing k are much larger on the left side of the graph than on the right side. Using the performance analysis of section 9.3.5, explain the reasons for this observed property.

13. Indicate the modifications needed to run the Jacobi Relaxation program of Figure 9.13 on a Ring multicomputer instead of a Hypercube. Show the required changes to the general performance analysis for this program. Derive a new general expression for the program execution time.

14. In the Jacobi Relaxation programs of Chapter 6, the main issue was the implementation of the barriers for synchronizing the iterations. Explain why this issue of barrier synchronization does not arise in the multicomputer version of the program.

15. In the Jacobi Relaxation program of Figure 9.13, each process i is assigned $inchan(GrayCode[i])$ as communication port. Suppose this were changed to $inchan[i]$. What errors or performance problems will result when the program is run?

16. Using a two-dimensional partitioning method for the Jacobi Relaxation program, explain in detail why only the boundary points need to be communicated to the neighboring processors.

17. The two-dimensional partitioning method for the Jacobi Relaxation program reduces the amount of data communicated, provided that n is sufficiently large. However, it also increases the number of communication steps for each process from two to four. Analyze the performance of both partitioning methods, and determine under what conditions the two-dimensional method is superior.

10

Replicated Workers

In most parallel algorithms, the number of computing tasks is known in advance, and they can be partitioned among the available processors in a reasonably balanced manner. This task partitioning is usually based on the structure of the data, with a portion of the data being assigned to each processor. This type of data parallelism is used both on multiprocessors and multicomputers.

However, there is an important class of algorithms in which the specific computing tasks are not known in advance, but are generated dynamically as the program runs. Combinatorial search algorithms are typically in this category—a problem solution space is being searched with partial search paths being created and discarded dynamically. The well-known Traveling Salesman Problem is an example of such a combinatorial search problem. As the Traveling Salesman program progresses, various partial tours are generated and eliminated in a dynamic fashion. Graph search algorithms also have this property of dynamic creation of computing tasks. A typical example is the Shortest Path Problem, during which partial paths through the graph are gradually extended or replaced by shorter paths.

In such algorithms with dynamic task creation, the computing cannot be initially partitioned among the processors. To achieve a balanced load, the computing tasks must be assigned to processors in a dynamic manner as they are generated during the execution of the program. This is best achieved by using a new type of parallel programming paradigm called *Replicated Workers*. Identical worker processes are assigned to run on each physical processor, and computing tasks are dynamically assigned to the workers as the program is being executed.

In the Replicated Worker paradigm, an abstract data structure called a *Work Pool* is used. A Work Pool is a collection of task descriptors, with each descriptor specifying a particular computing task that may be performed by any of the workers. When a Worker

Process becomes idle, it retrieves a new task descriptor from the Work Pool and then performs the required computation. During the processing of a task descriptor, the Worker Processes may generate new tasks, which are added to the Work Pool.

The main focus of this chapter is the implementation of Replicated Workers and Work Pools on shared-memory multiprocessors. Chapter 11 deals with Replicated Workers on multicomputers. For multiprocessor implementations, Multi-Pascal channels can be used as the basis for the Work Pools, because channels have the ability to collect and distribute data items. However, an important efficiency problem must be overcome: channel contention. If a single channel is used by all the Worker Processes, contention will limit the total number of workers. This contention problem is solved by decentralizing the Work Pool into a number of separate channels. The main implementation issue then becomes one of load balancing among the separate channels, so that all the Worker Processes are kept busy.

The other important implementation issue is termination of the Replicated Workers. The workers must terminate when they are all idle and the Work Pool is empty. As the Work Pool itself becomes more decentralized, this termination problem becomes more difficult. It is important to minimize the additional computing overhead created by the termination test, and also to make sure that the termination test does not produce any memory contention. When one implements Replicated Workers on multicomputers, the distributed termination issue becomes especially interesting. This is the main topic of Chapter 11.

This chapter begins with a general overview of the Replicated Worker programming paradigm and the concept of a Work Pool. Then a specific example algorithm is given that uses Replicated Workers: a parallel Shortest Path algorithm. The remainder of the chapter discusses various implementation issues for Work Pools, with the main focus on load balancing and termination. A simple multiprocessor implementation is given, which avoids contention and achieves a reasonable load balance. The performance of this implementation is analyzed in the context of the parallel Shortest Path algorithm.

10.1 WORK POOLS

The Replicated Worker programming paradigm is best illustrated through a simple diagram, as shown in Figure 10.1. A group of n identical worker processes share access to a centralized *Work Pool*. The worker processes run in parallel on different processors. Whenever any worker becomes idle and available for performing a new computing task, the worker performs a *Getwork* operation to retrieve a new task descriptor from the Work Pool. In the process of performing a computing task, a worker may generate additional computing tasks, which it adds to the Work Pool, using the *Putwork* operation. When the Work Pool is eventually empty, then all the worker processes will terminate and a final answer will be assembled.

If all the computing tasks are already known at the start of the program, then there is no need for a Work Pool—the tasks can simply be divided equally among all the processes. This has been done repeatedly throughout many of the algorithms presented in earlier chapters. For example, in the Rank Sort program, each process is intially given a portion of the array to be sorted, and all subsequent computing consists of processing these array

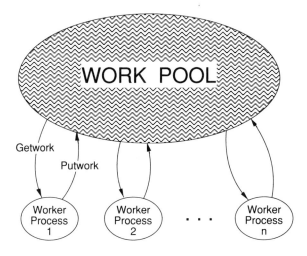

Figure 10.1 Replicated workers.

elements. A Work Pool becomes necessary only when all of the computing tasks are not known initially, and each worker process can continue to generate new tasks. In this case, there must be some system for coordinating the distribution of computing tasks to worker processes throughout the execution of the program. This is the purpose of the Work Pool and its associated operations *Getwork* and *Putwork*.

In Multi-Pascal, the Replicated Workers may be created with a *FORALL* statement, just as in most of the example algorithms in previous chapters. The code for each worker will usually consist of a loop that calls *Getwork* at the start to get the next computing task descriptor from the Work Pool. During the subsequent computation, the worker may possibly generate several new computing tasks and call *Putwork* several times to add these tasks to the Work Pool. In addition to the Work Pool, there may also be some other shared data structures that are used by the worker processes. Access to this shared data will be coordinated by using the same data-sharing techniques described in previous chapters. In multicomputer algorithms, the shared data structures will often have to be partitioned among the local memories, using techniques presented in previous chapters on multicomputer programming.

After determining that a given algorithm requires a Replicated Worker approach, the first step in planning the program is to decide on the format for the task descriptors in the Work Pool. In Multi-Pascal, each task descriptor will usually be a Pascal *record* structure, although in some cases the task descriptors may be *arrays*, or possibly even simple *integer* values for some algorithms. Based on the format of the task descriptors, the next step is to design the structure of a Worker process, considering the Work Pool as just a predefined abstract data structure. Finally, the Work Pool itself must be implemented by using Multi-Pascal channels, and procedures must be written for the *Getwork* and *Putwork* operations.

There are three main issues that arise in the implementation of Work Pools: contention, load balancing, and termination. Contention naturally arises because of the centralized nature of the Work Pool. Since the Work Pool globally collects and distributes task descriptors, it is constantly being accessed by all the worker processes. To achieve large speedups, large numbers of workers are needed, and this produces the potential for contention during access to the Work Pool. The obvious solution is to partially decentralize the Work Pool into portions that can be accessed in parallel. However, this necessary decentralization may lead to imbalances in the distribution of tasks among the portions of the Work Pool, and subsequently to load imbalances among the tasks available to different worker processes. The method used to decentralize the Work Pool and distribute the tasks among the workers must be carefully designed to minimize the potential load imbalances.

Termination becomes a problem because it is a *global* property, which depends on the state of the Work Pool and all the workers at the same time. Naturally, a Replicated Worker algorithm wants to terminate when there is no more work to do, that is, when there are no more task descriptors to be processed. Of course, the Work Pool must be empty in order to terminate. However, even when the Work Pool is empty, an active worker process may still add some new computing task to the Work Pool. Therefore, the termination condition is that the Work Pool is empty *and* all worker processes are idle (waiting for the next computing task). This termination condition is tricky to test for in a running parallel algorithm, especially in the case of multicomputers. The goal of any implementation is first to make the termination testing efficient, so that it does not slow down the algorithm or cause a performance bottleneck. A secondary goal is to make the termination test simple and elegant, to minimize the programming effort and reduce the potential for bugs in the code.

10.2 SHORTEST PATH ALGORITHM

To illustrate the Replicated Worker parallel programming paradigm, this chapter uses the *Shortest Path Algorithm* for finding the shortest path between vertices of a graph. Specifically, we will consider the *single-source* shortest path problem of finding the shortest distance between a given source vertex and every other vertex of the graph. First, a sequential shortest path algorithm will be described, and then a simple parallel version using a Work Pool. Subsequent sections will describe the implementation of the Work Pool for multiprocessors.

Graphs have proved to be useful conceptual and mathematical tools for modeling various aspects of natural law. They are used extensively in many branches of engineering, natural science, and social science. Fundamentally, a graph is an extremely simple object: a finite set of *vertices* and a finite set of *edges* that connect pairs of vertices. In a *directed* graph, each edge has an orientation and goes from one vertex to another. In a *weighted* graph, each edge has an associated *weight*, which is a number. Figure 10.2 shows an

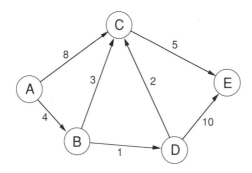

FIGURE 10.2   Weighted directed graph.

example of a *weighted directed graph* with five vertices (A, B, C, D, E) and seven edges, each with a positive integer weight.

A graph could be used to represent air fares between cities, where each vertex is a city, and each weight is the air fare between a pair of cities. Alternately, the weights could represent distances between the cities, or travel times by automobile between the cities. A graph might also represent alternate methods for achieving a goal, where each edge represents some task to be performed and the corresponding weight represents the manpower requirements for performing that task. In all of these example applications, it would be useful to know the *shortest* path from a given source vertex to other destination vertices. In the case of the air fares, the shortest path in the graph would tell the minimum air fare for traveling between two cities. In the case of the task–manpower graph, the shortest path would indicate the proper series of tasks to perform in order to achieve a goal with the minimum manpower requirements.

10.2.1 Sequential Shortest Path Algorithm

To formulate a shortest path algorithm, first a data structure is needed to represent the directed graph. The vertices of graph can be numbered from 1 to n, and the weights represented by a two-dimensional array *weight*, in which the weight of an edge from vertex i to j is stored at position *weight*$[i, j]$. If there is no edge from vertex i to j, then *weight*$[i, j]$ is "infinity." The number of edges n and the two-dimensional *weight* array are sufficient to represent any weighted directed graph. Following is the *weight* array for the graph of Figure 10.2:

inf	4	8	inf	inf
inf	inf	3	1	inf
inf	inf	inf	inf	5
inf	inf	2	inf	10
inf	inf	inf	inf	inf

Vertex numbering:

$$A = 1; \quad B = 2; \quad C = 3; \quad D = 4; \quad E = 5$$

The *weight* array has one noninfinite entry for each edge in the graph. Two more data structures are needed to express the shortest path algorithm. The algorithm will compute the shortest distance from the source vertex (assumed always to be vertex number 1) to every other vertex in the graph. An array *mindist* is used to record the shortest distance to each vertex. As the algorithm progresses, *mindist* records the shortest distance found so far to each vertex. The elements of this array are continually being updated until the algorithm finally terminates with the correct answers. Also, a queue is needed to hold vertex numbers. Vertices are continually being removed and added to this queue during the running of the algorithm.

To understand the shortest path algorithm, consider a particular moment during its execution in which *mindist* records the shortest distance found so far to each vertex. Then suppose a new shorter distance has just been found to vertex x and stored into *mindist*$[x]$. Now consider some outgoing edge from vertex x to vertex w with weight *weight*$[x, w]$. The path to vertex x can now be extended to vertex w along this edge, and this path will have distance: *newdist* := *mindist*[x] + *weight*[x, w]. This *newdist* is then compared with the current value of *mindist*[w]. If it is less, then a new shorter distance has been found to vertex w, and *mindist*[w] is updated with this new value *newdist*. At this time, the outgoing edges of vertex w now have to be examined also. However, first the remaining outgoing edges from vertex x must be examined, so vertex w is put onto the vertex queue.

Each time a new shorter distance is found to any vertex in the graph, it is put onto the queue. Vertices are removed from the queue one at a time, and all their outgoing edges are examined. This may result in new vertices being added to the queue. Gradually, as all the shortest paths are discovered, the size of the queue will shrink. When the queue is empty, the algorithm terminates. Following is a more precise description of this sequential *Shortest Path Algorithm*:

```
Initialize mindist array to infinity;
Initialize queue to contain source vertex 1;
mindist[1] := 0;
While queue is not empty do
  Begin
    x := head of queue;
    For w := 1 to n do
      Begin
        newdist := mindist[x] + weight[x,w];
        If newdist < mindist[w] then
          Begin
            mindist[w] := newdist;
            If w not in queue then append w to queue;
          End;
      End;
  End;
```

10.2.2 Parallel Shortest Path Algorithm

In the sequential algorithm, a queue is used to save the vertices for later consideration. However, there is no reason these queue entries must be considered in any particular sequence. In fact, there is no reason why queued vertices could not be all considered in *parallel*. This observation is the key to formulating a parallel version of this shortest path algorithm. The vertex queue can be transformed into a *Work Pool* of vertex numbers. A group of parallel *Worker* processes can remove vertices from the Work Pool, process them, and add new vertices to the Work Pool. When the Work Pool is empty, the algorithm terminates.

The code for each Worker Process in the parallel version of the algorithm is almost identical to the sequential program shown above. This activity of sequentially considering vertices one at a time is just replicated among the Worker Processes, with each identical worker executing essentially the same code. The procedure for the Worker Processes is shown in Figure 10.3. Each Worker is given a unique identification number *me*. This is passed to the *Getwork* and *Putwork* routines as an additional parameter. In subsequent sections of the chapter that deal with implementation of Getwork and

```
PROGRAM Shortpath;
CONST n = ... ;            (*number of vertices*)
      numworkers = ... ; (*number of Worker processes*)
      infinity = 32000;
TYPE worktype = INTEGER; (*Each item in Work Pool is vertex no.*)
VAR weight: ARRAY [1..n,1..n] OF INTEGER;
    i,j: INTEGER;
    mindist: ARRAY [1..n] OF INTEGER;  (*Min. dist to each vertex*)
    L: ARRAY [1..n] OF SPINLOCK;
    inflag: ARRAY [1..n] OF BOOLEAN; (*True if vertex in Work Pool*)
    startvertex: worktype;


  PROCEDURE Getwork(me: INTEGER; VAR item: worktype);
    ...  (*Read a task descriptor into "item"*)


  PROCEDURE Putwork(me: INTEGER; item: worktype);
    ...  (*Add "item" to work pool*)


PROCEDURE Worker(me: INTEGER);
VAR  vertex: worktype;
     w,newdist: INTEGER;
BEGIN
  Getwork(me,vertex);  (*Get a new vertex number to examine*)
  WHILE vertex <> -1 DO
    BEGIN
      inflag[vertex] := FALSE;  (*Vertex is removed from Work Pool*)
      FOR w := 1 TO n DO (*Consider all outgoing edges of "vertex"*)
        BEGIN
          IF weight[vertex,w] < infinity THEN
            BEGIN (*See if this is a shorter path to w*)
               newdist := mindist[vertex] + weight[vertex,w];
               Lock(L[w]); (*mutual exclusion on "mindist[w]*)
               IF newdist < mindist[w] THEN
                 BEGIN
                   mindist[w] := newdist; (*Update distance to w*)
                   Unlock(L[w]);
                   IF not inflag[w] THEN  (*If w not in Work Pool*)
                     BEGIN
                       inflag[w] := TRUE;
                       Putwork(me,w);     (*Put w into Work Pool*)
                     END;
                 END
               ELSE Unlock(L[w]);
            END;
        END;
    END;
```

FIGURE 10.3 Parallel shortest path algorithm.

```
        Getwork(me,vertex); (*Get new vertex number*)
      END;
END;


BEGIN (*Main*)

   ... (*Read in values for weight array*)

  FOR i := 1 TO n DO  (*Initialize mindist and inflag*)
    BEGIN
      mindist[i] := infinity;
      inflag[i] := FALSE;
    END;
  mindist[startvertex] := 0;
  inflag[startvertex] := TRUE;
  FORALL i := 1 TO numworkers DO  (*Create Replicated Workers*)
    Worker(i);

   ... (*Final answers found in "mindist" array*)

END.
```

FIGURE 10.3 (continued)

Putwork, it will be seen that these process identification numbers are helpful in load balancing of the Work Pool.

Each Worker Process begins with a call *Getwork*(*me, vertex*) to read a vertex number from the Work Pool into local variable *vertex*. When the Work Pool is empty and all the Workers are waiting on this empty Work Pool, then the Getwork routine will return a termination flag (−1) to all the Workers. Each Worker has a *WHILE* loop that continues processing vertices from the Work Pool until the termination flag is received. The remainder of the Worker Procedure is essentially the same as the sequential shortest path algorithm shown earlier. The only difference is that when a new shorter distance is discovered to a vertex *w*, the vertex number is put into the Work Pool by using *Putwork*(*me, w*), rather than into the queue as in the sequential version.

At the heart of the Worker procedure is a "test-and-modify" operation on *mindist*[*w*]. Since this operation is being performed by all the parallel Workers, mutual exclusion is required on *mindist*[*w*]. This is provided with Lock and Unlock operations on spinlock *L*[*w*]. An interesting aspect of the Worker procedure is the use of the array *inflag* to indicate whether each vertex is already in the Work Pool. Since there is a test-and-modify operation on *inflag*[*w*], mutual exclusion could be used here to make it an atomic operation. Since it is not an atomic operation, it is possible for two copies of the same vertex number to be put into the Work Pool. However, this unlikely event causes only some extra computation and does not result in any errors. Therefore, the extra overhead of mutual exclusion is not justified in this case.

If the particular graph is *dense*, with each vertex directly connected to most other vertices, then the two-dimensional *weight* array is a suitable data structure for representing the graph. However, if the graph is *sparse*, with each vertex having a relatively small number of outgoing edges, a more efficient data structure can be used: an edge list for each vertex. The Worker Procedure could then be modified to iterate through the edge list for its given vertex. This minor modification to the Worker Procedure is considered in one of the exercises at the end of this chapter.

10.3 IMPLEMENTATION OF WORK POOLS

In the parallel Shortest Path Algorithm, the Work Pool is used to replace the queue in the sequential algorithm. Therefore, it would be a natural impulse to consider implementing the Work Pool with a *channel*, which is in essence just a parallel-access queue. Just as the sequential algorithm adds and removes vertices from the queue, the parallel algorithm can add and remove vertices from the channel. *Putwork(me, item)* can simply write *item* into the channel, and *Getwork(me, item)* can read a value from the channel into *item*. Since a Multi-Pascal channel is already set up for parallel access by many reader and writer processes, there are no concurrency errors when one allows all the Replicated Workers to access the Work Pool in parallel. The Work Pool itself can then just be declared as follows:

```
VAR workpool:  CHANNEL OF worktype;
```

Now consider the termination issue. In the sequential algorithm, termination testing is handled by simply testing whether the queue is empty. However, this is *not* sufficient in the parallel case, because some Worker Processes may still be active. A given Worker *A* may find at some time that the Work Pool is empty. However, another Worker *B* may be in the middle of computing and then later add several new items to the Work Pool. Thus, if Worker *A* just waits for a while, it will receive some work to do. As was mentioned earlier, the termination condition for the Replicated Worker algorithm is as follows:

Termination Condition:

1. The Work Pool is empty.

2. All Worker Processes are idle.

If both these conditions are met, then there is no possibility of any more computation by the Worker Processes. It is assumed during a Replicated Worker algorithm that no items can be added to the Work Pool by any outside processes, except at the very beginning when the Work Pool is being initialized to get the computation started. In the Shortest Path Algorithm, the Work Pool must be initialized with the source vertex for computing the paths (vertex 1 is used here for simplicity).

Both of these termination conditions can be tested by using a counter variable indicating the total number of items in the Work Pool. *Putwork* increments the counter and *Getwork* decrements the counter. When the counter reaches value 0, then the Work Pool is empty, which satisfies termination condition 1. Actually, the only way in which a Worker Process can become idle is by calling *Getwork* when the Work Pool is empty. In this situation, the *Getwork* procedure must put the Worker into a *wait* state until some new items are written into the Work Pool by another active Worker. To detect termination condition 2, the *Getwork* procedure must keep a count of the total number of Worker Processes currently waiting on the empty Work Pool. When this number reaches the total number of Workers, then termination condition 2 is satisfied.

The count of waiting Workers can be maintained by using the same counter variable for items in the Work Pool. Even when the Work Pool is empty, *Getwork* will continue to decrement the counter when it is called by Workers. Thus, a positive counter will indicate the number of items in the Work Pool. A zero counter will indicate an empty Work Pool. A negative counter value will tell how many Worker Processes are waiting on the empty Work Pool. Since this counter value will be accessed and updated concurrently by the Workers, it requires a spinlock to guarantee that the update operations are atomic.

The Multi-Pascal code for the *Getwork* and *Putwork* procedures is shown in Figure 10.4. *Putwork* simply increments the Work Pool counter value stored in variable *count*, and then writes the new *item* into the *workpool* channel. The *Getwork* procedure begins by decrementing the Work Pool counter variable. If the counter value has reached the negative of the number of Worker Processes (*−numworkers*), then the computation must be terminated. Otherwise, an item is read from the *workpool* channel and returned to the calling Worker Process. If the Work Pool is empty at this time, then the attempt to read from it at the end of the *Getwork* procedure will cause the Worker Process to go into a *Blocked* state waiting on the channel *workpool*. When all of the Workers go into this waiting state, then the computation must be terminated. Actually, the last Worker Process to enter *Getwork* when all the others are waiting will find that the value of *count* has reached *−numworkers*. Then the *FOR* loop in *Getwork* will be activated to put termination messages into the Work Pool for all the waiting Worker Processes to read. Thus, all the Workers will receive the −1 termination code and terminate themselves (see Procedure Worker in Figure 10.3).

A few initialization instructions must be added in the body of the main part of the program, as shown in Figure 10.4. The source vertex 1 must be written into the Work Pool as the starting point for all paths. Since vertex 1 is the source, the shortest distance to itself must of course be 0, so *mindist*[*startvertex*] is initialized to 0. Since there is now one item in the Work Pool, the counter variable is initialized to 1.

10.4 ELIMINATING CONTENTION

The implementation of the Work Pool as shown in Figure 10.4 now provides a complete Multi-Pascal program for the Parallel Shortest Path algorithm. Now that a working program has been created, the next issue is to analyze its performance, and see if it is acceptable. As explained in Chapter 5, atomic operations may sometimes lead to performance problems because they can be executed by only one process at a time. Each Worker Process uses an atomic operation to update the *count* variable every time it accesses the Work Pool. Although the duration of the atomic operation is short, it will eventually lead to a performance bottleneck as the number of Worker Processes is increased. Let I denote the average time interval between Work Pool accesses by each process, and d denote the duration of the atomic operation on the *count* variable. The saturation point for the number of Worker Processes is I/d.

In previous chapters the general principle was presented that contention for a shared resource can be reduced through *decentralization* of that resource. Applying this principle

```
PROGRAM Shortpath;
CONST numworkers = ... ;
      ...

TYPE worktype =  INTEGER;
VAR workpool: CHANNEL OF worktype;
    count: INTEGER;  (*Work Pool counter*)
    M: SPINLOCK;
    startvertex: worktype;
     ...



PROCEDURE Getwork(me: INTEGER; VAR item: worktype);
VAR workcount: INTEGER;
BEGIN
  (*first read and decrement Work Pool counter*)
  Lock(M);
    workcount := count - 1;
    count := workcount;
  Unlock(M);
  IF workcount = -numworkers THEN
    BEGIN  (*Terminate Workers*)
      item := -1;
      FOR i := 1 TO numworkers-1 DO
          workpool := item;
    END
  ELSE item := workpool;  (*read item from Work Pool*)
END;



PROCEDURE Putwork(me: INTEGER; item: worktype);
VAR workcount: INTEGER;
BEGIN
  Lock(M);
    count := count + 1;  (*Increment Work Pool counter*)
  Unlock(M);
  workpool := item;
END;



PROCEDURE Worker(me: INTEGER);
  ... (*Worker Process - see Figure 10.3*)


BEGIN (*Main*)
count := 1;
startvertex := 1;
workpool := startvertex;   (*Source vertex 1 into Work Pool*)

  ... (*Other initializations as in Figure 10.3*)

FORALL i := 1 TO numworkers DO
  Worker(i);
END.
```

FIGURE 10.4   Implementation of Getwork and Putwork.

to Work Pools, the solution is to modify the implementation to contain several channels that can be accessed in parallel by different Workers. Each channel can have its own *count* variable, thus partially relieving the performance bottleneck. This can improve the performance, provided that another important issue is also considered: *load balancing*. Also, the decentralization of the Work Pool complicates the termination detection. The following two subsections presents a decentralized Work Pool implementation, and considers the two issues—load balancing and termination.

10.4.1 Load Balancing

The best approach is to leave the Worker Processes unchanged, with the same *Getwork* and *Putwork* calls to use the Work Pool as an abstract data structure. The multiple channels will be hidden inside the internal implementation of the Work Pool. With several channels to choose from, the implementation now must decide which channel to use for each *Getwork* and *Putwork* operation. There are several important issues in choosing a methodology for making this choice of channels. The first issue is to balance the computing load among the Worker Processes so that they all stay as busy as possible, avoiding situations where Workers are waiting on empty channels while other channels still contain items.

The second important issue is to be careful not to create any new sequential bottlenecks in the implementation. For example, if all the Worker Processes are still accessing some centralized counters or pointers, then this may still limit the performance despite the availability of many channels for storing the items. Finally, the third important issue is to make the implementation simple and elegant to reduce the programming difficulty and minimize the potential for concurrency bugs. There could be a wide range of implementations possible. One will be presented here, and others will be explored in the exercises at the end of this chapter.

The solution adopted here is to divide all the Worker Processes into equal-size groups and assign each group permanently to a single channel for its *Getwork* operations. For example, if there are four channels and 24 Workers, then a group of six Workers will be assigned to each channel. Each Worker will always access its assigned channel when performing a *Getwork* operation. If that channel is empty, then the Worker will go into the *Blocked* state waiting on the empty channel. This implementation technique is illustrated in Figure 10.5.

To help balance the work load among the groups, each Worker will rotate its *Putwork* operations among all the channels in a round-robin fashion. Each Worker will have an internal *channel pointer,* which will identify the target channel for the next *Putwork* operation. After each *Putwork* operation, this pointer will be moved on to the next channel. This may seem to be a rather crude method to balance the load, but it is found in practice to perform well for the Shortest Path algorithm and other *combinatorial* algorithms. For such algorithms, the work items build up very fast at the start of the algorithm and fill all the channels quickly. During the main body of the program, there are so many work items that even this simple round-robin distribution method is sufficient to keep all the channels filled. Load imbalance becomes a problem only in the very beginning and very end of the program, during which time there is a shortage of work items, allowing the possibility of some channels being empty while others have items. However, for most

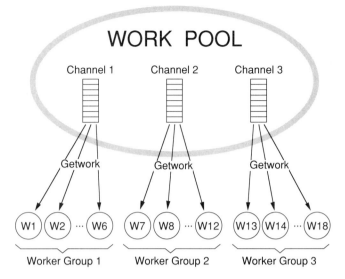

FIGURE 10.5   Multiple channel work pool.

combinatorial problems, these early and late stages are very short compared to the middle part of the program.

10.4.2 Termination Algorithm

In the original implementation of Work Pools using only one channel, there were two termination conditions: the Work Pool is empty, and all Worker Processes are idle. This condition was detected by using a *counter* value to record the number of items in the Work Pool and to record the number of waiting Workers when the Work Pool is empty. As shown in Figure 10.4, the *Getwork* operation decrements the counter, and the *Putwork* operation increments the counter. For the new implementation of the Work Pool using multiple channels, the two termination conditions are the same, except that these conditions are slightly more complex to detect.

Now the "Work Pool is empty" condition requires that all the channels of the Work Pool be empty. The "all Workers idle" condition requires that each group of workers be idle, which occurs only when all the Workers in that group are waiting on their assigned channel, and that channel is empty. With reference to Figure 10.5, when Channel 1 is empty and all the Workers of Group 1 are blocked in *Getwork* waiting on that channel, then Worker Group 1 is said to be *idle*. The termination condition is clearly that all Worker Groups are idle.

To detect when a Worker Group becomes idle, the same technique is used as in the one-channel implementation: a *counter* is maintained for the channel assigned to the Worker Group. Each channel in the Work Pool must have its own private counter. Whenever *Putwork* is applied to a given channel, its private counter is incremented. Whenever *Getwork* is applied to a given channel, its private counter is decremented. Thus, as was the case in the one-channel implementation, a positive counter indicates the number of work items in the channel, a zero counter indicates an empty channel, and a negative counter gives the number of blocked workers waiting on that empty channel. When the counter value for a specific channel reaches the negative of the size of the Worker Group, then this detects the condition "Worker Group idle." When all the Worker Groups are idle, then termination must occur.

To implement the termination detection, an array of counters is required with one counter for each channel in the Work Pool. These array counters are incremented and decremented throughout the program as *Getwork* and *Putwork* operations are performed. To detect the final termination condition, one additional *master counter* is used to record the total number of idle Worker Groups. This is illustrated in Figure 10.6. The individual components of the *count* array are updated frequently—each time a *Getwork* or *Putwork* is done on the corresponding channel. As in the previous implementation, the updating of a counter must be an atomic *operation*, and therefore requires a short time period of exclusive access by a single Worker Process. Since each channel has its own counter, the updating of counters should not cause a performance bottleneck.

There is only one *master counter*, which also requires *atomic* updating. However, the termination detection algorithm is organized so that accesses to the master counter are relatively infrequent. The master counter need be accessed only when a Worker Group changes state from "active" to "idle," or "idle" to "active." These transitions of the Worker Groups happen infrequently enough that the access to the *master counter* does not cause a serious performance bottleneck.

To ensure that access to the counter array and master counter do not cause bottle-necks, the number of channels in the Work Pool implementation must be chosen carefully. If the number of channels is too small, then there will be a large number of Worker Processes in each Worker Group, thereby introducing the same kind of performance bottleneck as in the one-channel case. However, if the number of channels is too large, then the work items must be dispersed over all these channels, and the load-balancing problem may cause performance degradation. Experience has shown that approximately 5 to 15 Workers per group is a good choice for a wide range of Replicated Worker algorithms. A detailed mathematical analysis of this issue is considered later.

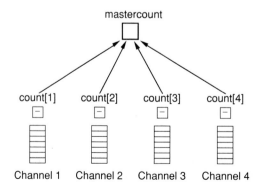

FIGURE 10.6   Termination counters.

Following is a high-level description of the required *Getwork* and *Putwork* procedures for this multiple-channel implementation of Work Pools:

```
Getwork(me,item):

  Compute my channel number in Work Pool;
  Decrement counter for the channel;
  If counter = -Worker_Group_size then
    begin (*my Worker Group is now idle*)
      Increment master counter;
      If master counter = number_of_Worker_Groups then
        (*Send a termination flag to each Worker Process*)
        For i := 1 to number_of_Worker_Groups do
          For j := 1 to Worker_Group_size do
            Put a termination flag into channel of Worker Group i;
    end;
  Read a task descriptor from my channel into "item";


Putwork(me,item):

  Move my pointer to the next channel in Work Pool;
  Increment counter for the target channel;
  If counter = -Worker_Group_size + 1 then
    Decrement master counter;  (*idle Worker Group now active*)
  Write "item" into the target channel;
```

In addition to reading and writing items from the Work Pool, the *Getwork* and *Putwork* routines must modify the counters and detect transitions of the Worker Groups from *idle* to *active* or visa versa. *Getwork* detects *active* to *idle* transitions. When the channel assigned to a Worker Group is empty, the Worker Processes of that group will get *blocked* as they try to read the empty channel. When the last active process of the Worker Group calls *Getwork* to read the channel, the counter for that channel will have reached the negative of the "Worker_Group_size." At this time, the *master counter* must be incremented to indicate that one additional Worker Group is now idle. If this happens to be the last Worker Group to become idle, then the *master count* will have reached the value "number_of_Worker_Groups." In this case, termination must take place, so the *Getwork* routine will send termination flags to all the Worker Processes by writing the flags into the channels of the Work Pool. Recall from Figure 10.3 that the Worker Processes check for a "−1" termination flag at the start of each iteration.

In addition to writing items into the channels using a *round-robin* technique, *Putwork* must detect *idle* to *active* transitions of the Worker Groups. When a Worker Group is idle, then all the Worker Processes of that group are waiting on the empty channel. However, a Worker Process from another group may put a new work item into that channel, thereby waking up the target Worker Group. If the target Worker Group is idle, its counter will have the value "−Worker_Group_size." Therefore, after incrementing the counter for the target channel, the *Putwork* routine must test the counter to see if it now has the value

"–Worker_Group_size + 1." If this is the case, then the target Worker Group has just become active, and the *master count* must be decremented.

10.4.3 Performance

The Multi-Pascal code for the *Getwork* and *Putwork* procedures is shown in Figure 10.7. These procedures simply replace the previous implementation of Work Pools. The Worker Processes are unchanged because they treat the Work Pool as an abstract data type: the Work Pool implementation is transparent to the Workers. In the variable declaration section at the start of Figure 10.7, it is seen that the Work Pool is an *ARRAY OF CHANNELS*, in which each channel holds a collection of vertices from the graph. The counters are declared as an array *count* with an array of spinlock *CL* for providing mutual exclusion. Recall that each Worker Process uses a rotating pointer to determine where to write vertices during the *Putwork* operation. These pointers for all the Worker Processes are stored in the global array *nextchan*.

The *Getwork* procedure in Figure 10.7 corresponds to the high-level description given earlier. At the beginning of the procedure, the entering Worker computes its channel number in the Work Pool, using its own worker identification number stored in variable *me*. These identification numbers are assigned to the Worker Processes when they are created. The *Putwork* procedure of Figure 10.7 also corresponds to the high-level description given earlier. One notable feature is the use of the *nextchan* array to hold the Work Pool channel pointers. At the start of *Putwork*, the pointer for the calling Worker Process is copied into variable *next*, and then used to index the *count* and *workpool* arrays. At the end of *Putwork*, the pointer is moved to the next channel in the Work Pool.

The performance of this Shortest Path program will be very much dependent of the characteristics of the particular graph, which will determine the amount of available concurrency. Since the primary focus of this chapter is on the Work Pool implementation, a sample graph has been chosen with a large number of vertices. This provides ample potential for concurrent computation, so that any observed losses in speedup can be attributed to inefficiencies in the program. The most interesting performance issue in this Work Pool implementation is the interplay between channel contention and load balancing as the number of channels in the Work Pool is varied. Smaller numbers of channels tend to increase contention, while large numbers of channels tend to imbalance the load.

Figure 10.8 shows a performance curve of the speedup of the Shortest Path program for a sample graph with 2800 vertices. The horizontal axis shows the total number of channels in the Work Pool implementation (the parameter *num_worker_groups* in the program of Figure 10.7). The total number of Worker Processes is held constant at 60, which is therefore the maximum possible speedup. For the case of one channel only, all of the 60 Workers use this same channel, resulting in a severe contention problem, as indicated by the very low speedup (9.5). It appears that the frequency of access to the Work Pool causes a single channel to saturate at about 10 Workers. In the figure, as the number of channels is gradually increased, the speedup at first increases rapidly, then begins to level off, and eventually decline.

The initial rapid increase in speedup at the left side of the performance curve results from the reduced contention as the number of channels is increased. Increasing the number

```
PROGRAM Shortpath_1;
CONST num_worker_groups = 5;
      worker_group_size = 10;
      numworkers = num_worker_groups * worker_group_size;
        ...


TYPE worktype = INTEGER;
VAR workpool:  ARRAY [1..num_worker_groups] OF CHANNEL OF worktype;
    count: ARRAY [1..num_worker_groups] OF INTEGER;
    CL: ARRAY [1..num_worker_groups] OF SPINLOCK;
    mastercount: INTEGER;
    M: SPINLOCK;
    nextchan: ARRAY [1..numworkers] OF INTEGER;
    i,j: INTEGER;       startvertex: worktype;
      ...



PROCEDURE Getwork(me: INTEGER; VAR item: worktype);
VAR workcount,emptycount,mychan: INTEGER;
BEGIN
  mychan := (me-1) DIV worker_group_size + 1; (*my channel number*)
  Lock(CL[mychan]);
    workcount := count[mychan] - 1;              (*decrement count*)
    count[mychan] := workcount;
  Unlock(CL[mychan]);
  IF workcount = -worker_group_size THEN
    BEGIN (*my work group is now completely idle*)
      Lock(M);
        emptycount := mastercount + 1;       (*increment master count*)
        mastercount := emptycount;
      Unlock(M);
      IF emptycount = num_worker_groups THEN
        BEGIN   (*terminate all the workers*)
          FOR i := 1 TO num_worker_groups DO
            FOR j := 1 TO worker_group_size DO
              workpool[i] := -1;
        END
    END;
  item := workpool[mychan];
END;


PROCEDURE Putwork(me: INTEGER; item: worktype);
VAR workcount,emptycount,next: INTEGER;
BEGIN
  next := nextchan[me]; (*Get destination channel no.*)
  Lock(CL[next]);
```

FIGURE 10.7   Work pool with no contention.

```
      workcount := count[next] + 1;        (*increment count*)
      count[next] := workcount;
   Unlock(CL[next]);
   IF workcount = - worker_group_size + 1 THEN
     BEGIN
       Lock(M);
         emptycount := mastercount - 1;   (*decrement master count*)
         mastercount := emptycount;
       Unlock(M);
     END;
   workpool[next] := item; (*Write item into Work Pool*)
   nextchan[me] := next MOD num_worker_groups + 1; (*Next destination*)
END;


PROCEDURE Worker(me: INTEGER);
VAR ...

BEGIN
  nextchan[me] := (me-1) DIV worker_group_size + 1;

  ...  (*Worker Process same as in Figure 10.3*)

END;


BEGIN (*Main*)
startvertex := 1;
workpool[1] := startvertex;  (*Source vertex 1 into Work Pool*)
(*Initialize all counters*)
count[1] := 1;
for i := 2 to num_worker_groups do
   count[i] := 0;
mastercount := 0;

  ...  (*Other initializations as in Figure 10.3*)

FORALL i := 1 TO numworkers DO
   Worker(i);

END.
```

FIGURE 10.7   (continued)

of channels from one to two increases the speedup by 8.5, which is near the saturation limit of a single channel. The third channel increases speedup by (7.5). As the number of channels continues to increase, the marginal reduction in contention from each additional channel begins to decline, causing the performance curve to rise less steeply. Also, another performance factor starts to become significant—load balancing. This problem is espe-

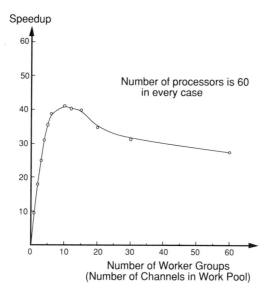

FIGURE 10.8 **Performance of replicated workers.**

cially acute in the initial and final phases of the program execution, when the total number of items in the Work Pool is so low that even a slightly uneven distribution among the channels may result in idle Worker Processes.

As the number of channels is increased, the decreasing marginal improvement in contention, combined with increasing load-balancing problems, eventually causes the performance curve to turn downward. The maximum speedup of 41 results from 10 channels, which has 6 of the 60 Workers assigned to each channel. This means that each channel is operating at an average 60 percent of capacity. According to standard queuing theory, a "server" with mean service time d operating at a fraction f of its capacity will cause the following expected queuing delay for arriving individuals:

$$\text{Queuing Delay:} \quad \frac{fd}{1-f}$$

This formula assumes that the arrivals are a Poisson process and the service time is exponentially distributed, which is not the case in this program. Nevertheless, the formula can be used to get a rough approximation of the expected performance degradation resulting from contention. Substituting $f = .6$ gives an expected delay of $(1.5d)$. If the average time interval between accesses to the Work Pool by each process is denoted by I, then the saturation point for a single channel is I/d. Since the observed saturation point in this case is 10 Workers, then $d = (.1I)$. Thus, the expected delay experienced by each Worker every time it accesses the Work Pool is $(.15I)$. Since these Work Pool accesses occur every I time units, the expected performance degradation from contention is about 15 percent. In Figure 10.8, the observed loss of speedup for the 10 channel case is 32 percent. The above analysis shows that about 15 percent can be attributed to channel contention, and therefore the remaining 17 percent must result from load imbalances.

To investigate the nature of the load imbalance problem, a special "monitor" process can be added to the Shortest Path program. This process periodically reads and prints out the *count* array, which indicates how many items are currently in each channel, or how many idle processes are waiting on a given channel. The monitor process has the following general structure:

```
FOR i := 1 TO num_samples DO
  BEGIN
    Duration(Interval);         (*Wait "Interval" time units*)
    FOR j := 1 TO num_worker_groups DO (*Write count array*)
      Write(count[j]);
    Writeln;
  END;
```

This process will sample the *count* array every "Interval" time units. Since the process runs on a separate processor and does not use any spinlocks or access any channels, it does not interfere with the ordinary program execution in any way. For Interval size 450, the resultant output is shown in Figure 10.9. Each row represents a sample of the counts across the 10 channels in the Work Pool. The relative sizes of the counts in each row indicate the degree of load imbalance at that point in the program execution. Recall that zero or negative count values indicate the number of Workers waiting on that empty

−3	−4	−5	−6	−6	−6	−2	0	0	0
−2	4	10	14	7	1	−5	−6	−6	−6
−5	−3	9	16	22	28	34	25	11	−1
25	8	9	14	16	27	33	40	46	44
51	50	46	44	37	36	36	37	42	43
50	42	50	68	74	74	66	62	58	56
70	64	56	64	72	78	81	87	91	81
96	97	81	82	98	94	95	102	102	98
108	106	98	104	114	122	115	111	112	107
120	116	118	118	127	143	139	142	140	125
148	141	133	135	138	154	157	150	153	153
164	157	160	158	157	161	168	165	171	173
179	170	163	173	173	184	193	190	187	184
194	178	160	183	182	189	198	213	211	208
206	176	154	194	184	181	203	200	212	210
192	148	126	175	175	172	195	190	214	208
170	116	88	148	149	153	169	169	201	194
135	78	48	108	111	118	133	133	175	171
93	37	8	64	67	72	91	91	141	135
48	−6	−6	22	24	26	46	45	99	94
2	−6	−6	−6	−6	−6	−1	0	54	48
−6	−6	−6	−6	−6	−6	−6	−6	10	3

FIGURE 10.9   **Channel counts for shortest path.**

channel. It can be clearly seen in the figure that some performance degradation occurs in the initial and final stages of execution, resulting from a combination of lack of sufficient work and slightly uneven distribution of the work items. Since the negative counts indicate idle processes, these samples can be used to estimate the average number of idle processes during the program execution. The resultant value of 14 percent gives a rough estimate of the size of the performance degradation resulting from load imbalances and lack of work. This is close to the 17 percent that was predicted from the above analysis of contention.

(*Note*: In computing the average in Figure 10.9, one important correction has to be made. Since there are 60 processes, it takes about 900 time units for all the processes to be created. Therefore, the first sample row, which occurs after 450 time units, will find the five rightmost channels with no processes at all. Thus, the rightmost numbers in the first row must all be corrected to –6 during computation of the average.)

Throughout this chapter, the Shortest Path algorithm has been used to illustrate the Replicated Worker parallel programming paradigm. The implementation of Work Pools developed in this section is presented in the context of a Shortest Path program. However, the implementation is quite general and is not limited to the Shortest Path. This multiple-channel implementation of Work Pools can be used in a wide variety of Replicated Worker programs on multiprocessors. The procedures *Getwork* and *Putwork* can be lifted from the program of Figure 10.7 and used in any Replicated Worker program. The Worker Process code must be changed for each program, but the same implementation of the Work Pool can be used. The only modification needed is to change the format of the "task descriptor" record used in the Work Pool.

10.5 N-QUEENS PROBLEM

To illustrate the ease with which the Work Pool implementations given in this chapter can be adapted to new Replicated Worker programs, another example will be considered: the N-Queens Problem. Because of its simplicity and its purely combinatorial nature, this problem has become very popular as an example in the computer science literature on parallel programming. The problem is to find a placement of *n* Queens on an *n* by *n* chessboard, such that none of the queens is attacking any other. The best way to solve such a problem is just to do a combinatorial search of possible placements for the Queens, and reject those in which Queens are attacking each other. Because of the large number of combinations resulting from even a small value of *n*, the problem can keep a large number of parallel processors busy, resulting in a good speedup.

Two Queens on a chessboard are *attacking* each other if they are in the same row, column, or diagonal. Figure 10.10 shows a Queen on an 8 by 8 chessboard. The "Q" shows the location of the Queen, and the "x" marks show all the squares attacked by that Queen. Notice that this includes all the squares in the same row and all the squares in the same column. It also includes all *diagonal* squares going in all four possible diagonal directions. Figure 10.11 shows a solution for *n* = 7.

To solve this problem by hand, one might take an *n* by *n* chessboard and a pile of *n* Queens and then start placing the Queens one at a time on the chessboard. One would always add each new Queen in such a way that it did not attack any of the other Queens already on the board. If a situation were ever reached in which it was impossible to add a

FIGURE 10.10 Attack area of queen.   **FIGURE 10.11** Solution for 7 queens.

new Queen without attacking the others, then one would *backtrack* by removing one or more Queens, and then continue from there to try alternatives not yet explored. This kind of combinatorial searching is easily computerized in such a way that all possible alternatives are explored in a systematic way. In a parallel computer, the search space can be divided among the available processors.

Since a Queen always attacks all squares in the same row, it is obvious that there cannot be two Queens in the same row. Since the number of rows of the chessboard is n, and there are also n Queens, then any solution must clearly have exactly one Queen in each row of the board. Thus, a systematic solution procedure would be to place the first Queen in row number 1, considering all n possibilities. For each of these placements of Queen 1, then place Queen 2 in the second row, considering all those positions that are not attacked by Queen 1. The result would be a set of tuples $(Q1, Q2)$, where $Q1$ gives the column number of the Queen in row 1, and $Q2$ gives the column number of the Queen in row 2. Now each of these tuples can be extended by considering all valid positions for Queen 3 in row 3. The result would be a set of tuples of the form $(Q1, Q2, Q3)$. This search procedure could be continued up to n, resulting in a collection of *n-tuples* of the form $(Q1, Q2, ..., Qn)$. Each of these *n-tuples* is then a solution to the N-Queens problem.

In a Multi-Pascal program for the N-Queens problem, each of these tuples can be represented by the following data structure:

```
TYPE worktype =

    RECORD
      len: INTEGER; (*number of Queens so far*)
      queens: ARRAY [1..n] OF INTEGER; (*positions on board*)
    END;
```

In a Replicated Worker program, the Work Pool can contain all the tuples created so far. When a Worker Process removes an item from the Work Pool, it adds one more Queen to the tuple in the next empty row. Each possible position in the row is considered, looking for those that are not attacked by Queens already on the board. For each such valid position, the new Queen is placed on the board, and the corresponding work item is written back into the Work Pool. As time progresses, the tuples in the Work Pool will gradually grow until they all reach length *n*. These remaining *n-tuples* are all the solutions to the original N-Queens problem.

A high-level description of the Worker Process is as follows:

```
Worker Process:

    Getwork(myboard); (*Get a tuple from Work Pool*)
    While myboard <> Doneflag Do
      Begin
        If myboard.len = n then "A Solution is Found"
        Else Begin
           newrow := len + 1;
           For col := 1 To n Do
             Begin
               Is position (newrow,col) attacked by any of the
                  previous Queens on "myboard"?
               If answer is "no" then
                 Begin
                   create "newboard" by adding Queen
                       in position (newrow,col);
                   Putwork(newboard);
                 End;
             End;
        End;
      Getwork(myboard);
    End;
```

The complete Multi-Pascal program is shown in Figure 10.12. The code for the Worker Procedure closely follows the above high-level description. The termination flag for the Workers will be a "–1" in the *myboard.len*, so each Worker continues looping until this flag is detected. All the solutions to the N-Queens problem are collected in a shared channel called *solutions*. The only tricky part of the code is the method used to test positions for the new Queen to see if they are attacked by any of the existing Queens. This is done for each of the existing Queens by computing its distance in rows (*rowdist*) and columns (*coldist*) from the test position.

The Work Pool implementation already developed in the context of the Shortest Path program can be used directly here. The *Getwork* and *Putwork* procedures used in this N-Queens program are identical to those in Figure 10.7. Recall that in this implementation, the Work Pool contains a small number of separate channels, with a group of Worker Processes assigned to each channel. This implementation avoids channel contention in the Work Pool. Load balancing is achieved by having *Putwork* distribute work items to the channels in a *round-robin* fashion. All of these internal implementation details, including the termination detection, are completely hidden in the *Getwork* and *Putwork* procedures of Figure 10.7. This new N-Queens program is written by simply considering the Work Pool as an abstract data structure, as shown in Figure 10.1. Naturally, the Worker Process had to be custom designed to solve the N-Queens problem, but no changes to the Work Pool implementation are required.

```
PROGRAM NQueens;
CONST n = 8; (*Number of Queens*)
      num_worker_groups = 5;
      worker_group_size = 6;
      numworkers = num_worker_groups * worker_group_size;
TYPE board = ARRAY [1..n] OF INTEGER;
     worktype = RECORD
                     len: INTEGER;  (*No. queens so far*)
                     queens: board; (*Positions of queens*)
                  END;
VAR workpool:  ARRAY [1..num_worker_groups] OF CHANNEL OF worktype;
    i: INTEGER;     startitem: worktype;
    solutions: CHANNEL OF board; (*Collects final solutions*)
       ...  (*Work Pool counter declarations as in Figure 10.7*)



PROCEDURE Getwork(me: INTEGER; VAR item: worktype);

   ... (* same as Figure 10.7 *)



PROCEDURE Putwork(me: INTEGER; item: worktype);

   ... (* same as Figure 10.7 *)



PROCEDURE Worker(me: INTEGER);
VAR myboard: worktype; row,col,coldist,rowdist: INTEGER;
    samecol,samediag,ok: BOOLEAN;
BEGIN
  Getwork(me,myboard);
  WHILE myboard.len <> -1 DO
    BEGIN
      WITH myboard DO
        IF len = n THEN solutions := myboard.queens
        ELSE BEGIN (*add new queen to board*)
          len := len + 1;
          FOR col := 1 TO n DO
            BEGIN (*See if ok to place queen in this column*)
              ok := true;
              FOR row := 1 TO len-1 DO
                BEGIN
                  rowdist :=  Abs(len - row);
                  coldist :=  Abs(col - queens[row]);
                  samecol :=  coldist = 0;
                  samediag :=  coldist = rowdist;
                  IF samecol OR samediag THEN ok := false;
                END;
```

FIGURE 10.12   N-Queens program for multiprocessor.

```
                IF ok THEN
                  BEGIN
                   queens[len] := col;
                   Putwork(me,myboard); (*add to Work Pool*)
                  END;
              END;
          END;
       Getwork(me,myboard);  (*new work item to consider*)
     END;
END; (*Worker*)


BEGIN (*Main*)
startitem.len := 0;
workpool[1] := startitem; (*Initialize Work Pool with empty board*)

  ... (*Initialize Work Pool counters as in Figure 10.7*)

FORALL i := 1 TO numworkers DO (*Create Worker Processes*)
  Worker(i);

  ... (*All answers are found in channel "solutions"*)

END.
```

FIGURE 10.12 (continued)

10.6 SUMMARY

The purpose of this chapter has been to describe an important parallel programming technique: the Replicated Worker paradigm. This technique is required for programs in which computational activity is generated dynamically in an unpredictable way as the program progresses. For such programs, simple nested *FORALL* loops as used in previous chapters is not sufficient. The program must be organized to store and distribute the large number of computational tasks as they are dynamically generated. For this purpose, the concept of the *Work Pool* was introduced. Each required unit of computation is represented by a *task descriptor* that is stored in the Work Pool. A group of identical *Worker Processes* continually reads and writes task descriptors from the Work Pool. When a Worker Process is free, it will read a task descriptor from the Work Pool and perform the required computation. During this computation, new task descriptors may be generated by the Worker and added to the Work Pool.

The major focus of the chapter was to describe the implementation of the Work Pool for multiprocessors. The first implementation issue was *contention* by the Worker Processes. To avoid channel contention, the Work Pool was decentralized into a small number of channels, each with its own local group of Worker Processes. This decentralization introduced the issue of *load balancing* because of the potential for some Worker groups to be idle while others have too many work items. In practice it is found that this problem can be overcome by a very simple distribution technique for the work items, such as having each Worker use a round-robin distribution among all the channels in the Work Pool.

Termination detection is also an interesting issue that arises in Replicated Worker programs. The program must terminate when the Work Pool is empty and all the Worker Processes are waiting for more work. As the Work Pool becomes more decentralized, this condition becomes more difficult to detect. For the decentralized multiprocessor implementation presented in this chapter, termination is detected by using an array of counters, one for each channel, that record the number of idle Workers waiting on that channel.

As an example of the Replicated Worker paradigm, a parallel Shortest Path program was presented for computing the shortest distance in a weighted graph from a single source to all other vertices. As the program progresses, new shorter distances are continually being discovered to vertices. These form the task descriptors or *work items* for the Work Pool. A Worker Process reads a new shorter distance from the Work Pool, and computes new test distances to all immediate neighbors of that vertex. If a shorter distance is found for any neighbors, then a new work item is generated and added to the Work Pool. This Shortest Path example was chosen just to illustrate the Replicated Worker paradigm and serve as a basis for describing Work Pool implementation techniques.

There are a wide variety of other examples for which the Replicated Worker paradigm is the best solution. These include many graph algorithms and combinatorial search problems. One simple example is the N-Queens problem given at the end of this chapter. It was shown that the Work Pool implementations developed in the context of the Shortest Path program can also be used for a Replicated Worker solution to the N-Queens problem. The only modification needed is to change the definition of the "work item" to make the Work Pool suitable for this problem.

In the programming projects that follow in this chapter, two additional examples are given: the Traveling Salesman problem and a Maze Search program. For these programs and many others, the Replicated Worker parallel programming paradigm is suitable, and the Work Pool implementations described in this chapter can easily be used with only minor modification.

REFERENCES

The Replicated Worker parallel programming paradigm appears in Ahuja, Carriero, and Gelernter [1986] with reference to the parallel programming language Linda. There are several parallel programming systems that have implemented special features to help support the creation of Replicated Workers. These include the Uniform System used in the BBN Butterfly multiprocessor [Thomas, 1988], and the macros of Boyle, et al. [1987], which have a "Getwork" macro to manage the work pool.

The sequential shortest path algorithm presented in this chapter originally appeared in Moore [1959]. Quinn [1987] presents a parallel version of this algorithm using a single shared queue, which is similar to the first parallel version presented in this chapter with only one channel in the Work Pool. The performance of this single-queue algorithm was tested on the Denelcor HEP by Deo, Pang, and Lord [1980]. They found that queue contention became severe with more than six processors.

Quinn and Deo [1984] present a survey of parallel shortest path algorithms in the computer science literature. Several parallel versions of the shortest path appear in Bertsekas and Tsitsiklis [1989]. Chandy and Misra [1988] have a chapter devoted to a parallel version of the Floyd–Warshall algorithm for solving the "all-pairs" shortest path problem.

Quinn [1987] describes a parallel Traveling Salesman program based on the original sequential algorithm of Little [1963]. The performance of two parallel versions of the Traveling Salesman program are given in Mohan [1983] for the Cm* parallel computer. Brawer [1989] presents parallel programs for the Maze Search problem and Traveling Salesman problem on the Encore shared-memory multiprocessor.

PROGRAMMING PROJECTS

1. MAZE SEARCH

In this project you will write and run a parallel Maze Search program for a multiprocessor. The Replicated Worker parallel programming paradigm described in this chapter will be the basis for designing the program. You will be able to use the Work Pool implementation developed in this chapter. Therefore, the main task is to decide on the format of the *task descriptors* for the Work Pool and write the Worker Procedure in Multi-Pascal.

Basically, each task descriptor will be a partially completed path through the maze. After a Worker Process reads this partial path from the Work Pool, the Worker will extend the path to the next "branch point," where a choice must be made. The Worker will then create a new partial path for each choice and write them all back into the Work Pool. Before reaching a "branch point," the Worker may find that a "dead end" is reached. In this case, the partial path is simply discarded. Also, the Worker may reach the "goal" position in the maze, in which case the current path becomes a *solution path* for the maze.

The maze has one "starting point" and one "goal." The starting point is put into the Work Pool as the first partially completed path. As the Replicated Worker program progresses, new partial paths will be created by extending the old paths. As new paths are created, some will be discarded and others will continue to be extended. Eventually, one path will hit the goal. The input to your program should be a description of the maze, and the output should be a path from the starting point to the goal.

One additional refinement in the search algorithm for greater efficiency is for the Workers to place a special "mark" at the branch points of the maze itself as a path grows through that branch point. This will prevent other paths from exploring that same branch point again later on. This will eliminate duplication of effort and also prevent unending "circular" paths from being created.

The maze can be represented by an *undirected* graph. Each corridor of the maze corresponds to an edge in the graph, and each branch point in the maze corresponds to a vertex in the graph. Your program should begin by reading in a data structure describing the structure of the graph, including a specification of the starting vertex number and the goal vertex number. In testing your program, begin with a small maze. However, to keep a lot of processors busy and get a good speedup, a very large maze with lots of alternate paths will be needed.

After developing a working program, use a combination of mathematical analysis and experimental observation to determine what portion of the total loss of speedup results from each of the following factors: lack of available work, contention, and load imbalance.

2. TRAVELING SALESMAN PROBLEM

The Traveling Saleman Problem is a classic computer problem, that has received a great deal of attention in the computer science literature. It is one example of an *NP-Complete* problem, which means that there is no known solution technique that performs substantially better than simply just searching through all possible alternatives. Given a group of cities with a fixed travel distance between each pair, the problem is to find the shortest *tour* that visits each city exactly once.

Like the N-Queens problem discussed in this chapter, the Traveling Salesman problem can be solved through a combinatorial search of all possible tours. Therefore, it is well suited for a Replicated Worker solution. As partially completed tours are generated during the search, they can be stored in the Work Pool. Each Worker Process removes a partial tour from the Work Pool, computes all possible extensions of the tour to one more city, and then writes all these new partial tours back into the Work Pool.

The cities are numbered from 1 to *n*, and the travel distances are given by a two-dimensional array *distance*, such that *distance*[i, j] gives the travel distance from city *i* to city *j*. For simplicity, assume that all the tours start at city 1, then visit all the other cities exactly once, and return to city 1 at the end. The Traveling Saleman problem is to find the tour with the minimum total travel distance.

A partial tour is just a sequence of city numbers beginning with city 1. Associated with each partial tour is the *travel distance* for that tour. To extend a partial tour, one must consider all the remaining cities not yet in the tour: each of these is a potential candidate for the next city to be visited in the partial tour. Each Worker Process will read a partial tour from the Work Pool, compute all possible one-city extensions of the tour, and then write them all back to the Work Pool.

A global minimum is maintained for the shortest complete tour found so far. Whenever any Worker finds a complete tour, it compares the travel distance with this global minimum, and replaces the global minimum if necessary. After the Replicated Worker program terminates, this global minimum is the final answer.

The algorithm described above is suitable for writing a Replicated Worker program for the Traveling Salesman problem. However, the performance can be improved through a minor modification. In the above algorithm, each tour is extended by one city and then returned to the Work Pool. Thus, all the partial tours grow gradually, one city at a time. As the algorithm progresses, the number of such partial tours will grow explosively, requiring a large amount of computation, and possibly even overwhelming the storage system.

This combinatorial explosion can be reduced by using a *heuristic* search technique, which attempts to find *good* tours first, and then uses these to eliminate *bad* tours at early stages of their creation. When a Worker Process reads a partial tour from the Work Pool, it will select the next city for the tour as the nearest of the remaining cities. Partial tours for the other cities will also be computed, but these will be immediately written back into the Work Pool. Then the Worker will extend its partial tour by one more city, by finding the nearest of the cities that still remain unvisited. The Worker will keep pushing forward with its partial tour in this way until all the cities are visited, and a complete tour is generated.

This algorithm is really almost identical to the one described previously. The Worker still computes all possible one-city extensions to each partial tour. However, instead of immediately writing all of them back to the Work Pool, the shortest of these partial tours is retained and extended, while the others are written back to the Work Pool. In this way, each Worker will push forward quickly to find some reasonably good tours, which will be recorded in the global minimum.

Then the global minimum can be used to eliminate many partial tours before they are completed. As each new partial tour is generated, its travel distance is compared to the global minimum. In this way, many bad tours that jump long distances between cities will be eliminated in their early stages. This simple *heuristic* will greatly reduce the number of partial tours generated. Also, it will reduce storage requirements for the Work Pool, because the Workers will continue to push partial tours quickly towards complete tours, and thus eliminate them from the Work Pool.

After developing a working program, use a combination of mathematical analysis and experimental observation to determine what portion of the total loss of speedup results from each of the following factors: lack of available work, contention, and load imbalance.

EXERCISES

1. Give a brief definition of the Replicated Worker parallel programming paradigm.

2. Explain in a general way why any implementation of Work Pools for multiprocessors has to be careful about the contention problem.

3. For the sample graph of Figure 10.2, show in detail the steps of the Sequential Shortest Path algorithm, including the values of the *mindist* array and the vertex queue at each stage of computation.

4. In the Worker Process shown in Figure 10.3, the spinlock $L[w]$ is used to perform mutual exclusion on the access to *mindist*[w].
   (a) Consider a version of this Worker Process in which the spinlock is not present, and there is no mutual exclusion. Give a detailed scenario that results in an error in the computation.
   (b) Although mutual exclusion is performed on *mindist*[w], there is a reference to *mindist*[*vertex*] that is outside the exclusion region. Show in detail that this cannot cause any errors in the computation.

5. In the parallel Shortest Path algorithm of Figure 10.3, the graph is represented by the two-dimensional *weight* array. Consider an alternate representation of the graph in which each vertex has a linked list of outgoing edges. Each edge in the list is a RECORD containing the destination vertex and the distance to that vertex. You are to rewrite the Worker Procedure, using this new graph representation. You may use the following definitions:

```
TYPE edgepnt = ^edge;

    edge =  RECORD
                destination: INTEGER; (*vertex number*)
                weight: INTEGER;      (*distance*)
                link: edgepnt;  (*pointer to next edge*)
            END;

VAR graph:  ARRAY [1..n] OF edgepnt; (*pointer to edge list*)
```

The *graph* array contains pointers to the edge list for each vertex. For a vertex *i*, *graph*[*i*] points to the start of the edge list for vertex *i*.

6. In the text it is stated that Figure 10.4 may result in contention. Describe in detail a situation that can arise in this program in which several Worker Processes may be kept waiting. Specify exactly which lines of code are being executed, why the Workers are waiting, and how long they have to wait.

7. In the multiprocessor Work Pool implementation of Figure 10.7, what properties of the Worker Processes will determine a good choice of the Worker Group Size? Explain why some Replicated Worker algorithms would require a lower or higher group size than the Shortest Path algorithm.

8. Describe a Replicated Worker algorithm for searching a tree by examining every node and leaf. Give a detailed design for the Worker Procedure.

9. In some Replicated Worker programs, it may be useful to terminate the program even while there are still items in the Work Pool. For example, this situation may occur in a tree or graph search when the goal of the search is achieved. For this purpose, a new procedure "Terminate" can be added to the Work Pool implementation, which can be called by any Worker Process to immediately terminate the computation.

    Give a detailed design for this Terminate Procedure, as well as any needed modifications to the *Getwork* and *Putwork* procedures.

10. In the multiprocessor Work Pool implementation described in section 10.4, a Worker Process will be suspended if the channel assigned to its Worker Group is empty. Consider the following modificiation: if a Worker finds its own channel is empty, then it scans through the other channels to find one with some work items. Rewrite the high-level descriptions of *Getwork* and *Putwork* to implement this modification.

11. Consider a modification to the multiprocessor Work Pool implementation of Figure 10.7 in which the initial value for the *nextchan* pointer of each Worker is computed randomly. Discuss the advantages of this modification. Describe the detailed changes necessary to the program of Figure 10.7 to implement this modification.

12. Figure 10.8 shows a 42 percent loss of speedup, using 20 Worker Groups. Use some theoretical analysis to approximate how much of this is due to channel contention.

13. Assume that a Replicated Worker program has saturation limit S for the size of a work group. If the actual size of the work groups is $.5S$, what is the expected performance degradation from channel contention? (Your answer should be in terms of S.)

14. Using Figure 10.9, estimate how much performance degradation results from lack of sufficient work, and how much from load imbalances.

15. In an alternate formulation of the Replicated Worker paradigm, the Work Pool can be replaced by recursion in the Worker Processes. In this formulation, the Worker Procedure has one parameter—the vertex on which it will operate. After finishing with this one input vertex, the Worker process terminates. This removes the need for calling *Getwork*. Also, instead of calling

Putwork(me, w) to put each vertex *w* into the Work Pool, the Worker executes the following to create a new Worker Process:

```
FORK Worker(w);   (*Create new Worker Process for vertex w*)
```

Discuss the advantages and disadvantages of this recursive method, as compared to the Work Pool method presented in this chapter. Which method is easier to use? Which method is more efficient? Give detailed reasons for your answers to these questions.

16. Find a solution by hand to the N-Queens Problem for $n = 4$.

17. For the N-Queens program of Figure 10.12, use the Multi-Pascal system to experimentally estimate the saturation limit for Worker Processes in a single work group. Use two different measurement methods to make sure your estimate is accurate. Your measurement technique has to be carefully thought out to make sure you are actually measuring the saturation limit, and not something else.

11

Distributed Termination Detection

The Replicated Worker paradigm allows a parallel program to generate computing tasks dynamically as the program runs. These tasks are stored in a Work Pool, where they can be accessed by the Worker Processes. The previous chapter showed how to implement this programming paradigm on shared memory multiprocessors. The Replicated Worker paradigm is also applicable to multicomputers. However, the basic concept must be slightly modified because of the localized nature of the memory in the multicomputers. The Work Pool can no longer be considered as a centralized and shared pool of common work items that can be freely retrieved by the identical worker processes. The Work Pool must be partitioned and distributed across the local memories of the multicomputer. Because of this conceptual change and the resultant new implementation issues that arise, a new name will be used for this parallel programming technique on multicomputers: *Distributed Workers*.

To implement Distributed Workers, the most difficult issue is the termination detection. A new and somewhat more complex *distributed termination algorithm* is required. The whole issue of distributed termination is an important general topic in multicomputer programming, and is the main subject of this chapter. Another important area of consideration for Distributed Workers is the method of distributing the work items. The Work Pool is completely partitioned among the Workers, and therefore each work item must be sent directly to a specific Worker. In the Replicated Worker paradigm, Workers are assumed to be essentially indistinguishable, so that any Worker could in principle receive any work item. However, for Distributed Workers it is often the case that the Workers are not indistinguishable, and it is necessary for certain work items to go to specific Workers. This requirement results from the *data partitioning* that is often necessary in multicomputer algorithms.

In Replicated Worker programs, the Workers often use some additional shared data structures besides the Work Pool itself. For example, in the Shortest Path program, the

Workers use an array that records the shortest distance found so far to each vertex in the graph. To promote more efficient access and minimize communication delays in a multicomputer implementation, these shared data structures usually must be partitioned among the local memories. In most Distributed Worker programs, this will mean that the work items can no longer be distributed to any Worker Process. The work items may refer to a specific partition of the shared data structure, and therefore must be sent to the Worker that has local access to that particular partition.

As in the previous chapter, the Shortest Path algorithm will be used as the primary vehicle to illustrate and develop the Distributed Worker parallel programming paradigm. First the issue of *data partitioning* will be considered, and then the termination detection algorithm. The most interesting aspect of this termination detection algorithm is the use of *message acknowledgments* to inform a sender that a message has been properly received. This allows it to function correctly despite arbitrarily large message transmission delays in the communication network. The algorithm is quite general and has application beyond Distributed Worker programs. The chapter concludes with a consideration of asynchronous iterative algorithms, which hold promise for the future of parallel computing. These algorithms can be implemented within the Distributed Worker paradigm.

11.1 MULTICOMPUTER SHORTEST PATH PROGRAM

The first issue to consider in this chapter is how to adapt the Shortest Path program to multicomputer execution. Recall the sequential Shortest Path algorithm described in the previous chapter (see Figure 10.3). The algorithm keeps a queue of vertex numbers that need to be examined. Another data structure (array *mindist*) records the shortest distance found so far to each vertex. After a vertex number x is read from the queue, it is necessary to look at several *mindist* elements: *mindist*[x] and also the elements corresponding to the vertices directly connected to vertex x. If a shorter distance is to find any of the vertices connected to x, then the corresponding *mindist* element is updated.

Since the *mindist* array elements change dynamically during the program execution, there must be only one shared copy of this array in the parallel version of the algorithm. In the multiprocessor algorithm developed in the previous chapter, several Workers could potentially try to access the same element of *mindist* in parallel. Therefore, a spinlock was used for each array element to guarantee *atomic* updating. Now in the multicomputer case, the *mindist* array presents something of a difficulty.

Since Worker Processes read the vertices from a central Work Pool, any Worker could conceivably receive any vertex in the graph, and therefore require access to any elements in the *mindist* array. Since there must be only one copy of the *mindist* elements, this raises the issue of where to locate the *mindist* array elements. No matter how cleverly they are distributed around the local memories, it will be difficult to guarantee that each Worker Process always has the required *mindist* elements in its own local memory. The result will be a frequent requirement to communicate *mindist* values between the processors.

To avoid this problem in the multicomputer program, a reorganization of the parallel algorithm is required. In past chapters this same problem has arisen in other multicomputer programs when shared data structures were updated dynamically. Recall that the solution adopted was always *data partitioning*: divide the elements of the shared data structure among the local memories, and try to organize the algorithm so that each process primarily focuses on its own partition of the data. In the case of the Shortest Path program, this means that the *mindist* array must be partitioned among the local memories of the multicomputer. The program presented here will simply place one element of *mindist* in each local memory. This is possible as long as the number of vertices in the graph is less than the number of processors. For larger graphs, several *mindist* elements will have to be assigned to each local memory.

Each Worker Process i will now find that it has local access to $mindist[i]$, which is the shortest distance found so far to vertex i. The Shortest Path algorithm can be modified to completely avoid the need for communicating these *mindist* values. Each Worker i will deal only with vertex i of the graph. Whenever vertex i is put into the Work Pool, the Work Pool implementation will make sure that this work item goes to Worker Process i.

In the Shortest Path algorithm, a consideration of a given vertex i by Worker i involves computing a new *trialdistance* to each neighboring vertex w and then comparing this with the current value of $mindist[w]$. But $mindist[w]$ is located in the local memory of Worker w. So Worker i will simply send the *trialdistance* for w to Worker w, where it will be compared to $mindist[w]$. With this new organization for the parallel algorithm, all the work items will be *trial distances*. Each work item will consist of a vertex number w and a *trial distance* for that vertex. When Worker w receives this work item, he will compare this *trial distance* to the current value of $mindist[w]$, which is located in his own local memory. If the *trial distance* is less, then *mindist* is updated. Worker w will then consider all the adjacent vertices to its vertex w and send them all new *trial distances* based on its new lower value of $mindist[w]$.

The multicomputer Shortest Path program is shown in Figure 11.1. The implementation of the Work Pool is not shown here and will be described in subsequent sections of this chapter. As before, the structure of the graph is represented by the two-dimensional *weight* array: element $weight[i,j]$ is the weight assigned to the edge from vertex i to j. If there is no edge from i to j, then the value is "infinity." Therefore, row i of the array contains the weights for all the edges originating from vertex i. Since all the processing for vertex i is done by Worker i, this row of the *weight* array is passed as a "value" parameter when Worker i is created.

The Worker Process begins by reading an initial item from the Work Pool. The Work Pool implementation guarantees that Worker Process i will receive only work items referring to vertex i. Therefore, the "vertex number" is omitted from the *Getwork* call— only the *distance* portion of the work item is returned. Once it has received this new *trialdistance* for vertex i, Worker i must compare this to the shortest distance found so far to vertex i, which is stored locally in variable *mindistance*. The collection of these local *mindistance* values from all the Workers is just the *mindist* array as discussed earlier. These *mindist* values are partitioned among the Workers.

If the new *trialdistance* is in fact less than the current shortest distance to vertex i, then *mindistance* is updated. Also, for each outgoing edge from vertex i to a destination vertex w, a new work item is generated containing a new *testdistance* for *vertex w* (see Figure 11.1). The Work Pool implementation will guarantee that this work item reaches Worker Process w. Each Worker Process continues looping until it detects a termination flag. Before terminating, the Worker sends the final value of *mindistance* back to the main process through the *VAR* parameter *answer*.

```
PROGRAM Shortpath_2;
ARCHITECTURE HYPERCUBE(6);
CONST n = 63; (*Number of vertices in the graph*)
      numworkers = 63;
      infinity = 32000;   done = -1;
TYPE weightrow = ARRAY [1..n] OF INTEGER;
VAR weight: ARRAY [1..n] OF weightrow; (*edge weights in graph*)
    i: INTEGER;
    finaldist: ARRAY [1..n] OF INTEGER; (*final solution*)


PROCEDURE Worker(me: INTEGER; myweight: weightrow;
                        VAR answer: INTEGER);
VAR mindistance: INTEGER; (*shortest distance to my vertex "me"*)
    w,trialdistance: INTEGER;

  PROCEDURE Getwork(VAR inputdistance: INTEGER);
      ...


  PROCEDURE Putwork(vertex, outputdistance: INTEGER);
      ...


BEGIN (*worker*)
  mindistance := infinity;
  Getwork(trialdistance);
  WHILE trialdistance <> done DO
    BEGIN
      IF trialdistance < mindistance THEN
        BEGIN (*Shorter distance to my vertex has been found*)
          mindistance := trialdistance;
          FOR w := 1 TO n DO (*for each adjacent vertex*)
            IF myweight[w] < infinity THEN
                Putwork(w, mindistance + myweight[w]);
        END;
      Getwork(trialdistance);
    END;
  answer := mindistance; (*final shortest distance*)
END;


BEGIN  (*Main*)

  ... (*Read in values for weight array to define the graph*)

  FORALL i := 1 TO numworkers DO (*Create Distributed Workers*)
   (@i) Worker(i, weight[i], finaldist[i]);

  ... (*answers are in finaldist array*)

END.
```

FIGURE 11.1 Shortest path algorithm for multicomputer.

11.2 WORK POOL IMPLEMENTATION

Now consider the implementation of the Work Pool for this multicomputer Shortest Path program. In the multiprocessor case, all the Workers were essentially equivalent, and therefore any work item could go to any Worker. The Work Pool could then be implemented by a small number of shared channels, with many Workers assigned to each channel. However, in the multicomputer program, each Worker is assigned a specific vertex of the graph, and therefore each work item must go to a specific Worker. The simplest implementation of the Work Pool is just to allow each Worker Process to have its own input channel for receiving work items. The Work Pool will contain an array of channels, and Worker Process i will be assigned channel $workpool[i]$ as its communication port for receiving work.

This Work Pool implementation is illustrated in Figure 11.2. The Work Pool is still treated as an abstract data structure by the Worker Processes. Each Worker uses *Getwork* and *Putwork* to access the Work Pool. However, internally the Work Pool has assigned one channel to each Worker as a communication port. *Getwork* for Worker i simply reads a work item from channel i, which is its own communication port. When any Worker calls *Putwork* with a given work item, the *Putwork* routine determines which vertex number the work item refers to, and then writes the work item into the appropriate channel. In this implementation of the Work Pool, the reading and writing of work items is quite straightforward. However, the termination detection is more complex than in the multiprocessor case.

11.2.1 Message Acknowledgments

Multicomputers pose a problem to termination detection because of the delays in message transmission between the processors. In a multicomputer, all communication between the processors and all remote memory access is done by message passing through the proces-

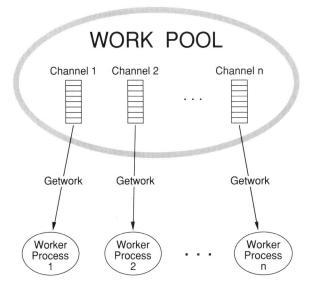

FIGURE 11.2 **Multicomputer work pool.**

sor communication network. There will always be some delays involved in this message passing. This means that there may be periods of time in which some data already sent by a source process has not yet been received by the destination process. In the Shortest Path program, this means that there may be periods of time in which work items are "in transit" between processors. Since the program wants to terminate only after all work items are consumed, these "in-transit" work items pose something of a difficulty. It may be that all Workers are idle at a given time, and yet some work items are still moving through the communication network on the way to their destination.

To illustrate in more detail the nature of this problem and its solution, consider using a termination detection procedure that is similar to the one used in the multiprocessor program. A *master count* is used to record the total number of idle Worker Processes. When this count reaches the total number of Workers (n), then termination messages are sent to all the Workers. Since the master count is one single value, it must be located in the local memory of some processor—assume that this is processor 0. Whenever any Worker Process finds that its Work Pool input channel is empty, the Worker will send a "+1" message to be added to the master count at processor 0, indicating that the Worker has gone from the active state into the idle state. Whenever an idle Worker Process receives a new work item into its empty queue, it will send a "−1" message to be added to the master count, indicating that the Worker is no longer idle.

At processor 0, the incoming "+1" and "−1" messages are simply added to the master count as they arrive. When the count reaches n, then it is known that all the Workers must be idle, and the algorithm can terminate. The reader may already have seen the fatal flaw in this termination detection method. Consider the following scenario. All the Workers are idle except Worker i. The master count is therefore $n − 1$. Worker i is processing its last work item, and then goes into the idle state itself and sends out a "+1" message to the master count. However, before becoming idle, Worker i sends out one last work item destined for Worker j running on processor j. There are two possible outcomes now that depend on the delays encountered by these two messages: the "+1" message on its way to processor 0, and the work-item message on its way to processor j.

When the work item is received by Worker j, it immediately sends out a "−1" message to the master count, indicating that it has just gone from the idle state into the active state. If this "−1" message reaches processor 0 before the "+1" that has already been sent from Worker i, then the master count will first go to $n − 2$ and then to $n − 1$ again: the master count will know that one Worker is still active. However, if the "+1" message arrives at processor 0 first, then the master count will go to n, thereby erroneously indicating that all of the n Worker processes are idle.

One obvious solution to this *critical race* situation is to delay the termination decision long enough to allow any in-transit messages to arrive. After the program detects that the master count has reached the value n, it will wait D time units for additional messages before initiating the termination procedure. The time delay D must be long enough to allow an in-transit work item to reach its destination Worker Process, and the "−1" message to be generated by the Worker and then travel to processor 0. In practical work on a real multicomputer, it may be possible to determine the needed value of D to guarantee correctness of the program. However, a general algorithm should be robust enough to run correctly in any multicomputer environment, assuming arbitrary message transmission delays.

In the following sections of this chapter, a theoretically sound termination algorithm is presented, which will work correctly independent of the duration of any message delays or computational delays in the multicomputer. The algorithm is based on the principle of *message acknowledgments*: each message sent to a remote processor will generate an *acknowledgment* back to the source processor. In this way the source processor can be sure that the message has been received and is no longer still in transit. Since the source processor knows the acknowledgment will come eventually, it can wait an arbitrarily large amount of time, thus allowing for the possibility of arbitrarily large delays in message transmission.

In the context of the Shortest Path algorithm, the application of this principle means that every work item sent from a source Worker process to a destination Worker process must generate an acknowledgment, which travels from the destination Worker back to the source Worker. In this way, each Worker process will know when all the work items it has sent have actually been received at their destination Worker. Each Worker will wait for all return acknowledgments before going into an "idle" state. This will prevent all the Workers from going idle prematurely while some work items are still moving through the message-passing network toward their destination.

The use of these acknowledgments can be completely hidden in the Work Pool implementation, so that the Worker procedure is unchanged, just as in Figure 11.1. The Work Pool is still treated as an abstract data structure, being accessed through simple calls to *Getwork* and *Putwork*. The acknowledgments and the termination detection is handled completely inside the Work Pool implementation, which will send the necessary termination flags to all the Workers. Using the message acknowledgments, we can now modify the above termination method to work correctly. The modification of this *master-count* method will be dealt with in the exercises at the end of this chapter. However, there is a more elegant and simpler technique, which is described in the next section.

11.2.2 Termination Detection Algorithm

In this termination detection algorithm, each Worker Process is always in one of two states: idle or active. An *idle* Worker has an empty work-pool input channel and is currently waiting for a new work item. An *active* Worker is currently computing. The key to this algorithm is the dynamic creation of an *active-worker tree* of all the active Worker processes. The only way any Worker can go from the idle to the active state is to receive a work item in its work-pool channel. When this transition takes place, the Worker will look at the source of the work item—the Worker Process that generated the work item. This source Worker then becomes the *parent* in the *active-worker tree*.

At every moment during the parallel computation, each active Worker Process will have exactly one *parent*. This parent-child relationship therefore defines a *tree* among the active Workers. The only way any idle Worker *y* can become active is for some active Worker *x* already in the tree to send a work item to Worker *y*. When Worker *y* receives this work item and thereby makes the transition from idle to active, it will record that its parent is Worker *x*. Thus, Worker *y* is now added to the tree with Worker *x* as its unique parent. Worker *y* may now send some work items to other idle Worker Processes, thereby making them its children in the tree. As work items are sent around by all the active Workers, the tree will grow dynamically and will always contain all the active Worker Processes, such that each Worker has exactly one parent Worker in the tree.

Figure 11.3 shows a typical snapshot of the tree during the execution of the Distributed Worker program. Eleven of the 20 Worker Processes are in the active state and are therefore found in the tree, each with a unique parent Worker. The remaining nine Worker Processes are in the idle state waiting for a new work item. Whenever an *active* Worker finds that its work-pool input channel is empty, it must go into the *idle* state. However, there is one important restriction: the Worker is not allowed to go into the idle state until it has received all required acknowledgments. It will remain in the *active* state until all acknowledgments are received, even though its work-pool input channel may be empty.

Each Worker Process expects to receive an acknowledgment for every work item that it puts into the Work Pool. When each work item is received by its destination Worker, an acknowledgment is generated and sent back to the source Worker. Each Worker will wait to receive all these acknowledgments before going into the idle state, even if it has no more work items to process. Therefore, each *idle* Worker will always have the following important property: the Worker is waiting for more work on an empty work-pool input channel, *and* all work items sent out by this Worker have been received at their destination. It is obvious that if all the Worker Process are in the idle state, then the computation must be terminated, because the following three properties must be true:

1. The Work Pool is completely empty.
2. No work items are in transit.
3. All of the Workers are waiting for work.

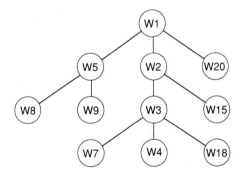

ACTIVE WORKER TREE

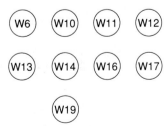

IDLE WORKERS

FIGURE 11.3 **Active and idle workers.**

Recall that property 2 above was the one that caused problems in the previous analysis of termination in multicomputers. The use of work-item acknowledgments will now solve this problem and guarantee that no work items are in transit. This is because a Worker will not go into the idle state until it has received all its acknowledgments, and is therefore certain that all work items have been received at their intended destination.

The one remaining issue to complete the termination detection algorithm is how to determine when all the Worker Processes are in the *idle* state. The *active-worker tree* is used for this purpose. It has already been stated that each Worker Process must acknowledge the source of each work item it receives. These acknowledgments are all sent out immediately upon receiving the work item, with one important exception: the work item from the parent Worker is not acknowledged immediately. When a Worker Process is idle, the first work item it receives will define its parent, which is defined as the source of this work item. The Worker will not acknowledge this work item from its parent as long as it remains in the active state. Only when a Worker makes its transition from active to idle will it finally acknowledge its parent.

This acknowledgment policy for parents will ensure that active Workers will keep their parents active also, since the parent must remain active until it receives all its acknowledgments. Since the parent of every active Worker is also active, this means that the root Worker of the *active-worker* tree will remain active as long as any other Worker Process is active. If any Worker Process is still active, then its parent will still be active, and therefore its grandparent will still be active, and so on back up the tree to the root. Therefore, to detect when all the Worker Processes are idle, simply watch the root of the *active-worker tree* to see when it becomes idle.

The behavior of each Worker Process is summarized in Figure 11.4. Each Worker begins in the *IDLE* state with its input work channel empty. When the first work item is

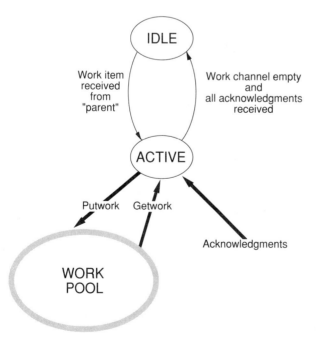

FIGURE 11.4   State diagram for worker.

Distributed Termination Detection   Chap. 11

received, a transition is made to the *ACTIVE* state. The source Worker of this first work item is recorded as the *parent*. Once in the *ACTIVE* state, the Worker will continue to call *Getwork* and *Putwork* to read and write work items to the Work Pool. For each item written into the Work Pool using *Putwork*, the Worker will expect to receive an acknowledgment from the destination Worker Process. Also, for each work item read from the Work Pool using *Getwork*, the Worker will send an acknowledgment to the source. When the Worker finds that its work-pool input channel is empty and all its expected acknowledgments have been received, then it makes a transition from the *ACTIVE* state back to the *IDLE* state. Only at this time does the Worker send an acknowledgment to its parent. Once it is in the *IDLE* state, a new work item may be received, causing the Worker again to make a transition to the *ACTIVE* state.

11.3 GETWORK AND PUTWORK

This distributed termination algorithm based on message acknowledgments is quite general and can be used in a wide variety of multicomputer programs. When used in Distributed Worker programs, the details of the termination algorithm are completely hidden inside the Work Pool implementation. The generation and processing of acknowledgments and the state transitions are generated inside the *Getwork* and *Putwork* procedures, so that the Work Pool still appears as the simple abstract data structure as originally shown in Figure 10.1. The required Worker Process for the Shortest Path program is just as shown in Figure 11.1. The Worker just expects to receive a termination flag of –1 from the Work Pool implementation when the computation is finished. All aspects of work item distribution and termination detection are handled inside the *Getwork* and *Putwork* procedures.

In the following discussion, first a high-level description of the *Getwork* and *Putwork* procedures will be given, and then the Multi-Pascal code, which will integrated with the Worker procedure of Figure 11.1 to complete the multicomputer Shortest Path program. The internal structure of the Work Pool has already been described and is illustrated in Figure 11.2. The Work Pool is an array of channels, with one channel assigned as a communication port for each Worker Process. The Worker Processes produce work items that consist of a new distance to a specific vertex. *Putwork* will use the vertex number to find the proper destination communication port: a new distance to vertex i will go into channel *workpool*[i], which is assigned to Worker i.

Since each Worker already knows to which vertex it is assigned, there is no reason to retain the vertex number in the work items—the new distance is sufficient. However, as part of the termination algorithm, the *source* Worker must be acknowledged after each work item is received. Thus, it is necessary for each work item to contain the number of the source Worker Process. After the *Getwork* procedure reads a work item from a channel, it will send an acknowledgment to the source Worker. In the Shortest Path program there is only one version of the *Getwork* and *Putwork* procedures, but when the program is running on a multicomputer, each local memory will have its own copy of the procedures. Thus, each Worker Process calls its own local copy of *Getwork* and *Putwork*. To properly implement the termination detection, *Getwork* and *Putwork* must have access to the following values for the calling Worker:

Variable Name	Interpretation
me	The identification number of the Worker
active	The state of the Worker (active or idle)
ackcount	The number of work items sent out that are still unacknowledged
parent	The identification number of the parent Worker Process

The Putwork procedure is by far the simpler of the two. *Putwork* is given a destination vertex number and a new trial distance for that vertex. It builds a work item containing this trial distance plus the source Worker's identification number, then writes the work item into the destination Worker's communication port in the Work Pool:

```
Putwork(vertex, outputdistance):

    Increment ackcount;
    Build work item consisting of (me,outputdistance);
    Write work item into workpool[vertex];
```

The state transition diagram of Figure 11.4 can be used as the basis for writing the *Getwork* procedure. The simplest code for *Getwork* will result from an implementation that uses the same input channel to receive incoming work items and acknowledgments. Items can be read from this single channel and then processed differently, depending on whether they are work items or acknowledgments. Since each Worker Process i already has an assigned channel *workpool*[i], this communication port is used for all incoming work items and acknowledgments destined for Worker i.

The basic activity of the *Getwork* procedure is to read items from the Worker's port looking for the first work item. As acknowledgments are encountered in the port, they are simply discarded and the *ackcount* for the Worker is decremented. When the first work item is found, then an acknowledgment is sent to the source Worker, and the *distance* portion of the work item is returned to the calling Worker. If it is found that all acknowledgments have been received and the work pool channel is empty, then the state of the Worker is changed from Active to Idle. Following is a high-level description of the *Getwork* procedure:

```
Getwork:

    Repeat
      If Worker in Active State AND Work Channel empty
         AND all acknowledgments received Then
        Begin
          Acknowledge current parent;
          Go into Idle State;
        End;
      Read new item from Work Pool;
      If new item is acknowledgment then decrement ack. count;
    Until work item is received;

    If Worker in Active State Then
        send acknowledgment to source of work item
```

```
Else Begin
  Go into Active State;
  Set new parent from source of this work item;
End;

Return "distance" part of work item to calling Worker;
```

The actual Multi-Pascal code for the *Getwork* and *Putwork* procedures is shown in Figure 11.5, along with all required variable definitions and initializations. This code is to be combined with the Worker Procedure of Figure 11.1 to complete the multicomputer Shortest Path program. The definition of the Work Pool as an array of channels is contained at the start of the program. Each work item is a record containing the source vertex number and a new distance. The Work Pool is initialized at the start of the main program by placing the first work item into the channel for vertex 1. Since this is the starting vertex for all the paths, the *distance* is initialized to 0. The code for *Getwork* and *Putwork* corresponds closely to the high-level descriptions given above. Notice that these procedures are physically located inside the Worker Procedure, giving them access to the local variables of the Worker: *me*, *ackcount*, *parent*, and *active*.

One aspect of Figure 11.5 that has not been previously discussed is the *Monitor* Procedure. The sole purpose of this procedure is to detect when the Active Worker Tree becomes empty, and then to send a termination flag to each Worker Process. Refer back to Figure 11.3 for a diagram of the Active Worker Tree. As Workers continue to change from the Active to Idle state throughout the computation, the tree will grow and shrink dynamically. Since the Work Pool is initialized to give Worker Process 1 the first work item, it will always be the first Active Worker and therefore always the root of the Active Worker Tree (as in Figure 11.3). Worker Process 1 will become Idle only when all of its descendants are Idle. Thus, when Worker 1 goes into the Idle state, this means that all the Workers are Idle.

Therefore, termination detection simply consists of determining when Worker 1 goes from the Active state into the Idle state. Whenever any Worker makes this transition, it always sends an "acknowledgment" to its parent. Since Worker 1 has no parent, a dummy Worker Process 0 is created to act as the parent of Worker 1. This dummy Worker 0 just sits and waits for the acknowledgment to come from Worker 1, and when it does, then this is the signal for termination. This dummy Worker 0 is created from the Monitor Procedure, using a *FORK* statement in the main program. This Monitor Process starts with an instruction to read channel 0 in the Work Pool. This channel will be empty until Worker 1 sends its acknowledgment, indicating that all the Workers are now finally Idle and the computation must be terminated.

As with the multiprocessor Work Pool implementation, this multicomputer Work Pool implementation is quite general and can be used in a wide variety of Distributed Worker programs. To adapt the *Getwork* and *Putwork* procedures to a different problem, the format of the work item must be changed. Also, the method of distributing work items in *Putwork* may have to be modified. In the Shortest Path program, the destination vertex number is used to select the proper Worker Process to receive each work item. This technique is based on the assignment of one vertex from the graph to each Worker. In other Distributed Worker programs for different problems, this distribution technique may have to be modified, but all the other aspects of the Work Pool implementation can remain unchanged.

```
PROGRAM Shortpath_2;
ARCHITECTURE HYPERCUBE(6);
CONST numworkers = 63;
     done = -1; ack = -2; (*special message codes*)
     ...


TYPE worktype = RECORD      (*format of item in work pool*)
                    source: INTEGER;
                    distance: INTEGER;
                END;
     ...


VAR workpool:  ARRAY [0..numworkers] OF CHANNEL OF worktype;
    i: INTEGER;     startwork: worktype;
     ...



PROCEDURE Monitor;
   (*Waits for Active Worker Tree to disappear*)
VAR i: INTEGER;
    workitem: worktype;
BEGIN
  workitem := workpool[0]; (*Wait here*)
  workitem.source := done;  workitem.distance := done;
  (*Now send termination flag to all Workers*)
  FOR i := 1 TO numworkers DO
    workpool[i] := workitem;
END;



PROCEDURE Worker(me: INTEGER; myweight: weightrow;
                    VAR answer: INTEGER);
VAR ackcount,parent: INTEGER;
    active:  boolean;  (*Current status of Worker*)
     ...

PROCEDURE Getwork(VAR inputdistance: INTEGER);
VAR inwork,ackwork: worktype;
BEGIN
  ackwork.source := ack;
  REPEAT
    IF active AND (ackcount = 0) AND (NOT workpool[me]?) THEN
      BEGIN (*Transition from active to idle state*)
        active := False;
        workpool[parent] := ackwork; (*Acknowledgement to parent*)
      END;
    inwork := workpool[me];   (*Read item from Work Pool*)
    IF inwork.source = ack THEN ackcount := ackcount - 1;
```

FIGURE 11.5   Implementation of the work pool.

```
      UNTIL inwork.source <> ack; (*Read until actual work item is received*)
      IF active THEN workpool[inwork.source] := ackwork (*Ack to source*)
        ELSE BEGIN  (*Transition from idle to active state*)
          active := True;
          parent := inwork.source;  (*Set new parent from source*)
        END;
      inputdistance := inwork.distance; (*Return work item to caller*)
    END; (*Getwork*)


    PROCEDURE Putwork(vertex, outputdistance: INTEGER);
    VAR outwork: worktype;
    BEGIN
      ackcount := ackcount + 1;
      outwork.source := me;  (*"me" is my assigned vertex number*)
      outwork.distance := outputdistance;
      workpool[vertex] := outwork;  (*Put into Work Pool*)
    END;

    BEGIN (*worker*)
     ackcount := 0;
     active := false;

        ...  (*Worker Procedure same as in Figure 11.1*)

    END;


    BEGIN (*Main*)
      ...

    startwork.source := 0;
    startwork.distance := 0;
    workpool[1] := startwork; (*Start with vertex 1*)
    FORK (@0 PORT workpool[0]) Monitor;

    FORALL i := 1 TO numworkers DO (*Create Distributed Workers*)
      (@i PORT workpool[i]) Worker(i, weight[i], finaldist[i]);

    END.
```

FIGURE 11.5   (continued)

The distribution technique for work items will depend on the partitioning of the shared data structures among the Worker Processes. In some Distributed Worker programs, the shared data can simply be duplicated for each Worker with no partitioning. In this case, all the Workers are essentially equivalent, and any work item may be distributed to any Worker by the Work Pool implementation. However, when the shared data is partitioned, then each work item can go only to a Worker that has the proper partition for that work item. Then the *Putwork* procedure must examine the work item and make sure that it is sent to the right Worker Process.

11.4 PERFORMANCE ANALYSIS

11.4.1 Factors Influencing Performance

The performance of the Shortest Path program will be partially dependent on the characteristics of the particular input graph. If there is some limitation in the available concurrency of the graph, then this will be reflected in an observed loss of speedup in the performance of the program. Since our main focus here is on the general performance of this Distributed Worker implementation, a sample graph has been chosen with enough concurrency to keep all the Workers busy. The graph has 31 vertices and 500 edges, and therefore requires a Hypercube with 32 processors. Figure 11.6 shows a performance profile for the execution of this Shortest Path program with the basic communication delay set to 0.

The profile does not show the process creation and initial data distribution phase of the program, since this performance issue has already been thoroughly discussed in Chapter 9. The overall speedup achieved by this computational portion of the program is 19, using 31 Workers. From the profile, it can be seen that there are several factors producing this observed 38 percent loss in speedup. At the beginning, it takes some time for enough work to be generated to engage all the Workers. Recall that the source vertex 1 is the only work item when execution begins. Worker 1 will gradually generate new work items from this and distribute them to the appropriate Workers, who will also begin to generate new work items.

Another factor reducing the performance is load imbalance in the distribution of work items among the Workers. This is observed in Figure 11.6 by the unequal lengths of the active portion of the Workers. Work items in this program always refer to a specific vertex, and thus must be sent to a specific Worker Process. Therefore, the particular structure of the graph and the dynamics of the program may generate load imbalances. One additional factor causing some performance degradation is the time required for termination detection. This is seen in Figure 11.6 by the last line of the profile, in which only processor 0 is active. The Monitor process, which performs the termination detection, is the only one running at this time. The magnitude of the influence of each performance overhead can be estimated by counting the idle Workers in each region of the profile of Figure 11.6. The observed 38 percent loss of speedup can thus be explained as follows:

Initial work creation:	12%
Load imbalance:	20%
Termination detection:	6%

11.4.2 Communication Delay

The performance profile of Figure 11.6 was made with the basic communication delay set to 0. Now it will be interesting to conceptually analyze the expected influence of the communication delay on the program performance. Communication delay will cause a

```
0 1 2 3 4 5          10          15          20          25          30
  .  *  +  .  .  .   .   .   .   .   .   .   .   .   .   .   .   .   .   .
  .  *  *  *  *  +  -  -   .   .  -   .   .   .   .   .   .   .  *   .   .   .   -
  .  *  *  *  *  *  *  *  *  *  *  *  *  +  +  -   .   .   .  *  +  -  -   .   .   .   .   *
  .  *  *  *  *  *  *  *  *  *  *  *  *  *  *  *  *  *  *  *  *  *  *  *  *  +  -  -   .  *
  .  -  *  *  *  *  *  *  *  *  *  *  *  *  *  *  *  *  *  *  *  *  *  *  *  *  *  *  *
  .  .  *  *  *  *  *  *  *  *  *  *  *  *  *  *  *  *  *  *  *  *  *  *  *  *  *  *  .
  .  .  -  *  *  *  *  *  *  *  *  *  *  *  *  *  *  *  *  *  *  *  *  *  *  *  *  *  *
  .  .  .  *  *  *  *  *  *  *  *  *  *  *  *  *  *  *  *  *  *  *  *  *  *  *  *  *  *
  .  .  .  .  *  *  *  *  *  *  *  *  *  *  *  *  *  *  *  *  *  *  *  *  *  *  *  *  *
  .  .  .  .  .  +  *  *  *  *  *  *  *  *  *  *  *  *  *  *  *  *  *  *  *  *  *  *  .
  .  .  .  .  .  .  -  *  *  *  *  *  *  *  *  *  *  *  *  *  *  *  *  *  *  *  *  +  .
  .  .  .  -  .  .  .  .  +  *  *  *  *  *  *  *  *  *  *  *  *  *  *  *  *  -   .   .   -
  .  .  .  .  .  .  .  .  -  +  *  *  *  *  *  *  *  *  .  *  *  *  *  +  -   .   .   .   -
  .  .  .  .  .  .  .  .  .  -  *  *  *  *  *  *  *  *  -  *  *  -   .   .   .   .   .   .
  .  .  .  .  .  .  .  .  .  .  .  -  -  +  *  *  *  -   .   .   .   .   .   .   .   .   .
  .  .  .  .  .  .  .  .  .  .  .  .  .  .  .  .  .  .  .  .  .  .  .  .  .  .  .  .  .
  *  -  .  .  .  .  .  .  .  .  .  .  .  .  .  .  .  .  .  .  .  .  .  .  .  .  .  .  .
```

Scale: 300 time units per line

FIGURE 11.6 **Shortest path program with no delay.**

time lag between the sending and receiving of the work items. If the destination Worker is idle and waiting for the work item to arrive, then this communication delay will increase the idle time, resulting in some performance degradation. However, if the Worker is actively computing, perhaps with several waiting work items already in its communication port, then the communication delay will not affect the Worker's computation. Thus, communication delay becomes a problem only when work items are relatively sparse, which is mainly in the initial and final stages of program execution. During the middle stage, which is the dominant portion of the program, there are enough work items to keep all the Workers busy, so that communication delays are not noticed.

Even with no communication delay, it has already been observed that there is some time required at the beginning to generate enough work items to engage all the Workers. This initial time will be increased by communication delays in the multicomputer because of the additional delay required for the first work item to reach each Worker. The size of this additional delay can be understood by considering the initial *Active Worker Tree*, created as the Workers receive their first work items. Recall that when an idle Worker receives a work item, the source of the item becomes the *parent* in the Active Worker Tree. Figure 11.3 shows a typical Active Worker Tree. During the initial phase of the program, all the Workers become active, and therefore the Active Worker Tree will contain all the Workers.

The position of a given Worker in the Active Worker Tree will indicate how much it has been affected by the communication delay. Each Worker receives its first work item from its parent in the tree, who receives its first work item from its parent, and so on up the tree. A Worker at level 3 of the tree must wait for three communication steps before it receives its first work item. For example, in Figure 11.3, Worker W18 will wait for three communication steps: W1 to W2, W2 to W3, W3 to W18. The form of this Active Worker

Tree will depend on the structure of the particular input graph, and also on the dynamics of the program. To get some general idea of the expected performance degradation over a wide range of programs, let us make the following simple assumptions:

1. The Active Worker Tree is a complete binary tree.
2. Each Worker is equally likely to appear anywhere in the Tree.

These assumptions permit a precise analysis using probability theory to compute the expected performance degradation resulting from communication delays. From assumption 2, the expected delay for each communication step in the Tree will be the average communication delay between all pairs of processors in the multicomputer. For a Hypercube multicomputer with dimension d and basic communication delay D, this expected delay is $dD/2$. Therefore, a Worker at level i will experience an expected delay from the root: $idD/2$. This results from the fact that the expectation of a sum of random variables is the sum of the expectations.

To find the expected delay from the root over all the Workers, the expression $idD/2$ must be averaged over the entire Tree. Since i is the level in the tree, this average can be computed as $dD/2$ times the average depth of the tree. From assumption 1, it is a complete binary tree. A Hypercube of dimension d has 2^d processors, and therefore will yield a binary tree of depth $d - 1$. A very good approximation to the average depth of any complete binary tree is the total depth minus 1, yielding $d - 2$ in this case. Thus, the expected communication delay experienced by each Worker in receiving its first work item is as follows:

$$\text{Expected Tree Creation Delay:} \quad \frac{(d - 2)dD}{2}$$

A similar situation occurs at the end of the program during termination detection, except that the communication is moving *up* the Active Worker Tree instead of *down*. The last Worker to enter the Idle state will send an acknowledgment to its parent, who will then send an acknowledgment to its parent, and so on up the Tree to the root. The expected communication delay for this upward communication is simply the average depth of the Tree multiplied by the expected commmunication delay between a Worker and its parent. This is the same as the *expected communication delay* already computed for the initial Tree creation:

$$\text{Expected Tree Destruction Delay:} \quad \frac{(d - 2)dD}{2}$$

After the Active Worker Tree is gone, Worker 1 will send a signal to the Monitor process running of processor 0, which will then send termination messages to all the Worker Processes (see Figure 11.5). After termination, each Worker sends a message back to the Main Process on processor 0. Thus, the total communication delay during this final phase of termination is just twice the diameter of the communication network: $2dD$. Adding this to the expected tree creation and destruction delays gives the total expected communication delay:

$$\text{Expected Total Communication Delay:} \quad Dd^2$$

This expression gives a general idea of the expected increase in overall program execution time that results from communication delays in the multicomputer. It will be interesting now to look at the actual observed delays in the Shortest Path program. With the same sample graph used to generate the performance profile of Figure 11.6, the Multi-Pascal system was used to determine the program execution time for a range of communication delays. The results are shown in Figure 11.7. The horizontal axis is the basic communication delay D, varying from 0 to 100. The vertical axis shows the execution time of the computational portion of the program, excluding the process creation and initial data distribution, as is also the case in the profile of Figure 11.6.

With the "Congestion OFF" option, the performance curve appears to be linear with slope 23. Our mathematical analysis above was also done without consideration of congestion. Since the Hypercube has dimension 5, the analysis predicts an expected increase of execution time $25D$. This predicted slope of 25 is surprisingly close to the observed slope 23, considering that our analysis was based on the assumption that the Active Worker Tree is a complete binary tree, which actually turns out to not be the case in this program. Nevertheless, the actual delay in Tree creation and destruction is close to the predicted expectation.

With the "Congestion ON" option, the figure shows a significant increase in the execution time, especially at the higher values of the basic communication delay. This congestion occurs during the final phase of termination when the Monitor process sends termination messages to all the processes. If the basic communication delay is large, some congestion is created as all these messages leave process 0. A similar congestion also results after the processes terminate and their final termination signals converge back on

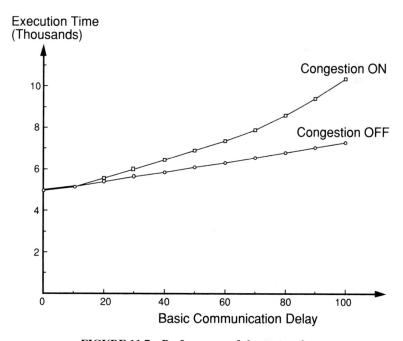

FIGURE 11.7 **Performance of shortest path.**

the Main process running on processor 0. This congestion problem can be greatly reduced by changing the Monitor process to use a Hypercube broadcast for the termination messages. This issue is considered in one of the exercises at the end of this chapter.

11.4.3 Load Balancing

One thing that will help to improve the processor utilization in this multicomputer Shortest Path program is to assign several vertices to each Worker. The version presented here assigned exactly one vertex to each Worker because this simplified the program for pedagogical purposes. Generally, in a real application problem, the number of vertices in the graph will be very much larger than the number of available processors in the multicomputer, thus requiring this multiple vertex assignment. This will increase the workload on the processors, and thereby increase the duration of the "middle" portion of the program when all the Workers are kept busy. All of the major performance overheads are associated with the initial and final phases of the program execution. The overheads, including process creation, active worker tree creation, and termination, depend only on the total number of Workers, and do not increase if many vertices are assigned to each Worker. Therefore, as the number of vertices per Worker is increased, the overheads become a smaller percentage of the total execution time, thus improving the processor utilization and increasing the speedup.

One important issue to consider in this regard is the effect of increased workload on the load-balancing problem. In the sample profile of Figure 11.6, load imbalances resulted in a 20 percent loss of speedup. It also turns out that load imbalances become less as the workload increases. To consider the load-balancing issue analytically, let us consider the random distribution of n work items among p Workers. If there are a large number of vertices assigned to each Worker, this random distribution may be a reasonable model. In any case, it will be useful to gain some insights into the nature of the load-balancing problem. Focusing on a single Worker, each of the n work items will be assigned to this Worker with probability $1/p$. Thus, the total workload assigned to the Worker is the sum of n Bernoulli trials, each with probability $1/p$. From the standard properties of Bernoulli trials, the expected size of the workload is n/p. This corresponds to our intuition that the average workload is just the total number of work items divided by the number of Workers.

The load imbalances arise from variations in the actual number of work items assigned to each Worker. If some Workers receive a much larger number of work items, then they will have to execute for a longer time, while other Workers finish much earlier. The result is a period of time when many Workers are idle, thus reducing average processor utilization and increasing program execution time. In this Bernoulli model of the workload distribution, a good measure of the expected variation in the workload assigned to the Workers is the *standard deviation*, which in this case is approximately $(n/p)^{1/2}$. This means that the actual magnitude of the variation is expected to increase as the total workload n increases. However, the expected variation *decreases* as a percentage of the average workload per Worker. The average workload increases linearly with n, but the variation increases only as the square root of n. Therefore, the performance losses associated with load imbalances should decrease as the total workload is increased for a given number of Workers.

11.5 WORK COMPRESSION

Distributed Worker programs usually go through a middle phase in which the work items are being generated faster than they can be processed by the Workers. The result is that the work items begin to queue up in the communication ports of the Workers. For some Distributed Worker programs, this presents an opportunity to improve the performance by compressing the work items in some way, and delivering them as a single unit to the Worker. Assuming that the time for compressing the work items is less than the time for processing them individually, this will save a lot of processing time by the Worker. Also, since the Worker is processing fewer work items, the creation of new work items is expected to be less, thereby reducing the computation time.

11.5.1 New Getwork Implementation

The Shortest Path program presented in this chapter offers this opportunity for work compression. Each work item received by a Worker is simply a new distance to the vertex assigned to that Worker. Referring back to the Worker procedure of Figure 11.1, each incoming "trial distance" is compared with the minimum distance found so far to that vertex. If the trial distance is less, then it becomes the new minimum, and new trial distances are sent to all the neighboring vertices. Clearly, if there are several trial distances queued in the communication port of a Worker, it is enough to consider only the minimum of these. When the Worker calls *Getwork* to receive the next trial distance, all the work items can be read from the communication port, with only the minimum one being returned to the Worker.

This new implementation of *Getwork* requires some internal modification. The previous version of *Getwork* reads items from the communication port until the first work item is found. The new version must read work items until the port is empty. As each work item is encountered, it is sent to a special "Compression" procedure supplied by the Worker. In this case the Compression procedure will just record the minimum of the work items. As the work items are read from the port, *Getwork* may also encounter acknowledgments, which also must be removed. When the port is finally completely empty, then *Getwork* returns the compressed work item to the Worker. The termination detection and the Active Worker Tree must, of course, still be part of the *Getwork* computation.

The simplest way to describe the structure of the new Getwork procedure is a state transition diagram, as shown in Figure 11.8. The three states are *Ready*, *Active*, *Idle*. Each arc representing a potential state transition is labeled with the "condition" that will cause that transition, plus the "action" that will be taken as part of the transition. The "condition" is shown first in capital letters, and refers to the type of item currently found at the front of the communication port. The "action" that occurs during the transition is shown in parentheses. The Worker request for a new work item enters the diagram in the *Ready* state, indicating that it is "ready" to receive a new work item. The first work item received will cause a transition to the *Active* state, during which all work items will be removed from the port and compressed. When the port is finally empty, the *Getwork* procedure will return to the Worker.

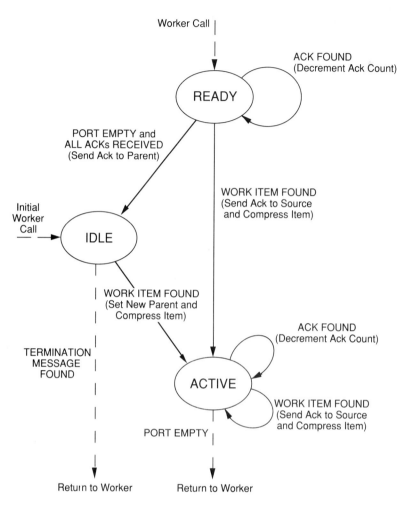

FIGURE 11.8   Getwork with work compression.

Termination detection occurs through the *Idle* state in the same way as before. Each Worker has a specific parent in the Active Worker Tree, which is acknowledged only when the Worker becomes completely idle with all its own acknowledgments already received. From the *Ready* state, if the port is empty and all acknowledgments have been received, a transition is made to the *Idle* state, and an acknowledgment is sent to the parent. From the *Idle* state, any new work item reactivates the Worker by causing a transition into *Active* state. The source of this work item becomes the new parent in the Active Worker Tree. Termination occurs when a termination message is received in the *Idle* state and returned to the Worker. Notice that there is no transition possible from *Active* to *Idle*. This is because the *Active* state is entered only after at least one work item has been found in the port. This work item must be returned to the Worker for processing before any termination might be required.

11.5.2 Asynchronous Algorithms

The Distributed Worker paradigm with work compression can be used to implement an important class of parallel algorithms called *asynchronous iterative algorithms*. Chapter 6 discussed the implementation of *synchronous* iterative algorithms, often used for solving systems of equations. In such algorithms, there is a state vector $X = (x_1, x_2, \ldots, x_n)$, whose value is iteratively recomputed until the change becomes less than some desired tolerance. The final value of X becomes the solution to the equations. This type of iterative algorithm is easily parallelized by assigning one or more items from the state vector to each processor. With this method, the processors must synchronize after each iteration to make sure all the values in the new state vector are computed before proceeding to the next iteration.

When such algorithms are implemented on multicomputers, the synchronization step is replaced by a *communication* step, in which each processor broadcasts to all other processors a copy of its assigned items from the state vector. Before beginning the next iteration, each processor must wait for all the new values of the state vector. The communication time required between iterations will therefore be equal to the time to transmit a message between the most distant processors in the multicomputer communication network. Since the processors cannot begin the next iteration until all values are received, there is no possibility for overlapping computation with communication.

To increase the efficiency, one can consider the possibility of allowing the processors to continue to the next iteration even before all the new values are received. Any values that did not arrive in time are then used in subsequent iterations. This type of algorithm is called *asynchronous*, because there is no synchronization occurring after each iteration. The main difficulty of such *asynchronous* algorithms is that the conditions required for convergence may be more restrictive. Nevertheless, there are many important parallel algorithms that can be formulated in this asynchronous manner. For further details the reader is referred to Bertsekas and Tsitsiklis [1989].

To facilitate further discussion on the implementation of asynchronous algorithms, assume that there are n processors, and each processor i is assigned value x_i from the state vector X. Each processor has its own local copy of the state vector, and recomputes x_i from this local state vector during each iteration. After this recomputation, processor i broadcasts the new value of x_i to all the other processors. In the asynchronous formulation, the processor does not need to wait for all the new values of the state vector. The processor just reads in all the new values that have arrived and moves ahead with the recomputation of x_i. In this way, new values of the state vector are constantly moving through the communication network, and being absorbed by processors as they arrive. No processor ever waits for any values to arrive. Thus, computation is fully overlapped with communication, thereby reducing the overall execution time.

To facilitate termination of the program, one additional constraint is placed on each processor i. After computing a new value for x_i, this value is compared with the old value. If the change is less than some desired tolerance specified as a program input, then the new value is thrown away. Each newly computed value of x_i is broadcast to the other processors, only if its deviation from the old value of x_i is greater than this tolerance. This restriction will prevent the generation of useless values, and also allow the program to terminate. The program will continue execution only so long as some processor is computing new values. When the magnitude of computed changes in the state vector at all the processors goes below the specified tolerance, then no further messages are generated, and the computation can terminate.

The Distributed Worker paradigm with work compression can be used to implement this type of asynchronous iterative computation. Each new state vector value sent to a processor is considered as a work item. The general activity of each Worker process *i* is as follows:

```
Worker Process i:

  VAR X: ARRAY [1..n] OF REAL;  (*Local copy of state vector*)

  BEGIN
    REPEAT
      Compute new x_i from current state vector X;
      IF ABS(new x_i - old x_i) > tolerance THEN
        BEGIN
          FOR destination := 1 TO n DO (*Send copy to everyone*)
            Putwork(destination, new x_i);
          Copy new x_i into X[i];
        END;
      Call Getwork to read all state vector values from my port;
    UNTIL done;
  END;
```

For the Shortest Path program, the work compression operation is to record the minimum of the work items read from the port. For this asynchronous iteration, the work compression operation consists of writing each work item into its proper position in the local state vector *X*. Each work item must have two parts, the index in the state vector and the new value itself. The activity of the *Getwork* procedure is just as previously shown in Figure 11.8, including the termination detection. The *Putwork* procedure is essentially the same as the original version developed in the context of the Shortest Path program without work compression (see Figure 11.5). It is interesting that the Distributed Worker paradigm can be adapted to implement asynchronous algorithms, even though at first glance they appear to be quite different. One of the programming projects at the end of this chapter deals with writing a Distributed Worker program for asynchronous solution of a system of linear equations.

11.6 SUMMARY

Distributed Workers is a parallel programming paradigm for multicomputers, in which work items are dynamically created and exchanged by a set of identical Worker processes. These programs consist of a Worker procedure supplemented with a *Getwork* procedure to retrieve work items, and a *Putwork* procedure to dispatch work items to other Workers. The Worker procedure may vary greatly, depending on the specific application area of the program. However, the *Getwork* and *Putwork* procedures can be viewed as utilities that are the same in all Distributed Worker programs.

There are actually a few major classes of Distributed Worker programs that will determine the specifi~ ~ ~entation of *Getwork* and *Putwork*. The *Putwork* implemen- ~ ~he Workers are *indistinguishable* or not. If the Workers are ~ ~rk item may in principle be sent to any Worker. Therefore, ~ ~o distribute the newly created work items with the goal of ~ ~Workers. One example of such a program is the N-Queens ~ ~0 in the context of Replicated Workers on multiprocessors. ~ ~istribution technique used in that chapter can easily be ~ ~ implementation of the N-Queens problem, or to any other ~ ~th indistinguishable Workers. Another example of such a ~ ~an Problem, which is assigned as one of the programming ~ ~r.

~ ~ does not fit into this category, and requires Workers that ~ ~ement results from the partitioning of the main data ~ ~m distance to each vertex in the graph. Since each new ~ ~tex, it must be sent to the Worker who is assigned to that ~ ~onal load imbalances for some graphs. However, if the ~ ~y vertices can be assigned to each Worker, then this is ~ ~ n a general performance analysis of Distributed Worker ~ ~ ~ ~an assumption that distribution of work items is random, it can be shown that the problem of load imbalance becomes gradually less severe as the total number of work items is increased.

The *Getwork* procedure does not depend on whether the Workers are indistinguishable or not. The important factors in *Getwork* implementation are the method of termination detection and whether work compression is used. If it can be assumed in a specific machine that the communication delay for messages has a known upper bound, then there are several simple termination detection methods that may be used. This is explored in the exercises of this chapter. However, for the termination detection to be robust, it should allow the possibility of arbitrary communication delays. The most important topic of this chapter is the implementation of such a robust termination detection algorithm for Distributed Worker programs.

The problem of arbitrary communication delays is solved by using *message acknowledgments*, sent by *Getwork* back to the source of each received work item. *Getwork* must keep a count of all unacknowledged messages, and will not allow termination until all the acknowledgments are received, as an indication that none of the work items is still in transit between Workers. Termination is detected through the use of an Active Worker Tree, in which each active worker is assigned a parent according to the source of its first work item. The use of message acknowledgments combined with this Active Worker Tree allows the termination condition to be detected: all Workers are waiting for work, and there are no work items in transit between Workers.

For some Distributed Worker program, *work compression* may be used to improve the performance. The same termination detection method can be used by *Getwork* in this case. However, the internal implementation of *Getwork* must be modified to allow the reading of everything in the work queue before returning to the Worker. This work compression technique can be used in a Distributed Worker implementation of asynchronous algorithms, which may be important in the future development of multicomputer programming.

Sec. 11.6   Summary   **315**

Handwritten note:

Shortest Path

n vertices

weight = [[ ], [ ],]

matrix → # edges

array → mindist = [ ]

queue → vertices = [ ]

REFERENCES

The distributed termination algorithm presented in this chapter was developed by Dijkstra and Sholten [1980], and also is described in Bertsekas and Tsitsiklis [1989]. Apt [1986] gives a summary of correctness proofs for distributed termination algorithms. Chandy and Misra [1988] contains a detailed discussion of the termination issue.

Some of the issues regarding the implementation of Distributed Workers on multicomputers are examined in Ranka, Won, and Sahni [1988] for a hypercube. A good reference for the basic concepts from probability theory used in the performance analysis of this chapter is Trivedi [1982]. Asynchronous iterative algorithms originated with Chazan [1969] in the context of solving a system of linear equations. A comprehensive discussion of recent results in asynchronous algorithms is found in Bertsekas and Tsitsiklis [1989].

PROGRAMMING PROJECTS

1. ASYNCHRONOUS SOLUTION OF LINEAR EQUATIONS

Programming Project 3 in Chapter 8 describes a *synchronous* method for parallel solution of a system of linear equations. In this project your job is to write a program that uses *asynchronous iteration* to solve a system of linear equations. To implement the asynchronous iteration, use Distributed Workers with work compression as described in section 11.5 of this chapter. The condition *row diagonal dominance* described in Chapter 8, will guarantee that your sample system of equations for testing does converge using the asynchronous method.

Using a Hypercube topology, run your program for a variety of values of the basic communication delay. Determine how the communication delay affects the three major portions of the program: process creation and data distribution, iterative computation of the solution, and termination. If you have also done Project 3 in Chapter 8, it will be interesting to compare the performance of the synchronous and asychronous methods.

2. TRAVELING SALESMAN PROBLEM

In this project, you will write a Distributed Worker program for the Traveling Salesman problem on a multicomputer. The algorithm used is basically the same as that described for Replicated Workers on a multiprocessor (see Chapter 10, Programming Project 2). By allowing each Worker to have its own complete copy of the *distance* array, the need for data partitioning is avoided. The result is a situation in which the Workers are *indistinguishable*. Therefore, each work item can freely be distributed to any Worker, thus reducing the potential for load imbalances.

The main area of difference with the multiprocessor Traveling Salesman program is in the implementation of the global minimum tour. In the multiprocessor program, the global minimum is shared by all the Workers and is easily accessible to them all (although there is a possibility of contention, which must be avoided). However, this presents a problem in the multicomputer. Where do we store the global minimum? It is too inefficient for each Worker to keep reading the global minimum from a remote memory. The solution will be for each Worker to keep a local copy of the global minimum and use that for testing its own tours. If any new minimum is found, the Worker will send it to a central *Monitor* process, which will then broadcast this new global minimum to all the other Worker Processes, so they can update their own local copies.

With this method, the Worker's local copies may be slightly outdated. To deal with this problem, the *Monitor* process will maintain the real global minimum itself. Whenever a Worker sends a new minimum, the Monitor will first compare it with the current real global minimum to see if it is actually a new minimum tour. In this way, errors are avoided.

The Traveling Salesman problem results in an enormous number of potential tours for even a small number of cities. Therefore, while debugging your program, use a small number of cities. Then increase the number later on to get good speedup for a large number of processors.

EXERCISES

1. In the Shortest Path program given in this chapter, only one vertex is assigned to each Worker. Describe the necessary changes to the program to assign several vertices to each Worker.
   (a) Describe the changes to the Worker procedure.
   (b) Describe the changes to the *Getwork* and *Putwork* procedures.

2. For the same input graph, the multicomputer Shortest Path (Figure 11.1) will create many more work items than the multiprocessor version (Figure 10.3). Explain in detail the reason for this.

3. In section 11.2.1, a *master-count* termination method is described, including the reasons why it may not work correctly. It is stated that a long time delay at the master count can correct the problem for practical purposes on some real machines. Give a high-level description of the required *Getwork*, *Putwork*, and *Monitor* procedures for this termination method. You may use the Multi-Pascal *Duration* statement, as described in Appendix B.

4. In section 11.2.1, a *master-count* termination method is described for multicomputers, including the reasons why it may not work correctly. It is stated that it can be corrected through the use of *message acknowledgments*. Describe in detail the implementation of this *master-count* termination method using acknowledgments. Give a high-level description of the *Getwork*, *Putwork*, and *Monitor* procedures.

5. Suppose the distributed termination algorithm of section 11.2.2 is modified so that each Worker acknowledges its parent immediately just as any other work item is acknowledged. Explain in detail how this can give rise to an erroneous termination.

6. In the Distributed Worker implementation of Figure 11.5, each Worker continues to read its communication port every time it needs a new work item. If the port is empty, then it will wait for the empty port. It appears that a *deadlock* may result, in which all the Workers are waiting for an empty port. Explain in detail why this deadlock can never occur in Figure 11.5.

7. In the Work Pool implementation described in section 11.3, both acknowledgments and work items come into the same input channel. Rewrite the high-level description of *Getwork*, assuming that there are two ports for each Worker: a port *workpool[me]* for receiving work items, and a port *acknowledge[me]* for receiving acknowledgments. Be especially careful of the situation when both ports are empty, but there are still some outstanding acknowledgments not yet received. To make the algorithm function correctly, the Worker may have to do some busy waiting by continually checking both ports for input.

8. In the Work Pool implementation of Figure 11.5, the Monitor process reads an item from *workpool*[0]. Since there is no vertex number 0 in the graph, how is it that any work items ever get written into this channel? (Explain.)

9. Section 11.4.2 derives a general expression for the communication delays associated with creating the initial Active Worker Tree on a Hypercube. Describe in a general way how this derivation must be modified for different multicomputer topologies.

10. The performance analysis of the distributed termination algorithm showed that some congestion results if the basic communication delay is large. This congestion occurs during the distribution of final termination messages by the *Monitor* process.
   (a) Explain in detail the cause of this congestion.
   (b) Show that this congestion can be greatly reduced by using a standard Hypercube broadcast algorithm to distribute the termination messages.
   (c) Describe the necessary changes to the *Getwork* procedure to implement this broadcast of the termination messages.

11. Consider the random distribution of *n* work items to *p* Workers. In the performance analysis of section 11.4, it was explained that the expected work load for each Worker is $m = n/p$, and the standard deviation of the work load is $m^{1/2}$. The work load for each Worker can therefore be approximated as a Normal Distribution with mean *m* and standard deviation $m^{1/2}$. Using this model, the expected maximum work load among all the *p* Workers can be calculated to have the following form:

$$\text{Expected Maximum: } m + km^{1/2}$$

The value of *k* depends on *p* according to the following table:

p	10	20	30	40	50	60	70	80
k	1.55	1.87	2.04	2.16	2.24	2.31	2.37	2.42

   (a) Derive a general expression for the expected time required for the Workers to process all their work items. Assume a constant time *T* for processing each work item. Also, assume that Workers never have to wait for work items to arrive.
   (b) Using the same assumptions as part (a), derive a general expression for the ideal minimum time for the processing of the work items, assuming a perfectly balanced load.
   (c) The expected loss of performance due to load imbalance can be approximated by dividing the ideal minimum time of part (b) by the expected time of part (a). Draw a graph of this expected loss vs. the number of Workers, using $m = 1000$. Draw a similar graph for $m = 10,000$.
   (d) What general conclusions can be inferred from these performance graphs about the effect of load-balancing problems on performance of Distributed Workers?

12. A multiprocessor program for the N-Queens Problem is given in Figure 10.12. Describe in detail the modifications necessary for a multicomputer implementation using Distributed Workers. You should use the Work Pool implementation given in Figure 11.5. Show any necessary changes to this Work Pool implementation, and also any changes to the N-Queens Worker Procedure of Figure 10.12.

13. Figure 11.8 shows a state transition diagram for the *Getwork* procedure with work compression. Draw a similar state transition diagram for the *Getwork* procedure without work compression, as shown in Figure 11.5. Include "condition" and "action" on each transition arc.

14. Figure 11.8 gives a state transition diagram for the *Getwork* procedure with work compression. Write this *Getwork* procedure in Multi-Pascal.

15. Assuming that there is a known upper limit L on the communication time between any processors in a multicomputer, it is possible to use a *polling* technique for termination detection of Distributed Workers. In this technique, a *Monitor* process regularly sends a "polling" message to each Worker, causing the Worker to send a return "status" message back to the Monitor. With this method, the work item acknowledgments and the Active Worker Tree can be eliminated.

Describe the detailed implementation of this polling techique for termination detection. Include a high-level description of the detailed behavior of the Monitor process and the *Getwork* and *Putwork* procedures. Your implementation should allow for the possibility of variations in processor speeds.

16. In the high-level description of the Worker process for asynchronous iteration (section 11.5.2), every new value is sent to all the Workers. Some systems of equations will be "sparse," which means that the computation of a new value for each x_i is based on the values of only a few elements from the state vector. Thus, each Worker does not need to have a copy of the full state vector, but only those elements that are required for recomputation of its assigned component. Give a detailed high-level description for this new type of Worker process for sparse systems.

Appendix A

Advanced Multi-Pascal Features

This appendix discusses some of the more sophisticated aspects of the Multi-Pascal programming language. A more complete discussion of environments for parallel processes is given, including the capability of creating many generations of child processes. There is also a section about advanced usage of channel variables in expressions or as procedure parameters. None of these advanced features are used in the example programs of this text. However, they are available in version 2.0 of the Multi-Pascal interactive software system that accompanies this text.

A.1 ENVIRONMENTS

This section describes the rules for determining the environment in multiprocessor implementations of Multi-Pascal. In ordinary Pascal, the environment for the execution of each statement depends on the static scope rules and the sequence of procedure and function calls. Each call of a procedure (or function) will create a new *activation record* containing a new copy of the local variables and parameters of that procedure (or function). At any given time during program execution, variable names will be interpreted according to the current *environment stack*, which consists of a stack of activation records. A variable name is first looked up in the top record of the environment stack; if it is not there, the next record in the stack is searched, and so on down the stack. Each procedure call or return will alter this environment stack. The detailed rules for the use and alteration of the environment stack can be found in any Pascal textbook and will not be reviewed here.

The standard rules for determining the environment in Pascal are the same in Multi-Pascal, with a few additions to account for parallel processes. The major additional rule is as follows:

Environment Inheritance Rule:

At the time of process creation, the environment stack of a child process is initialized with its parent's current environment stack.

The child process is not given a copy of the parent's environment, but it actually shares the use of the same activation records found in the parent's stack. This is the origin of shared variables in Multi-Pascal—the child process actually physically shares the same activation records with its parent, and therefore can read or write the same variables. Other child processes created by the same parent will also share the parent's environment stack, thus allowing sibling processes to have shared variables also.

The above rule determines the initial environment stack of every process. The following rule determines the evolution of this environment:

Environment Evolution Rule:

Every procedure (or function) call or return by a process will add and remove activation records from its own environment stack according to the standard Pascal rules.

The major consequence of this rule is that processes may create their own *local* variables by calling procedures or functions. These local variables will not be visible to the parent process or any of the sibling processes. Thus, the environment stack of any process will consist of two portions: the bottom portion of the stack contains the shared records inherited from its parent at the time of process creation, and the top portion of the stack contains all local activation records created by its own procedure or function calls.

In all of the example programs used in this text, all of the process creation statements are contained in the body of the main program. Applying the environment *inheritance* and *evolution* rules to this specialized situation results in the following two rules, which were already stated in Chapter 2:

All variables declared at the start of the main program are shared by all processes.

All procedure or function calls by any process creates local variables, accessible only by that process.

The Multi-Pascal language allows process creation statements to occur anywhere in the program, including inside procedure or function bodies, or within child processes. To understand more fully the implications of the environment inheritance and evolution rules, a few simple examples will be considered. The following program shell shows the creation of two child processes:

```
PROGRAM Sample;
VAR ...

    PROCEDURE A;
    VAR ...
    BEGIN
```

```
      ...

   END; (*A*)

   PROCEDURE B;
   VAR ...

      PROCEDURE C;
      VAR ...
      BEGIN

         ...

      END; (*C*)

   BEGIN (*Body of B*)
      ...

      FORK A; (*Child process 1 calls procedure A*)
      FORK C; (*Child process 2 calls procedure C*)
      ...

   END; (*B*)

BEGIN (*Body of Main*)
   ...

   B; (*Main calls procedure B*)
   ...

END.
```

In this example, the main process 0 leaves the body of the main program by calling procedure *B*, where it creates two child processes that call procedures *A* and *C*, respectively. Both children will inherit their parent's environment stack, containing two activation records: the *Main* variables and the procedure *B* variables. Child process 2 calls procedure *C* and adds this new activation record onto the local portion of its environment stack. Child process 1 calls procedure *A* and adds this to its stack, and in so doing loses access to *B*, according to the usual Pascal scope rules. The resultant environment stack for each process is shown below (the stack grows downward):

Main Process 0	Process 1	Process 2
Main	Main	Main
B	A	B
		C

Since the child processes are created with *FORK* operators, the parent process continues its own execution, and may eventually return from procedure *B* back to the body of the main program. If it is assumed the children have not yet terminated, the environment stacks will be as follows:

Main Process 0	Process 1	Process 2
Main	Main	Main
	A	B
		C

Notice now that Process 2 is the only one with access to the activation record of procedure *B*. Ordinarily in Pascal a procedure return will cause the corresponding activation record to be deallocated and discarded. However, in Multi-Pascal an activation record may be shared by many processes. Therefore, Multi-Pascal has the following rule for extending the lifetime of activation records:

Lifetime Extension Rule:

The lifetime of every activation record is extended as long as it is accessible by any nonterminated process.

In the above example program, this rule causes the lifetime of the activation record for procedure *B* to be extended even after the main process returns from that procedure call to *B*.

Since process creation statements may occur anywhere in a Multi-Pascal program, it is possible for child processes to create their own children, thus possibly producing many generations of child processes. A simple example of such a program is shown below:

```
PROGRAM Sample;
VAR ...

      PROCEDURE D(i,j: INTEGER);
      VAR ...
      BEGIN
        ...

      END; (*D*)

      PROCEDURE E(i: INTEGER);
      VAR ...
      BEGIN
        ...

        FORK D(i,1);  (*Create child 1*)
        FORK D(i,2);  (*Create child 2*)
        ...

      END; (*E*)
```

```
BEGIN (*Body of Main program*)
  ...

  FORALL i := 1 TO 3 DO
    E(i);   (*Create three child processes*)

END.
```

In this program, the main process 0 creates three children in the usual way, using a *FORALL* statement that calls procedure *E*. Inside procedure *E*, each of these three children creates two of its own children, resulting in a total of six grandchildren of the main process. The resulting environment for all of these processes is most easily understood by a tree diagram of the procedure activation records, as shown in Figure A.1. In the figure, each box represents an activation record of that procedure, showing the procedure argument values in parenthesis. The top of the environment stack for each process *Pi* is indicated by a label *Pi* in the figure. The entire stack for each process consists of the path from its label back up the tree to the root.

Process *P0*, the main process, has only one activation record in its stack—the *MAIN* record. Processes *P1*, *P2*, *P3* are created by the *FORALL* statement, and therefore each has two records in its environment stack—one record for procedure *E* at the top of stack and then the shared *MAIN* record at the bottom of the stack. All the third generation processes have three activation records in their stack. For example, the top of the stack for process *P6* is the record created by calling procedure *D* with parameters (2, 1). The next stack record is *E*(2), which is also shared by process *P7*. The *MAIN* activation record is at the bottom of the stack for every process, and therefore is shared by all processes.

One of the important properties of multiple generations of process creation is the availability of shared variables with limited scope. This is indicated by the *E* activation

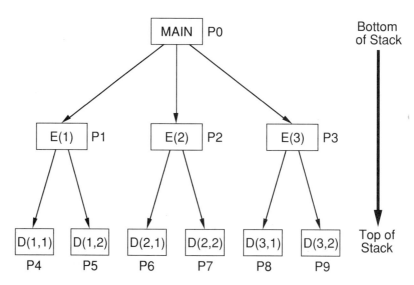

FIGURE A.1   Multiple generations of processes.

records in Figure A.1. The variables in each of these records are shared by three processes only, and are not visible to any of the other processes. In all the examples in this textbook, each variable is either shared by all the processes, or completely local to one specific process. This results from the fact that all process creation statements are in the body of the main program. However, the general rules for environments in Multi-Pascal, as described above, allow a much richer variety of possibilities for multiple generations of processes, and multiple levels of shared variables.

A.2 CHANNEL VARIABLES

A.2.1 Channel Variables in Expressions

Any channel variable name may also be part of an expression on the right side of an assignment, as in the following example for channel variable C:

```
VAR C:  CHANNEL OF INTEGER;
    x,r: INTEGER;

    . . .

BEGIN
    . . .

  x := C * 2 + r;
```

In the above assignment, the next value is read from the front of channel C, multiplied by 2, added to r, and then written into x. A channel variable may be used in any valid Pascal expression on the right side of any assignment statement, provided that the component type of the channel is appropriate in that context. For example, in the above assignment, since variables x and r have type INTEGER, then the channel C is expected to be of type *CHANNEL OF INTEGER*.

Each reference to a channel variable on the right side of an assignment, whether the channel name appears alone on the right or as part of an expression, will read one value from the channel. If the channel is empty, then the whole process will be delayed. In the above assignment, if channel C is empty, then the whole process executing that assignment will be suspended until some other process writes a value into channel C. Thus, a reader process will always be suspended when attempting to read an empty channel. However, writer processes will never be suspended; channels have unlimited capacity and can hold any number of values.

In the examples in this text, channel variables are used only in simple assignment statements. However, the Multi-Pascal language actually allows channel variables to be used in any expression in the program, provided that the component type matches the context in the expression. The general rule is that wherever an ordinary variable of a given type may be used in an expression, a channel variable with that same component type may be used. Thus, channel variables may be used even in Boolean conditions or array subscripts, as in the following examples:

```
VAR
  C: CHANNEL OF INTEGER;
  D: CHANNEL OF REAL;
  i: INTEGER;   x,y: REAL;
  a: ARRAY [1..20] OF REAL;
BEGIN
  ...

  IF 2*x > D/5 THEN   x := y;
  a[C+i] := 34.5;
```

In the above *IF* statement, a value will be read from channel D, divided by 5, and compared with $2*x$. If channel D is empty, the process execution is suspended until some other process writes a value into channel D. In the above assignment to array a, channel C is read as part of the subscript computation; the next integer value is read from the front of channel C and then added to i to compute the subscript for array a. The general rule is that any expression context in which an *INTEGER* variable is valid, a *CHANNEL OF INTEGER* may also be used, and similarly for *REAL*, *BOOLEAN*, and *CHAR*.

Although channel variables may be used in the same context as ordinary variables, they behave quite differently, since values are queued inside the channel variable during writing and then removed during reading. Thus, each time a channel variable is read, it produces a different value. Consider the following use of a channel C:

```
x := C + C + C;
```

In the above assignment, it appears that the same value is being added three times, but since C is a channel variable, a new value is read from it each time it is evaluated in the expression. Thus, this statement reads three values from channel C, adds them, and stores the resultant value into variable x. Each channel read operation is independent, and will cause the process to be suspended if the channel is empty at that time.

One restriction on channel variable usage is that they are not permitted in *Read* or *Write* statements.

A.2.2 Channel Variables as Parameters

Since an expression may be used to compute a value to pass to a procedure or function parameter, channel variables may be used as part of these expressions. For example consider a procedure *Compute* that has a parameter of type *REAL*:

```
VAR  D: CHANNEL OF REAL;

    PROCEDURE Compute( r: REAL);
      ...

  BEGIN
    ...

  Compute( 2*D );
```

In the above call to procedure *Compute*, a *REAL* value is read from channel *D*, multiplied by 2, and then passed to the procedure as a value for parameter *r*. Note that in this case, the parameter *r* must be a *value* parameter. If *r* were a *VAR* parameter, the compiler would generate a type mismatch error. Since *D* has a component type of *REAL*, a call of the form *Compute*(*D*) would also be valid, since *D* is treated as an expression in this context, causing a *REAL* value to be read from *D*.

In some applications, it is also useful for procedures or functions to have parameters that are themselves channels. For example, consider the following program segment with a procedure *Eval* having a channel parameter:

```
PROGRAM Sample;
TYPE chanytp = CHANNEL OF INTEGER;
VAR C: chantyp;

   PROCEDURE Eval( VAR P: chantyp );
     . . .

BEGIN
  . . .

  Eval( C );
```

The above call to procedure *Eval* passes channel variable *C*, which has the same type as the parameter *P*. Recall that in standard Pascal, a *VAR* parameter causes the parameter name in the procedure to become an *alias* for the actual variable that really exists in the calling program. Thus, a *VAR* parameter causes a single variable cell to have two different names. When a channel variable is used in Multi-Pascal as a *VAR* parameter, the same rule is applicable. In the above example, there is one *CHANNEL OF INTEGER*, called *C* in the main program. During the procedure call to *Eval*, the parameter name *P* becomes an *alias* for this same channel. Thus, after the call to procedure *Eval* returns, any values that were written into parameter *P* will now be contained in channel variable *C*.

Channel parameters used in the definition of a procedure or function must be *VAR* parameters. Thus, the following procedure header will generate a compiler error, because the channel is a *value* parameter:

```
PROCEDURE Eval( P: chantyp );
```

A.2.3 Combining Channels with Arrays, Records, and Pointers

Channel variables may be composed with the other structured types in Pascal—Array and Record. Several examples in the text show the use of channels whose component type is either Array or Record. Also, some examples use an "Array of Channels." A Record may have a component that is a channel. This composition of channels with arrays and records may go to any depth, provided the following simple rule is satisfied:

The component type of a channel must be a valid type in standard Pascal.

This rule precludes the possibility of a channel that has more channels as part of its component type. Thus, a "channel of channel" is not permitted by this rule. Such a possibility would not make any sense semantically in the language. The following illustrates a more complex example of the usage of channels with arrays and records:

```
TYPE  arraytyp = ARRAY [1..5] OF INTEGER;
VAR  R: RECORD
          x,y: INTEGER;
          c: CHANNEL OF arraytyp;
        END;
      a: arraytyp;
    ...

BEGIN
    ...

    a := R.c;
```

The above assignment to variable *a* reads an array from channel *R.c* and writes it into *a*.

Multi-Pascal also permits channels to be composed with pointers. A channel may have a component type "pointer." Also, pointers to a channel type are allowed. This provides a mechanism for dynamic creation of channels using the *NEW* operator on the pointer. Consider the following example:

```
VAR  pnt: ^CHANNEL OF INTEGER;
    ...

BEGIN
    ...

    NEW(pnt);
    pnt^ := 23;
    pnt^ := 24;
```

In the above variable *pnt* is declared as a pointer to *CHANNEL OF INTEGER*. The *NEW(pnt)* instruction dynamically creates a new channel that is referenced with the expression *pnt^*. In the next two lines of the above example, the values 23 and 24 are written into this channel.

In Multi-Pascal, channel types may be composed with all the standard Pascal types *INTEGER, REAL, BOOLEAN, CHARACTER, ARRAY, RECORD*, and pointer, as illustrated in the examples in this appendix and in other portions of the text. The general rule is that the component type of a channel type may be any valid type from standard Pascal. Channel types may appear at any level of a structured type. The only restriction is that the component type of a channel may not contain any channels: a "channel" of channels is not permitted in Multi-Pascal.

Appendix B

The Multi-Pascal Interpreter and Debugging Tool User's Manual

The Multi-Pascal interpreter and debugging tool runs on a wide variety of small and large computers, including IBM PC-compatibles. The interpreter allows Multi-Pascal programs to be checked for syntax errors and executed to see if they produce the desired results. The debugging tool allows the programmer to interactively set breakpoints in the Multi-Pascal program and examine the value of variables as a debugging aid. There are also features in the debugging tool to keep track of the status and location of parallel processes and monitor the performance of the program as a whole. The user may specify some characteristics of the target parallel computer architecture, including whether it is a multiprocessor or a multicomputer.

Interactive debugging tools are widely used for ordinary sequential programming and have been found to be very useful by programmers during program development. Parallel programs have an additional level of debugging complexity over sequential programs because of the interaction between parallel processes. Thus, a well-designed debugging tool is even more essential for parallel programming than for sequential programming. The easy-to-use Multi-Pascal debugging tool and performance monitor is an enormous aid in parallel program development. Its use should be thoroughly understood by anyone writing Multi-Pascal programs. Not only does the tool allow bugs in the program to be isolated and removed, but it also has features to help locate performance bottlenecks and thereby reduce execution time.

This chapter serves as a complete reference manual for the Multi-Pascal interpreter and interactive system that accompanies this text. It begins with general instructions on using the Multi-Pascal interpreter to run programs. Then each command of the interactive debugging tool is described. To learn practical parallel programming, it is vital that programs be tested for correctness and performance characteristics. This is the purpose of the Multi-Pascal interpreter and debugging tool: supplying a simple environment for each student to run and test his programs. After reading the appendix to get an overview of the system, it is recommended that the student run some test programs on the Multi-Pascal system and practice using each of the commands.

B.1 GETTING STARTED

The Multi-Pascal program must first be created as a text file in the computer by using any normal text editor or word processor that creates a standard ASCII text file. For the PC-version, the Multi-Pascal system is started with the command "MULTI" at the DOS prompt. When the Multi-Pascal system is started, it begins by prompting the user for the name of the program file as follows:

```
Program File Name:
```

The user then types the name of the Multi-Pascal program text file followed by a carriage return. The program will be compiled and checked for syntax errors, which will be indicated on the screen to the user. For a list of syntax error messages and their meaning, see Appendix C. The syntax errors in each line will be located on the terminal screen with a "^" character under the position where the error occurs, plus a number indicating the type of the error. For each error number code, a brief note will appear at the end of the program, indicating the reason for the error. More detailed explanation of error code numbers are found in Appendix C.

Figure B.1 shows an actual program listing produced by the Multi-Pascal interpreter indicating two syntax errors. The misspelling of the keyword *REAL* in line 3 causes the compiler to interpret it as a type identifier that has not been defined. This is error code 0, indicated in the following line. Then at the end of the program under the heading "KEY WORDS," the error code 0 is further explained as "UNDEF ID," which stands for undefined identifier. In line 10 the ":" is missing from the ":=" thus generating an error code 51, which is identified at the end of the program as a ":=" error. Notice that for both line 3 and line 10, the "^" indicating the source of the error occurs just beyond the actual error. This is because the compiler usually does not notice the error until it has passed the actual source of the error. In some cases this will cause the error to be flagged on the following line. This will happen in the case of a missing ";" at the end of a line.

When the Multi-Pascal program does not have any compiler errors, then the interpreter will prompt the user with a "*". To run the program simply type the following:

```
*RUN
```

After running the program to completion, the interpreter will then prompt the user again with a "*". To leave the Multi-Pascal interpreter system, type the following:

```
*EXIT
```

```
   1 PROGRAM Test;
   2 VAR i, j: INTEGER;
   3    r: REEAL;
****              ^ 0
   4    a: ARRAY [1..10] OF INTEGER;
   5
   6 BEGIN
   7   FOR i := 1 TO 10 DO
   8      Readln( a[i] );
   9   Writeln('Here is a copy of the list: ');
  10   FOR j = 1 TO 10 DO
****            ^51
  11      Writeln( a[j] );
  12 END.


COMPILATION ERRORS

KEY WORDS
0   UNDEF ID
51   :=
```

1ss 2: 1524

FIGURE B.1   Multi-Pascal program listing with syntax errors.

B.2 LIST AND INPUT–OUTPUT OPTIONS

When entering the name of the Multi-Pascal program file, the user may include several options to influence the listing of the program and to redirect the standard input and output to files. The general form of these options is as follows:

```
Program File Name: file.prg/list=file.lis/input=file.inp/output=file.out
```

"file.prg" is the name of the Multi-Pascal program file. The rest of the line may contain up to three options in any sequence, each preceded by a "/" as shown. The "list" option will cause the Multi-Pascal program to be listed to the file "file.lis". If the "=file.lis" is omitted from the "list" option, then the program will be listed to the screen. If the "list" option is not used, then only the program lines with syntax errors will be listed on the screen.

The current version of the Multi-Pascal interpreter does not allow any text or data files for program input and output. All input and output are done to the standard system input and output devices, which are usually the keyboard and the terminal screen. However, the user may redirect the input or output to files with the "input" and "output" options, as shown above. The "input=file.inp" option causes all *READ* statements in the Multi-Pascal program to get their input from the text file "file.inp". The "output=file.out" option causes all *WRITE* statements in the Multi-Pascal program to output to the text file "file.out". The "input" and "output" options are especially important and useful when the input or output data of the program is very long. In the options list, the file names may, of course, be replaced by any other valid file names.

Using the "input" or "output" options does not redirect the interactive I/O of the interpreter and debugging tool. Only the I/O of the Multi-Pascal program itself is affected. If the user desires to redirect the I/O of the interpreter and debugger, then this can be done at the system level by using operating system commands. For PC-compatible computers, consult the MS-DOS reference manual for this purpose.

B.3 OVERVIEW OF INTERACTIVE COMMANDS

The following is a list of the important interactive commands in the Multi-Pascal system to assist the programmer in testing the program and isolating bugs. A brief description of each command is included. These commands are all issued directly to the Multi-Pascal system in response to the system prompt "*".

*RUN—Starts execution of the whole program from the beginning.

*EXIT—Terminates the Multi-Pascal interactive system.

*LIST *n:m*—Lists program source lines *n* through *m* on the monitor screen.

*BREAK *n*—This command sets a breakpoint at program line *n*. Program execution will be suspended whenever any process attempts to execute this line of the program.

*CLEAR BREAK *n*—Clears the breakpoint from program line *n*.

*CONT—Continues execution of the program after a breakpoint has been encountered.

*STEP *n*—Continues execution for *n* lines in the current process, then suspends program execution again.

*WRITE *p name*—At any given time during program execution, each process has an execution environment including certain program variables. This WRITE command will display the current value of variable "name" in process *p*. This command may be used to display entire data structures or any portion of these structures.

*TRACE *p name*—This command makes variable "name" a trace variable. Whenever any process attempts to read or write a trace variable, the program execution is suspended.

*DISPLAY—Displays list of breakpoints and trace variables.

*CLEAR TRACE *m*—Clears the trace from memory location *m*.

*STATUS *p*—This command displays some information about the current status of process *p*, including its current execution point in the program, and whether it is currently running.

*VARIATION ON (OFF)—Creates randomly chosen variations in the speed of each processor, to help the user determine whether the program has timing-dependent bugs.

The following is a list of important interactive commands that are useful for monitoring the performance of the program, and locating performance bottlenecks:

*TIME—Gives the elapsed time since the start of program and since the most recent breakpoint. This command can be used to time portions of the program between breakpoints.

*UTILIZATION p—Processor utilization is defined as the percentage of time a given physical processor is actually executing any portion of the program. This UTILIZATION command gives the utilization percentage for physical processor p.

*PROFILE p t—A utilization profile is a graph that shows the processor utilization as a function of time. This PROFILE command generates a utilization profile for physical processor p, using successive time intervals of duration t.

*ALARM t—Sets an alarm to go off after t time units from the beginning of program execution. Program execution is suspended when the alarm goes off.

*DELAY d—For multicomputer architectures, this command sets the basic communication delay between processors with a direct communication link.

*CONGESTION ON (OFF)—For multicomputer architecture, the Congestion option uses a more sophisticated and more realistic method of determining the communication time for messages.

In the remainder of this appendix, the use of all of these commands will be explained in complete detail. As is the case with all software system reference manuals, there is a great deal of detail that must be covered. During the first reading, the student may prefer to read for general ideas. Then later while actually using the Multi-Pascal system, the student can refer to various sections for reference on how to use particular commands.

Note: There are a few of the standard Pascal features that are not currently supported in the version of the Multi-Pascal system that accompanies this text. These details are given in Appendix C. The reader is advised to consult Appendix C before using the Multi-Pascal software.

B.4 SETTING BREAKPOINTS

There are several useful features in the Multi-Pascal system for helping the user isolate bugs in the program. Some of the features are similar to traditional sequential program debugging features, while other features are novel and unique to parallel programming. One of the most important features for helping to locate bugs in a program is the ability to set a breakpoint: a point in the program code where execution is automatically interrupted. Breakpoints are set in the Multi-Pascal system by referring to program line numbers. The user may get a listing of the program with line numbers by using the "list" option when entering the name of the program (see previous section). Also, once the program has been compiled, the user may at any time get a listing of the entire program (including line numbers) with the following command:

```
*LIST
```

To get a listing of a portion of the program with line numbers, indicate a range "n:m" of line numbers as in the following command:

```
*LIST 30:45
```

A breakpoint may be set on any executable line of the Multi-Pascal program with the following command:

```
*BREAK <line-number>
```

Up to ten breakpoints may be set in the program through repeated use of the *BREAK* command. To get a list of the location of all breakpoints, use the following command:

```
*DISPLAY
```

Individual breakpoints may be removed one at a time as follows:

```
*CLEAR BREAK <line-number>
```

Once some breakpoints are set in the program, the user may start executing the program from the beginning with the *RUN* command. The program will run until any line of the program with a breakpoint is encountered. The execution will be suspended immediately *prior* to the execution of the line with the breakpoint. Then the "*" prompt will appear, and the user may then set or remove breakpoints, examine the values of program variables, or use any of the other debugger commands at this point. To continue execution of the program to the next breakpoint, use the following command:

```
*CONTINUE
```

B.5 PROCESSES AND PROCESSORS

As the Multi-Pascal program creates processes with *FORALL* and *FORK*, the interpreter assigns a unique identification number to each process. The main program is always process number 0, and additional processes are numbered sequentially beginning with number 1. Process numbers are never reused even after the corresponding process terminates.

As each process is created, it is also automatically assigned to a physical processor by the Multi-Pascal system. It is important to understand clearly the difference between a *process* and a *processor*. A *process* is a sequence of Multi-Pascal instructions, which must always be executed by a *processor*. To help emphasize the difference, we will sometimes use the term *physical processor* in place of the term *processor*, but they have the same meaning.

The total number of physical processors is fixed by the architecture of the underlying computer hardware. However, processes can be created and terminated dynamically in any numbers by the Multi-Pascal program. Chapter 8 discusses how to control the assignment of processes to physical processors in the Multi-Pascal language. For most purposes, the default processor assignment mechanism in the Multi-Pascal software system is sufficient.

The physical processors are numbered from 0 up to some maximum (255 for the PC-version of the Multi-Pascal software and 511 for versions on larger machines). The main program is always assigned to run on physical processor number 0. As each new process is created, it is assigned to the first free physical processor beginning with processor number 1. When a physical processor becomes idle due to the termination of the process it is currently running, it becomes a candidate for assignment of a newly created process.

In most of the examples in this text, the total number of processes will never exceed the total number of physical processors. However, the Multi-Pascal system allows for this possibility by permitting more than one process to be assigned to run on each physical processor. When all the available physical processors have already been assigned processes, then additional processes will be evenly distributed among the processors. When a new process is created, it will be assigned to the physical processor with the smallest total number of processes. However, once a process is assigned to a physical processor, it executes there until it is terminated: processes are not moved during their execution.

Whenever the execution of a Multi-Pascal program is suspended due to a breakpoint, the user can examine the status of all the processes. As a sequential program is executing, there is one "execution point" that moves from one statement to the next and may be located anywhere within the body of the main program or within the body of any procedure or function. However, for a parallel program, each process has its own individual execution point that moves from one statement to the next in parallel with all the other processes. For example, refer to the Parallel Rank Sort program of Figure 2.3. Each processor is executing its own call to the procedure PutinPlace. Therefore, each process will have its own "execution point" in the procedure, which may be different from other processes.

To determine the overall status of this Parallel Rank Sort while it is running, one would need to know the execution point of each process. When encountering a breakpoint (or any other event causing suspension of program execution), the user may use the following command to determine the status and current execution point of each active process:

*STATUS

The Multi-Pascal system will then display a table of the processes. For the Parallel Rank Sort program of Figure 2.3, the following would be a typical example:

PROCESS #	PROCEDURE	LINE NUMBER	STATUS	PROCESSOR
0	RANKSORT	20	BLOCKED	0
1	PUTINPLACE	12	RUNNING	1
2	PUTINPLACE	13	RUNNING	2
3	PUTINPLACE	12	RUNNING	3
4	PUTINPLACE	14	RUNNING	4
5	PUTINPLACE	13	RUNNING	5

Actually, the above display shows only the first six processes. The actual display would contain all 100 processes (unless the display is restricted by using a technique described below). Process 0 is the main program, which is the parent of all the other processes. The "procedure" name for the parent in the above display is just the overall program name "RANKSORT." It is on physical processor 0, but is currently in the "BLOCKED" state waiting for all of its children to finish execution. Each of the child processes 1–5 is running somewhere inside the procedure "PUTINPLACE." The above display shows the specific line number where each child is currently executing.

The following shows another typical example from the execution of a different parallel program:

PROCESS #	PROCEDURE	LINE NUMBER	STATUS	PROCESSOR
0	ODDEVEN	29	RUNNING	0
1	ODDEVEN	28	BLOCKED	0
2	COMPARE	15	RUNNING	1
3	COMPARE	14	RUNNING	2
4	COMPARE	10	RUNNING	3
5	ODDEVEN	29	READY	4

In this example there are six processes, numbered 0 to 5. The name of the program is "ODDEVEN," and there is one procedure called "COMPARE." Process 0 is executing in the main program "ODDEVEN" at line number 29. The process is in the "RUNNING" state on physical processor number 0. Process number 1 is also executing in the main program "ODDEVEN" at line 28, but is currently in the "BLOCKED" state on physical processor 0. A process is "BLOCKED" when it is waiting for some external event that must be caused by another process. For example, a parent process is "BLOCKED" while waiting for its children to terminate.

Processes 2–4 are all executing in procedure "COMPARE" and are in the "RUN-NING" state. Process 5 has just been created and assigned to physical processor 4, but has not yet started to run and is therefore currently in the "READY" state. Notice in this example that the process numbers do not correspond to the processor numbers. Both processes 0 and 1 are assigned to physical processor 0, where one of them is running and the other is blocked. The remaining processes are assigned to physical processors 1–4.

There are five possible states for any active process: READY, RUNNING, BLOCKED, DELAYED, SPINNING. At any given time there can only be one RUNNING process on a given physical processor since the processor is essentially sequential and can execute only one process at a time. A process is READY if it is currently available for execution but is not currently being executed on its physical processor. When a process is first created, it is put into the READY state. When a running process gets to a point in its execution where it has to wait for something from another process, it goes into the BLOCKED state. One such example is when a parent process creates a group of children in a *FORALL* statement and then must wait for them all to terminate. The parent is in the BLOCKED state while it is waiting for its children. Processes may also become blocked while waiting for a value from an empty *CHANNEL* variable, as is discussed thoroughly in Chapter 4.

The DELAYED state is almost the same as the BLOCKED state, except that the event being waited for has already occurred. However, due to communication delays in the physical computer architecture, the event has not yet arrived at the BLOCKED process. Since the Multi-Pascal system is a simulator, it knows that the needed event has already occurred at a distance, and therefore changes the status of the BLOCKED process to DELAYED as a debugging aid to the user. When the needed event actually arrives at a BLOCKED or DELAYED process, the process is put into the READY state and then becomes a candidate to be executed by its physical processor. The DELAYED state will only occur in multicomputers because of communication delays between physical processors. The DELAYED state will never occur in multiprocessors. The SPINNING state has to do with the use of spinlocks, as described in Chapter 5. When a process is trying to perform a "Lock" operation on a spinlock that is already in the locked state, the process will assume a form of "busy-waiting" indicated by the SPINNING state.

There may be many processes on a given physical processor in the READY, BLOCKED, DELAYED, or SPINNING state, but only one in the RUNNING state at a given time. If there are many processes in the READY state on a given physical processor, the processor will continue to switch back and forth between the processes, running each one for a short time interval. If it has no other READY processes, then a physical processor will continue running the same process until it goes into the BLOCKED state or terminates. Once a process terminates, it no longer appears in the STATUS table.

The STATUS command gives the user a snapshot of the current situation with respect to all the parallel processes. As each breakpoint is encountered during program execution, the user can use STATUS to see what the processes are doing. When the number of processes gets very large, the user can choose to view only a range of processes as in the following command for displaying the status of processes 30 to 50:

```
*STATUS 30:50
```

B.6 STEPPING THROUGH A PROCESS

Each breakpoint is valid for all the processes. A breakpoint is assigned to a specific line of code in the program. When any running process tries to execute a line in the program with a breakpoint, the whole program execution will be suspended, including the execution of all the processes. The Multi-Pascal system will display a message telling the user the line number where the breakpoint was encountered and the process number that tried to execute that breakpoint, as in the following example:

```
Break at 26 In Procedure ODDEVEN
Process Number 0
```

At this point, the execution of the whole program may be continued (with the CONTINUE command) until the next breakpoint is encountered by any process. To focus on the execution of a specific process, the STEP command may be used to follow the execution of that process line by line. Whenever a breakpoint is encountered by a given process, that process automatically becomes the current "Step-Process." All STEP commands refer to the current Step-Process. The current Step-Process may be changed, as in the following example that changes the Step-Process to process number 7:

```
*STEP PROCESS 7
```

To focus attention on the Step-Process, the STEP command can execute a specified number of lines in the Step-Process and then suspend execution. The following command will execute three lines of the Step-Process:

```
*STEP 3
```

The lines for execution are counted according to the line numbering scheme in the program listing. Thus, if the Step-Process is currently at line 15 and no loop back is encountered, the above STEP command will execute the program until the Step-Process hits line 18 in the program. The STEP command counts just executable lines in the program listing, independent of how many statements are contained on a given line. For program loops, the total number of lines executed is counted until the number reaches the STEP command count. Program lines that contain only *BEGIN* or *END* statements are counted as executable lines in the STEP command, but blank lines, comment lines, and declarations are not counted. As the Step-Process is executed by the STEP command, all the other processes also continue to execute in parallel, so they also will be advancing in execution. However, during a STEP command, breakpoints are ignored. Breakpoints are valid only during the CONTINUE command or the RUN command.

B.7 WRITING AND TRACING VARIABLES

Whenever the execution of the Multi-Pascal program is suspended, the user may examine the current value of variables in the current environment of each process. In an ordinary sequential Pascal program, the "environment" is statically defined for each statement in the program. The scope rules of Pascal specify that when a variable name is used in a statement, first the declarations of the immediate enclosing procedure are searched for that name. If the variable name is not found there, then the next outer enclosing procedure is searched, and so on, until the main program declarations are reached. If the declaration of the given variable name is not found in this hierarchical search, then the variable is flagged as "undefined" by the compiler.

In a Multi-Pascal program, each process has its own individual execution point and therefore its own environment. At a given time during program execution, different processes may be executing inside different procedure bodies and therefore may have completely different environments. When program execution is suspended, the Multi-Pascal system allows the user to display the value of any variable in the current environment of each process with a command of the following general form:

```
*WRITE  <process-number>  <variable-name>
```

The <process-number> must be the number of some active process that appears in the STATUS command list. The process may be READY, RUNNING, BLOCKED, DELAYED, or SPINNING, but cannot be terminated. The chosen process will have an environment that depends on the current line number that it is executing in the program. The <variable-name> is located in the environment of that process and the value displayed.

B.7.1 Writing Standard Variables

To illustrate the use of the WRITE command, consider the partial program shown in Figure B.2. Assume that process 0 is currently executing the *FORALL* statement in line 80 of the main program. Then the following is a valid command to determine the current value of variable *j*:

```
*WRITE 0 j
```

If it is assumed that process 1 is currently executing in line 30 in the middle of procedure COMPARE, then the following command will display the value of variable *temp*, since it is in the environment of process 1:

```
*WRITE 1 temp
```

```
1    PROGRAM Oddeven;
2    VAR  i, j: INTEGER;
3         a: ARRAY [1..10] OF REAL;
4         item:  RECORD
5                  first: INTEGER;
6                  second: INTEGER;
7                END;
8         itemlist: ARRAY [1..3] OF item;
     . . .

20        PROCEDURE Compare(k: INTEGER);
21        VAR  index: INTEGER;
22             temp: REAL;
23        BEGIN
     . . .      . . .

40        END;

41        PROCEDURE Tree(value: REAL);
42        VAR  b: ARRAY [1..10] OF REAL;
43        BEGIN
     . . .      . . .

70        END;

71    BEGIN
     . . .      . . .

80        FORALL i := 1 TO 10 DO
81          Compare(i);
     . . .      . . .

100  END.
```

FIGURE B.2   Segment of a Multi-Pascal program.

However, the command "WRITE 0 temp" is not valid, since *temp* is not in the current environment of process 0. In response to this command, the Multi-Pascal system will display the error message "Name Not Found." Assume that there is a process number 2 currently executing inside procedure Tree in line 50. Then process 2 has variables *value* and *b* in its environment. Notice that all the processes 0, 1, and 2 share the variables declared at the beginning of the program. Therefore, the following commands are all valid and refer to the same variable *j*:

```
*WRITE 0 j

*WRITE 1 j

*WRITE 2 j
```

B.7.2 Writing Structured Variables

In the WRITE command, it is also permitted to refer to a specific item of an array or a component of a record as in the following commands:

```
*WRITE 0 a[4]

*WRITE 0 item.second

*WRITE 2 b[3]
```

Any array or record may be qualified as it would be in a normal Pascal statement, except that array subscripts must be integer literals. By using the name of a record, the whole record will be displayed, including the names and values of all its components as in the following example:

```
*WRITE 0 item

  RECORD
     FIRST: 3
     SECOND: 45
```

A range of indices in an array may be displayed by requesting to WRITE the whole array as follows:

```
*WRITE 0 a
```

The system will then respond with the prompt message "Index Range:," after which the user may specify any range of indices in the array as in the following example:

```
*WRITE 0 a
```

```
Index Range: 3:6
      3--> 56
      4--> 70
      5--> -3
      6--> 0
```

To display the entire array, the user responds with a carriage return after the "Index Range" prompt. For variables that have many levels of structure using arrays, records, and pointers, the user may qualify the variable name to many levels in the WRITE command as in the following example (refer to the declaration of *itemlist* in Figure B.2):

```
*WRITE 0 itemlist[2].first
```

For any variable with several levels of structure formed by arrays, records, or pointers, the system will attempt to follow all the levels and display the entire structure on the screen for the user. For example, consider the following command and the resultant display for *itemlist*, which is an array of records:

```
*WRITE 0 itemlist
```

```
Index Range:
      1-->   RECORD
                  FIRST: 1
                  SECOND: 4
      2-->   RECORD
                  FIRST: 3
                  SECOND: -10
      3-->   RECORD
                  FIRST: 0
                  SECOND: 14
```

To help in describing how the WRITE command works with respect to pointer variables, consider the following declarations:

```
TYPE
   itemtyp = RECORD
                  first, second: INTEGER;
               END;
   nodepnt = ^node;
   node = RECORD
                  data: INTEGER;
                  next: nodepnt;
              END;
VAR
   itempnt: ^itemtyp;
   root: nodepnt;
```

When a pointer is referenced in a WRITE command without a qualifier, the Multi-Pascal system automatically follows the pointer and displays the data value that is pointed to, as in the following example:

```
*WRITE O itempnt

   POINTER
     TO^:    RECORD
                FIRST: 3
                SECOND: 45
```

The pointer may also be qualified by using the "^" primitive in the same way it is used in ordinary Pascal statements, as follows:

```
*WRITE O itempnt^.second

   45
```

When the user attempts to WRITE the value of a variable with many levels of pointers, such as in a linked list, the Multi-Pascal system will continue to display each level and follow the pointers to several levels. For example, assume that the variable *root* declared above points to a linked list with two items. Then the following will be the result of a WRITE command:

```
*WRITE O root

   POINTER
     TO^:    RECORD
                DATA: 124
                NEXT: POINTER
                        TO^:    RECORD
                                  DATA: 30
                                  NEXT: NIL POINTER
```

The above display shows that the variable *root* is a pointer to a record with a data value of 124 and a link pointer to another record. The final record in this linked list has data value 30 and a "NIL" pointer. If the linked list is long, the system will display only the first three or four levels. The user can also qualify the variable *root* to any number of levels, as in an ordinary Pascal variable reference:

```
*WRITE O root^.next^.data

30
```

The use of *CHANNEL* variables is described in detail in Chapter 4. A *CHANNEL* variable contains a queue of values with new values added at the tail and removed from the head. Using the WRITE command, the current contents of any *CHANNEL* variable may be displayed as in the following example for a variable *c* declared as *CHANNEL OF INTEGER*:

```
*WRITE c

CHANNEL
        > 13
        > 11
        > 56
        > -100
        > 0
```

The channel contents are written with the head at the top and the tail at the bottom. If the chosen target architecture is a multicomputer, then it is possible that some values sent to a channel from a remote processor may still be traveling through the communication network, and have not yet reached the channel. For such "in-transit" values, the Multi-Pascal system will list them as part of the contents of the channel, but use a special "**" notation to indicate that they have not yet physically arrived at the channel. The following is an example:

```
*WRITE c

CHANNEL
       > 6
       > 34
       > -13
     **> 41
     **> 10
```

B.7.3 TRACE Command

To debug a program, the user must interrupt the execution at various points and then examine the status of the processes and values of the variables. Setting a breakpoint or using the STEP command are two important techniques discussed so far for interrupting program execution. Another technique is to use the TRACE command to put a trace flag on any variable. Whenever that variable is referenced during subsequent program execution, the program will be suspended as it is for breakpoints. Since variables may be referenced by many different processes in a variety of locations, the TRACE command provides a useful tool for the user to focus on the use of key program variables. The general form of the TRACE command is as follows:

```
*TRACE <process-number> <variable-reference>
```

The <process-number> plays the same role as in the WRITE command to identify the process and environment. The <variable-reference> is also similar to the WRITE command with one important difference: the <variable-reference> must be a fully qualified reference that evaluates to a scalar variable of type *INTEGER*, *REAL*, *CHAR*, *BOOL-*

EAN, or a single *CHANNEL* or *SPINLOCK*. Individual elements of an array or record may be traced, but one cannot use a single TRACE statement for an entire array or record. With reference to the sample program of Figure B.2, the following are all valid TRACE commands:

```
*TRACE 0 j

*TRACE 0 a[4]

*TRACE 0 a[1]

*TRACE 0 item.first

*TRACE 0 itemlist[2].second
```

However, the following commands are erroneous, since they refer to whole arrays or records:

```
*TRACE 0 a
 Cannot Trace a Whole Array or Record

*TRACE 0 item
 Cannot Trace a Whole Array or Record
```

A TRACE command results in a flag being put onto a specific memory cell corresponding to the variable reference. In Figure B.2, the variable j is assigned by the system to a specific memory location where values of that variable are stored and retrieved. The command "TRACE 0 j" puts a flag on that memory cell. During subsequent program execution, any reference to that memory cell by any statement in any process will cause program execution to be suspended. Similarly, the command "TRACE 0 a[4]" will put a flag on the memory cell corresponding to a[4]. During program execution, the use of procedure calls with VAR parameters may cause different variable names to be associated with the same memory cell. For example, variable j may be passed as a VAR parameter to a procedure that uses the name p. If variable j has a trace on it, then a reference to p will also cause the program to be suspended.

To get a list of the currently active trace variables, use the DISPLAY command, which displays the breakpoint locations and the trace locations as in the following example:

```
*TRACE 0 j

*TRACE 0 a[4]

*BREAK 23

*DISPLAY

Breakpoints at Following Lines:
23
```

```
List of Trace Variables:
Variable Name              Memory Location
  A[4]                          13
  J                              9
```

To remove a trace from a variable, refer to the *Memory Location* rather than the name. The following command will remove the trace from variable *J*:

```
*CLEAR TRACE 9
```

It is possible to put a trace on a pointer variable. However, the flag is put on the memory location corresponding to the pointer variable itself. Whenever that pointer variable is referenced, the program will be suspended. The flag is not put on the thing pointed to. Thus, a pointer variable *itempnt* may point to a record. The command "TRACE 0 itempnt" will put a flag on *itempnt* but not on the record to which it points.

As with the WRITE command, a TRACE command must refer to variables that already exist in the environment of some process. Thus, if process 1 is executing in line 30 of procedure Compare in Figure B.2, then the following command is valid:

```
*TRACE 1 index
```

B.8 PROGRAM PERFORMANCE STATISTICS

As the Multi-Pascal system executes a program, it keeps track of the relative timing of all the processes and generates a range of performance statistics to help the user understand the behavior of the program. When a Multi-Pascal program is run on a real multiprocessor computer, it is first compiled to machine language that is executed by the processors of that computer. In the Multi-Pascal simulation system, the program is also compiled into a pseudo-machine code called "p-code," which is interpreted rather than directly executed. As the Multi-Pascal system interprets this p-code, it uses an estimated execution time for each p-code instruction and keeps a running total of the execution time of the program. The time charged for each p-code instruction varies from 1 to 6 time units, depending on the relative complexity of the instruction. A simple instruction such as moving the value of a variable onto the stack is counted as one time unit, and a complex instruction such as creating a new process descriptor is counted as six time units.

Using these estimated execution time values, the Multi-Pascal system is able to simulate the performance of the program on a real multiprocessor or multicomputer. At the end of the program execution, the system will display the total program execution time called the "PARALLEL EXECUTION TIME": the estimated value of the actual running time of the program on the target multiprocessor. The Multi-Pascal system also keeps track of another statistic called the "SEQUENTIAL EXECUTION TIME": an estimate of the execution time on a uniprocessor computer. If there are ten processors executing continuously for 1000 time units each, then the PARALLEL time is simply 1000, but the SEQUENTIAL time is the sum of all the execution times of all the processors: 10,000. In the final program statistics, the Multi-Pascal system also displays the total number of processors used during program execution and the "SPEEDUP": the SEQUENTIAL time divided by the PARALLEL time. Following is a typical display by the Multi-Pascal simulation system at the end of program execution:

```
SEQUENTIAL EXECUTION TIME: 123711
PARALLEL EXECUTION TIME: 9857
SPEEDUP:  12.5
NUMBER OF PROCESSORS USED:   16
```

For these sample statistics, the estimated running time of the program is 9857 time units. For many of the typical multiprocessor systems, one time unit of simulated time is approximately equivalent to one microsecond of real execution time on a multiprocessor. Thus, the estimated running time of this program is 9.86 milliseconds. The estimated total sequential execution time (uniprocessor execution time) is 123711 time units. The speedup of 12.5 is calculated by dividing the SEQUENTIAL time by the PARALLEL time. Any processor that is used at all during the program execution is counted in the total of "NUMBER OF PROCESSORS USED." Since the use of these 16 processors resulted in an overall speedup of 12.5, then the average processor utilization was approximately 12.5/16 = 78 percent.

B.8.1 TIME Command

In addition to these overall program performance statistics given at the end of the execution, the Multi-Pascal system has several commands to help the user monitor the performance during various phases of the program. One of these is the TIME command, which can be used whenever program execution is suspended to give the total elapsed time since the beginning of the program. Following is a typical display resulting from the TIME command:

```
*TIME

Since Start of Program:
    Elapsed Time:  3450
    Number of Processors Used:   14
    Speedup:  10.7
```

The "Elapsed Time" of 3450 time units is the total execution time consumed by the program so far: similar to the "PARALLEL EXECUTION TIME" discussed above. The "Number of Processors Used" and the "Speedup" are the same measures as discussed above, except that they refer only to the portion of program execution that has taken place so far. As a result of the simulation technique used by the Multi-Pascal system, the "time" always moves forward in steps of 10 time units. Thus, the "Elapsed Time" will always be a multiple of 10.

To focus attention on the performance of localized portions of the program, the user can set a breakpoint in the program and then after hitting this breakpoint, run the program up to a second breakpoint. Using the TIME command will then provide information about the performance of the program between the breakpoints. For example, the following is a typical sequence of commands to use this capability:

```
*BREAK 24

*BREAK 28

*RUN

Break at 24   In Procedure ODDEVEN
Process Number  0

*CONTINUE

Break at 28   In Procedure ODDEVEN
Process Number  0

*TIME

Since Start of Program:
    Elapsed Time: 2890
    Number of Processors Used:   20
    Speedup:   5.4

Since Last Breakpoint:
    Elapsed Time: 670
    Speedup: 18.3
```

In this sequence of commands, the user has determined the program performance between program lines 24 and 28. Breakpoints are set at both lines 24 and 28. The program is run from the beginning until the breakpoint at line 24 is encountered. Then execution is continued until the breakpoint at line 28 is encountered. Using the TIME command at this point will not only give the performance statistics since the beginning of the program, but also since the last breakpoint. Thus, this display shows that the program performance between lines 24 and 28 is considerably better than since the beginning of the program. Between lines 24 and 28, a speedup of 18.3 is achieved. This probably means that the early portion of the program must have a lot of sequential code that is reducing the overall speedup to only (5.4).

This technique of using the TIME command between breakpoints is useful for focusing attention on the performance of localized segments of the program. One of the important uses of this technique is to remove the effects of data initialization from the overall performance statistics. For example, consider determining the speedup achieved by the Parallel Rank Sort program given in Chapter 2. To run a test requires that some initial data values be read into the array at the beginning of the program. This sequential reading of a large number of data values may consume a lot of program execution time. Running this program with the time-consuming sequential initialization at the beginning and the parallel sorting at the end will result in a reduced speedup due to the predominance of the sequential part at the beginning. To focus attention on the parallel sorting only, the user can set breakpoints at the beginning and end of the sorting phase. Using the above technique of running the program from the beginning, the first breakpoint will be encountered after the array is already initialized. Continuing from this point, the second breakpoint will be encountered after the parallel sorting is complete. The TIME command at this second breakpoint will then tell the user the speedup achieved by the parallel sorting portion of the program.

Another useful technique for focusing attention on the performance of localized portions of the program is the STEP command. After each STEP command, the Multi-Pascal system will display the time required for this step and the percentage of this time that the *Step-Process* was actually running. The following is a typical example:

```
*STEP 4

Break at 24 In Procedure COMPARE
Step Time is 50.  Process running 100 percent.
```

This break message indicates that the execution of the requested four lines in the Step-Process took 50 time units. During these 50 time units, the Step-Process was running 100 percent of the time. If the Step-Process had become blocked or delayed during the four steps and then continued to complete the steps, the percentage would be less than 100 percent. Thus, this timing of the STEP command can help the user time various portions of the program and locate delays in process execution.

The execution time is also available to the Multi-Pascal program itself in the program statements using the Built-in parameterless function *CLOCK*, which evaluates to the total elapsed time since the beginning of the program. The Built-in function *SEQTIME* evaluates to the estimated sequential time to execute up to this point in the program on a uniprocessor computer. Both functions evaluate to real numbers, not integers. The user can insert these functions along with *Write* statements at various points in the program to display performance statistics about the different phases of program execution. For example, these functions can be used to determine performance of the computational portion of a program, without considering the data initialization that occurs at the beginning. For this purpose, the body of the main program in the Parallel Rank Sort of Figure 2.3 can be modified as follows:

```
PROGRAM RankSort;
VAR  ...
    parstart,seqstart: REAL;

  PROCEDURE PutinPlace( src: INTEGER);
    ...

BEGIN (*Main*)
FOR  i := 1 TO n DO
  Readln( values[i] );  (*initialize values to be sorted*)
parstart := CLOCK; seqstart := SEQTIME;
FORALL  i := 1 TO n DO
    PutinPlace(i);  (*find rank of values[i] and put in position*)
Writeln('Speedup is ', (SEQTIME-seqstart)/(CLOCK-parstart));
END.
```

B.8.2 UTILIZATION Command

Processor utilization is sometimes taken as a measure of how efficiently a given program uses a particular multiprocessor architecture. The utilization of a given physical processor is defined as the proportion of the time the processor is actually running. Any time the program execution is suspended, the user may give the UTILIZATION command to get a complete table of the utilization of all processors up to that point in the execution. This command will also give the processor utilization since the last breakpoint: the proportion of time since the last breakpoint that each processor is actually running. For example, the following is a typical display from this command:

```
*UTILIZATION

                    PERCENT UTILIZATION
PROCESSOR     SINCE START     SINCE LAST BREAK
    0             63                51
    1             61                76
    2             62                79
    3             64                84
    4             66                89
    5             67                91
    6             67                91
    7             66                89
    8             65                88
```

The above display shows that the average utilization of all the processors is about 65 percent since the beginning of the program, but the higher-number processors have been used more heavily since the last breakpoint. Processor 0 has only a 51 percent utilization since the last break, but processors 4–8 have an average utilization of 90 percent since the last break. When using the UTILIZATION command, the display will automatically include all processors that have been used at all since the start of the program. Other processors not listed all have zero utilization. If the list of processors is too long, the user may qualify the command with a range of processors as follows:

```
*UTILIZATION 20:30
```

The command may also be abbreviated "UTIL."

B.8.3 Sequential Execution Time

For parallel programs, the most common definition of the "Sequential Execution Time" is the time required to execute a sequential version of the same program, using the same general algorithm. The SEQUENTIAL time automatically computed by the Multi-Pascal system is an attempt to approximate the actual Sequential Execution Time, which can really be accurately determined only by writing and running a sequential version of the program. To help make the SEQUENTIAL time statistic more accurate, the Multi-Pascal system does not include the process management activity in the SEQUENTIAL time. Process management activities such as process creation, dispatching the process to its target processor, and process termination are all computational activities that require some computing time by a physical processor. Since a sequential version of the program would have no processes, these process management functions would not be required. Therefore, the Multi-Pascal system does not include this process management in the SEQUENTIAL time statistic.

In addition to these primitive activities of process creation and termination, the program may also have segments that perform some high-level process management function, such as synchronization or communication between processes. In Chapter 6, a Barrier Procedure is described, whose function is to synchronize a group of parallel processes. In a sequential version of the program, this synchronization activity is not required. To help the user increase the accuracy of the SEQUENTIAL time statistic, there is a special primitive that may be inserted into the Multi-Pascal program itself to exclude certain portions of code from the SEQUENTIAL time. The primitive %SEQOFF may appear in any position in the program that an ordinary statement could appear. The execution of this primitive by a process will cause all subsequent instruction execution by that process to be excluded from the SEQUENTIAL time. This exclusion will continue until that process executes a %SEQON primitive. These primitives will affect only the process that executes them, and not other processes.

For example, the following structure will eliminate the Barrier Procedure from inclusion in the SEQUENTIAL time:

```
PROCEDURE Barrier;
VAR ...
BEGIN
  %SEQOFF;

   ... (*Ordinay Body of Barrier Procedure*)

  %SEQON;
END;
```

Since the SEQUENTIAL time is used by the Multi-Pascal system to compute the program SPEEDUP, this important performance statistic will also become more accurate by increasing the accuracy in the SEQUENTIAL time.

B.8.4 ALARM Command

As an aid in debugging or performance analysis of a program, it is sometimes useful to be able to stop the program execution at a specific time. This is done with the ALARM command, which will automatically suspend program execution when a certain time is reached. This is similar to setting an alarm on a ordinary watch or clock. To set an alarm to go off at 1500 time units into the execution of the program, use the following command:

```
*ALARM 1500
```

The alarm time is always measured from the start of program execution initiated with the RUN command. When the program time reaches 1500, the execution will be suspended and the following message will be displayed:

```
Time is 1500. Alarm Went Off.
```

The technique used by the Multi-Pascal system for simulating program execution sometimes causes time to take jumps. Thus, in some cases the program may actually stop slightly after the specified alarm time. Once set with the ALARM command, the alarm setting will continue to remain valid. The alarm may be reset to a new time if desired, or the alarm may be turned off entirely with the following command:

```
*ALARM OFF
```

The DISPLAY command, in addition to listing the breakpoints and trace variables, will also show the alarm setting if it is on.

B.8.5 VARIATION Command

In writing parallel programs, the programmer must assume that the relative processor speeds may vary. The program should be robust enough to work correctly, independent of the relative processor speeds. To help the user test for this property, the Multi-Pascal system has the VARIATION command to vary the relative processor speeds. The "Variation" option may be turned on with the following command:

```
*VARIATION ON
```

After this command is issued, the program may be executed by using the RUN command as usual. When the RUN command is issued, the Multi-Pascal system will prompt the user for an integer "Random Number Seed." This will be used to create a random number e_i between 0 and 1 for each physical processor i that will be used to increase the speed by a factor of $1/e_i$. This randomly selected speed factor for each processor will remain in effect throughout the subsequent program execution, until another RUN command is issued, at which time a new Random Number Seed will be requested to select a new set of random speed factors for the processors. The particular random speed factors chosen are completely dependent on the Random Number Seed: using the same Seed again will result in the same set of processor speed factors.

To test a program for a range of relative processor speeds, the user first turns on the VARIATION option, then RUNs the program many times, using a different Random Number Seed each time. During and after each run, the user can check to see if the program is producing correct results. If any error is found, then it is possible to reproduce that same execution pattern by running the program again with the same Random Number Seed. This reproducibility is useful as an aid in isolating the source of the error with the help of the usual debugging commands, such as Breakpoints or Variable Tracing.

During this debugging, the user may notice that certain processors are much faster than others, and move ahead through large portions of the program very quickly. Since the random speed factors will change the program execution time, all of the usual program performance statistics are meaningless when the VARIATION option is on, and should be ignored. The Variation option is turned off as follows:

```
*VARIATION OFF
```

B.8.6 DURATION Statement

The Multi-Pascal programming language has a built-in operation to allow any process to suspend its own execution for a specified time period. This operation is an ordinary executable statement and has the following general form:

```
DURATION( <expression> );
```

The <expression> is any valid Multi-Pascal expression that evaluates to an integer. The process executing the DURATION statement will be delayed by the number of microseconds determined by the evaluation of <expression>. When the Multi-Pascal interactive software is used, the DURATION statement will cause the process to be put into the DELAYED state for the exact number of time units specified by <expression>.

The DURATION statement is especially useful during program performance evaluation to focus attention on the computational portion of the program by ignoring the process creation time. As each process is created, it begins to run immediately, even before the other processes are created. This means that there is an overlap between the process creation and computational portion of the program. Thus, it is not possible to ignore the process creation time by simply subtracting it from the total program execution time. This problem can be solved by using the DURATION statement to delay the start of every process until the creation portion of the program is completed.

Consider a program with the following process creation statement:

```
BEGIN (*Body of Main program*)
  ...

  FORALL i := 1 TO 50 DO
    Compute(i);
  ...

END.
```

The first step is to use the Multi-Pascal performance monitoring features to determine the time at which the process creation is finished. Assume that in this program it is 3000 time units. All that is necessary now is to use a DURATION statement to delay the start of every process until after 3000 time units as follows:

```
PROCEDURE Compute(i: INTEGER);
VAR ...
BEGIN
  DURATION(TRUNC(3000 - CLOCK));
    ...

END;
```

When the DURATION statement is executed by a process, the current value of CLOCK will be the current time. By waiting exactly "3000-CLOCK" time units, the process will be waiting until time 3000 before starting its execution. Thus, all the processes will simply wait until time 3000 and then all start together. To determine the execution time of the rest of the program, run the program to its end in the usual way, and then subtract 3000 from the final program execution time. With this little trick, it is possible to ignore the process creation time, and focus attention on the performance of the computational portion of the program.

B.9 PROGRAM PERFORMANCE PROFILE

The Multi-Pascal system has a powerful PROFILE command to create a visual performance profile, that will help the user understand the program performance in a glance. Figure B.3 is a typical example of a performance profile, showing the processor utilization during successive time intervals of program execution. The processor numbers are given horizontally across the page. Time advances vertically down the page from top to bottom. In this case, each successive line of the display represents a time interval of duration 20 time units. The marks indicate the processor utilization during each time interval: "*" indicates 75–100 percent utilization, "+" indicates 50–75 percent utilization, "–" indicates 25–50 percent utilization, and "." indicates 0–25 percent utilization. These particular marking symbols were chosen so that a glance at the profile gives a pictorial view of the processor utilization patterns, with darker areas being higher utilization areas.

In the profile of Figure B.3, the body of the main program is running by itself on processor 0 for some time, doing initialization. Then the main program begins executing a *FORALL* statement that gradually creates 10 parallel processes to run on processors 1–10. After the processes are created, the main program on processor 0 goes into a blocked state (indicated by the low utilization of processor 0 in the lower half of the profile). The processes continue executing in parallel for some time and terminate individually. After they are all terminated, then the main program on processor 0 continues to run for some time at the end of the program. If the profile is very long and runs off the terminal screen, the Multi-Pascal system will break the profile every 20 lines and display the current time as a reference point.

To create a performance profile, the user first must set up the profile parameters, using the PROFILE command in the following general form:

```
*PROFILE p:q t
```

```
TIME: 0
0 1 2 3 4 5         10
*
*
*
* + .
* * * -   .
* * * * + -
* * * * * + -
* * * * * * *   .   .
* * * * * * * * * +   .
* * * * * * * * * * *
* * * * * * * * * * *
. * * * * * * * * * *
. * * * * * * * * * *
. * * * * * * * * * *
. * * * * * * * * * *
. * * * * * * * * * *
. * * * * * * * * * *
. * * * * * * * * * *
. * * * * * * * * * *
. * * * * * * * * * *
. * * * * * * + * * +
. * * + + - + - . * .
. + - . . . . . * .
+ . . . . . . . . .
* . . . . . . . . .
* . . . . . . . . .
```

FIGURE B.3   Performance profile of a program.

The parameter "p:q" is the range of processor numbers to be displayed in the profile (the range must be continuous). The parameter "t" is the size of the time interval used for each line of the profile. A maximum of 40 processors is allowed in a single profile, and the minimum time interval size is 10 time units. The sample profile of Figure B.3 was created with the following command:

```
*PROFILE 0:10 20
```

Once the PROFILE command is used to set the parameters, then the profile will be automatically displayed on the terminal screen whenever the program is executed. If a breakpoint is encountered, the profile is temporarily interrupted and then continued when program execution is continued. Thus, the user may do a profile of the whole program using the RUN command, or do profiles of short portions of the program by using breakpoints. By using a relatively long time interval in the profile, the user can get an overall view of the major phases of the program execution and the performance during each phase. Then the user can focus on short segments of the program by using a shorter time interval and setting program breakpoints. In this way, performance bottlenecks and periods of low processor utilization can be isolated as a basis for improving program performance. The PROFILE command will remain active until the following command is given:

```
*PROFILE OFF
```

If the program outputs values to the terminal using "Write" statements, then these outputs may be intermixed with the profile, causing a messy display. This problem can be remedied by using the "output=filename" option in the original command line to redirect the program output to a file. The profile itself is not affected by this "output" option.

B.10 SIMULATION OF PARALLEL ARCHITECTURES

When the Multi-Pascal simulation system is used, the default architecture is a shared-memory multiprocessor with a maximum of 512 processors available (256 in the MS-DOS version). For pedagogical purposes of learning parallel programming techniques, this architecture is the simplest and should be used for the programming laboratories in Chapters 2–6. The programmer may override this default and specify a wide range of other architectures, including many of the common multicomputer topologies. This allows the performance of Multi-Pascal programs to be simulated on a wide range of parallel computer architectures according to the choice of the programmer.

B.10.1 Specifying the Architecture

In addition to the shared-memory multiprocessor, the multicomputer architectures available in Version 2.0 of the Multi-Pascal system include Hypercube, 2D-mesh, 3D-mesh, Ring, and Torus. A detailed discussion of the structure of each of these multicomputer topologies is found in Chapter 7, "Multicomputer Architecture." To specify a given architecture in a Multi-Pascal program, the keyword *ARCHITECTURE* must be used at the very beginning of the program, followed by the name of the chosen architecture. Each architecture will also have one numeric parameter that specifies the total number of processors. In the following simple example, a shared-memory multiprocessor with 64 processors is chosen:

```
PROGRAM Sample;
ARCHITECTURE SHARED(64);
VAR
  x, y, z: INTEGER;
  a: ARRAY [1..10] OF REAL;
  ...
```

After the *ARCHITECTURE* specification in the above example, the remainder of the program follows as usual. This *ARCHITECTURE* specification must be immediately after the *PROGRAM* line, even prior to the *CONST* declarations. A shared-memory architecture in the Multi-Pascal simulation system means that all variables are stored in one central shared memory, and all processors may access the shared memory in one time unit. For the

SHARED architecture option, the number inside the parenthesis (64 in the above example) specifies the number of processors available in the target architecture. This number may not exceed 512 (256 in the MS-DOS version). Actually, the default architecture for the Multi-Pascal system is *SHARED*(512).

The general form of the architectures available in Version 2.0 of the Multi-Pascal system is as follows:

SHARED(p)
LINE(n)
RING(n)
MESH2(m)
TORUS(m)
MESH3(m)
HYPERCUBE(d)
FULLCONNECT(p)

Following the name of each architecture is an integer-valued parameter that must be specified by a literal number. For the *SHARED* architecture, the parameter p specifies the total number of available processors. Following is a brief explanation of each multicomputer topology.

LINE(n)   The parameter n specifies the total number of processors in this Line multicomputer topology. The processors are always numbered from 0 to $n - 1$, as illustrated in Figure 7.5 for $n = 8$.

RING(n)   A *RING* multicomputer topology is identical to a *LINE*, except that the last processor in the line is connected back to processor 0, as shown in Figure 7.6. The parameter n specifies the total number of processors (numbered 0 to $n - 1$).

MESH2(m)   This is a 2-D Mesh topology with m rows and m columns: a total of m^2 processors. The processors are always numbered in row-major order with processor 0 in the upper left corner, as illustrated in Figure 7.7.

TORUS(m)   The *TORUS* multicomputer topology is almost identical to the 2-D Mesh topology (*MESH*2). The only difference is that the processors at each boundary have direct connections to the corresponding processors on the opposite boundary, as illustrated in Figure 7.8.

MESH3(m)   This 3-D Mesh topology for a multicomputer is similar to *MESH*2, except that the processors are arranged in a three-dimensional structure, as illustrated in Figure 7.9. The parameter m specifies the number of rows, number of columns, and also the depth. A 3-D Mesh topology may be visualized as a series of 2-D meshes, one behind the other. For subsequent discussion of the *MESH*3 topology, each 2-D mesh will be referred to as a *plane*.

The *MESH*3 topology will have a total of m^3 processors, numbered sequentially from 0 to $m^3 - 1$. The processors in each plane are numbered in row-major order from the upper left corner to the lower right corner. The front plane 0 in the 3-D Mesh will begin with processor number 0 in the upper left, and end with processor $m^2 - 1$ in the lower right. In Figure 7.9 this means that plane 0 will contain processors 0 to 8. The next plane 1 will begin with processor m^2 in the upper left (in Figure 7.9, this is processor 9). The numbering of processors in each plane is continued sequentially in this way.

HYPERCUBE(d)   This is a Hypercube topology with dimension specified by the parameter d. Thus, the total number of processors is 2^d.

FULLCONNECT(p)   This is a "fully connected" multicomputer topology, in which each processor has a direct physical communication link to every other processor. Although this topology may not be practical for real multicomputers, it is often useful as a conceptual tool to help evaluate program performance properties, especially the impact of communication delays.

B.10.2 Communication Delays

If the architecture specified in the Multi-Pascal program is a multicomputer, then the user may interactively set an important parameter called the *basic communication delay*, which is the basic time to communicate a small message packet between two processors with a direct physical communication link. It is set to 10 time units by default, when initially entering the Multi-Pascal system. It may be changed to any positive integer value with a command as follows:

```
*DELAY 30
```

After this command, the basic communication delay (denoted D) will be set at 30 time units during all subsequent program execution.

When any message is generated, it is first divided into packets. Data values are bundled into packets with three values per packet. The communication time to send a message with k packets along a path with m physical communication links is as follows:

$$\text{Communication Delay: } \left[m + \frac{(k-1)}{2} \right] D$$

A discussion of this formula and further details on the communication model can be found in Chapter 8. The above formula for the communication delay is adequate when the message traffic is low enough that there is no interference between messages that might result in congestion delays. Some programs have more frequent communication that travels longer paths in the network, resulting in the potential for message congestion and resultant delays that may degrade program performance. For simulating the execution of such programs, the Multi-Pascal software system has a "congestion" option, in which every individual message packet is followed as it moves through the communication network. The system keeps track of which communication links and interfaces are busy at various times. When a packet requires use of a link or interface that is currently busy, the movement of the packet is delayed.

It is assumed that processing by each interface can occur concurrently with transmission on any of the connecting links. Furthermore, it is assumed that each communication link is capable of simultaneous bidirectional communication—the link can transmit in both directions simultaneously. However, transmission in each direction is sequential. A packet being transmitted will make the link busy for the entire duration of the transmission, which is $D/2$ time units. Also, each communication interface can process only one packet at a time. When any packet is being processed, the interface is busy for the entire $D/2$ time units required for processing. Every packet arriving at an interface must be processed by the interface before it can travel any further. If packets arrive at an interface faster than they can be processed, they will be queued inside the interface until they are processed. The processsing of queued packets is done in a first-come-first-served manner. For simplicity, it is assumed that there is no limit to the buffer space for queued packets in each interface.

Another important issue is the routing technique used for messages. To ensure that packets and messages sent from the same source to a specific destination will always arrive in the same order that they were sent, the same route is always used for any given source–destination pair. This route is chosen to minimize the *path length*, as measured by the total number of communication links in the path. For some of the topologies, there may be several minimum-length paths to choose from. The following describes the routing method used for each multicomputer topology:

FULLCONNECT—Since there is a direct link between every pair of processors, this link is always the chosen route for every source–destination pair.

LINE—A direct path from the source to destination is always used.

RING—The minimum length path is chosen by comparing the relative positions of the source and destination on the Ring. This path will be in either the clockwise or counterclockwise direction.

MESH2—The message first travels horizontally from the source, moving either left or right, until it reaches the same column as the destination. Then the message travels vertically, either up or down, to the destination.

TORUS—The routing technique is the same as MESH2, except that the end-around links are used to minimize the horizontal and vertical distance traveled.

MESH3—The routing technique is similar to the MESH2. Movement first occurs in the horizontal direction, then vertical, then in the third (depth) dimension.

HYPERCUBE—A standard Hypercube routing technique is used. When a message with destination Q arrives at an intermediate processor P, the corresponding bits of the binary form of Q and P are compared from right to left. Using this right-to-left comparison, let m be the first bit position in which Q and P differ. The message is now sent to a new processor, whose number is determined by reversing the mth bit of P. The path length for this routing algorithm will just be the number of bit positions in which the source and destination processors differ. This is clearly a minimum length path.

When the Multi-Pascal simulation system is used, the "Congestion" option is turned off initially. This means that the communication delays will be determined by the formula described above. These delays will be independent of the current traffic in the communication network. The user may turn on the "Congestion" option with the following command:

```
*CONGESTION ON
```

After this command, any subsequent execution of the Multi-Pascal program will determine all communication delays by using a detailed simulation of packets through the communication network, as described above. To turn off this "Congestion" option again, use the following command:

```
*CONGESTION OFF
```

This is available as an option in the Multi-Pascal system for two reasons. First, it gives the opportunity to determine if there is any performance degradation resulting from congestion in the communication network. This is done by running the program with "Congestion" off and then on. Second, the detailed simulation of message flow in the network is very time consuming, and therefore may significantly increase the program simulation time. For programs that do not suffer from congestion problems, the user can turn this option off to make the simulation run more quickly. The current settings for this basic communication delay and the congestion option can be determined with the "DIS-PLAY" command, which is also used to view the current breakpoint settings.

Recall that the Multi-Pascal system computes the *Sequential* execution time of every program, defined as the time to execute the program on a single processor. In a multicomputer this means that the *Sequential* execution time is not affected by the communication delays between processors. However, as the above discussion illustrates, the *Parallel* execution time may be greatly increased by the communication delays. Recall that the Multi-Pascal system computes the speedup of every program: the *Sequential* time divided by the *Parallel* time. For multicomputers, it is therefore actually possible for a poorly designed program to have a Parallel time *greater* than the Sequential time, resulting in a speedup that is less than 1.

B.11 SUMMARY OF COMMANDS

The Multi-Pascal interactive system contains a variety of commands to help the programmer isolate bugs and performance bottlenecks. Breakpoints may be set at any line in the program, or the programmer may step through the program a few lines at a time. Whenever program execution is suspended, the programmer may examine the current values of program variables as an aid in locating errors. As an alternate to placing breakpoints on specific lines of code, the programmer may make certain program variables into "trace" variables. Whenever any process reads or writes a trace variable, the program execution is suspended.

There are several useful features in the Multi-Pascal system for helping the programmer monitor the program performance. The system will simulate the actual timing behavior of the program as it would run on the target multiprocessor hardware. The programmer can view various performance statistics such as elapsed execution time, parallel speedup factor, and processor utilization. A detailed visual profile of processor utilization may also be generated to help the programmer understand the dynamics of program performance.

The Multi-Pascal interactive system was created to accompany this text for the purpose of allowing the student to run and test Multi-Pascal programs. It is only through this practical experience of writing and running real programs that the student will master the variety of practical parallel programming techniques presented in this text. Following is a summary of available commands in the Multi-Pascal system as produced by the HELP command:

```
*RUN — Initialize and run the program from the beginning.
*EXIT — Terminate the Multi-Pascal system.
*LIST n:m — Lists program source lines n through m.
*BREAK n — Sets a breakpoint at program line n.
*CLEAR BREAK n — Clears the breakpoint from line n.
*CONT — Continues program execution after a breakpoint.
*STATUS p:q — Displays status of processes p through q.
*STEP n — Continues execution for n lines in current STEP process.
*STEP PROCESS p — Sets current STEP process number to p.
*WRITE p name — Writes out value of variable "name" in process p.
*TRACE p name — Makes variable "name" a trace variable.
*DISPLAY — Displays list of breakpoints, trace variables, and alarm.
*CLEAR TRACE m — Clears the trace from memory location m.
*TIME — Gives elapsed time since start of program and since last break.
*UTILIZATION p:q — Gives utilization percentage for processors p to q.
*PROFILE p:q t — Causes utilization profile to be generated for processes
                 p to q every t time units.
*PROFILE OFF — Turns off profile.
*ALARM t — Sets alarm to go off at time t.
*ALARM OFF — Disables alarm from going off in future.
*VARIATION ON (OFF) — Turns variation option on (off).
*CONGESTION ON (OFF) — Turns congestion option on (off).
*DELAY d — Sets the basic communication delay to d time units.
```

REFERENCES

The first publication about the Multi-Pascal interpreter and interactive system is Lester and Guthrie [1987]. It is also described in Lester and Guthrie [1988]. The creation of this software package began with an interpreter for a subset of Pascal developed by Wirth [1975]. Wirth's interpreter was used as the backbone for building the Multi-Pascal software.

Appendix C

Multi-Pascal Error Messages

FEATURES NOT SUPPORTED

Version 2.0 of the Multi-Pascal interpreter and debugging system does not support the following standard features of Pascal:

> enumerated data types
> subrange data types
> sets
> packed arrays
> variant records
> files

In addition, there is a restriction on the length of identifier names. The identifiers may have any number of characters, but only the first 10 characters are used to differentiate them from each other. Therefore, all identifier names should be unique in the first ten characters.

It is important to understand that the above restrictions do not refer to the Multi-Pascal language itself, but only the current version of the Multi-Pascal software system.

ERROR CODES

> 0. UNDEF ID—The definition of the identifier is missing.
> 1. MULTI DEF—The identifier has multiple definitions.

361

2. IDENTIFIER—An identifier was expected but not found.

3. PROGRAM—The keyword PROGRAM is missing.

4.) —A right parenthesis was expected but not found.

5. : —A colon was expected but not found.

6. SYNTAX—A different symbol is required at the indicated position.

7. IDENT, VAR—An identifier or the symbol VAR is expected to begin each item in a formal parameter list of a procedure or function.

8. OF—The keyword "OF" was expected but not found.

9. (—A left parenthesis was expected but not found.

10. ID, ARRAY—The first word in each type definition must be an indentifier or one of the following: ARRAY, RECORD, ^, CHANNEL.

11. [—A left bracket was expected but not found.

12.] —A right bracket was expected but not found.

13. .. —A ".." was expected but not found.

14. ; —A semicolon was expected but not found.

15. FUNC. TYPE—Functions must have one of the following types: INTEGER, REAL, CHAR, BOOLEAN.

16. = —An equal sign was expected but not found.

17. BOOLEAN—The indicated expression must evaluate to a BOOLEAN type.

18. CONVAR TYP—In a FOR or FORALL statement, the index variable must be of type INTEGER, CHAR, or BOOLEAN.

19. TYPE—The expression must evaluate to the same type as the index variable of the FOR or FORALL statement.

20. unused

21. TOO BIG—The number has too many digits or the exponent is too large. In the PC version, a maximum of eight significant digits is allowed. Exponents must be in the range 127 to –127. Integers have a range 32765 to –32765. For larger computers, these limits will be higher.

22. . —A period was expected at the end of the program but not found.

23. TYP (CASE)—Following the keyword "CASE," an expression of type INTE-GER, BOOLEAN, or CHAR is required.

24. CHARACTER—An illegal character in this context.

25. CONST ID—Constants must be defined by a literal or a previously defined constant identifier.

26. INDEX TYPE—The array index does not match the type declared in the array definition.

27. INDEXBOUND—The bounds of the index in the array definition exhibits one of the following errors: lower bound exceeds upper bound, types of bounds do not match, type is real, index range exceeds the limit 32767.

28. NO ARRAY—Attempt to index a nonarray variable.

29. TYPE ID—The identifier must be a "type indentifier."

30. UNDEF TYPE—The type identifier has not yet been defined.

31. NO RECORD—Attempt to use a field selector with a nonrecord variable.

32. BOOLE TYPE—A Boolean type is required for the following operators: AND, OR, NOT.

33. ARITH TYPE—The type of the expression does not match the context.

34. INTEGER—An INTEGER type is required for DIV or MOD.

35. TYPES—Two values must be of the same type to be compared, with the exception of comparing integers with reals.

36. PARAM TYPE—The parameter of a procedure or function call does not match the type in the procedure or function definition. Also, channels can only be VAR parameters.

37. VARIAB ID—A variable identifier was expected but not found.

38. STRING—An empty string is not permitted.

39. NO.OF PARS—The number of parameters in a procedure or function call does not match the number of parameters in the procedure or function definition.

40. TYPE—For a READ operation, the variable must have one of the following types: INTEGER, REAL, CHAR.

41. TYPE—For a WRITE operation, the expression must evaluate to one of the following types: INTEGER, REAL, CHAR, BOOLEAN.

42. REAL TYPE—In a statement of the form WRITE(v:x:y), the expression "v" must evaluate to a REAL type.

43. INTEGER—In a statement of the form WRITE(v:x:y) or WRITE(v:x), both expressions "x" and "y" must be INTEGER.

44. VAR, CONST—The indicated identifier should be a variable or constant identifier.

45. VAR, PROC—A statement must begin with a variable or procedure identifier, except for assigning the result of a function.

46. TYPES (:=)—The types on the left and right sides of the assignment are not compatible.

47. TYP (CASE)—The type of a CASE label does not match the type of the expression following the keyword "CASE."

48. TYPE—The parameter of the built-in function is of the wrong type.

49. STORE OVFL—The storage required by the variables declared at the beginning of the main program is too large.

50. CONSTANT—A constant was expected but not found.

51. := —A ":=" was expected but not found.

52. THEN—The keyword "THEN" was expected but not found.

53. UNTIL—The keyword "UNTIL" was expected but not found.

54. DO—The keyword "DO" was expected but not found.

55. TO DOWNTO—The keyword "TO" or "DOWNTO" was expected but not found.

56. BEGIN—The keyword "BEGIN" was expected but not found.

57. END—The keyword "END" was expected but not found.

58. FACTOR—Error in the indicated expression.

59. CHAN. ERR—One of the following illegal use of channels: nested channel definition, indexing a channel, applying a field selector to a channel.

60. NO POINTER—The symbol ^ must follow a pointer variable.

61. COEND—The keyword "COEND" was expected but not found.

62. unused

63. unused

64. POINTER—NEW and DISPOSE can be used only with pointer variables.

65. NO TOPOLOGY—A built-in multicomputer topology was expected but not found.

66. TYPE—Multicomputer architecture parameters must be positive integer values.

67. unused

68. INTEGER—The expression following the keyword "GROUPING" must evaluate to an INTEGER.

69. UNDEF FRWD—Somewhere in the TYPE declarations, a pointer is defined to a type that is undefined.

70. FORAL INDX—It is not permitted to modify the value of a FORALL index variable. A FORALL index may not appear on the left side of an assignment, in a READ statement, or as a VAR parameter.

PC VERSION

In addition to the above error codes, the PC version has the following runtime error codes:

Runtime error 002—the specified input file name cannot be found.
Runtime error 203—insufficient memory space is available(at least 450K is needed).

REFERENCES

The creation of the Multi-Pascal interactive software system began with an interpreter for a subset of Pascal developed by N. Wirth [1975]. Most of the above error codes are the same as in this original document by Wirth.

References

AHUJA, S., CARRIERO, N., and GELERNTER, D. 1986. Linda and friends. *Computer* 19, 8 (August), pp. 26–34.

AMDAHL, G. M. 1967. Validity of the single processor approach to achieving large-scale computing capabilities. In *AFIPS Conference Proceeedings 1967*, 30, AFIPS Press, Montvale, N.J., p. 483.

APT, K. R. 1986. Correctness proofs of distributed termination algorithms. *ACM Transactions on Programming Languages and Systems* 8, 3 (July), pp. 388–405.

ATHAS, W. C., and SEITZ, C. L. 1988. Multicomputers: Message-passing concurrent computers. *Computer* 21, 8 (August), pp. 9–25.

BAASE, S. 1988. *Computer Algorithms: Introduction to Design and Analysis, 2nd edition.* Reading, Mass.: Addison-Wesley.

BALLARD, D. H., and BROWN, C. M. 1987. *Computer Vision.* Englewood Cliffs, N.J.: Prentice Hall.

BBN. 1985. Butterfly parallel processor overview. Version 1. Tech. Rept., BBN Laboratories, Inc. (December), Cambridge, Massachusetts.

BEN-ARI, M. 1982. *Principles of Concurrent Programming.* Englewood Cliffs, N.J.: Prentice Hall.

BERTSEKAS, D. P., and TSITSIKLIS, J. N. 1989. *Parallel and Distributed Computation: Numerical Methods.* Englewood Cliffs, N.J.: Prentice Hall.

BITTON, D., DEWITT, D. J., HSAIO, D. K., and MENON, J. 1984. *ACM Computing Surveys* 16, 3 (September), pp. 287–318.

BOKHARI, S. H. 1987. Multiprocessing the sieve of Eratosthenes. *Computer* 20, 4 (April), pp. 50–60.

BONOMO, J. P., and DYKSEN, W. R. 1989. Pipelined iterative methods for shared memory machines. *Parallel Computing* 11, pp. 187–199.

BOYLE, J., BUTLER, R., DISZ, T., GLICKFIELD, B., LUSK, E., OVERBEEK, R., PATERSON, J., and STEVENS, R. 1987. *Portable Programs for Parallel Processors.* New York: Holt, Reinhart, and Winston.

BRAWER, S. 1989. *Introduction to Parallel Programming.* New York: Academic Press.

BRINCH HANSEN, P. 1973. *Operating System Principles.* Englewood Cliffs, N.J.: Prentice Hall.

BRINCH HANSEN, P. 1975. The programming language Concurrent Pascal. *IEEE Transactions on Software Engineering* SE-1, 2 (June), pp. 199–206.

BRINCH HANSEN, P. 1977. *The Architecture of Concurrent Programming.* Englewood Cliffs, N.J.: Prentice Hall.

BRINCH HANSEN, P. 1978. Distributed processes: A concurrent programming concept. *Communications of the ACM* 21, 11 (November), pp. 934–941.

BRINCH HANSEN, P. 1981. Edison: A multiprocessor language. *Software Practice and Experience* 11, 4 (April), pp. 325–361.

CARRIERO, N., and GELERNTER, D. 1989. Linda in context. *Communications of the ACM* 32, 4 (April), pp. 444–459.

CHAN, T. E., and SAAD, Y. 1986. Multigrid algorithms on hypercube multiprocessors. *IEEE Transactions on Computers*, Vol. C-35 (November), pp. 969–977.

CHANDLER, K. C. 1987. Modern science and Vedic science: An introduction. *Modern Science and Vedic Science* 1, 1 (January), pp. 5–28.

CHANDY, K.M., and MISRA, J. 1988. *Parallel Program Design: A Foundation.* Reading, Mass.: Addison-Wesley.

CHAZAN, D., and MIRANKER, W. L. 1969. Chaotic relaxation. *Linear Algebra and Applications*, 2, pp. 199–222.

CHOPRA, D. 1990. *Perfect Health: The Complete Mind/Body Guide.* New York: Harmony Books.

CHU, E., and GEORGE, A. 1989. QR factorization of a dense matrix on a shared-memory multiprocessor. *Parallel Computing* 10, pp. 55–71.

DEO, N., PANG, C. Y., and LORD, R. E. 1980. Two parallel algorithms for shortest path problems. In *Proceedings of the 1980 International Conference on Parallel Processing* (August), IEEE Press, New York, pp. 244–253.

DESROCHERS, G. R. 1987. *Principles of Parallel and Multiprocessing.* New York: McGraw-Hill.

DIJKSTRA, E. W. 1968a. Cooperating sequential processes. In *Programming Languages*, F. Genuys, ed. New York: Academic Press.

DIJKSTRA, E. W. 1968b. The structure of the THE multiprogramming system. *Communications of the ACM* 11, 5 (May), pp. 341–346.

DIJKSTRA, E. W., and SHOLTEN, C. S. 1980. Termination detection for diffusing computations. *Information Processing Letters* 1, pp. 1–4.

FELDMAN, J. A. 1979. High level programming for distributed computing. *Communications of the ACM* 22, 6 (June), pp. 353–368.

FILMAN, R. E., and FRIEDMAN, D. P. 1984. *Coordinated Computing: Tools and Techniques for Distributed Software.* New York: McGraw-Hill.

FOX, G., JOHNSON, M., LYZENGA, G., OTTO, S., SALMON, J., and WALKER, D. 1988. *Solving Problems on Concurrent Processors, Vol. I: General Techniques and Regular Problems.* Englewood Cliffs, N.J.: Prentice Hall.

HAGELIN, J. S. 1987. Is consciousness the unified field? A field theorist's perspective. *Modern Science and Vedic Science* 1, 1 (January), pp. 29–88.

HAGEMAN, L. A., and YOUNG, D. M. 1981. *Applied Iterative Methods.* New York: Academic Press.

HALSTEAD, R. 1985. Multilisp: An overview and working example. *ACM Transactions on Programming Languages and Systems* 7, 4 (October), pp. 501–538.

HELLER, D. E. 1978. A survey of parallel algorithms in numerical linear algebra. *SIAM Review* 20, 4, pp. 740–777.

HILLIS, W. D. 1986. *The Connection Machine.* Cambridge, Mass.: MIT Press.

HOARE, C. A. R. 1974. Monitors: An operating system structuring concept. *Communications of the ACM* 17, 10 (October), pp. 666–677.

HOARE, C. A. R. 1978. Communicating sequential processes. *Communications of the ACM* 21, 8 (August), pp. 666–677.

HOCKNEY, R. W., and JESSHOPE, C. R. 1988. *Parallel Computers 2: Architecture, Programming, and Algorithms*. Bristol, England: Adam Hilger.

HORIGUCHI, S., and MIRANKER, W. L. 1989. A parallel algorithm for finding the maximum value. *Parallel Computing* 11, pp. 101–108.

HUBEL, D. H. 1984. The brain. *Scientific American Offprint*. San Francisco, California: W. H. Freeman.

HWANG, K., and BRIGGS, F. A. 1984. *Computer Architecture and Parallel Processing*. New York: McGraw-Hill.

INMOS, 1985. *The Occam Programming Manual*. Englewood Cliffs, N.J.: Prentice Hall.

JENNINGS, A. 1977. *Matrix Computation for Scientists and Engineers*. New York: John Wiley and Sons.

JONES, D. W. 1989. Concurrent operations on priority queues. *Communications of the ACM* 32, 1 (January), pp. 132–137.

KARP, A. H. 1987. Programming for parallelism. *Computer* 20, 5 (May), pp. 43–57.

KARP, A., and BABB, R. G. 1988. A comparison of 12 parallel Fortran dialects. *IEEE Software* (September), pp. 52–67.

LESTER, B. P. 1987. Unified field based computer science: Towards a universal science of computation. *Modern Science and Vedic Science*, 1, 3 (July), pp. 220–271.

LESTER, B. P., and GUTHRIE, G. R. 1987. A system for investigating parallel algorithm architecture interaction. In *Proceedings of the 1987 International Conference on Parallel Processing* (August), IEEE Press, New York, pp. 667–670.

LESTER, B. P., and GUTHRIE, G. R. 1988. Multi-Pascal: A language and runtime debugging environment for teaching concurrent programming. In *Proceedings of 12th Western Educational Computing Conference* (November).

LISKOV, B. L., and SCHEIFLER, R. 1982. Guardians and actions: Linguistic support for robust, distributed programs. In *Proceedings of the 9th ACM Symposium on Reliability in Distributed Software and Database Systems* (July). IEEE, New York, pp. 53–60.

LITTLE, J. D. C., MURTY, K. G., SWEENEY, D. W., and KAREL, C. 1963. An algorithm for the traveling salesman problem. *Operations Research* 11, 6 (November–December), pp. 972–989.

MOHAN, J. 1983. Experience with two parallel programs solving the traveling salesman problem. In *Proceedings of the 1983 International Conference on Parallel Processing* (August), IEEE Press, New York, pp. 191–193.

MOORE, E. F. 1959. The shortest path through a maze. In *Proceedings of the International Symposium on the Theory of Switching*, Volume 2, pp. 285–292.

NELSON, P., and SNYDER, L. 1987. Parallel programming paradigms. In *The Characteristics of Parallel Algorithms*, L. H. Jamieson, D. Gannon, and R. Douglas, eds. Cambridge, Mass.: MIT Press, pp. 1–20.

ORTEGA, J. M., and VOIGHT, R. G. 1985. Solution of partial differential equations on vector and parallel computers. *SIAM Review*, 27, p. 149.

PAWLEY, G. S., BAILLIE, C. F., TENENBAUM, E., and CELMASTER, W. 1989. The BBN Butterfly used to simulate a molecular liquid. *Parallel Computing* 11, pp. 321–329.

QUINN, M. J. 1987. *Designing Efficient Algorithms for Parallel Computers*. New York: McGraw-Hill.

QUINN, M. J., and DEO, N. 1984. Parallel graph algorithms. *ACM Computing Surveys* 16, 3 (September), pp. 319–348.

RANKA, S., and SAHNI, S. 1989. Hypercube algorithms for image transformations. In *Proceedings of the 1989 International Conference on Parallel Processing*, Vol. III (August), Pennsylvania State University Press, University Park, pp. 24–31.

RANKA, S., WON, Y., and SAHNI, S. 1988. Programming a hypercube multicomputer. *IEEE Software* (September), pp. 69–77.

RITCHIE, D. M., and THOMPSON, D. 1974. The UNIX timesharing system. *Communications of the ACM* 17, 7 (July), pp. 365–375.

ROMAN, G., and COX, K. C. 1989. A declarative approach to visualizing concurrent computations. *Computer* 22, 10 (October), pp. 25–37.

SAAD, Y. and SCHULTZ, M. H. 1988. Topological properties of hypercubes. *IEEE Transactions on Computers* 37, pp. 867–872.

SEITZ, C. L. 1985. The cosmic cube. *Communications of the ACM* 28, 1 (January), pp. 22–33.

SHAPIRO, E. Y. 1985. Systolic programming: A paradigm of parallel processing. Tech. Rept. CS84–16, Weizmann Institute of Science, Rehovot, Israel.

SHAPIRO, E. Y. 1986. Concurrent Prolog: A progress report. *Computer* 19,8 (August), pp. 44–58.

SHAW, A. C. 1974. *The Logical Design of Operating Systems*. Englewood Cliffs, N.J.: Prentice Hall.

SHILOACH, Y., and VISHKIN, U. 1981. Finding the maximum, merging and sorting in a parallel computation model. *Journal of Algorithms,* Vol. 2, pp. 88–102.

SIEGEL, H. J. 1984. *Interconnection Networks for Large-Scale Multiprocessing: Theory and Case Studies.* Lexington, Mass.: Lexington Books.

SNYDER, L., and SOCHA, D. 1986. Poker on the cosmic cube: A first retargetable parallel programming language and environment. In *Proceedings of the 1986 International Conference on Parallel Processing*, IEEE Press, New York.

STERLING, T. L., MUSCIANO, A. J., CHAN, E.Y., and THOMAE, D. A. 1987. Effective implementation of a parallel language on a multiprocessor. *IEEE Micro* (December), pp. 46–62.

STONE, H. S. 1987. *High-Performance Computer Architecture*. Reading, Mass.: Addison-Wesley.

STOROY, S. 1989. Holistic algorithms: A paradigm for multiprocessor programming. *Parallel Computing* 10, pp. 221–229.

TANENBAUM, A. S. 1989. *Computer Networks*. Englewood Cliffs, N.J.: Prentice Hall.

THOMAS, R. H. 1988. The uniform system: An approach to runtime support for large scale shared memory parallel processors. In *Proceedings of the 1988 International Conference on Parallel Processing* (August), Pennsylvania State University Press, University Park, pp. 245–254.

TRIVEDI, K. S. 1982. *Probability and Statistics with Reliability, Queueing and Computer Science Applications*. Englewood Cliffs, N.J.: Prentice Hall.

ULLMAN, J. D. 1984. *Computational Aspects of VLSI*. Rockville, Md.: Computer Science Press.

UNITED STATES DEPARTMENT OF DEFENSE. 1981. *Programming Language Ada: Reference Manual,* Vol. 106, *Lecture Notes in Computer Science*. New York: Springer-Verlag.

WALLACE, R. K. 1986. *The Maharishi Technology of the Unified Field: The Neurophysiology of Enlightenment*. Fairfield, Iowa: MIU Neuroscience Press.

WIRTH, N. 1975. *The Pascal-S Compiler*. Institut fur Informatic, ETH, Report Nr. 12 (June), Zurich, Switzerland.

WIRTH, N. 1977. Modula: A language for modular multiprogramming. *Software Practice and Experience* 7, pp. 33–35.

Index

acknowledge count, 302 (*see also* termination)
activation record, 320
  lifetime extension, 323
active worker tree, 298, 303
  creation, 307–308
  destruction, 308
  performance, 308
ADA language, 8
address spreading, memory, 61
aggregate function, 143
aggregation:
  hypercube, 173
  line, 170
  mesh, 171–172
  multicomputer, 168–174
  multiple, 204–207
  parallel, 140–142
  ring, 171
alarm command, Multi-Pascal, 332, 350
Alliant computer, 3
Amdahl's law, 44–46, 54
architecture keyword, Multi-Pascal, 197, 355
Argus language, 8
array of channels, 79, 192, 276, 328
arrival phase, 130
astrophysics, 22
asynchronous:
  algorithms, 313–314
  communication, 189
  solution of linear equations, 316
@ primitive, 196, 198–199
atomic operations, 98–102

back substitution, 80–85
  pipeline, 82–84
  sequential, 82
backtracking, 282
barrier:
  binary tree, 130–136
  definition, 127
  linear, 128–130
  local, 151–152
  performance, 134, 139
  releasing processes, 133
  spinlock implementation, 129
  synchronization, 126–128
  tournament technique, 131
basic communication delay, 201

BBN computer, 3, 286
Bernoulli trials, 310
binary split, 88–89
binary tree:
  barrier, 130–136
  communication, 206
bitonic list, 88
bitonic merge sort, 88–90, 93
blocked state, 113, 336
blocking communication, 189
break command, Multi-Pascal, 332, 334
breakpoints, 333–334
broadcast:
  barrier, 143
  execution time, 174
  hypercube, 173, 208–211
  line, 169
  mesh, 171–172
  multicomputer, 168–174
  multinode, 181
  multiple, 208–211
  ring, 171
  tournament technique, 182
bucket sort, 116
buffered communication, 189
bus bandwidth, 56
bus-oriented systems, 56–60
busy-waiting, 113, 337
butterfly, 136, 205
  network, 64

cache coherence, 3, 60, 71
cache memory, 4
  multiprocessor, 58–60
  uniprocessor, 57–58
channel:
  of array, 86, 328
  of channels, 328
  comparison with spinlocks, 112
  component type, 87, 327–328
  counts, 280
  declarations, 76
  empty, 76
  exclusive access, 112
  in expressions, 325
  in-transit values, 343
  parameters, 236–327
  read or write statements, 326

channel (*cont'd*)
  reading, 76
  of record, 87, 328
  saturation, 276, 279
  variables, 75–76
  work pool implementation, 269–274
  writing, 76
child process, 20, 321–322
  multiple generations, 324
circulating partition, 226
clear bit operation, 132
clear break command, Multi-Pascal, 332, 334
clear trace command, Multi-Pascal, 332, 345
clock function, 348
Cm* computer, 287
combinatorial search, 261
commands, Multi-Pascal, 332
Communicating Sequential Processes, 8
communication:
  asynchronous, 189
  bandwidth, 155
  buffered, 189
  channels, multicomputer, 185–186
  congestion, 158–159, 202
  delay, 159–161, 199–203, 357
  error detection, 156
  interface, 154–155
  link, 154–155
  main program, 193–195
  message header, 157
  message transmission, 160
  multicomputer, 199–203
  network, 156–159
  overhead, 220–222
  phase, 221, 243
  phased-array, 88
  pipeline, 160
  ports, 184–190
    implementation, 215
  processing time, 159, 161
  routing, 156–157
  software overhead, 202
  synchronous, 189
  transmission time, 159
compiler errors, 361–364
computation phase, 221, 242
compute, aggregate, and broadcast, 121, 140
Concurrent Pascal, 8
congestion, 158–159
  in broadcast, 210
  option, Multi-Pascal system, 202, 332, 359
  shortest path, 309
Connection Machine, 12
connectivity, multicomputer topology, 161

contention:
  in histogram, 107
  performance degradation, 279
  in work pool, 270–272
continue command, Multi-Pascal, 332
convergence testing, 140
  multicomputer, 247–248
count:
  array, 280
  variable, 128, 150, 270
counters, termination, 274
critical race, 297
critical regions, 101
cross-product algorithm, 222
crossbar network, 63
cut-through routing, 160

data distribution:
  multicomputer, 194
  time, 243–244
data initialization, 347
deadlock, 118, 317
decentralization, 109, 115, 130, 272
declaration, port, 187, 191–192, 197
delay command, Multi-Pascal, 332
delayed state, 336
delayed write, 187–188
Denelcor HEP computer, 286
departure phase, 130
diameter, multicomputer topology, 161
difference equation, 121–124
dimension of hypercube, 165
direct memory access, 155
directed graph, 264
display command, Multi-Pascal, 332, 334
Distributed Processes, 8
distributed workers:
  asynchronous algorithms, 313–314
  definition, 292
  load imbalance, 310
  performance analysis, 306–310
  shortest path program, 295
  termination detection, 298–300
  work compression, 311–314
  work pool implementation, 296–300 (*see also* work pool)
dot product, 234
duration statement, 352

efficiency, definition, 251
embedding:
  definition, 174
  hypercube, 233
Encore computer, 3

ENIAC computer, 2
environment:
    evolution rule, 321
    inheritance rule, 321
    stack, 320, 322
error codes, 361–364
error detection, communication, 156
error messages, 361–364
exchange sort, 213
exit command, Multi-Pascal, 332

factorial program, 216
fields, 2
floating-point systems, 3
Floyd–Warshall algorithm, 287
forall indices, scope of, 39
fork operator, 40–41
fullconnect topology, 357 (*see also* topology)
fully connected topology, 203, 357

Gaussian elimination, 148–149 (*see also* linear
    equations)
    multicomputer, 258
generations of processes, 324
getwork procedure:
    multicomputer, 301–305
    multiprocessor, 275, 277
    work compression, 311–312
    (*see also* work pool)
global minimum, 288–289
global synchronization, 218
graph:
    representation, 265, 290
    shortest path algorithm, 264–268
    undirected, 287
gravitational force, 223–224
Gray code, 175–177, 243, 249
grouping primitive, 24
group size, optimal 24–26

help command, Multi-Pascal, 360
heuristic search, 288
hierarchical memory, 72
histogram:
    contention, 107
    parallel, 106
    sequential 105
hot spots, memory, 68–69
human brain, 17–18
human computer, 17–18
Hypercube:
    aggregation, 204–207
    broadcast, 208–211
    congestion, 210

definition, 165–167
dimension, 165
embedding, 174–178, 233
Multi-Pascal system, 357
recursive rule, 167
routing, 358
solving linear equations, 214, 316

idle workers, 273 (*see also* worker process)
image processing:
    histogram, 105–106
    ray-tracing, 2
    region growing, 256–257
    smoothing algorithm, 51
inheritance rule, environment, 321
initial data distribution, 194
initialization overhead, 45–46
input option, Multi-Pascal, 331
insertion sort, 198
    performance, 203
integration, numerical, 108
Intel, 3
interconnection networks, 63–65 (*see also*
    network)

Jacobi relaxation:
    convergence, 141–144, 246–247
    definition, 121–122
    Hypercube, 248–249
    improving performance, 145–146
    iteration time, 251
    local synchronization, 138
    mesh, 258
    multicomputer program, 245–254
        performance, 250–252
    multiprocessor, 125
    sequential, 121–123
join statement, 42–43

Laplace's equation, 121
lifetime extention rule, 323
Linda programming language, 8, 286
line topology:
    definition, 162
    Multi-Pascal system, 356
    routing, 358
    sorting, 199
linear equations:
    back substitution, 81–82
    definition, 80
    Gaussian elimination, 148–149
    lower triangular, 81
    solution (*see* solution of linear equations)
    upper triangular, 149

linked list insertion, 118
list command, Multi-Pascal, 332
list option, Multi-Pascal, 331
list processing, parallel, 43
load balancing:
  distributed workers, 310
  performance analysis, 318
  replicated workers, 272
  (*see also* work pool)
load factor, 107
load imbalance, 15
local barrier, 151–152 (*see also* barrier)
local synchronization, 136–138
local variables, 34–35, 183
lock operation, 103 (*see also* spinlocks)
long-range interaction, 222
lower triangular system, 81

Maharishi International University, 10
master counter, 274
master count termination, 297, 317
matrix multiplication:
  definition, 32
  memory contention, 67–68
  multicomputer, 234–245
    partitioning, 235–236
    performance, 242–244
    speedup, 244
    torus implementation, 236–241
  multiprocessor, 31–34
matrix partitioning, 235, 253–254
maze search, 287
memory:
  address spreading, 61
  contention, 3, 56
  direct access, 155
  hierarchical, 72
  hot spots, 68–69
  multiple modules, 60–63
merge sort, 88
merging sorted lists, 50
mesh topology:
  definition, 163–165
  embedding, 176–177
  Multi-Pascal system, 356
  numerical integration, 214
  routing, 358
  three-dimensional, 165
  two-dimensional, 163
message:
  acknowledgments, 298, 303 (*see also* work pool)
  header, 157
  transmission, 160, 201 (*see also* communication)
minimum, in array, 118
Modula language, 8

monitor procedure, 303–304
monitor process, 280, 317
monitors, 101
multicomputer:
  aggregation, 168–174
  broadcasting, 168–174
  communication (*see also* communication):
    channels, 185–186
    overhead, 220–222
    ports, 184–190
  connectivity, 232–233
  data distribution, 193–194, 243–244
  definition, 5–7
  distributed workers (*see* distributed workers)
  Jacobi relaxation, 245–254
  linear equations, 214, 316
  matrix multiplication (*see* matrix multiplication, multicomputer)
  N-body program, 222–231
  pipeline, 197–199
  shortest path program, 293–295
  spinlocks, 191
  topology (*see* topology)
  traveling salesman problem, 316
  work pool, 296–301 (*see also* work pool)
Multilisp language, 8
multinode broadcast, 181
multipacket message, 201
multiple aggregation, 204–207, 248
multiple broadcast, 208–211
multiple channel work pool, 273 (*see also* work pool)
multiple port communication, 204–211
multiplication, matrix (*see* matrix multiplication)
multiplying polynomials, 49
mutual exclusion, 97, 116

N-body program, 222–231
  execution time, 230
  multicomputer, 226–228
  optimal processors, 229
  overlapping computation and communication, 231–232
  performance, 228–230
  shared memory, 223–226
N-queens problem, 281–285
  definition, 281
  program, 284–285
  worker process, 283
natural law, 18
Navier–Stokes equations, 2
nested loops, 29–31
network:
  butterfly, 64
  crossbar, 63

interconnection, 63–65
shuffle-exchange, 65
neural networks, 17
Newton's law of gravitation, 223
nonblocking write, 187
NP-complete problem, 288
numerical integration:
definition, 108
mesh, 214
parallel, 111
sequential, 109

Occam language, 91, 190
operating sytems, 8
order notation, 29
output option, Multi-Pascal, 331
overlapping communication and computation, 231

p-code, 346
packet size, optimal, 180
parallel efficiency, definition of, 251
parallel execution time, definition of, 10, 345
parent process, 20, 321–322
parent worker, 298, 302–303
partial differential equation, 121 (*see also* Jacobi
    relaxation)
particle physics, 2
partitioning, row, 253–254
partitioning, two-dimensional, 253–254
%Self function, 196, 213
%seqoff directive, 350
%seqon directive, 350
performance analysis:
barrier implementation, 139
broadcasting, multicomputer, 174
communication overhead, 221–222
histogram program, 107
insertion sort, 203
Jacobi relaxation, 250–252
matrix multiplication, 242–244
multiple broadcast, 210–211
N-body program, 228–230
shortest path program:
    multicomputer, 306–310
    multiprocessor, 279–281
performance profile, 85, 307, 353–354
permanent partition, 226
phased-array communication, 88
pipeline:
back substitution program, 82–84
communication, 160
insertion sort program, 198
multicomputers, 197–199
parallelism, 77–80
performance, 94, 95

pivot element, 149
pixels, 256 (*see also* image processing)
Poker language, 92
polling, termination detection, 319
polynomials, multiplication, 49
port:
communication, 184–190
declaration, 187, 191–192, 197
examples, 192
multiple, 204–211
reading and writing, 187–188
table, 215
prime number sieve, 92
process:
child, 20
concept, 7
creation, 20–22
granularity, 22–24
Multi-Pascal interpreter, 334–336
numbering, 334
parent, 20
pipeline, 79
state, 336
synchronization by termination, 124
termination, 41–42
worker, 262–264
processor:
allocation, 196
communication, 154–161 (*see also* communica-
    tion)
utilization, 10
producer-consumer, 75, 78
profile command, Multi-Pascal, 332, 353–354
profile, performance, 85, 307, 353–354
putwork (*see also* work pool):
multicomputer, 301–305
multiprocessor, 275, 278

quantum physics, 17
queen, attack area, 282
queuing delay, 279

random number seed, 351
rank sort, 8–10, 26–28, 66–67
ray-tracing, 2
ready state, 113, 336
receive operation, 189, 215
recurrence relations, 147
recursive worker creation, 290–291 (*see also*
    worker process)
red-black relaxation (*see also* Jacobi relaxation):
definition, 148
mesh, 258
redirecting input and output, 331
region growing, 256–257

relaxation, 245 (*see also* Jacobi relaxation)
relaxed algorithms, 13, 20, 68
remote procedure call, 195
remote-var parameter, 194, 197, 199
ring topology:
    definition, 162
    Multi-Pascal system, 356
    N-body program, 226–230
    routing, 358
RISC processors, 2
round-robin distribution, 272, 283 (*see also* work
      pool)
routing:
    algorithm, 180
    communication network, 156–157
    cut-through, 160
    dynamic, 157
    hypercube topology, 358
    line topology, 358
    mesh topology, 358
    Multi-Pascal system, 358
    ring topology, 358
    static, 157
    torus topology, 358
    worm-hole, 160
row diagonal dominance, 215, 316
row partitioning, 253–254
row-major order, 164
RPC, 195
run command, Multi-Pascal, 332
running state, 113, 336
runtime errors, Multi-Pascal system, 364

saddle point of matrix, 116
searching an array, 99
semaphores, 114, 150
send operation, 189, 215
seqtime function, 348
Sequent computer, 3
sequential execution time, definition of, 10, 345, 349
set bit operation, 134
shared data:
    contention, 104–107
    error, 99
shared variables, 11, 28, 34–35
shortest path program:
    algorithm, 264–269
    all-pairs, 287
    congestion, 309
    multicomputer, 293–295
    multiprocessor, 266–268
    performance profile, 307
    sequential, 265–266
    (*see also* distributed workers; work pool)

shuffle-exchange network, 65 (*see also* network)
sieve of Eratosthenes, 92–93
signal operation, 114
smoothing algorithm, 51
snake-like order, 174
snooping cache, 3 (*see also* cache coherence)
solution of linear equations:
    asynchronous, 316
    hypercube, 214
    sparse, 319
sorted lists, merging, 50
sorting:
    bitonic merge, 88–90, 93
    bucket, 116
    exchange, 213
    insertion, 198
    line toplogy, 199, 213
    parallel, 48, 88–90
    rank sort, 8–10, 26–28, 66–67
sparse graph, 268
sparse system of equations, 319
speedup, Multi-Pascal system, 346
spinlocks:
    array, 103
    in barrier implementation, 129
    comparison with channels, 112
    implementation, 102
    multicomputer, 191
    pointer, 104
    structured types, 103–104
spinning state, 113, 336
square root, parallel, 21–22
state diagram, 300, 312 (*see also* work pool)
statement blocks, 35–39
status command, Multi-Pascal, 332, 335–336
step command, Multi-Pascal, 332, 337–338
step process, Multi-Pascal, 337
synchronization:
    by process termination, 124
    delay, 15
    global, 218
    local, 136–138
    penalty, 14
synchronous communication, 189 (*see also*
      communication)
syntax errors, Multi-Pascal system, 361–364

task descriptor, 263 (*see also* work pool)
termination:
    algorithm, 273–275
    condition, 269, 299
    counters, 274
    detection:
        active worker tree, 298–301

master count method, 297
performance, 306, 308
polling method, 319
replicated workers, 264
test and set instruction, 102, 118 (*see also* spinlocks)
three-dimensional mesh, 165, 356 (*see also* mesh topology)
time command, Multi-Pascal, 332, 346
timing-dependent error, 99
tolerance, 141 (*see also* convergence testing)
topological embedding, 174
topology:
  connectivity, 168
  diameter, 168
  fully connected, 203
  line, 162, 356
  mesh, 163–164
  ring, 162, 356
  torus, 164, 356
  tree, 181, 216
torus topology:
  definition, 164
  Multi-Pascal system, 356
  routing, 358
tournament technique:
  barrier implementation, 131
  hypercube broadcast, 182
  multiple aggregation, 204
trace command, Multi-Pascal, 332, 343–345
transmission time, 159, 200 (*see also* communication)
transputer, Inmos, 190
traveling salesman problem:
  multicomputer, 316
  multiprocessor, 288
tree topology, 181, 216
tuples, for N-queens program, 282
two-dimensional mesh, 163, 356 (*see also* mesh topology)
two-dimensional partitioning, 253–254

undirected graph, 287
unified field, 18
uniform system, 286
UNIX, 48
UNIX pipes, 91
unlock operation, 103 (*see also* spinlocks)
upper triangular matrix, 149, 258
utilization command, Multi-Pascal, 332, 349

variables:
  channel, 75–76
  local, 34–35, 183
  shared, 11, 28, 34–35
variation command, Multi-Pascal, 332, 351
vector processing, 3
vector product, 31
virtual ring, 225–226, 231–233
virtual topology, 231–233
VLSI processors, 2
voltage on metal sheet, 122 (*see also* Jacobi relaxation)

wait operation, 114
weighted directed graph, 264–265
work compression, 311–312
work pool:
  definition, 262–264
  contention, 270–272, 277
  implementation, 269–270
  load balancing, 272
  multicomputer, 296–305
  multiple channel, 273, 296
  performance:
    multicomputer, 306–310
    multiprocessor, 276–281
  round-robin distribution, 272, 283
  saturation, 270, 276, 291
  termination detection, 270
worker process:
  active and idle, 299, 303
  definition, 262–264
  distributed, 292
  indistinguishable, 292, 315
  N-queens program, 284–285
  recursive method, 290–291
  shortest path program (*see* shortest path program)
  state diagram, 300
  work compression, 314
workload distribution, 310
worm-hole routing, 160 (*see also* routing)
wraparound connections, 164
wraparound mesh, 180
write command, Multi-Pascal, 338–343
  channels, 343
  pointers, 342
  records, 341
  standard variables, 339
  structured variables, 340–343
write-back technique, 58
write-through technique, 58, 60

IBM® PC DISKETTE to Accompany THE ART OF PARALLEL PROGRAMMING

Prentice Hall

ISBN 0-13-045923-2